# The Pursuit of History

# The Pursuit of History

Aims, methods and new directions in the
study of modern history

FOURTH EDITION

John Tosh with Seán Lang

PEARSON
Longman

Harlow, England • London • New York • Boston • San Francisco • Toronto • Sydney • Singapore • Hong Kong
Tokyo • Seoul • Taipei • New Delhi • Cape Town • Madrid • Mexico City • Amsterdam • Munich • Paris • Milan

PEARSON EDUCATION LIMITED

Edinburgh Gate
Harlow CM20 2JE
United Kingdom
Tel: +44 (0)1279 623623
Fax: +44 (0)1279 431059
Website: www.pearsoned.co.uk

First published 1984
Second edition 1991
Third edition 2002
**Fourth edition published in Great Britain in 2006**

© Pearson Education Limited 1984, 2006

The rights of John Tosh and Seán Lang to be identified as
authors of this work have been asserted by them in accordance
with the Copyright, Designs and Patents Act 1988.

ISBN-13: 978-1-4058-2351-7
ISBN-10: 1-4058-2351-8

*British Library Cataloguing in Publication Data*
A CIP catalogue record for this book can be obtained from the British Library

*Library of Congress Cataloging in Publication Data*
Tosh, John.
    The pursuit of history : aims, methods, and new directions in the study of
modern history / John Tosh with Seán Lang. – 4th ed.
        p. cm.
    Includes bibliographical references and index.
    ISBN-13: 978-1-4058-2351-7 (pbk. )
    ISBN-10: 1-4058-2351-8 (pbk. )
1. Historiography. 2. Great Britain – Historiography. I. Lang, Seán. II. Title.

    D13.T62 2006
    07.2'041 – dc29

                                                                    2005044588

10  9  8  7  6  5  4  3  2
10  09  08  07  06

Set by 3 in 10pt Sabon
Printed in Great Britain by Henry Ling Ltd, at the Dorset Press, Dorchester, DT1 1HD.

*The Publisher's policy is to use paper manufactured from sustainable forests.*

*For Nick and William*

# Contents

# Publisher's acknowledgements

The publishers are grateful to the following for permission to reproduce copyright material:

Getty Images/AFP for Chapter 1: State Opening of Parliament; Getty Images/J.A. Hampton/Hulton Archive for Chapter 1: St Paul's Cathedral; Bridgeman Art Library/Capitol Collection, Washington, USA for Chapter 1: Declaration of Independence; Topfoto/Topham/UPP for Chapter 2: R.H. Tawney; Topfoto/Louise Gubb/Image Works for Chapter 2: South Africa's Truth and Reconciliation Commission; Getty Images/Time Life Pictures for Chapter 3: Archivist; Mary Evans Picture Library for Chapter 3: Agrarian revolts; AKG-images for Chapter 3: Vincenz of Beauvais and Chapter 6: Clio; M. Square Visions/Photographers Direct for Chapter 4: National Archive Building, Kew; Paul Shawcross/Photographers Direct for Chapter 4: Montaillou; Bridgeman Art Library/Private Collection for Chapter 4: Edward Gibbon; Mary Evans Picture Library for Chapter 5: French barricades and Chapter 8: Levellers; Chris Gibson/Photographers Direct for Chapter 5: Co-Operative shop; Topfoto/Topham/Picturepoint for Chapter 6: A.J.P. Taylor, Chapter 10: Jack the Ripper and Chapter 11: Campbell Road; Corbis/James Leynse for Chapter 7: Bookshop history shelves; Alamy/ICP for Chapter 8: Marx and Engels; Corbis/Bettmann for Chapter 8: Feminist march and Chapter 9: Communion; Corbis/Hulton-Deutsch Collection for Chapter 9: Census; Topfoto/James Marshall/Image Works for Chapter 11: Interview.

In some instances we may have been unable to trace the owners of copyright material, and we would appreciate any information that would enable us to do so.

# Preface to the Fourth Edition

In this edition the main text is unchanged. Supplementary material has been added in the margins and at the beginning and end of each chapter to facilitate student use of the book. I am most grateful to Seán Lang for preparing this material.

*John Tosh*
*August 2005*

# Preface to the Revised Third Edition

This book belongs to a genre of writing about the discipline of history which can be said to have begun with the publication of E.H. Carr's book, *What Is History?* in 1961. The fortieth anniversary was marked by the reissue of the original text in 2001, together with Carr's notes towards a second edition and a new introduction by Richard Evans.[1] *What Is History?* has never been out of print, and it has been a reliable fixture on student reading lists since it first appeared. Its reissue with all the editorial trappings of a classic invites reflection on the current standing of the discipline of history.

In some ways, the continuing popularity of *What Is History?* is surprising. Carr stood at an oblique angle to the historical profession. He was not trained as a historian and he never taught history; only in later life did he devote himself primarily to the writing of history (in his multi-volume *History of Soviet Russia*); before the 1950s he was much better known as an authority on international relations. *What Is History?* originated as a set of lectures delivered in the History Faculty of Cambridge University. It is a strongly polemical work. The title was something of a provocation, considering Carr's position as an outsider. While he demonstrated a respect for the great historians of the past, he was dismissive towards the current practitioners of the craft, and he could not resist the temptation of settling old scores. The book also bears the imprint of a political context which seems a world away from today's. It was written against the background of the Cold War, though at a moment when the prospects for accommodation between the two power blocs looked better than for many years. Carr himself strongly sympathized with the Soviet Union, especially its ruling élite; he also believed that the coming of independence to large areas of Asia and Africa represented a major step in human progress. In short, the book is very much rooted in its time and place.

It is hardly surprising, then, that *What Is History?* did not prove to be a charter for the future of historical studies. Some of Carr's central concerns raise barely a flicker of interest today. His treatment of the theme of society and the individual seems remote, and his interpretation of historical objectivity idiosyncratic. Conversely many features of today's historical practice are not even mentioned in the book. In Carr's view history is the property of literate and powerful élites. There is no sense that history might be claimed by the dispossessed or marginal, and hence no intimation of what later came to be known as 'history from below'. It is probably safe to say that Carr would have been bemused by the arrival of gender history, and dismissive of oral history. Above all he would have been angered by the Postmodernist assault. For all his scepticism, Carr did not dispute the historicity of textual evidence, and his conception of history was founded on the 'grand narratives' of progress and power. Both have become the target of the deconstructionists.

The claim of *What Is History?* to continuing significance rests on two grounds. First, it virtually established a new genre. Searching questions about the nature of history had been asked since Graeco-Roman times, but they had mostly been posed (and answered) by philosophers. Indeed the history of this kind of enquiry can be written convincingly with virtually no mention of historians.[2] Historians themselves, on the rare occasions when they stepped back from their researches, wrote guides to method rather than reflections on the nature of history. Carr bridged the gap. He was well read in philosophy; at the same time he was enough of a historical practitioner to root his analysis in real problems of historical enquiry. The outcome is a book which pithily captures many of the unstated assumptions of the historian's work and subjects them to withering critique. At the same time the polemical tone of the book itself stimulates a critical response, since several of its arguments are distorted by the requirements of rhetoric. That iconoclastic quality has been much less evident in the books which have followed in the wake of

*What Is History?* But 1961 was clearly a watershed in the writing of historiography. The issues which Carr raised became part of the intellectual milieu in which historians worked. His views could not be ignored. They were vigorously debated by a succession of historians – G.R. Elton, Arthur Marwick, Gordon Connell-Smith, H.A. Lloyd, and so on.[3] More recent writers – like Ludmilla Jordanova for example[4] – may make few explicit references to Carr, but they occupy a space which was first opened up by *What Is History?*

The second reason why Carr's work has continuing resonance is that the most obvious and pressing message of the book continues to be so relevant. Carr stated that history was 'an unending dialogue between the past and the present'.

> To learn about the present in the light of the past means also to learn about the past in the light of the present. The function of history is to promote a profounder understanding of both past and present through the interrelation between them.[5]

Carr emphasized the conclusion which logically flows from this proposition – that the priorities and findings of historical enquiry inevitably change over time. This argument was partly directed against the unreflecting empiricism which was much commoner among historians then than it is now. Carr wanted to dispose of the idea that following the trusted procedures of the professional will yield authentic or objective knowledge of the past. He showed that at every level of historical enquiry, from the choice of source materials through to the finished work of history, the present intrudes on the reconstruction of the past. What the most casual reader will carry away from reading *What Is History?* is the idea that historians do not stand outside or above history; some rise above the preoccupations of their contemporaries better than others, but even the most objective remain fundamentally 'part of the procession'.

For a historical profession confined within very limited notions of the subject matter of history, Carr's outlook was little short of revolutionary, and it provoked predictably sharp reactions, for and against. It was hardly a coincidence that the appearance of *What Is History?* was quickly followed by the establishment of new strands of history which deliberately sought to address present need: social history in the mould of E.P.

Thompson, the new urban history, and the history of Africa, for example. It was as if Carr's dynamic vision of the relationship between past and present had released a new creative energy among younger historians. In that sense the shape of academic history today bears the unmistakable stamp of Carr's influence. That history continues to be characterized by a high degree of variety – both of theme and method – is a sure sign of health, as is the steady flow of writing which critiques the practice of history in the tradition created by Carr himself.[6]

What, meanwhile, of the impact made by history and historians on the wider public? The record here is much more mixed. The coming of the third millennium in January 2000 provided a convenient vantage point from which to weigh the current social significance of historical enquiry. Temporal landmarks of this kind are as much about evaluating the past as about mapping out the future: indeed the two are indissolubly linked, since any conception of the future is defined in relation to the past (as Carr emphasized). One might, for example, have expected some reflection on Britain's relationship with mainland Europe a thousand years on from the Roman occupation, or a reassessment of our social and cultural life based on a long view of continuity and change. Instead the public celebration of the Millennium in Britain was almost empty of historical content: the tone was set by the exhibition in the Millennium Dome at Greenwich, where major themes of human experience and achievement were presented in a historical vacuum. Historians appear to have played no part in planning the celebrations.

It was therefore in keeping with the millennial atmosphere that historical perspective proved singularly lacking with respect to the most epoch-making event in the twenty-first century so far: the attacks on New York and Washington on September 11 2001. Confronted by a disaster on this unprecedented scale, most Americans – and many of their overseas friends – were overwhelmed by feelings of visceral fear, moral revulsion and a desire for revenge. These responses were entirely understandable, but by themselves they did not furnish the basis for a rational policy towards terrorism. September 11 represented a point where many historical strands became intertwined: the growth of Islamic fundamentalism (linked to notions of a *jihad*, or holy war); the simmering crisis in Palestine; the collapse of central state power in a number of Islamic countries; the rising tide of resentment in the Middle East against US interventionism; and the unstable world order since the end of the Cold War.[7] Analytical thinking along these lines requires not only a well-stocked fund of historical knowledge but also cool-headed detachment; it is likely to be the first casualty in a situation which is defined for most people in terms of panic and rage. One of the key questions in the post-September 11 world is how quickly American policy becomes tempered by a sense of historical perspective.

However, loss of historical awareness is not the prerogative of nations caught up in catastrophe. At present the British government is particularly resistant to any critical perspective derived from the past. The Conservative administrations of the 1980s and 1990s had had a vision of the national past which was variously invoked in opposition to European integration, constitutional devolution within the United Kingdom and other issues. Margaret Thatcher had urged the nation to measure itself against the achievements of its Victorian forebears, and her government devoted closer attention to history than to any other subject in the National Curriculum. The advent of Tony Blair in 1997 marked a significant shift. True to its name, New Labour has struck a pose of commitment to novelty, unburdened by the past. The centenary of the Labour Party in 2001 was barely acknowledged, as if a backward glance might stir up memories of its earlier radicalism and thus jeopardize the reinvention of the party. The few public references which Blair has made to the role of history have tended to be negative: during the talks leading up to the Good Friday Agreement in Northern Ireland, for example, he expressed the hope that 'the burden of history' could be lifted.[8] Certainly New Labour regards history as a cultural asset to be lightly worn. The space planned for history in the National Curriculum by the Tories has been curtailed in order to accommodate more pressing requirements, such as 'citizenship'. It remains to be seen whether, in vacating the terrain of history, Blair has handed his opponents powerful cultural resources whose loss he may live to regret.

In sharp contrast to the indifference towards history which prevails at the top levels of government, a wide range of cultural institutions encourage an interest in the past, and many of them receive public funds for this purpose: one thinks of the great national museums, the historical monuments maintained by

English Heritage, and the BBC. This is the domain of what has come to be called 'public history', meaning the past as it is represented for public consumption, and at present it is unquestionably booming. Museums have recently experienced an impressive increase in the number of their visitors, only partly explained by the decision to abolish entrance charges. History now occupies a significant place in the most influential medium of popular culture – television. There are more history programmes than ever before, giving rise to the quip that history is 'the new gardening'. The subject matter is skewed to the Second World War and the history of the English monarchy, and the programmes vary sharply in quality, but at their best they bring the past to life and invite some kind of personal identification with it.

Of course any manifestation of mass culture is conditioned by commercial considerations. The objection can be made that, for example, museums and ancient monuments are promoted less for their contribution to historical education in the broadest sense than as an adjunct to tourism; hence the very mixed reactions to the term 'heritage'. The political assumptions of public history are also suspect: under the guise of entertainment popular images of the past pander to a lowest common denominator of sentimentalism, nostalgia and national pride.[9] But both these criticisms fall wide of the mark because they overstate the ability of the guardians of public history to determine popular response to their products. The important point about the current craze for historical material on the tourist trail or in the media is that it reflects varied forms of engagement that go far beyond the negative stereotypes. The quest for personal roots, the need for a perspective on present-day cultural identities, securing a better purchase on social problems – all these and more shape the popular fascination with the past. And they are expressed not only through the consumption of materials in the public sphere but also in creative individual pursuits, such as research into family history and collecting old photographs of particular genres or places.[10]

Most historians look askance at these popular uses of the past, believing that they are a diversion from the real job of reconstructing and interpreting the past. But professional and popular priorities are not mutually exclusive. On certain historical topics there is so much at stake in political or cultural terms that meticulous scholarship comes to be regarded as the final arbiter. This is most strikingly true of the Holocaust. The social memory of European Jewry, the moral obligations of the German nation and the legitimacy of the state of Israel are all closely bound up with the historicity of this event. Did six million Jews perish under Nazi rule? Did Hitler plan and order their extermination? Or was the Holocaust a propaganda myth devised by the victorious powers at the end of the war? These issues were brought to trial in Britain in unique circumstances in 2000. A leading 'revisionist' historian, David Irving, claimed that Deborah Lipstadt, an American academic, and her publisher, Penguin Books, had libelled him by describing him as a 'Holocaust denier' who suppressed and distorted the documentary record. In order to rebut the charges, the defence needed to prove both that Irving was dishonest in his use of evidence, and that the historical events which he denied had actually taken place. As a result the views of professional historians were as central to the case as the arguments of legal counsel. Several leading academics either testified in court or were commissioned to write reports on the historical issues at stake. One historian, Richard Evans, was retained specifically to investigate the validity of Irving's research procedures. In his later account of the case, Evans posed the question, 'How do we know when a historian is telling the truth?'[11] The answer was, by tracing his or her statements back to the sources on which they were purportedly based. For three months the court heard a mountain of evidence of this kind. The verdict, delivered in a 350-page judgement, was an unequivocal defeat for Irving: he was found to have flouted accepted research methods and to have manipulated the evidence to suit his political prejudices.

The Irving case was obviously important in diminishing the credibility of Holocaust denial. But it had a wider significance. It showed that what professional historians do matters, that some events in the past can be authenticated beyond reasonable doubt, and that society has a vested interest in the maintenance of scholarly standards. Each of these propositions has been a matter of debate in recent years. History has been dismissed by Modernists as an antiquarian irrelevance, and by Postmodernists as a self-serving fiction. Historians have sometimes felt that the scholarly claims of their profession have been locked in a losing battle with sceptical voices from outside. The Irving case may well prove to be unique: perhaps no other historical issue could lead to such a sharply focused confrontation between scholarship and propaganda. But it nevertheless provides a sober reminder that the most accurate history possible is a social necessity.

That in a nutshell is the position argued in *The Pursuit of History*. The book begins by drawing a distinction between a professionally informed historical awareness and other, more instrumental versions of the past. It concludes by asserting that historians will continue to merit the support of the societies in which they work as long as they acknowledge the validity of relevant history. The intervening chapters support these claims by defining the evidential base of the subject, by outlining its characteristic themes, which have often been soundly practical in origin, and by exploring the limits of reliable and disinterested historical knowledge. For all its infatuation with the modern and the new, contemporary society continues to regard the past as a source of legitimacy and inspiration. It is easy to criticize that focus on the past when, as is so often the case, it is acknowledged in a backhanded fashion, through an entirely present-centred relativism. The Irving case reminds us that there are vital historical issues which transcend the preoccupations of cultural politics, and which place professional expertise at a premium. For as long as that is so, there will be a need for the skills and insights described in this book.

*John Tosh*
*April 2002*

## Notes

1 E.H Carr, *What Is History?*, with a new introduction by Richard J. Evans (Palgrave, 2001).

2 See for example B.A. Haddock, *An Introduction to Historical Thought* (Arnold, 1980).

3 G.R. Elton, *The Practice of History* (Fontana, 1969); Arthur Marwick, *The Nature of History* (Macmillan, 1970); Gordon Connell-Smith and Howell A. Lloyd, *The Relevance of History* (Heinemann, 1972).

4 Ludmilla Jordanova, *History in Practice* (Arnold, 2000).

5 Carr, *What Is History?*, p. 62.

6 See for example Richard J. Evans, *In Defence of History* (Granta, 1997); Ludmilla Jordanova, *History in Practice* (Arnold, 2000); Alun Munslow, *Deconstructing History* (Routledge, 1997). For a recent anthology, see John Tosh (ed.), *Historians On History* (Longman, 2000).

7 For a preliminary analysis, see Fred Halliday, *Two Days That Shook the World* (Saqi Books, 2002).

8 Tony Blair, quoted in *The Guardian*, 11 April 1998.

9 Patrick Wright, *On Living In An Old Country: the National Past in Contemporary Britain* (Verso, 1985).

10 For a passionate demonstration of this point, see Raphael Samuel, *Theatres of Memory*, vol. I (Verso, 1994).

11 Richard J. Evans, *Telling Lies About Hitler: History, Holocaust, and the David Irving Trial* (Basic Books, 2001), p. 1.

# Preface to the Third Edition

The word *history* carries two meanings in common parlance. It refers both to what actually happened in the past and to the representation of that past in the work of historians. This book is an introduction to history in the second sense. It is intended for anyone who is sufficiently interested in the subject to wonder how historical enquiry is conducted and what purpose it fulfils. More specifically, the book is addressed to students taking a degree course in history, for whom these questions have particular relevance.

Traditionally history undergraduates were offered no formal instruction in the nature of their chosen discipline; its time-honoured place in our literary culture and its non-technical presentation suggested that common sense combined with a sound general education would provide the student with what little orientation he or she required. This approach leaves a great deal to chance. It is surely desirable that students consider the functions served by a subject to which they are about to devote three years of study or more. Curriculum choice, which is a great deal more bewildering than it was twenty years ago, will be a hit-and-miss affair unless based on a clear grasp of the content and scope of present-day historical scholarship. Above all, students need to be aware of the limits placed on historical knowledge by the character of the sources and the working methods of historians, so that at an early stage they can develop a critical approach to the formidable array of secondary authorities which they are required to master. It is certainly possible to complete a degree course in history without giving systematic thought to any of these issues, and generations of students have done so. But most universities now recognize that the value of historical study is thereby diminished, and they therefore provide introductory courses on the methods and scope of history. I hope that this book will meet the needs of students taking such a course.

Although my own research experience has been in the fields of African history and gender in modern Britain, it has not been my intention to write a manifesto for 'the new history'. I have tried instead to convey the diversity of current historical practice and to situate recent innovations in the context of mainstream traditional scholarship, which continues to account for a great deal of first-rate historical work and to dominate academic syllabuses. The scope of historical studies is today so wide that it has not been easy to determine the precise range of this book; but without some more or less arbitrary boundaries an introductory work of this length would lose all coherence. I therefore say nothing about the history of science and very little about the history of art or environmental history. My treatment of historical sources is in practice limited to verbal materials (both written and oral) because it is in this sphere that the claims of historians to special expertise lie. In general I have confined my choice to those themes which are widely studied by students today, as distinct from promising directions which may unfold in the future.

Even within these limits, however, my territory is something of a minefield. Anyone who imagines that an introduction to the study of history will express a consensus of expert opinion needs to be promptly disabused. One of the distinguishing features of the profession is its heated arguments concerning the objectives and limitations of historical study. This book inevitably reflects my own views, and it is appropriate to declare them at the outset. The salient points are that history is a subject of practical social relevance; that the proper performance of its function depends on a receptive and discriminating attitude to other disciplines, especially the social sciences; and that all historical enquiry, whatever the source of its inspiration, must be conducted in accordance with the rigorous critical method which is the hallmark of modern academic history. At the same time, I have tried to place these claims – none of which is of course original – in the context of recent debate among historians, and to give a fair hearing to views with which I disagree.

This book is intended to explore a number of general propositions about history and historians, rather than provide a point of entry into any one field or specialism. But since I anticipate that most of my readers will be more familiar with British history than any other, I have relied for my illustrative material mostly on that field, with some additional examples from Africa, Europe and the United States. The book is meant to be read as a whole, but I have included a certain amount of cross-referencing in the text to assist the reader who wishes to pursue only one theme.

The third edition makes substantial changes to the text. The intellectual milieu in which history is practised has changed considerably since 1984. The rise of Postmodernism has lent a new sharpness to the longstanding debate about the status of historical enquiry. In Chapter 7, I now take full account of the Postmodernist intervention while resisting its more destructive tendencies. A new chapter on 'Theories of meaning' assesses the cultural turn in history, including cultural tendencies in the study of gender. The book now opens with a much fuller account of how scholarly history differs from other renditions of the past, and this leads on to an expanded treatment of the social relevance of history in Chapter 2. Elsewhere I have amended and updated the text at numerous points.

In ranging so far beyond any one person's experience of research and writing, this book is more dependent than most on the help of other scholars. This latest edition has benefited from the advice of Michael Pinnock, Michael Roper and the late Raphael Samuel. I hope that the text still bears the imprint of those who cast a critical eye over earlier editions, particularly Norma Clarke, Ben Fowkes, David Henige, Tim Hitchcock and the late Peter Seltman. Over the years the University of North London has provided generous support, as well as an indispensable teaching context in which the ideas in this book have been developed. The dedicatees, Nick Tosh and William Tosh, continue to take a lively interest in the fortunes of a book that has existed for almost as long as they have. In the final stages Caroline White gave me timely encouragement and much else besides.

*John Tosh*
*London, March 1999*

# CHAPTER ONE

# Historical awareness

This chapter looks at the difference between memory, whether
individual or collective, and the more disciplined approach
towards the past that characterizes an awareness of *history*. All
groups have a sense of the past, but they tend to use it to reinforce
their own beliefs and sense of identity. Like human memory,
collective or social memory can be faulty, distorted by factors such
as a sense of tradition or nostalgia, or else a belief in progress
through time. Modern professional historians take their cue from
nineteenth-century *historicism*, which taught that the past should
be studied on its own terms, 'as it actually was'. However, this
more detached approach to the past can put historians in conflict
with people who feel their cherished versions of the past are under
threat.

'Historical awareness' is a slippery term. It can be regarded
as a universal psychological attribute, arising from the
fact that we are, all of us, in a sense historians. Because our
species depends more on experience than on instinct, life cannot
be lived without the consciousness of a personal past; and
someone who has lost it through illness or ageing is generally
regarded as disqualified from normal life. As individuals we draw
on our experience in all sorts of different ways – as a means of
affirming our identity, as a clue to our potential, as the basis for
our impression of others, and as some indication of the possibilities that lie ahead. Our memories serve as both a data bank and
a means of making sense of an unfolding life story. We know that
we cannot understand a situation without some perception of

where it fits into a continuing process or whether it has happened before. The same holds true of our lives as social beings. All societies have a collective memory, a storehouse of experience which is drawn on for a sense of identity and a sense of direction. Professional historians commonly deplore the superficiality of popular historical knowledge, but *some* knowledge of the past is almost universal; without it one is effectively excluded from social and political debate, just as loss of memory disqualifies one from much everyday human interaction. Our political judgements are permeated by a sense of the past, whether we are deciding between the competing claims of political parties or assessing the feasibility of particular policies. To understand our social arrangements, we need to have some notion of where they have come from. In that sense all societies possess 'memory'.

But 'historical awareness' is not the same thing as social memory. How the past is known and how it is applied to present need are open to widely varying approaches. We know from personal experience that memory is neither fixed nor infallible: we forget, we overlay early memories with later experience, we shift the emphasis, we entertain false memories, and so on. In important matters we are likely to seek confirmation of our memories from an outside source. Collective memory is marked by the same distortions, as our current priorities lead us to highlight some aspects of the past and to exclude others. In our political life especially, memory is highly selective, and sometimes downright erroneous. It is at this point that the term 'historical awareness' invites a more rigorous interpretation. Under the **Third Reich** those Germans who believed that all the disasters in German history were the fault of the Jews certainly acknowledged the power of the past, but we would surely question the extent of their historical awareness. In other words, it is not enough to invoke the past; there must also be a belief that getting the story right matters. History as a disciplined enquiry aims to sustain the widest possible definition of memory, and to make the process of recall as accurate as possible, so that our knowledge of the past is not confined to what is immediately relevant. The goal is a resource with open-ended application, instead of a set of mirror-images of the present. That at least has been the aspiration of historians for the past two centuries. Much of this book will be devoted to evaluating how adequately historians achieve these

**Third Reich**
The technical term for the National Socialist (Nazi) regime in Germany, 1933–45. Reich (roughly 'Empire') was used to denote the original medieval German Empire and the unified German Empire (the Second Reich), which lasted from 1871 to 1919.

ends. My purpose in this opening chapter is to explore the different dimensions of social memory, and in so doing to arrive at an understanding of what historians do and how it differs from other sorts of thinking about the past.

# I

## Social memory: creating the self-identity of a group

For any social grouping to have a collective identity there has to be a shared interpretation of the events and experiences which have formed the group over time. Sometimes this will include an accepted belief about the origins of the group, as in the case of many nation-states; or the emphasis may be on vivid turning points and symbolic moments which confirm the self-image and aspirations of the group. Current examples include the vital significance of the **Edwardian suffrage movement** for the women's movement, and the appeal of the **'molly house'** sub-culture of eighteenth-century London for the gay community in Britain today.[1] Without an awareness of a common past made up of such human detail, men and women could not easily acknowledge the claims on their loyalty of large abstractions.

The term 'social memory' accurately reflects the rationale of popular knowledge about the past. Social groupings need a record of prior experience, but they also require a picture of the past which serves to explain or justify the present, often at the cost of historical accuracy. The operation of social memory is clearest in those societies where no appeal can be made to the documentary record as a corrective or higher authority. Pre-colonial Africa presents some classic instances.[2] In literate societies the same was true for those largely unlettered communities which lay outside the élite, such as the peasantries of pre-modern Europe. What counted for historical knowledge here was handed down as a narrative from one generation to the next, often identified with particular places and particular ceremonies or rituals. It provided a guide for conduct and a set of symbols around which resistance to unwelcome intrusion could be mobilized. Until quite recently popular memory in a largely illiterate Sicily embraced both the Palermo rising of 1282 against the Angevins ('the Sicilian

**Edwardian suffrage movement**
The movement in the period before the First World War to obtain the parliamentary vote ('suffrage') for women. It is best known for campaigns of the militant suffragettes, although it was the more moderate suffragists who finally obtained votes for women in 1918.

**molly house**
An eighteenth-century covert meeting house for homosexual men. Molly houses remained little known until Mark Ravenhill's play *Mother Clapp's Molly House* (2001) was staged to widespread acclaim at the Royal National Theatre.

Vespers') and the nineteenth-century *mafia* as episodes in a national tradition of avenging brotherhood.[3]

But it would be a mistake to suppose that social memory is the preserve of small-scale, pre-literate societies. In fact the term itself highlights a universal need: if the individual cannot exist without memory, neither can society, and that goes for large-scale technologically advanced societies too. All societies look to their collective memories for consolation or inspiration, and literate societies are in principle no different. Near-universal literacy and a high degree of residential mobility mean that the oral transmission of social memory is now much less important. But written accounts (such as school history books or popular evocations of the World Wars), film and television perform the same function. Social memory continues to be an essential means of sustaining a politically active identity. Its success is judged by how effectively it contributes to collective cohesion and how widely it is shared by members of the group. Sometimes social memory is based on consensus and inclusion, and this is often the function of explicitly national narratives. It can take the form of a **foundation**

Foundation myth: the Declaration of Independence by America's 'Founding Fathers' in 1776 remains an iconic moment in American history of immense symbolic importance. American school history books still present it in resolutely heroic terms.
(Bridgeman Art Library/Capitol Collection, Washington, USA)

**myth**, as in the case of the far-seeing Founding Fathers of the American Republic, whose memory is still invoked today in order to shore up belief in the American nation. Alternatively consensual memory can focus on a moment of heroism, like the story of Dunkirk in 1940, which the British recall as the ingenious escape that laid the foundations of victory.

## Social memory of past oppression

But social memory can also serve to sustain a sense of oppression, exclusion or adversity, and these elements account for some of the most powerful expressions of social memory. Social movements entering the political arena for the first time are particularly conscious of the absolute requirement of a past. Black history in the United States has its origin in the kind of strategic concern voiced by Malcolm X in the 1960s. One reason why blacks were oppressed, he wrote, was that white America had cut them off from their past:

> If we don't go into the past and find out how we got this way, we will think that we were always this way. And if you think that you were in the condition that you're in right now, it's impossible for you to have too much confidence in yourself, you become worthless, almost nothing.[4]

The purpose of much British labour history has been to sharpen the social awareness of the workers, to confirm their commitment to political action, and to reassure them that history is 'on their side' if only they will keep faith with the heroism of their forebears. The historical reconstruction of working people's experience was, as the inaugural editorial of *History Workshop* put it, 'a source of inspiration and understanding'.[5] Working-class memories of work, locality, family and politics – with all the pride and anger so often expressed through them – were rescued before they were pushed out of popular consciousness by an approved national version.

The women's movement of the past thirty years has been if anything more conscious of the need for a usable past. For feminists this requirement is not met by studies of exceptional women such as Elizabeth I who operated successfully in a man's world; the emphasis falls instead on the economic and sexual exploitation which has been the lot of most women, and on the efforts of

**foundation myth**
A story, usually much-treasured, about the foundation of a group or people. One of the most famous is the biblical story of the Creation. Nations often have semi-'official' versions of their origins, usually involving national hero figures, but foundation myths can be found in schools, army regiments, even companies. 'Myth' need not imply that the story is entirely false, merely that it has developed into a simplistic, usually rosy, version of events.

**History Workshop**
History Workshop was a collaborative research venture set up by a group of left-wing historians led by Raphael Samuel (1934–96) at Ruskin College, Oxford, to encourage research and debate in working-class and women's history.

**patriarchy**
A social system based on
the dominance of fathers,
and, by extension, of men
in general.

activists to secure redress. According to this perspective, the critical determinant of women's history was not nation or class, but **patriarchy**: that is, the power of the household head over his wife and children and, by extension, the power of men over women more generally. Because mainstream history suppresses this truth, what it offers is not universal history but a blinkered account of half the human race. These are the themes which, to quote from the title of a popular feminist text, have been 'hidden from history'.[6] As one American feminist has put it:

> It is not surprising that most women feel that their sex does not have an interesting or significant past. However, like minority groups, women cannot afford to lack a consciousness of a collective identity, one which necessarily involves a shared awareness of the past. Without this, a social group suffers from a kind of collective amnesia, which makes it vulnerable to the impositions of dubious stereotypes, as well as limiting prejudices about what is right and proper for it to do or not to do.[7]

For socially deprived or 'invisible' groups – whether in a majority such as workers and women, or in a minority such as blacks in America and Britain – effective political mobilization depends on a consciousness of common experience in the past.

# II

## Historicism – liberating the past from the present

But alongside these socially motivated views of the past has grown up a form of historical awareness which starts from quite different premises. While social memory has continued to open up interpretations that satisfy new forms of political and social need, the dominant approach in historical scholarship has been to value the past for its own sake and, as far as possible, to rise above political expediency. It was only during the nineteenth century that historical awareness in this more rigorous sense became the defining attribute of professional historians. There were certainly important precursors – in the ancient world, in Islam, in dynastic China, and in the West from the Renaissance onwards. But it was not until the first half of the nineteenth century that all the elements of historical awareness were brought together in a historical practice which was widely recognized as the proper way to study the past. This was the achievement of the intellectual movement known as *historicism*, which began in Germany and soon spread all over the Western world (the word comes from the German *Historismus*).

The fundamental premise of the historicists was that the autonomy of the past must be respected. They held that each age is a unique manifestation of the human spirit, with its own culture and values. For one age to understand another, there must be a recognition that the passage of time has profoundly altered both the conditions of life and the mentality of men and women – even perhaps human nature itself. Historians are not the guardians of universal values, nor can they deliver 'the verdict of history'; they must strive to understand each age in its own terms, to take on its own values and priorities, instead of imposing ours. All the resources of scholarship and all the historian's powers of imagination must be harnessed to the task of bringing the past back to life – or *resurrecting* it, to employ a favourite conceit of the period. But historicism was more than an antiquarian rallying cry. Its proponents maintained that the culture and institutions of their own day could only be understood historically. Unless their growth and development through successive ages were grasped, their true nature would remain elusive. History, in short, held the key to understanding the world.

## Seeing through the eyes of the past

Historicism was one facet of Romanticism, the dominant movement in European thought and art around 1800. The most influential Romantic literary figure, Sir Walter Scott, aimed to draw readers of his historical romances into the authentic atmosphere of the past. Popular interest in the surviving remains of the past rose to new heights, and it extended to not only the ancient world but also the hitherto despised Middle Ages. Historicism represented the academic wing of the Romantic obsession with the past. The leading figure in the movement was Leopold von Ranke, a professor at Berlin University from 1824 until 1872 and author of over sixty volumes. In the preface to his first book, he wrote,

> History has had assigned to it the task of judging the past, of
> instructing the present for the benefit of the ages to come. To such

lofty functions this work does not aspire. Its aim is merely to show how things actually were (*wie es eigentlich gewesen*).[8]

By this Ranke meant more than an intention to reconstruct the passage of events, though this was certainly part of his programme.[9] What was new about the historicists' approach was their realization that the atmosphere and mentality of past ages had to be reconstructed too, if the formal record of events was to have any meaning. The main task of the historian became to find out why people acted as they did by stepping into their shoes, by seeing the world through their eyes and as far as possible by judging it by their standards. **Thomas Carlyle** believed more fervently in historical recreation than any other nineteenth-century writer; whatever the purpose of historical work, 'the first indispensable condition', he declared, was that 'we *see* the things transacted, picture them wholly, as if they stand before our eyes'.[10] And this obligation extended to *all* periods in the past, however alien they might seem to modern observers. Ranke himself strove to meet the historicist ideal in his treatment of the wars of religion in the sixteenth and seventeenth centuries. Others tackled the Middle Ages in the same spirit.

Ranke's much-quoted preface is also important as a disclaimer of relevance. Ranke did not maintain that historical research served no purpose outside itself; indeed, he was probably the last major historian to believe that the outcome of studies such as his own would be to reveal the hand of God in human history. But he did not look for practical lessons from the past. Indeed he believed that detachment from present-day concerns was a condition of understanding the past. His objection to previous historians was not that they lacked all curiosity or **empathy** but that they were diverted from the real task by the desire to preach, or to give lessons in statecraft, or to shore up the reputation of a ruling dynasty; in pursuing immediate goals they obscured the true wisdom to be derived from historical study. In the next chapter I will consider more fully the question of whether relevance is necessarily incompatible with historical awareness. But during the first half of the nineteenth century, when Europe experienced a high degree of turbulence in the aftermath of the **French Revolution**, history was politically contentious, and unless a special virtue had been made of detachment, it is hard to see how a scholarly historical practice could have become estab-

**Carlyle**
Thomas Carlyle (1795–1881) was a popular, though controversial, Victorian writer and historian, author of a long, colourful account of the French Revolution.

**empathy**
The ability to enter into the feelings of others (not to be confused with sympathy, which denotes actually sharing them). The term is often used to describe a historian's approach to the 'foreignness' of past societies. In the 1980s there was an ultimately ill-fated attempt to assess children's ability to empathize with people in the past for examination purposes.

**French Revolution**
The tumultuous political events in late eighteenth-century France which overturned the monarchy and established a republic based upon the principles of the Rights of Man. It involved considerable violence and chronic political instability, until Napoleon staged a military *coup* in 1799.

lished. Though very few people read Ranke today, his name continues to stand for an **Olympian** impartiality and a duty to be true to the past before all else.

## The 'otherness' of the past

Historical awareness in the sense understood by the historicists rests on three principles. The first, and most fundamental, is *difference*; that is, a recognition of the gulf which separates our own age from all previous ages. Because nothing in history stands still, the passage of time has profoundly altered the way we live. The first responsibility of the historian is to take the measure of the difference of the past; conversely one of the worst sins is **anachronism** – the unthinking assumption that people in the past behaved and thought as we do. This difference is partly about the material conditions of life, a point sometimes forcibly made by the surviving remains of the past such as buildings, implements and clothing. Less obviously but even more importantly, the difference is one of mentality: earlier generations had different values, priorities, fears and hopes from our own. We may take the beauties of nature for granted, but medieval men and women were terrified of forests and mountains and strayed from the beaten track as little as possible. In late eighteenth-century rural England, separation and remarriage were sometimes achieved by means of public wife-sale; although this was in part a reaction to the virtual impossibility of legal divorce for the poor, it is hard for the modern reader not to dwell on the extreme patriarchal values implied in the humiliation of a wife led to market by her husband and held by a halter.[11] During the same period public hangings in London regularly drew crowds of 30,000 or more, both rich and poor, and usually more women than men. Their motivation varied: it might be to see justice done, to draw lessons from the deportment of the condemned man or to register indignation at his death; but all shared a readiness to gaze on an act of cold-blooded cruelty from which most people today would recoil in horror.[12] More recent periods may not be so strange, but we still have to be alert to many evidences of difference. In mid-Victorian England it was possible for a thoughtful educated person to describe the teaming poor of East London as a 'trembling mass of maggots in a lump of **carrion**'.[13] Historical empathy, which has been much vaunted in classroom practice in recent years, is often taken to mean a recognition of the common humanity we share with our forebears; but a more realistic (and also more rigorous) interpretation of empathy dwells on the effort of imagination needed to penetrate past mentalities, which are irremediably removed from anything in our experience. As the novelist **L.P. Hartley** remarked, 'The past is another country'.[14] Of course, like all foreign lands, the past is never entirely alien. As well as the shock of revulsion, historians experience the shock of recognition – as when they come across unaffected spontaneity in the behaviour of parents towards children in seventeenth-century England, or uncover the consumerist culture of eighteenth-century London. 'All history', it has been said, 'is a negotiation between familiarity and strangeness'.[15] But in any scholarly enquiry it is the otherness of the past that tends to come to the fore because the passage of time has made exotic what once seemed commonplace.

## Putting 'otherness' in context

Merely to register such instances of difference across the gulf of time can give a salutary jolt to our modern assumptions. But historians aim to go much further than this. Their purpose is not only to uncover the strangeness of the past but to explain it, and that means placing it in its historical setting. What may seem bizarre or disturbing to us becomes explicable – though not necessarily less shocking – when interpreted as a manifestation of a particular society. To recoil in horror from the grisly details of witchcraft accusations in Early Modern Europe is certainly to acknowledge the gulf which separates that time from ours, but this is no more than a point of departure. The reason why we understand this phenomenon so much better now than we did thirty years ago is that historians have positioned it in relation to beliefs about the human body, the framework of popular religious belief outside the Church, and the tensions in the position of women.[16] *Context* is thus the second component of historical awareness. The underlying principle of all historical work is that the subject of our enquiry must not be wrenched from its setting. Just as we would not pronounce on the significance of an archaeological find without first recording carefully its precise location in the site, so we must place everything we know about the past

**L.P. Hartley**
British novelist (1895–1972). His novel *The Go-Between*, about a young boy who carries messages between a pair of lovers, is told through the memory of the boy grown to adulthood. The novel's opening line 'The past is a foreign country; they do things differently there' has been adopted by historians trying to put across the dangers of imposing modern assumptions on previous ages.

in its contemporary context. This is an exacting standard, requiring a formidable breadth of knowledge. It is often what distinguishes the professional from the amateur. The enthusiast working on family history in the local record office can, with a little technical guidance, substantiate a sequence of births, marriages and deaths, often extending over many generations; the amateur will come to grief not over factual omissions but because of an inadequate grasp of the relevant economic or social settings. To the social historian, the history of the family is not fundamentally about lines of descent, or even about plotting average family size down the ages; it is about placing the family within the shifting contexts of household production, health, religion, education and state policy.[17] Everything in the historian's training militates against presenting the past as a fixed single-track sequence of events; context must be respected at every point.

## The historical continuum

But history is more than a collection of snapshots of the past, however vivid and richly contextualized. A third fundamental aspect of historical awareness is the recognition of historical *process* – the relationship between events over time which endows them with more significance than if they were viewed in isolation. For example, historians continue to be interested in the application of steam power to cotton spinning in the late eighteenth century, not so much because it is a striking instance of technical and entrepreneurial ingenuity but because it contributed so much to what has come to be called the Industrial Revolution. Specific annexations during the **Scramble for Africa** attract attention because they formed part of a large-scale imperialism by the European powers; and so on. Apart from their intrinsic interest, what lies behind our concern with these instances of historical process is the much bigger question of how we got from 'then' to 'now'. This is the 'big story' to which so many more restricted enquiries contribute. There may be a gulf between 'us' and 'them', but that gulf is actually composed of processes of growth, decay and change which it is the business of historians to uncover. Thus the fuller understanding we now have of witchcraft in the sixteenth and seventeenth centuries begs the question of how this form of belief came into decline and disrepute, to the point where

**Scramble for Africa**
The term given to the process by which, in the 1880s and 1890s, almost the entire African continent was taken over by European powers. The term, which was used at the time, reflects distaste at the naked greed with which the Europeans jostled with each other to grab vast areas of land with no thought at all for the welfare of the African peoples who lived there.

**kinship systems**
Social systems based upon the extended family.

**venerable**
Worthy of respect and reverence, especially by virtue of age and wisdom.

in Western society today it is subscribed to by only a very few self-conscious revivalists. Historical processes have sometimes been marked by abrupt transitions when history, as it were, speeded up – as in the case of the great revolutions. At the other extreme, history may almost stand still, its flow only perceptible with the hindsight of many centuries, as in patterns of land use or **kinship systems** in many pre-industrial societies.[18] If historical awareness rests on the notion of continuum, this cuts both ways: just as nothing has remained the same in the past, so too our world is the product of history. Every aspect of our culture, behaviour and beliefs is the outcome of processes over time. This is true not only of **venerable** institutions such as the Christian churches or the British monarchy, which are visibly the outcome of centuries of evolution; it applies also to the most familiar aspects of everyday, such as marriage or personal hygiene, which are much less often placed in a historical frame. No human practice ever stands still; all demand a historical perspective which uncovers the dynamics of change over time. This is one reason why it is so important that students should study large swathes of history. At present in British schools and universities there is so much emphasis on the virtues of documentary study and narrow specialism that major historical trends tend to disappear from view.

# III

## Are professional historical awareness and popular social memory in opposition?

**autonomous**
State of self-governing independence.

In the sense understood by the historicists, then, historical awareness means respecting the **autonomy** of the past, and attempting to reconstruct it in all its strangeness before applying its insights to the present. The effect of this programme was to drive a bigger wedge between élite and popular attitudes to the past which has persisted until today. Professional historians insist on a lengthy immersion in the primary sources, a deliberate shedding of present-day assumptions, and a rare degree of empathy and imagination. Popular historical knowledge, on the other hand, tends to a highly selective interest in the remains of the past, is shot through with present-day assumptions, and is only incidentally concerned to understand the past on its own terms. Three recurrent features of social memory have particularly significant distorting effects.

## The distorting effects of tradition

The first of these is respect for *tradition*. In many areas of life – from the law courts to political associations, from churches to sports clubs – belief and behaviour are governed by the weight of precedent: an assumption that what was done in the past is an authoritative guide to what should be done in the present. Respect for tradition is sometimes confused with a sense of history because it involves an affection for the past (or some of it) and a desire to keep faith with it. But there is very little of the historical about appeals to tradition. Following the path laid down by the ancestors has a great deal to be said for it in communities which neither experience change nor expect it; for them present and past can scarcely be distinguished. That is why respect for tradition contributed so much to the cohesion of society among small-scale pre-literate peoples – and why indeed they are some-

The State Opening of Parliament. Much of the ritual at this annual ceremony has strong historical resonance, but this should not be confused with a professional, analytical sense of history. Such traditions can, in fact, conjure up the past to obscure the political reality of the present. (Getty Images/AFP)

times referred to by anthropologists as 'traditional societies'. But such conditions no longer exist. In any society with a dynamic of social or cultural change, as indicated by external trade or social hierarchy or political institutions, an uncritical respect for tradition is counterproductive. It suppresses the historical changes which have occurred in the intervening period; indeed it positively discourages any attention to those changes and leads to the continuance of outward forms which are really redundant – or which we might say have been 'overtaken by history'. One reason for the famed stability of parliamentary government in Britain is that Parliament itself enjoys the prestige of a 700-year-old history as 'the mother of parliaments'. This confers considerable legitimacy: one often hears it said that Parliament has stood the test of time, that it has been the upholder of constitutional liberties, and so on. But it also results in a reluctance to consider honestly how Parliament actually functions. The ability of the House of Commons to restrain the executive has declined sharply since the Second World War, but so far the immense tradition-based prestige of Parliament has blunted the demand for reform. Such is the authority of tradition that ruling groups have at various times invented it in order to bolster their prestige. Almost all the 'traditional' ceremonial associated with the Royal Family was improvised during the reign of Victoria, yet this rooting in specific historical circumstances is just what the whole notion of 'tradition' denies.[19] In modern societies tradition may hold a sentimental appeal, but to treat it as a guide to life tends to lead to unfortunate results.

## The invented traditions of nationalism

The consequences of respect for tradition are particularly disturbing in the case of nationalism. Nations are of course the product of history, and the same national designation has usually meant different things at different times. Unfortunately historians have not always kept this truth at the forefront of their minds. For all their scholarly principle, the nineteenth-century historicists found it hard to resist the demand for one-dimensional, nation-building history, and many did not even try. Europe was then the scene of bitterly contested national identities, as existing national boundaries were challenged by those many peoples whose sense of nationhood was denied – from the Germans and Italians to the Poles and Hungarians. Their claim to nationhood rested partly on language and common culture. But it also required a historical rationale, of past glories to be revived, or ancient wrongs to be avenged – in short, a tradition which could sustain the morale of the nation in the present and impress the other powers of Europe. Historians were caught up in popular nationalism like everyone else, and many saw no contradiction between the tenets of their profession and the writing of self-serving national histories. Frantisek Palacký was both a historian and a Czech nationalist. He combined his two great passions in a sequence of books which portrayed the Czechs as a freedom-loving and democratic people since the dawn of historical time; when he died in 1876 he was mourned as the father of the Czech nation.[20] Celebratory histories of this kind lend themselves to regular rituals of commemoration, when the national self-image could be reinforced in the popular mind. Every year the Serbs mark the anniversary of their epic defeat at the hands of the Turks on the field of Kosovo Polje in 1389, and in so doing reaffirm their identity as a brave but beleaguered people; they have continued to do so throughout the crisis in former Yugoslavia.[21] In such instances the untidy reality of history is beside the point. Nation, race and culture are brought together as a unified constant. Other examples span the modern world from the Nazis in Germany to the ideology of black separatism in the United States. **Essentialism** or 'immemorialism' of this kind produces a powerful sense of exclusive identity, but it makes bad history. Not only is everything in the past that contradicts the required self-image suppressed; the interval between 'then' and 'now' is telescoped by the assertion of an unchanging identity, impervious to the play of historical circumstance.

**essentialist**
Relating to the basic nature (the 'essence') of people or nations.

   The process of tradition-making is particularly clear in newly autonomous nations, where the need for a legitimizing past is strongly felt and the materials for a national past are often in short supply. Within two generations of the War of Independence Americans had come to identify with a flattering self-image: in taming the wilderness far away from the corruptions of the old society in Europe, their colonial forebears had developed the values of self-reliance, honesty and liberty that were now the heritage of all Americans: hence the enduring appeal of folk heroes such as Daniel Boone. More recently many African countries have faced the problem that their boundaries are the artificial outcome of the European partition of the continent in the late nineteenth century. In a few cases, such as Mali and Zimbabwe, descent can be claimed from a much earlier state of the same name. Ghana adopted the name of a medieval trading empire which did not include its present territory at all. Elsewhere in the continent political leaders have invoked timeless qualities from the pre-colonial past (like Julius Nyerere's *ujamaa*, or brotherhood) as a charter of identity. To forge a national identity without some such legitimizing past is probably impossible.

But appeals to an unchanging past are not confined to new or repressed nations. Nineteenth-century Britain had a relatively secure sense of nationhood, yet in the work of historians at that time is to be found an unchanging national essence as well as the idea of change over time. William Stubbs, usually regarded as the first professional historian in this country, believed that the reasons for the growth of the English constitution through the Middle Ages lay 'deep in the very nature of the people'; in this reading parliamentary government became the expression of a national genius for freedom.[22] Essentialist categories come readily to the lips of politicians, particularly at moments of crisis. During the Second World War Winston Churchill invoked a tradition of dogged resistance to foreign attack stretching back to Pitt the Younger and Elizabeth I. Liberal commentators were uncomfortably reminded of this vein of **rhetoric** at the time of the Falklands War in 1982. Pondering the lessons of the conflict, Margaret Thatcher declared,

**rhetoric**
Originally the ancient Greek art of public speaking, but more usually used nowadays to mean points that rely on the persuasive power of words or voice rather than actual argument.

> This generation can match their fathers and grandfathers in ability, in courage, and in resolution. We have not changed. When the demands of war and the dangers to our own people call us to arms – then we British are as we have always been – competent, courageous and resolute.[23]

Nationalism of this kind rests on the assertion of tradition, rather than an interpretation of history. It suppresses difference and change in order to uphold identity.

# IV

## Nostalgia – history as loss

Traditionalism is the crudest distortion of historical awareness, because it does away with the central notion of development over time. Other distortions are more subtle. One that has huge influence is *nostalgia*. Like tradition, nostalgia is backward-looking, but instead of denying the fact of historical change, it interprets it in one direction only – as change for the worse. Nostalgia is most familiar perhaps as generational regret: older people habitually complain that nowadays the young are unruly, or that the country is 'going to the dogs', and the same complaints have been documented over a very long period.[24] But nostalgia works on a broader canvas too. It works most strongly as a reaction to a sense of loss in the recent past, and it is therefore particularly characteristic of societies undergoing rapid change. Anticipation and optimism are never the only – or even the main – social responses to progress. There is nearly always regret or alarm at the passing of old ways and familiar landmarks. A yearning backward glance offers consolation, an escape in the mind from a harsh reality. It is when the past appears to be slipping away before our eyes that we seek to recreate it in the imagination. This was one of the mainsprings of the Romantic movement, and within historicism itself there was a sometimes unduly nostalgic impulse as scholars reacted against the industrialization and urbanization around them. It is no accident that the Middle Ages, with its close-knit communities and its slow pace of change, came into fashion just as the gathering pace of economic change was enlarging the scale of social life. Ever since the Industrial Revolution, nostalgia has continued to be one of the emotional reflexes of societies experiencing major change. One of its commonest expressions in Britain today is 'heritage'. When the past is conserved or re-enacted for our entertainment, it is usually (though not invariably) presented in its most attractive light. Bygone splendours, such as the medieval tournament or the Elizabethan banquet, naturally lend themselves to the pleasures of spectacle; but everyday life – such as the back-breaking routines of the early industrial craft shop or the Victorian kitchen – is also dressed up in order to be visually appealing. A sense of loss is part of the experience of visiting heritage sites.

**myopia**
Short-sightedness.

The image of the dome of St Paul's Cathedral standing intact through the devastating London Blitz of 1940 became a powerful symbol both of British defiance of Nazi Germany and of a particular approach to the distinctiveness of British history. More recent scholarship questions the extent to which the British people were united in the Blitz, but the popular social 'memory' of the 'Blitz spirit' shows no sign of diminishing.
(Getty Images/JA Hampton/Hulton Archive)

The problem with nostalgia is that it is a very lopsided view of history. If the past is redesigned as a comfortable refuge, all its negative features must be removed. The past becomes better and simpler than the present. Thus nineteenth-century medievalism took little account of the brevity and squalor of life or the power of a malign spirit-world. Present-day nostalgia shows a comparable **myopia**. Even a simulation of the London Blitz will prompt regret at the loss of 'wartime spirit' as much as horror at the effects of aerial bombardment. Champions of 'family values' who posit a golden age in the past (before 1939 or 1914 according to taste) overlook the large number of loveless marriages before divorce was made easier, and the high incidence of family break-up through the loss of a spouse or parent from natural causes. In such cases, as Raphael Samuel put it, the past functions less as history than as allegory:

> It is a testimony to the decline in manners and morals, a mirror to our failings, a measure of absence ... By a process of selective amnesia the past becomes a historical equivalent of the dream of primal bliss, or of the enchanted space which memory accords to childhood.[25]

This kind of outlook is not only an unreliable guide to the past but also a basis for pessimism and rigidity in the present. Nostalgia presents the past as an alternative to the present instead of as a prelude to it. It encourages us to hanker after an unattainable golden age instead of engaging creatively with the world as it is. Whereas historical awareness should enhance our insight into the present, nostalgia indulges a desire to escape from it.

# V

## Dismissing the past: history as progress

At the other end of the scale of historical distortion lies the belief in *progress*. If nostalgia reflects a pessimistic view of the world, progress is an optimistic creed, for it asserts not only that change in the past has been for the better but that improvement will continue into the future. Like process, progress is about change over time, but with the crucial difference that a positive value is placed on the change, endowing it with moral content. The concept of progress is fundamental to modernity, because for two hundred years it was the defining myth of the West, a source of cultural self-assurance and of outright superiority in its dealings with the rest of the world. In this sense progress was essentially the invention of the Enlightenment of the eighteenth century. Hitherto a limit on human development had always been assumed, either on account of the mysterious workings of Divine Providence or because the achievements of classical antiquity were regarded as unsurpassable. The Enlightenment of the eighteenth century placed its faith in the power of human reason to transform the world. Writers such as Voltaire, Hume and Adam Smith regarded history as an unfinished record of material and moral improvement. They sought to reveal the shape of history by tracing the growth of human society from primitive barbarism to civilization and refinement. The confidence of these historians may seem naïve and grandiose today, but for two hundred years some such structure has underpinned all varieties of progressive thought, including both liberal democracy and Marxism. As recently as the 1960s representatives of these two traditions – **J.H. Plumb** and E.H. Carr – wrote widely read manifestos for history informed by a passionate belief in progress.[26] That kind of faith is much rarer

**J.H. Plumb**
Sir John H. Plumb (1911–2001), a leading Cambridge historian specializing in the history of eighteenth-century Britain. Plumb was an influential figure, many of whose students went on to become high-profile historians.

today, given the misgivings aroused by economic, environmental and technological developments. But few of us are happy to live in a world of nostalgic regret all the time; the yearning for a lost golden age in one sphere is often balanced by the confident disparagement of 'the bad old days' in another.

That dismissal of the past points to the limitations of progress as a view of history. Whereas 'process' is a neutral term without an implicit value judgement, 'progress' is by definition evaluative and partial; since it is premised on the superiority of the present over the past, it inevitably takes on whatever values happen to be prevalent today, with the consequence that the past seems less admirable and more 'primitive' the further back in time we go. Condescension and incomprehension are the result. If the past exists strictly to validate the achievements of the present, there can be no room for an appreciation of its cultural riches. Proponents of progress have never been good at understanding periods remote from their own age. Voltaire, for example, was notoriously unable to recognize any good in the Middle Ages; his historical writings traced the growth of rationality and tolerance and condemned the rest. So if the desire to demonstrate progress is pressed too far, it quickly comes into conflict with the historian's obligation to re-create the past on its own terms. In fact historicism took shape very much as a reaction against the present-minded devaluation of the past which characterized many writers of the Enlightenment. Ranke regarded every age as being 'next to God', by which he meant that it should not be prejudged by modern standards. Interpreting history as an overarching story of progress involves doing just that.

Tradition, nostalgia and progress provide the basic constituents of social memory. Each answers a deep psychological need for security – through seeming to promise no change, or change for the better, or an escape into a more congenial past. The real objection to them is that, as a governing stance, they require the past to conform with a deeply felt and often unacknowledged need. They are about belief, not enquiry. They look for a consistent window on the past, and they end up doing scant justice to anything else.

# VI

## Challenging the conventional version

If social need so easily leads to distorted images of the past, it is hardly surprising that historians have on the whole kept their distance from it. At a practical level the stance of the professional historian towards social memory is not always consistent. Thus **Herbert Butterfield**, who made his name in the 1930s with an attack on present-minded history, wrote an impassioned evocation of the English historical tradition in 1944 which was clearly intended to contribute to wartime morale.[27] Today the newspapers quite often publish articles by leading historians who are tempted by the opportunity to influence popular attitudes towards the past. But the profession as a whole prefers to emphasize how different the purpose and approach of scholarly historical work are. Whereas the starting point for most popular forms of knowledge about the past is the requirements of the present, the starting point of historicism is the aspiration to re-enter or re-create the past.

It follows that one important task of historians is to challenge socially motivated misrepresentations of the past. This activity has been likened to 'the eye-surgeon, specializing in removing cataracts'.[28] But whereas patients are only too glad to have their sight corrected, society may be deeply attached to its faulty vision of the past, and historians do not make themselves popular in pointing this out. Many of their findings incur the odium of undermining hallowed pieties – as in the case of historians who question the efficacy of Churchill's wartime leadership, or who attempt a **nonsectarian** approach to the history of Northern Ireland. There is probably no official nationalist history in the world that is proof against the deflating effect of academic enquiry. The same is true of the kind of engaged history which underwrites the conflict between Left and Right. Politically motivated labour history in Britain has tended to emphasize political radicalism and the struggle against capital; yet if it is to provide a realistic historical perspective in which political strategies can be planned, labour history cannot afford to ignore the equally long tradition of working-class Toryism, still very much alive today. When Peter Burke told a conference of socialist historians, 'although I consider myself a socialist and a historian, I'm

**Herbert Butterfield**
Cambridge historian (1900–79) specializing in the eighteenth century. His analysis of 'The Whig Interpretation of History' attacked the tendency of 'Whig' historians to see history in terms of progress, thereby unjustly (and anachronistically) criticizing earlier ages as 'backward'.

**nonsectarian**
Avoiding allegiance to any particular religious group.

**untrammelled**
Unhindered.

**rolling back the state**
The role of the state grew enormously in twentieth-century Britain, especially after Clement Attlee's postwar Labour government (1945–51) nationalized heavy industry and the health service. The Conservative governments of Margaret Thatcher (1979–90) reversed this policy by returning nationalized industry to private ownership.

not a socialist historian', he meant that he wanted to study the real complexity of the historical record, not reduce it to an over-dramatized confrontation between Us and Them.[29] The same argument can be made with regard to distortion emanating from the Right. During the mid-1980s Margaret Thatcher tried to make political capital out of a somewhat self-serving image of nineteenth-century England. When she applauded 'Victorian values', she meant that **untrammelled** individualism and a **rolling back of the state** might once again make Britain great. She omitted to say that the essential precondition of the Victorian economic miracle had been Britain's global strategic dominance, and she did not dwell on the appalling social costs in terms of destitution and environmental damage. Historians were quick to point out that her vision was both unrealistic and undesirable.[30]

## The overlap between history and social memory

If this debunking activity would seem to put historians in the opposite camp from the keepers of social memory, it needs to be stressed that the distinction is by no means as hard and fast as I have depicted it up to this point. One strand of opinion (particularly associated with Postmodernism) holds that there is in fact no difference between history and social memory. According to this view, the aspiration to recreate the past is an illusion, and all historical writing bears the indelible impression of the present – indeed tells us more about the present than the past. I will evaluate the merits of this radically subversive position in Chapter 7. Here it is enough to point out that the collapsing of history into social memory appeals to a particular kind of sceptical theorist but commands very little support from historians. However, there are significant areas of overlap. It would be wrong to suppose that accuracy of research is the exclusive property of professional historians. As Raphael Samuel pointed out, there is an army of enthusiastic amateurs in this country, investigating everything from family genealogy to steam locomotives, whose fetish for accuracy is unsurpassed.[31] Academic historians may distance themselves from the distortions of social memory, but many well-established historical specialisms today have their origin in an explicit political need: one thinks of labour history, women's history and African history. It is not always possible to distinguish completely between history and social memory, because historians perform some of the tasks of social memory. Perhaps most important of all, social memory itself is an important topic of historical enquiry. It is central to popular consciousness in all its forms, from democratic politics to social mores and cultural taste, and no comprehensive social history can afford to ignore it; oral history represents in part an attempt to take account of this dimension (see Chapter 11). In all these ways history and social memory feed on each other.

Yet for all these points of convergence, the distinction that historians like to make between their work and social memory remains important. Whether social memory services a totalitarian regime or the needs of interest groups within a democratic society, its value and its prospects of survival are entirely dependent on its functional effectiveness: the content of the memory will change according to context and priorities. Of course historical scholarship is not immune from calculations of practical utility. Partly this is because we understand more clearly than Ranke did that historians cannot detach themselves completely from their own time. Partly also, as I will argue in the next chapter, the richness of history is positively enhanced by responding to topical agendas. Where most historians will usually part company from the keepers of social memory is in insisting that their findings should be guided by the historicist principles described in this chapter – that historical awareness should prevail over social need. This is a principle that can be defended on its own merits. But it must also be sustained if we are to have any prospect of learning from history, as distinct from finding there the mirror-image of our own immediate concerns. To that possibility I now turn.

## Myths of popular history

When the Germans invaded France in May 1940 the British Expeditionary Force was forced to retreat to the port of Dunkerque (Dunkirk), from where it had to be evacuated under heavy fire. Many in Britain mistakenly perceived it as a success, and the 'Dunkirk spirit' came to denote cheery optimism and resolution in the face of overwhelming odds.

▶

On Easter Tuesday 1282 the people of Palermo rose up against the French, massacring as many as they could find while they were at vespers (evening prayer). The 'Sicilian Vespers' became a symbol of the immense potential power of a popular uprising to strike without warning and to oust a foreign occupying force, and therefore had resonance far beyond its immediate historical context. The mafia also has its origins in medieval Sicily, where it was one of a number of clandestine brotherhoods operating a pseudo-feudal system outside the law. Mafia 'barons' ruled their neighbourhoods, often combining benevolence with ruthless enforcement of their authority. Elements of the mafia were caught up in large-scale Italian emigration to the United States in the late nineteenth century, where they moved into protection rackets and organized crime. The Italian-American mafia rose to public prominence through its involvement in supplying illegal alcohol during the years of Prohibition (1919–33), becoming part of American mythology in the process.

In 1776 representatives of the thirteen British colonies in North America, including John Adams, Thomas Jefferson and Benjamin Franklin, met in Philadelphia and signed the Declaration of Independence, renouncing British rule and founding the United States. Nowadays they are popularly revered and romanticized in America as the 'Founding Fathers'. It remains rare – indeed, it is considered almost unpatriotic – for Americans to subject the Founding Fathers to serious critical historical evaluation.

Malcolm X (1925–65), a leading figure in the radical black civil rights movement in the United States in the 1960s, called for a major reappraisal of the mythology of American history and of the rôle Africans played in it.

## Enlightenment and the Romantics

The Enlightenment of the eighteenth century grew out of the scientific revolution of the previous century, which had stressed the importance of learning through observation and deduction rather than by the unquestioning acceptance of past authority. Enlightenment thinkers such as Montesquieu and Rousseau applied these ideas to human society, teaching that man's 'natural' condition is to be free, and that human behaviour should be governed by reason rather than by irrational and 'unnatural' tradition or religious faith. Enlightenment philosophy was an important influence on the leaders of the French Revolution.

Romanticism was a cultural and intellectual movement in the early nineteenth century, heavily influenced by the ideas of the

French Revolution. It sought to give free range to the emotions, and thereby to attain eternal truths. The Romantics found inspiration in the romances and tales of the Middle Ages, for example the tales of King Arthur.

Nationalism, also originating in the French Revolution, emphasized the importance of a sense of collective national identity. Much of nationalism is concerned with preserving and cherishing 'traditional' national language and culture, but it is also closely identified with the idea of the nation-state, in which states are organized along national ethnic lines.

## Further reading

Michael Bentley, *Modern Historiography*, Routledge, 1999.

Beverley Southgate, *History: What and Why?*, 2nd edn, Routledge, 2004.

J.H. Plumb, *The Death of the Past*, Macmillan, 1969.

George G. Iggers & James Powell (eds), *Leopold Ranke and the Shaping of the Historical Discipline*, Syracuse UP, 1990.

James Fentress & Chris Wickham, *Social Memory*, Blackwell, 1992.

Stefan Berger (ed.), *Writing National Histories*, Routledge, 1998.

David Lowenthal, *The Past is a Foreign Country*, Cambridge UP, 1985.

David Lowenthal, *The Heritage Crusade and the Spirit of History*, Viking, 1997.

Raphael Samuel (ed.), *People's History and Socialist Theory*, Routledge & Kegan Paul, 1981.

Raphael Samuel, *Theatres of Memory*, vol. 1: *Past and Present in Contemporary Culture*, Verso, 1994.

## Notes

1 Rictor Norton, *Mother Clap's Molly House: the Gay Subculture in England, 1700–1830*, Gay Men's Press, 1992.

2 Jan Vansina, *Oral Tradition as History*, James Currey, 1985.

3 James Fentress and Chris Wickham, *Social Memory*, Blackwell, 1992, ch. 5.

4 Malcolm X, *On Afro-American History*, 3rd edn, Pathfinder, 1990, p. 12.

5 *History Workshop Journal*, **I**, 1976, p. 2 (editorial).

6 Sheila Rowbotham, *Hidden from History*, Pluto Press, 1973.

7 Sheila R. Johansson, "Herstory' as history: a new field or another fad?', in Berenice A. Carroll (ed.), *Liberating Women's History*, Illinois University Press, 1976, p. 427.

8 L. von Ranke, *Histories of the Latin and German Nations from 1494 to 1514*, extract translated in G.P. Gooch, *History and Historians in the Nineteenth Century*, 2nd edn, Longman, 1952, p. 74.

9 Unfortunately this is the impression conveyed by the most frequently cited translation, 'What actually happened': see Fritz Stern (ed.), *The Varieties of History*, 2nd edn, Macmillan, 1970, p. 57.

10 Thomas Carlyle, quoted in J.R. Hale (ed.), *The Evolution of British Historiography*, Macmillan, 1967, p. 42.

11 E.P. Thompson, *Customs in Common*, Penguin, 1993, ch. 7.

12 V.A.C. Gatrell, *The Hanging Tree: Execution and the English People, 1770–1868*, Oxford University Press, 1994.

13 Quoted in Gareth Stedman Jones, *Outcast London*, Penguin, 1976, p. 258.

14 L.P. Hartley, *The Go-Between*, Penguin, 1958, p. 7.

15 Simon Schama, 'Clio at the Multiplex', *The New Yorker*, 19 Jan. 1998, p. 40.

16 See, for example, James Sharpe, *Instruments of Darkness: Witchcraft in England, 1550–1750*, Hamish Hamilton, 1996; Jonathan Barry, Marianne Helster and Gareth Roberts (eds), *Witchcraft in Early Modern Europe*, Cambridge University Press, 1996.

17 See, for example, John Gillis, *For Better, For Worse: British Marriages, 1600 to the Present*, Oxford University Press, 1985.

18 Fernand Braudel, 'History and the social sciences: *la longue durée*', in his *On History*, Weidenfeld & Nicolson, 1980, pp. 25–52.

19 E.J. Hobsbawm and T.O. Ranger (eds), *The Invention of Tradition*, Cambridge University Press, 1982.

20 Richard G. Plaschka, 'The political significance of Frantisek Palacký', *Journal of Contemporary History*, **VIII**, 1973, pp. 35–55.

21 Noel Malcolm, *Kosovo: a Short History*, Macmillan, 1998.

22 William Stubbs, quoted in Christopher Parker, *The English Historical Tradition since 1850*, Donald, 1990, pp. 42–3.

23 Margaret Thatcher, speech in Cheltenham, 3 July 1982, reprinted in Anthony Barnett, *Iron Britannia*, Allison & Busby, 1982.

24 Geoffrey Pearson, *Hooligan: a History of Respectable Fears*, Macmillan, 1983.

25 Raphael Samuel, *Island Stories: Unravelling Britain*, Verso, 1998, pp. 337–8.

26 J.H. Plumb, *The Death of the Past*, Macmillan, 1969; E.H. Carr, *What Is History?* Macmillan, 1961.

27 H. Butterfield, *The Englishman and his History*, Cambridge University Press, 1944.

28 Theodore Zeldin, 'After Braudel', *The Listener*, 5 November 1981, p. 542.

29 Peter Burke, 'People's history or total history', in Raphael Samuel (ed.), *People's History and Socialist Theory*, Routledge & Kegan Paul, 1981, p. 8.

30 Eric M. Sigsworth (ed.), *In Search of Victorian Values*, Manchester University Press, 1988; T.C. Smout (ed.), *Victorian Values*, British Academy, 1992.

31 Raphael Samuel, 'Unofficial knowledge', in his *Theatres of Memory: Past and Present in Contemporary Culture*, Verso, 1994, pp. 3–39.

# CHAPTER TWO

# The uses of history

This chapter looks at some of the different ways in which historians have tried to explain the purpose of their work. Some see history as a study in itself which needs no wider justification; others see it in terms of the inexorable march across time of great forces, human or even divine, which explain both how we got to where we are and where we might be heading; others deny that history has any lessons for us at all. Historians explain the past in response to present-day concerns and questions. History can certainly allow us to experience situations and face alternatives that we would not otherwise encounter and in that sense it serves a useful purpose; it can also reveal that aspects of modern life are not as old, or as new, as we have assumed. But how can we learn any useful lessons from history – especially for the future – when so much depends on the details of the historical context? And if history does not repeat itself, what sort of a guide can it provide for the present?

None of the issues discussed in this book has drawn a greater variety of answers than the question 'what can we learn from history?' The answers have ranged from Henry Ford's celebrated aphorism 'history is bunk' to the belief that history holds the clue to human destiny. The fact that historians themselves give very different responses suggests that this is an open-ended question which cannot be reduced to a tidy solution. But anyone proposing to spend several years – and in some cases a lifetime – studying the subject must reflect on what purpose it serves. And one cannot get very far in understanding how historians set about their work, or in evaluating its outcome, without first considering the rationale of historical enquiry.

# I

## Metahistory – history as long-term development

At one extreme lies the proposition that history tells us most of what we need to know about the future. Our destiny is disclosed in the grand **trajectory** of human history, which reveals the world today as it really is, and the future course of events. This belief requires a highly schematic interpretation of the course of human development, usually known as *metahistory*. A spiritual version of it predominated in Western culture until the seventeenth century. Medieval thinkers believed that history represented the inexorable unfolding of **Divine Providence**, from the Creation through the redeeming life of Christ to the **Last Judgement**; the contemplation of the past revealed something of God's purposes and concentrated the mind on the reckoning to come. This view became less tenable with the gradual secularization of European culture from the eighteenth century onwards. New forms of metahistory developed which attributed the forward dynamic of history to human rather than divine action. The **Enlightenment belief in moral progress** was of this kind. But the most influential metahistory of modern times has been Marxism. The driving force of history became the struggle by human societies to meet their material needs (which is why the Marxist theory is known as 'historical materialism'). Marx interpreted human history as a progression from lower to higher forms of production; the highest form was currently industrial capitalism, but this was destined to give way to socialism, at which point human need would be satisfied abundantly and equitably (see Chapter 8). Since the fall of international Communism, belief in historical materialism has sharply declined, but metahistorical thinking continues to hold an appeal: Marxism has been turned on its head by certain free-market theorists, for whom the 1990s signal the global triumph of liberal democracy, or 'the end of history'.[1]

**trajectory**
The line of an object in flight. It can be applied, as here, to a perceived 'path' of a theme traced over a long period of time.

**Divine Providence**
The idea of a benevolent God who watches over and protects people on earth.

**Last Judgement**
In Christian, especially Catholic, theology the Last Judgement is the moment at the end of time when all humans come before God for judgement on their lives on earth, some being allowed to enter heaven, others being condemned for eternity to hell. It was a common theme in medieval art and is dramatically presented in Michelangelo's frescos in the Sistine Chapel in the Vatican.

**Enlightenment belief in moral progress**
The eighteenth-century Enlightenment believed that the exercise of human reason would liberate people from the mental and political oppression of organized religion and superstition. By aiming for greater human liberty and happiness, reason was thereby equated with moral progress.

## The rejection of history

**totalitarianism**
Dictatorship, associated particularly with European regimes of the 1920s and 1930s, which stressed the all-encompassing role of the state.

**Modernists**
In this context, those whose concerns are concentrated on the modern day to the exclusion of any consideration of the past.

*avant-garde*
(French) The troops at the front who spearhead an army's advance into battle. The term was applied to radical and pioneering artistic movements in the early twentieth century and has since come to denote any new or radical ideas.

**alarming instability of the world economy**
The international economic slump of the 1930s that followed on from the New York Stock Exchange crash of October 1929.

**root-and-branch**
Thorough-going. The term derives from a seventeenth-century religious group who wanted a comprehensive reform of the Church of England.

At the other extreme is the view that *nothing* can be learned from history: not that history is beyond our reach, but that it offers no guidance. This rejection of history takes two forms. The first is essentially a defence against **totalitarianism**. For many intellectuals during the Cold War, the practical consequences of invoking the past to legitimate Communist ideology had been so appalling that any idea that history might hold clues for the present became completely discredited; some historians recoiled so far from any idea of pattern or meaning that they refused to find in history anything more than accident, blunder and contingency.[2]

The second basis for rejecting history is a commitment to modernity: if one is committed to the new, why bother with the past? This point of view has a much longer pedigree. The equation of modernity with a rejection of the past was first put into effect during the French Revolution of 1789–93. The revolutionaries executed the king, abolished the aristocracy, attacked religion and declared 22 September 1792 the beginning of Year 1. All this was done in the name of reason, untrammelled by precedent or tradition. The early twentieth century was another high point in the **modernist** rejection of history. In *avant-garde* thinking human creativity was seen as opposed to the achievements of the past, rather than growing out of them; ignorance of history liberated the imagination. During the inter-war period these ideas became the dominant strand in the arts, under the banner of 'Modernism'. Fascism and Nazism adapted this language to the political sphere. They reacted to the catastrophe of the First World War and the **alarming instability of the world economy** by claiming the virtue of a complete break with the past. They lambasted the corruption of the old society and demanded the conscious creation of a 'new man' and a 'new order'.[3] Today **root-and-branch** totalitarianism is completely discredited. But 'modernism' retains some of its allure. It validates a technocratic approach to politics and society and underwrites the fascination with the new in the arts.

Neither metahistory nor the total rejection of history commands much support among practitioners of history. Metahistory may cast the historian in the gratifying role of prophet, but at the cost of denying, or drastically curtailing, the play of human

agency in history. Marxism has had great influence on the writing
of history over the past fifty years, but as a theory of socio-economic change rather than as the key to human destiny. Ultimately
the choice between free will and determinism is a philosophical
one. There are many intermediate positions. If most historians
would tip the balance in favour of free will, this is because determinism sits uncomfortably with the contingencies and rough
edges that loom so large in the historical record. Metahistory
involves holding on to one big conviction at the expense of many
less ambitious insights. It is an outlook profoundly at odds with
the experience of historical research.

Historians are no happier to have their findings dismissed as a
complete irrelevance. The rejection of history would obviously
limit its study to a self-indulgent **antiquarian** pursuit. In fact the
claims for historical awareness have for 200 years been asserted
in a continuing **dialectic** with the modernist rejection of history.
Historicism itself was to a considerable extent a reaction against
the French Revolution. To conservatives such as Ranke, the political excesses in France were a terrifying instance of what
happens when radicals turn their backs on the past; to apply first
principles without respect for inherited institutions was a threat
to the very fabric of the social order. As the Revolution went off
course, many of the radicals acquired a new respect for history
too. Those who still believed in freedom and democracy came to
realize that humans were not so free from the hand of the past as
the revolutionaries had supposed, that progressive change must
be built on the cumulative achievements of earlier generations.

Only a visionary would accept the full implications of metahistory; only an antiquarian would be content to surrender all claim
to practical utility. The most convincing claims of history to offer
relevant insights lie somewhere between these two extremes. And
they hinge on taking seriously the principles of historical awareness established by the nineteenth-century founders of the
discipline. The historicists have become a by-word for disinterested historical enquiry without practical application, but this is
not an accurate picture of their position. They did not disclaim all
claims to practical relevance but merely insisted that the faithful
representation of the past must come first. In fact the three principles of difference, context and process (discussed in the previous
chapter) point to the specific ways in which the scholarly study of

**antiquarian**
Interest in historical details
and artefacts without
reference to their wider
context or significance.

**dialectic**
The conflict of one idea
(the Thesis) and another
diametrically opposed to it
(the Antithesis). The
resulting amalgamation of
the two is known as the
Synthesis.

history can yield useful knowledge. The end result is not a master-key or an overall schema but rather an accumulation of specific practical insights consistent with a sense of historical awareness.

# II

## The uses of history – an inventory of alternatives

Historical *difference* lies at the heart of the discipline's claim to be socially relevant. As a memory-bank of what is unfamiliar or alien, history constitutes our most important cultural resource. It offers a means – imperfect but indispensable – of entering into the kind of experience that is simply not possible in our own lives. Our sense of the heights to which human beings can attain, and the depths to which they may sink, the resourcefulness they may show in a crisis, the sensitivity they can show in responding to each other's needs – all these are nourished by knowing what has been thought and done in the very different contexts of the past. Art historians have long been familiar with the idea that the creative achievements of the past are an inventory of assets whose value may be realized by later generations – witness the way that Western art has repeatedly reinvented and rejected the **classical tradition** of Greece and Rome. But creative energy can be drawn from the past in many other fields. History reminds us that there is usually more than one way of interpreting a predicament or responding to a situation, and that the choices open to us are often more varied than we might have supposed. Theodore Zeldin has written a magpie's feast of a book, called *An Intimate History of Humanity* (1994), ranging over such subjects as loneliness, cooking, conversation and travel. His aim is not to lay bare a pattern, still less to predict or prescribe, but to open our eyes to the range of options that past experience places at our disposal. Most historians probably have serious misgivings about a frag-mented exposition such as Zeldin's, which lacks any topographical or chronological coherence. But his rationale is not unusual. Natalie Zemon Davis – a leading cultural historian of Early Modern Europe – has said, 'I let [the past] speak and I show that things don't have to be the way they are now.... I want to show that it could be different, that it was different, and that there are alternatives'.[4] As the process of historical change

**classical tradition**
'Classical' refers to the ancient world of Greece and Rome. Their ideas and philosophy were often revived by later ages, notably during the fifteenth- and sixteenth-century Renaissance and again in the eighteenth century.

unfolds, old arguments or programmes may once more become relevant. This has been a persistent theme in the work of the foremost historian of the English Revolution, Christopher Hill:

> Since capitalism, the **Protestant ethic**, **Newtonian physics**, so long taken for granted by our civilization, are now at last coming under general and widespread criticism, it is worth going back to consider seriously and afresh the arguments of those who opposed them before they had won universal acceptance.[5]

The point is not to find a precedent but to be alert to possibilities. History is an inventory of alternatives, all the richer if research is not conducted with half an eye to our immediate situation in the present.

## Lessons from the familiar

Of course not all the past is exotic. In practice our reaction to a particular moment in the past is likely to be a mixture of estrangement and familiarity. Alongside features that have changed out of all recognition, we may encounter patterns of thinking or behaviour that are immediately accessible to us. The juxtaposition of these two is an important aspect of historical perspective, and it is often the point at which the more thoughtful professional scholar engages most directly with the claims of social relevance. Peter Laslett's path-breaking work on the history of the English family offers a striking instance. Since the 1960s – beginning with *The World We Have Lost* (1965) – he has written a succession of books about the nature of early modern English society. He emphasizes two general conclusions. First, the residential extended family, which we fondly believe existed in the premodern world, is a figment of our nostalgic imagination: our forebears lived in nuclear households seldom spanning more than two generations. Secondly, the care of the elderly was not notably more family-based than it is today, but the scale of the problem was vastly different – indeed old age was not regarded as a problem at all because few people survived for very long after their productive life was over. Our view of the nuclear family is changed when we recognize that it was not a response to industrialization but was rooted in much earlier English practice. On the other hand, policy towards the old will get nowhere if it is guided by past models: 'Our situation remains irreducibly novel,'

**Protestant ethic**
Also known as the Protestant work ethic. First analyzed in detail by Max Weber, *The Protestant Ethic and the Spirit of Capitalism* (1905), this held that Protestant theology, with its stress upon an individual relationship with God (as opposed to the Catholic stress on the collective community of the Church), was uniquely well suited to the development of an independent, self-reliant approach to work.

**Newtonian physics**
The understanding of the operation of the natural world developed by Sir Isaac Newton (1642–1727). Newton's theories were unchallenged until the writings of Albert Einstein (1879–1955).

R.H. Tawney (1880–1962). He saw a close link between the industriousness of Protestant people and their religious beliefs. He wrote of a 'Protestant work ethic' by which a religious faith which placed stress upon the individual's role in his or her own salvation also encouraged people to work industriously and save economically. His ideas were influential, but few nowadays think capitalist enterprise a peculiarly Protestant trait. (Topfoto/Topham/UPP)

**Puritanism**
A radical form of seventeenth-century Protestantism which sought to 'purify' the Church of England of its 'Catholic' features. Puritanism was also associated with political radicalism during the English Civil Wars.

**Restoration of 1660**
The monarchy was abolished in the political changes that followed the English Civil Wars, and England became a republic. In 1660 the monarchy was restored and King Charles II returned from exile to take up the throne.

writes Laslett; 'it calls for invention rather than imitation'.[6] He does not trace the evolution of family forms over time – the eighteenth and nineteenth centuries are missed out entirely. His point is rather that the first step to understanding is comparison *across* time, which throws into relief what is transient and what is enduring about our present circumstances.

The ability to distinguish between the enduring and the transient is vital to any realistic programme of social action in the present. This was the approach of R.H. Tawney, the foremost social historian of England between the two World Wars and an influential social reformer. In his best-known historical work, *Religion and the Rise of Capitalism* (1926), his purpose was to show how the disengagement of Christian social ethics from the conduct of business, which in his day was so total and (from Tawney's viewpoint) so disastrous, had first come about; the book traces the reciprocal relationship between **Puritanism** and the capitalist spirit during the seventeenth century, culminating in the triumph of economic individualism after the **Restoration of 1660**. As Tawney put it in a characteristically elegant metaphor:

> If he [the historian] visits the cellars, it is not for love of the dust, but
> to estimate the stability of the edifice, and because, to grasp the
> meaning of the cracks, he must know the quality of its foundations.[7]

History here is not being quarried for 'meaning' to validate particular values but is treated as an instrument for maximizing our control over our present situation. To be free is not to enjoy total freedom of action – that is a Utopian dream – but to know how far one's action and thought are conditioned by the heritage of the past. This may sound like a prescription for conservatism. But what it offers is a realistic foundation for radical initiatives. We need to know when we are pushing against an open door and when we are beating our heads against a brick wall. Grasping what one historian has called 'the distinction between what is necessary and what is the product merely of our own contingent arrangements' offers important practical dividends.[8]

## Facing up to pain: history as therapy

The concept of historical difference has one other rather surprising application – as a means of grappling with aspects of the very recent past which we might prefer to forget. It is a measure of the almost incredible extremes of human behaviour over the past century that a real effort of the imagination is now needed to understand what happened under the Third Reich or in the Soviet Union under Stalin (more recent instances include **Idi Amin**'s Uganda and **Pol Pot**'s Cambodia). In cases such as these the gulf between present and past is, as it were, compressed into a single life-span. Those who lived through these experiences of mass death, incarceration and forced removal suffer from a collective trauma. The line of least resistance may be to leave the past alone, and in the Soviet Union 'forgetting' was the official line for most of the period between the death of Stalin and the collapse of Communism. Individuals did not forget, but there was no way in which their pain could be shared or publicly marked. A nation that cannot face up to its past will be gravely handicapped in the future. This understanding was central to the policy of glasnost ('openness') proclaimed by **Mikhail Gorbachev** in the late 1980s. He realized how crippling the psychological burden of the past was as long as it remained buried. After some initial hesitation he opened up the archives to historians and allowed the Soviet

**Idi Amin (1925–2003)**
General Amin seized power in Uganda in 1971 in a military coup. He proved a brutal dictator and massacred large numbers of his own people. He expelled Uganda's entire Asian population and was finally overthrown by a military invasion by neighbouring Tanzania in 1979.

**Pol Pot (1925–1998)**
Communist leader of Cambodia 1975–9. He instituted a reign of terror in which the entire urban population was forced into the countryside and some two million people were massacred. He was overthrown by an invasion from neighbouring Vietnam.

**Mikhail Gorbachev (1931–)**
Soviet leader 1985–91. Gorbachev instituted the policy of glasnost (openness) in discussing the failures of the Soviet system, and of fundamental reconstruction (perestroika) of Soviet society. This precipitated the collapse of the Soviet Union, and Gorbachev resigned in the aftermath of an attempted coup in 1991.

people to acknowledge publicly the terrible sufferings of the Stalin era. Whatever else happens in Russia in the future, that collective owning of the past cannot be undone. James Joll saw this kind of painful engagement with the recent past in therapeutic terms:

> Just as the psycho-analyst helps us to face the world by showing us how to face the truth about our own motives and our own personal past, so the contemporary historian helps us to face the present and the future by enabling us to understand the forces, however shocking, which have made our world and our society what it is.[9]

Historical difference provides an indispensable perspective on the present, whether as an inventory of experience, as evidence of the transience of our own time, or as a reminder of the deeply alien elements in our recent past.

# III

## Understanding behaviour in its context

The practical applications of historical *context* are much less likely to make the headlines, but they are no less important. As explained in Chapter 1, the discipline of context springs from the historian's conviction that a sense of the whole must always inform our understanding of the parts. Even when historians write about specialized topics in economic or intellectual history, they should respect this principle, and they open themselves to major criticism if they fail to do so. The same principle informs the practice of **social anthropology**, where fieldwork is concerned as much with the entire social structure or cultural system as with particular rituals or beliefs. The problem both history and anthropology face is how to interpret behaviour that may be founded on quite different premises from our own. It would, for example, be a great mistake to suppose that commercial transactions in thirteenth-century England – or twentieth-century Polynesia – were guided solely by what we define as economic rationality; looking at these societies as wholes will give us a grasp of how trade and exchange were informed by religion, social morality and social hierarchy (to specify only the most likely dimensions). The reason why this mode of thinking has contemporary application is not, of course, that our own society is alien or 'different'. Rather, the

**social anthropology**
Academic discipline which analyzes small-scale societies by the techniques of participant observation.

problem today is the baffling complexity of society, which leads us to place exaggerated faith in specialist expertise, without proper regard to the wider picture. E.J. Hobsbawm deplores how modern policy-making and planning are in thrall to 'a model of scientism and technical manipulation'.[10] This is more than prejudice born of a demarcation dispute between arts and sciences (Hobsbawm himself has always been respectful of science and technology). The argument here is that the technical approach to social and political problems compartmentalizes human experience into boxes marked 'economics', 'social policy' and so on, each with its own technical lore, whereas what is really required is an openness to the way in which human experience constantly breaks out of these categories.

The lateral links between different aspects of society are much easier to discern with the benefit of hindsight. In our own time it is clearly harder to spot the connections, given our lack of detachment and our lack of hindsight. But at the very least a historical training should encourage a less blinkered approach to current problems. The **Gulf War in 1991** illustrates this point – if in a regrettably negative way. The history of Western imperialism has been the subject of some highly sophisticated analysis over the past thirty years. Historians do not see the process of European expansion merely as an expression of maritime flair and technical superiority. They link it to economic structures, patterns of consumption and international relations – and increasingly to codes of masculinity and constructions of racial difference as well. All too little of this kind of contextualization was applied by the media to the escalation of conflict in the Gulf. For most commentators it was hardly seen outside the frame of international law and the politics of oil. Historians can claim with some justice to be specialists in lateral thinking, and this has underpinned their traditional claim to train graduates for management and the civil service, where the ability to think beyond the boundaries of particular technical perspectives is at a premium. A similar case can be made in relation to the education of the participating citizen, who inevitably approaches most public issues as a non-specialist.[11]

**Gulf War in 1991**
In 1990 President Saddam Hussein of Iraq invaded and annexed the small oil-rich kingdom of Kuwait. The invasion was condemned by the United Nations, and the Iraqis were forced out of Kuwait the following year by a counter-invasion by a broad international coalition led by the United States.

**Winston Churchill
(1874–1965)**
As well as his multi-
volume histories of the
two World Wars, Churchill
also wrote a detailed
biography of his famous
ancestor, John Churchill,
Duke of Marlborough.

**Roy Jenkins
(1920–2003)**
Jenkins served as Home
Secretary and Chancellor
of the Exchequer under
the Labour Prime Ministers
Wilson and Callaghan, as
President of the European
Commission, and was one
of the founders of the
short-lived Social
Democratic Party (SDP).
He also found time to
write critically acclaimed
biographies of Gladstone
and Churchill.

**Machiavelli**
Niccolo Machiavelli
(1469–1527), Florentine
statesman and
philosopher. When
Florence overthrew the
ruling Medici dynasty and
declared itself a republic in
1493 Machiavelli served
the new regime, but he
was arrested and tortured
when the Medici returned.
Machiavelli is best known
for his book of advice for
rulers, *The Prince*, which
suggests that the most
successful rulers should
know how to deceive and
dissemble. It earned him a
quite unjust reputation as
a promoter of unprincipled
tyranny.

## Does history repeat itself?

Context is also the principle that historians invoke against the common, but mistaken, belief that history repeats itself. Human beings strive to learn from their mistakes and successes in their collective life just as they do in everyday individual experience. Historical biography is said to feature prominently in the leisure reading of British politicians. Indeed a few of them have written distinguished works of this kind – **Winston Churchill** and **Roy Jenkins**, for example.[12] That politicians have a lively interest in the historical context in which posterity will judge their own standing is only part of the explanation. The real reason for their study of history is that politicians expect to find a guide to their conduct – in the form not of moral example but of practical lessons in public affairs. This approach to history has a long pedigree. It was particularly pronounced during the Renaissance, when the record of classical antiquity was treated as a storehouse of moral example and practical lessons in statecraft. **Machiavelli**'s prescriptions for his native Florence and his famous political maxims in *The Prince* (1513) were both based on Roman precedent. He was justly rebuked by his younger contemporary, the historian Francesco Guicciardini:

> How wrong it is to cite the Romans at every turn. For any comparison to be valid, it would be necessary to have a city with conditions like theirs, and then to govern it according to their example. In the case of a city with different qualities, the comparison is as much out of order as it would be to expect a jackass to race like a horse.[13]

Guicciardini put his finger on the principal objection to the citing of precedent, that it usually shows scant regard for historical context. For the precedent to be valid, the same conditions would have to prevail, but the result of the passage of time is that what looks like an old problem or a familiar opportunity requires a different analysis because the attendant circumstances have changed. The gulf that separates us from all previous ages renders the citing of precedents from the distant past a fruitless enterprise.

Only in the case of the recent past have historians seriously attempted to draw on historical analogies, on the grounds that much of the context may remain essentially the same over a short period and that the changes which have occurred are comparatively well documented. During the later stages of the Cold War there was something of a vogue for 'applied' history of this kind.[14] But even here the task is a daunting one. Consider the case of the arms race. The decade before the Second World War is commonly regarded as an object lesson in the dangers of military weakness and of appeasing an aggressive power. But one could equally cite the precedent of the First World War, one of whose causes was the relentless escalation in armaments from the 1890s onwards. Which precedent is valid? The answer must be: neither as it stands. Even within the time-span of a hundred years, history does not repeat itself. No one historical situation has been, or ever can be, repeated in every particular. If an event or tendency recurs, as the arms race has done, it is as a result of a unique combination of circumstances, and the strategies we adopt must have regard primarily to those circumstances.[15] The key historicist notion of the 'otherness' of the past is not suspended merely because we stand at only two or three generations' distance from our object of study. As E.J. Hobsbawm has reminded us, the atmosphere of the 1930s (through which he lived) was utterly different from today's, which makes any comparison between the original Nazis and their imitators today pretty pointless.[16] At the same time, the drawing of historical analogies, often half consciously, is a habitual and unavoidable part of human reasoning to which people in public life are especially prone. It is not necessarily futile provided we do not look for a perfect fit between past and present, or treat precedent as grounds for closing critical debate about the options available now.

The truth that history never repeats itself also limits the confidence with which historians can predict. However probable it may seem that a recurrence of this or that factor will result in a familiar outcome, the constant process of historical change means that the future will always be partly shaped by additional factors which we cannot predict and whose bearing on the problem in hand no one could have suspected. Moreover, when people do perceive their situation as 'history repeating itself', their actions will be affected by their knowledge of what happened the first time. As E.H. Carr pointed out, historical precedent gives us some insight into what kind of conditions make for a revolution, but whether and when the revolution breaks out in a specific instance will depend on 'the occurrence of unique events, which cannot themselves be predicted'.[17] The dismal record of well-informed intelligent people who have made false predictions, or have failed to predict what with hindsight seems obvious, does however suggest one lesson of history: that control of the future is an illusion, and that living with uncertainty is part of the human condition.

## IV

## The way ahead: history and sequential prediction

*Process* – the third principle of historicism – is equally productive of insights into the present day. Identifying a process does not mean that we agree with it, or believe that it made for a better world. But it may help to explain our world. Situating ourselves in a trajectory that is still unfolding gives us some purchase on the future and allows a measure of forward planning. In fact this mode of historical thinking is deeply rooted in our political culture. As voters and citizens, almost instinctively, we interpret the world around us in terms of historical process. Much of the time our assumptions are not grounded in historical reality; they

South Africa's Truth and Reconciliation Commission provided a forum where those who had committed crimes in the name of apartheid could admit openly what they had done and receive forgiveness from their victims. This process of facing up to a painful recent past proved helpful in allowing South Africans to work together to face the future.
(Topfoto/Louise Gubb/Image Works)

may amount to little more than wishful thinking projected backwards. But if conclusions about historical process are based on careful research, they can yield modest but useful predictions. We might call these *sequential* predictions, in order to distinguish them from the discredited *repetitive* or *recurrent* variety. These prevailing beliefs about historical process need to be brought into the light of day, tested against the historical record, and if necessary replaced by a more accurate perspective.

One prediction based on historical process which has stood the test of time concerns the political destiny of South Africa. During the 1960s, when most colonies in tropical Africa were securing their political independence, it was widely assumed that majority rule would shortly come about in South Africa too. Despite the weight of white oppression, mass nationalism was visibly the outcome of a process that dated back to the foundation of the **African National Congress** in 1912, and that had been marked by a growing sophistication in both political discourse and techniques of mass mobilization. Moreover, the South African case could be seen as part of a worldwide phenomenon of anti-colonial nationalism which had been building up since the late nineteenth century. In that sense history might be said to be 'on the side' of African nationalism in South Africa. What could not be predicted was the form of the succeeding political order, and the manner in which it would be achieved, whether by revolution from below or by devolution from above: those were matters of detail which only the future could divulge. But the direction in which the historical process was unfolding in South Africa seemed clear. The time-scale turned out to be more extended than had been supposed – thus demonstrating the crablike way in which a historical process may unfold – but the general prediction was accurate enough.[18]

Sometimes identifying the valid and appropriate historical process is complicated by the presence of more than one possible trajectory. Take the current debate about the 'breakdown' of the family. Processual thinking is certainly very evident in the way the media handle this issue. The relevant process is generally seen to be the decline of personal morality, aided and abetted by misguided legislation, beginning with the **Matrimonial Causes Act** of 1857, which set in train the liberalization of divorce.[19] Historians, on the other hand, bring into play a much more fundamental and

**African National Congress**
The black South African political party, founded in 1912, which led resistance to apartheid.

**Matrimonial Causes Act**
This act enabled couples to seek divorce through the newly created divorce courts. Previously, it had only been obtainable through a specially passed Act of Parliament.

long-term process, namely the changing role of the home in production. Two hundred and fifty years ago most work was done in or adjacent to the home. In selecting a mate, prospective spouses were influenced as much by the home-making and bread-winning skills of their partners as by their personal attractions; the ending of a marriage through separation or desertion meant the end of a productive unit, and for this reason most marriages endured until death. The Industrial Revolution changed all this: the growth of the factory (and other large firms) meant that most production no longer took place in a domestic setting, and control over domestic dependants ceased to be economically central. Now that personal fulfilment is by far the most compelling rationale of marriage, there is far less reason for people to stay in family relationships which no longer bring them happiness. The decline of the productive household, rather than a collapse of individual morality, would seem to be the critical historical process involved here; and given that the separation of work from home shows little sign of being reversed, it is a reasonable prediction that our society will continue to experience a comparatively high rate of marital breakdown.[20]

## Questioning assumptions

But the most important role of processual thinking is in offering an alternative to the assumptions of permanence and timelessness that underpin so many social identities. As we saw in the last chapter, nations tend to imagine themselves as unchanged by the vicissitudes of time. The fallacy of essentialism does not hold up well against historical research. 'British', for example, was in the eighteenth century a newly minted category to take account of the recent **Union of Scotland and England**, and it was built on the exclusion of Roman Catholics and the French. At the close of the twentieth century, the cultural meaning of Britishness is probably less certain than it has ever been, while the British state seems set for disintegration as Scotland edges closer to independence.[21] In the same way, any notion of what it means to be German has to come to terms not only with the multitude of states under which most Germans lived until the mid-nineteenth century but also with the political calculations that led to the exclusion of many German-speaking lands (notably Austria) from the German

**Union of Scotland and England**

The Act of Union between England and Scotland was passed by both countries' parliaments in 1707. Although there were economic advantages to both sides, the English wanted it primarily to prevent the Catholic pretender, Prince James Edward Stuart, becoming king of Scotland. It only passed through the Scottish parliament with the help of wholesale bribery.

Empire in 1871. A historical perspective requires us to abandon the idea that nations are organic; it is nearer the truth to regard them, in the words of an influential recent text, as 'imagined communities'.[22]

The term 'race' raises similar problems. In its modern form 'race' was originally developed as a category that justified the growing ascendancy of the West over other peoples. It treated as fixed and biologically determined what is socially constructed, and it has been most strongly developed as a means of reinforcing political and economic control over subordinate groups (as in colonial Africa and Nazi Germany). The way in which an earlier generation of historians wrote about Western global expansion strongly implied that the 'native' peoples at the receiving end were inferior both in their indigenous culture and in their capacity to assimilate Western techniques; and these negative stereotypes served in turn to sustain a flattering self-image of the British – or French or German – 'race'. More recently minorities with a strong ethnic identity have constructed what might be called a 'reverse discourse'; they too embrace the concept of 'race', because the term brings biological descent and culture together in a powerful amalgam that maximizes group cohesion and emphasizes distance from other groups. Among blacks in America and Britain there is today rising support for Afrocentrism – the belief in an absolute sense of ethnic difference and in the transmission of an authentic cultural tradition from Africa to blacks of the modern **diaspora**. A stress on common ancestry and a downplaying of outside influences lead to a kind of 'cultural insiderism'. The appropriate response is to point out that no nation has ever been ethnically **homogeneous** and to stress the formative experience of slavery and other forms of culture contact between black and white in Europe and the New World. The purpose of historical work is not to undermine black identity but to anchor it in a real past instead of a mythical construction. The outcome is likely to bear a rather closer relation to the circumstances in which black and white people live today. The formation of racial and national identities is never a once-and-for-all event, but a continuous and contingent process.[23]

**diaspora**
The dispersal of a people over a wide area.

**homogeneous**
All of the same sort.

## Challenging notions of 'natural'

What is true of the nation applies still more to the 'natural'. When unwelcome changes in our social arrangements are afoot, we often express our attachment to what is being replaced by asserting that it has always been there – that what is changing is not one particular phase with a limited time-span but something traditional, or fundamental, or 'natural'. This is especially true of gender. The 'traditional' role of women looks less and less tenable when we read about the **entrepreneurial widow** of seventeenth-century England, or the groundswell of women's organizations which worked for the **abolition of slavery** in the nineteenth century, well ahead of the agitation for women's suffrage.[24] The new history of men and masculinity is equally unsettling of received truths. Traditional fatherhood is often thought to have combined an emotionally hands-off approach with a distinctly hands-on approach to family discipline. That is usually what is meant by 'Victorian' fatherhood. But in so far as the Victorians kept their distance from their children and meted out harsh punishments to them, this was a reaction *against* the past, rather than the climax of a long tradition. The celebrated political journalist William Cobbett recalled that his time as a young father was spent 'between the pen and the baby'; he remembered how he had fed and put his babies to sleep 'hundreds of times, though there were servants to whom the task might have been transferred'.[25] Cobbett was writing in 1830, just when the tide was beginning to turn against the close paternal involvement with young children that had been so common when he was a young man thirty years before. It makes a difference now to know that a fully engaged fatherhood today is not some Utopian fantasy but a pattern which has existed within English culture in the comparatively recent past. In fact codes of fatherhood have been in continuous flux throughout the past two hundred years, and probably earlier.[26] One of the most salutary influences on the practice of history in recent years has been the French historian and philosopher Michel Foucault. His cardinal principle was that no aspect of human culture is God-given or lies outside history, and in his historical work he plotted some of the major shifts that have occurred in the human experience of sexuality, sickness and insanity. In selecting major themes of this kind in pursuit of what

**entrepreneurial widow**
We now know that many widows in seventeenth- and eighteenth-century England ran their own businesses, and that it was by no means unusual for women to assume positions of influence which historians had long assumed were reserved for men.

**abolition of slavery**
The campaign for the abolition first of the transatlantic slave trade, then of slavery itself, and later of the internal African slave trade, constituted one of the most important and influential lobbying movements of the nineteenth century. Church groups and women played a prominent role in the process on both sides of the Atlantic.

he called 'an archaeology of the present' Foucault achieved an influence which extended far beyond academia.[27]

# V

## History for its own sake?

Granted, then, that history has a varied and significant practical relevance, the question remains whether this should influence the way in which historians set about their work. Prior to the Rankean revolution this question could hardly have arisen. Historians believed what their audience assumed, that a historical education offered a training for citizens and statesmen alike. They took it for granted that history furnished the basis for a rational analysis of politics; indeed, many of the best historians, from Guicciardini in the sixteenth century to **Macaulay** in the nineteenth, were active in public life. All this was changed by the professionalization of history. By the late nineteenth century the subject featured prominently in the university curriculum all over Europe, controlled by a new breed of historians whose careers were largely confined to academic life. Their subject's traditional claim to offer practical guidance seemed irrelevant – almost an embarrassment. They adhered strictly to the central tenet of historicism, that history should be studied for its own sake, without paying much attention to the practical benefits that could accrue from this approach. This attitude still represents the conventional professional approach among British historians. G.R. Elton was an outspoken champion of the prevailing orthodoxy:

> Teachers of history must set their faces against the necessarily
> ignorant demands of 'society' ... for immediate applicability. They
> need to recall that the 'usefulness' of historical studies lies hardly at
> all in the knowledge they purvey and in the understanding of specific
> present problems from their prehistory; it lies much more in the fact
> that they produce standards of judgement and powers of reasoning
> which they alone develop, which arise from their very essence, and
> which are unusually clear-headed, balanced and compassionate.[28]

Apart from providing an intellectual training, the study of history is represented as a personal pursuit which at most enables the individual to achieve some self-awareness by stepping outside his or her immediate experience; in the austere formulation of

**Macaulay**

Thomas Babington Macaulay (1800–59), British historian, poet and administrator. As well as writing a best-selling *History of England*, Macaulay served on the Council of the Governor-General of India, as MP for Endinburgh, and as Secretary at War in the government of Lord Melbourne.

V.H. Galbraith, 'the study of history is a personal matter, in which the activity is generally more valuable than the result.'[29] Neither of these justifications is peculiar to history: training the mind is part of all academic disciplines worth the name, while the claim to enlarge the individual's experience can be argued with equal, if not greater, conviction by teachers of literature.

One positive result of 'history for its own sake' is a whole-hearted commitment to the re-creation or resurrection of the past in every material and mental dimension. There are historians for whom a fascination with the past as it was really lived and experienced overrides all other considerations. A notable case was Richard Cobb, a leading historian of the French Revolution:

> The historian should, above all, be endlessly inquisitive and prying, constantly attempting to force the privacy of others, and to cross the frontiers of class, nationality, generation, period, and sex. *His principal aim is to make the dead live*. And, like the American 'mortician', he may allow himself a few artifices of the trade: a touch of rouge here, a pencil-stroke there, a little cotton wool in the cheeks, to make the operation more convincing.[30] [emphasis added]

Cobb's marvellously evocative studies of the seamy side of life in revolutionary France, notably **Death in Paris** (1978), certainly vindicate his approach. Probably all historians can trace their vocation back to a curiosity about the past for its own sake, often aroused in childhood by the visible relics of the past around them. And there will always, one hopes, be historians like Cobb with special gifts in the re-creation of the past. But it is quite wrong to suppose that historians in general should be content with this. For most of them it is the essential preliminary to *explaining* the past. Their purpose is to identify trends, to analyze causes and consequences – in short to interpret history as a process and not just as a series of brightly coloured lantern-slides. Thus historians of the English Revolution approach their work with a view to discovering not only what happened in the Civil War or what it felt like to be a soldier in the **New Model Army** but also why the war occurred and what changes it brought about in the nature of English politics and society. Or to take a more distant example: the events of the **Anglo-Zulu War** of 1879, which saw the dissolution of the Zulu kingdom and the destruction of an entire British regiment, were tragic enough; but a whole other dimension of irony and pathos is revealed when we consider the betrayals, the mutual misunderstandings and the

**Death in Paris**
Richard Cobb (1917–96) was a colourful British authority on the history of France. *Death in Paris* gives a glimpse of the social history of nineteenth-century Paris through a collection of police records relating to dead bodies fished out of the Seine.

**New Model Army**
The highly-trained professional army created by Parliament during the English Civil Wars (1642–9). It is usually credited with having turned the tide of the war against King Charles I.

**Anglo-Zulo War**
Also known as the Zulu War (1879). It began with a completely unprovoked British military invasion of Zululand in South Africa, after which an entire British army column was wiped out by the Zulus at Isandhlwana. In the end, superior technology and firepower enabled the British to defeat the Zulus.

culture conflict that set the two sides on a collision course.[31] This represents the other side of historicism. Without it history's practical explanatory functions could not be fulfilled at all. (The distinction between re-creation and explanation is further explored in Chapter 6.)

## The rejection of relevance

However, it is perfectly possible for historical explanation to be pursued without reference to the claims of social relevance, and this, rather than the strictly 'resurrectionist' position, represents the mainstream academic view. For explanation too can be sought 'for its own sake'. Topics such as the origins of the First World War or the social welfare provision of the Victorians can be tackled in an entirely self-contained way without any recognition that they might have a bearing on the choices available to us today. Academic syllabuses are sometimes drawn up on the assumption that history consists of a number of core themes and episodes of permanent significance which, because they have generated extensive research and debate, offer the best material for training the intellect. New areas of study such as the history of Africa or the history of the family are dismissed as passing fancies peripheral to 'real history'. Commenting on the gradual retreat from big, contentious topics in university teaching, David Cannadine writes:

> The belief that history provides an education, that it helps us understand ourselves in time, or even that it explains something of how the present world came into being, has all but vanished.[32]

It is hard not to detect a fundamental conservatism in these attitudes: if history is defined to exclude anything that smacks of 'relevance', it is less likely to call into question the dominant mythologies of today or suggest radical alternatives to current institutions. This explains why 'relevant' historical enquiry attracts charges of irreverent muckraking.[33] There can be little doubt that conservatives are disproportionately represented in the ranks of the historical profession. As noted earlier, the triumph of historicism during the nineteenth century owed much to the strength of the conservative reaction to the French Revolution. It remains the case that the study of the past often attracts those who are hostile to the direction of social and political change in their own day and who find comfort in an earlier and more congenial order. This outlook has been marked in English local history: the writings of W.G. Hoskins, a formative influence on this field, are suffused with a nostalgic regret for the passing of the old English rural society.[34]

Disclaimers of social relevance are not, however, usually couched in explicitly conservative terms. They are more commonly defended on the grounds that 'relevant' history is incompatible with the historian's primary obligation to be true to the past, and with the requirements of scholarly objectivity. This argument has a wide currency among academic historians, being supported by many who are not conservative in other respects but who see their professional integrity at stake. But whether grounded in a conservative attitude or not, the denial of practical relevance is unduly cautious. It is entirely understandable that the original champions of the new historical consciousness should have distanced themselves from topicality, because they were only too aware how severely their subject had suffered at the hands of prophets and propagandists in the past. But the battle for scholarly standards of historical enquiry within the profession has long since been won. Practical purposes can be entertained without sacrificing standards of scholarship – partly because professional historians are so zealous in scrutinizing each other's work for bias.

**crisis in America's cities**
The mid-1960s saw serious rioting in a large number of American cities. The riots began in 1965 in the Watts district of Los Angeles, where young working-class blacks were protesting against the poverty and squalor in which they lived, but soon spread across the whole nation. The country erupted in further violence after the assassination of Dr Martin Luther King in 1968.

## Relevant fields of historical study

Historians should, of course, strive to be true to the past; the question is, which past? Faced with the almost limitless evidence of human activity and the need to select certain problems or periods as more deserving of attention than others, the historian is entirely justified in allowing current social concerns to affect his or her choice. International history originated in the 1920s as a very positive contribution by historians to the new – if short-lived – ethos of internationalism. The notable broadening of the scope of historical enquiry during the past forty years is largely the result of a small minority of historians responding to the demands of topicality. **The crisis in America's cities** during the 1960s brought into being the 'new urban history', with its stress on the history of social mobility, minority group politics and inner-city deprivation. African history was developed at about the same time in Africa and the West by historians who believed that it was indispensable both to the prospects of the newly independent states and to the outside world's understanding of the 'dark continent'. More recently, women's history has grown rapidly as traditional gender roles have been modified in the family, the workplace and public life.

Obviously new areas of history which proclaim their relevance run the risk of being manipulated by ideologues. But the responsibility of historians in these cases is clear: it is to provide a historical perspective which can inform debate rather than to service any particular ideology. Responding to the call of 'relevance' is not a matter of falsifying or distorting the past but rather of rescuing from oblivion aspects of that past which now speak to us more directly. Historians of Africa, for example, should be concerned to explain the historical evolution of African societies, not to create a nationalist mythology, and one of the consequences of four decades of research and writing is that it is now much easier to distinguish between the two than it used to be. Our priorities in the present should determine the questions we ask of the past, but not the answers. As will be shown later in the book, the discipline of historical study makes this a meaningful distinction. At the same time, it is a fallacy to suppose that the aspiration to reconstruct the past in its own terms carries the promise of objectivity: no essay in historical re-creation is proof against the values of the enquirer (see Chapter 7).

But historians who renounce relevance in the cause of objective knowledge are not only pursuing a **chimera**; they are also evading a wider responsibility. Intellectual curiosity about the past for its own sake is certainly one reason why people read history, but it is not the only one. Society also expects an interpretation of the past that is relevant to the present and a basis for formulating decisions about the future. Historians may argue that since their expertise concerns the past not the present, it is not their job to draw out the practical import of their work. But they are in fact the only people qualified to equip society with a truly historical perspective and to save it from the damaging effects of exposure to historical myth. If professionally trained historians do not carry out these functions, then others who are

**dark continent**
The standard Victorian nickname for Africa. It referred both to the colour of Africans' skin and to the fact that so little was known in the West about the interior of the continent.

**chimera**
A creature of the imagination, an illusion.

less well informed and more prejudiced will produce ill-founded interpretations. What Geoffrey Barraclough, a veteran champion of contemporary values in history, said more than forty years ago applies with equal force today:

> Man is an historical animal, with a deep sense of his own past; and if he cannot integrate the past by a history explicit and true, he will integrate it by a history implicit and false. The challenge is one which no historian with any conviction of the value of his work can ignore; and the way to meet it is not to evade the issue of 'relevance', but to accept the fact and work out its implications.[35]

## The need for contemporary history

One clear implication is that contemporary history, which can be roughly defined as the period since 1945, has a strong claim on historians. It can be argued that scholars today are too close to the events of this period to achieve sufficient detachment, and that they are further handicapped by their limited access to confidential records (see Chapter 3). But although the job cannot be done as well as historians would like, it is important that they do it to the best of their ability. For it is the recent past on which people draw most for historical analogies and predictions, and their knowledge of it needs to be soundly based if they are to avoid serious error. The recent past has also often proved a fertile breeding ground for crude myths – all the more powerful when their credibility is not contested by scholarly work. Academic neglect of contemporary history therefore has dangerous consequences. But the fulfilment of history's practical functions does not mean the abandonment of more distant periods – far from it. So many facets of the contemporary scene are rooted in the remote past that the tradition of studying the classical, medieval and early modern epochs can never be given up: without it our historical perspective on current problems would be seriously defective. And as evidence of the range of human achievement and mentality in the past, those periods are indispensable.

Responding to society's expectations does not, therefore, impose a limitation as regards periods – or as regards countries. But it does suggest that the selection of themes for research should be influenced by a sensitivity to those areas of current concern that stand most in need of a historical perspective; examples such as the history of the family or the history of Africa already discussed could easily be multiplied. Finally, the proper performance of history's social role demands that historians take seriously the task of diffusing as widely as possible their findings and the practical implications to be drawn from them. Scholarly historical writing should not just be directed at the academic community, important though the critical scrutiny of other scholars is; it concerns all who want informed perspectives on the present. One of the criticisms that can most fairly be made of the historical profession today is that too little history is written with this wider audience in view (see Chapter 6).

# VI

## A cultural subject, or a social science?

The argument of this chapter can be briefly summed up by situating history in the context of its neighbours among the academic disciplines. Traditionally history has been counted, along with literary and artistic studies, as one of the humanities. The fundamental premise of these disciplines is that what mankind has thought and done has an intrinsic interest and a lasting value irrespective of any practical implications. The re-creation of episodes and ambiences in the past has the same kind of claim on our attention as the recreation of the thought expressed in a work of art or literature. The historian, like the literary critic and art historian, is a guardian of our cultural heritage, and familiarity with that heritage offers insight into the human condition – a means to heightened self-awareness and empathy with others. In this sense history is, in Cobb's phrase, 'a cultural subject, enriching in itself'[36] and any venture in historical reconstruction is worth doing.

By contrast the social sciences owe their position to their promise of practical guidance. Economists and sociologists seek to understand the workings of economy and society with a view to prescribing solutions to current problems, just as scientists offer the means of mastering the natural world. Historians who believe in their subject's practical functions habitually distance it from the humanities and place it alongside the social sciences. E.H. Carr did so in *What is History?* (1961):

> Scientists, social scientists, and historians are all engaged in different branches of the same study: the study of man and his environment, of the effects of man on his environment and of his environment on man. The object of the study is the same: to increase man's understanding of, and mastery over, his environment.[37]

On this reading, historical re-creation has value primarily as a preliminary to historical explanation, and the kinds of explanation that matter are those which relate to questions of social, economic and political concern.

In this discussion I have given pride of place to the practical uses of history because these continue to arouse such strong resistance among many professional historians. But the truth is that history cannot be defined as either a humanity or a social science without denying a large part of its nature. The mistake that is so often made is to insist that history be categorized as one to the exclusion of the other. History is a hybrid discipline which owes its endless fascination and its complexity to the fact that it straddles the two. If the study of history is to retain its full vitality, this central ambivalence must continue to be recognized, whatever the cost in logical coherence. The study of history 'for its own sake' is not mere antiquarianism. Our human awareness is enhanced by the contemplation of vanished eras, and historical re-creation will always exercise a hold over the imagination, offering as it does vicarious experience to writer and reader alike. At the same time, historians also have a more practical role to perform, and the history that they teach, whether to students in schools and colleges or through the media to the wider public, needs to be informed by an awareness of this role. In this way a historical education achieves a number of goals at once: it trains the mind, enlarges the sympathies *and* provides a much-needed perspective on some of the most pressing problems of our time.

## Marxism and the English Revolution

Marxism, the philosophy of Karl Marx (1818–83), was one of the most influential political and intellectual movements of the nineteenth and twentieth centuries. Marx held that all of human history can be explained in terms of *dialectic*, the conflict between different social classes for control of the main means of economic production. This produces a succession of stages from feudalism to capitalism, and from capitalism to a Communist society, in which workers enjoy the benefits of their own labour. The English Civil Wars (1642–9) were for many years understood essentially as a conflict for authority between king and Parliament. Marxist historians working in the twentieth century, notably Christopher Hill (1912–2003), saw it in much more radical terms, as an attempt to create a new society on principles of equality and individual liberty. In this sense it constitutes an English Revolution in the same way as the later revolutions in France and Russia, as a shift from aristocratic to bourgeois and even working-class hegemony.

## Renaissance

The Renaissance was a fifteenth-century European cultural and intellectual movement which began in Italy and eventually spread to France, Germany, the Netherlands and England. It drew inspiration from new discoveries in the art and writings of the ancient Greeks and Romans. Artists experimented with perspective and depth, while sculptors created remarkably lifelike reproductions of human and animal forms. Renaissance writers explored Greek philosophy and sought to marry its ideas with those of Christianity.

## Transformation: by peace and by war

In 1948 the white Afrikaaner government of South Africa imposed a policy of strict racial segregation known as *apartheid*. Black African resistance came to centre on the imprisoned African National Congress leader, Nelson Mandela. By the 1980s South Africa seemed close to civil war, but concessions by the government of F.W. de Klerk, and especially the release of Nelson Mandela in 1990, enabled the country to undergo a remarkable peaceful transition to democracy. In 1994 Nelson Mandela became the first black President of South Africa.

Nineteenth-century Germany consisted of a large number of separate states. German nationalists wanted to amalgamate them into a single, unified German empire, but Austria, the largest and most powerful German state, presented a problem, partly because it had a large non-German empire of its own, and partly because it had long dominated Germany and was unlikely to welcome the creation of a large, independent German state. In the event, in 1871 Germany was united into a single empire under the leadership of the militaristic north German kingdom of Prussia; Austria and her empire were excluded.

## Further reading

Gordon Connell-Smith & Howell A. Lloyd, *The Relevance of History*, Heinemann, 1972.

Beverley Southgate, *Why Bother With History? Ancient, Modern and Postmodern Motivations*, Routledge, 2000.

Jeremy Black, *Using History*, Arnold, 2005.

Michael Howard, *The Lessons of History*, Oxford UP, 1989.

Eric Hobsbawm, *On History*, Abacus, 1997.

Peter Mandler, *History and National Life*, Profile, 2002.

Marc Ferro, *The Use and Abuse of History*, Routledge & Kegan Paul, 1984.

Raphael Samuel, *Island Stories: Unravelling Britain*, Verso, 1998.

William H. McNeill, *Mythistory and Other Essays*, Chicago UP, 1986.

Richard E. Neustadt & Ernest R. May, *Thinking in Time: the Uses of History for Decision-Makers*, Free Press, 1986.

Stuart Macintyre (ed.), *The History Wars*, Melbourne UP, 2001.

## Notes

1 Francis Fukuyama, *The End of History and the Last Man*, Hamish Hamilton, 1992.

2 A.J.P. Taylor, *War by Time-Table: How the First World War Began*, Macdonald, 1969, p. 45; Richard Cobb, *A Second Identity*, Oxford University Press, 1969, p. 47.

3 George L. Mosse, *The Image of Man: the Creation of Modern Masculinity*, Oxford University Press, 1996, ch. 8.

4 Interview with N.Z. Davis in Henry Abelove *et al.* (eds), *Visions of History*, Manchester University Press, 1984, pp. 114–15.

5 Christopher Hill, *Change and Continuity in Seventeenth-Century England*, Weidenfeld & Nicolson, 1974, p. 284.

6 Peter Laslett, *Family Life and Illicit Love in Earlier Generations*, Cambridge, 1977, p. 181.

7 R.H. Tawney, *History and Society*, Routledge & Kegan Paul, 1978, p. 55.

8 Quentin Skinner, 'Meaning and understanding in the history of ideas', *History & Theory*, **VIII**, 1969, p. 53.

9 James Joll, *Europe since 1870*, Penguin, 1976, p. xii.

10 Eric Hobsbawm, *On History*, Weidenfeld & Nicolson, 1997, p. 27.

11 Gordon Connell-Smith and Howell A. Lloyd, *The Relevance of History*, Heinemann, 1972, pp. 29–31, 123.

12 W.S. Churchill, *Marlborough: His Life and Times* (4 vols), Harrap, 1933–38; Roy Jenkins, *Asquith*, Collins, 1964.

13 Francesco Guicciardini, *Maxims and Reflections of a Renaissance Statesman (Ricordi)*, Harper & Row, 1965, p. 69.

14 See, for example, Richard E. Neustadt and Ernest R. May, *Thinking in Time: the Uses of History for Decision-Makers*, Free Press, 1986; Paul Kennedy, *The Rise and Fall of the Great Powers*, Unwin Hyman, 1988.

15 David H. Fischer, *Historians' Fallacies*, Routledge & Kegan Paul, 1971, ch. 9.

16 Hobsbawm, *On History*, pp. 29, 233.

17 E.H. Carr, *What Is History?* 2nd edn, Penguin, 1987, p. 69.

18 These assumptions underpinned Donald Denoon, *Southern Africa Since 1800*, Longman, 1972, and many other texts of the time.

19 Mary Lyndon Shanley, *Feminism, Marriage and the Law in Victorian England, 1850–1895*, Princeton, 1989.

20 Michael Anderson, 'The relevance of family history', in Chris Harris (ed.), *The Sociology of the Family*, Keele, 1980.

21 Linda Colley, *Britons: Forging the Nation, 1707–1837*, Yale University Press, 1992; Raphael Samuel, *Island Stories: Unravelling Britain*, Verso, 1998, pp. 41–73.

22 Benedict Anderson, *Imagined Communities*, Verso, 1983.

23 Paul Gilroy, *The Black Atlantic: Modernity and Double Consciousness*, Verso, 1993.

24 Amy Louise Erickson, *Women and Property in Early Modern England*, Cambridge University Press, 1993; Clare Midgley, *Women Against Slavery*, Routledge, 1992.

25 William Cobbett, *Advice to Young Men*, Peter Davies, 1926, p. 176.

26 John Tosh, *A Man's Place: Masculinity and the Middle-Class Home in Victorian England*, Yale University Press, 1999.

27 For an introductory selection, see P. Rabinow (ed.), *The Foucault Reader*, Pantheon, 1984.

28 G.R. Elton, 'Second thoughts on history at the universities', *History*, LIV, 1969, p. 66. See also his *The Practice of History*, Fontana, 1969, pp. 66–8.

29 V.H. Galbraith, in R.C.K. Ensor *et al.* (eds), *Why We Study History*, Historical Association, 1944, p. 7; see also his *An Introduction to the Study of History*, C.A. Watts, 1964, pp. 59–61.

30 Cobb, *A Second Identity*, p. 47.

31 Jeff Guy, *The Destruction of the Zulu Kingdom*, Longman, 1979.

32 David Cannadine, 'British history: past, present – and future?', *Past & Present*, 116, 1987, p. 180.

33 See, for example, G.R. Elton, *Return to Essentials*, Cambridge University Press, 1990, pp. 84–7.

34 See W.G. Hoskins, *The Making of the English Landscape*, Penguin, 1970.

35 Geoffrey Barraclough, *History in a Changing World*, Blackwell, 1955, pp. 24–5.

36 Richard Cobb, *A Sense of Place*, Duckworth, 1975, p. 4.

37 Carr, *What is History?* p. 86.

CHAPTER THREE

# The raw materials

Students rarely work with historical sources in their original state. Examination papers and textbooks contain short, labelled extracts, which bear little resemblance to the originals. What sort of sources are available to the modern historian? How did they come to be made available, and how might this affect their usefulness? This chapter gives you a fuller idea of the provenance of, and problems with, the sort of sources historians habitually use.

S uch is the range of motives and the variety of interests which draw people to the past that history can be said to embrace the human experience of every place and period. No part of that past can be dismissed as falling outside the proper domain of historical knowledge. But how far it can be made the subject of well-founded research depends on the availability of historical evidence. Whether the historian's main concern is with re-creation or explanation, with the past for its own sake or for the light it can shed on the present, what he or she can actually achieve is determined in the first instance by the extent and character of the surviving sources. Accordingly it is with the sources that any account of the historian's work must begin. This chapter describes the main categories of documentary material, showing how they came into being, how they have survived down to the present, and in what form they are available to the scholar.

# I

## Specialist sources and skills

Historical sources encompass every kind of evidence that human beings have left of their past activities – the written word and the spoken word, the shape of the landscape and the material **artefact**, the fine arts as well as photography and film. Among the humanities and social sciences history is unique in the variety of its source materials, each calling for specialist expertise. The military historian of the English Civil War can examine the arms and armour surviving from the seventeenth century and the terrain over which the battles were fought, as well as the military dispatches of each side. A rounded picture of the **General Strike** of 1926 calls for a study of government and trade union records, the press and broadcasting, together with the collection of testimonies from survivors. The reconstruction of a pre-colonial kingdom in black Africa is likely to depend not only on the excavation of its capital but also on the contemporary observations of European or Arab visitors and the oral traditions handed down over many generations. No single historian can possibly master all these tools. The more technical of them have become the province of distinct specialisms. The excavation of ancient sites and the interpretation of the material remains found there is the business of the archaeologist, assisted these days by the aerial photographer and the chemical analyst. The art historian has established a comparable hold over the study of the visual arts. The historian frequently draws on the findings of archaeologists and art historians, and he or she may feel qualified to draw inferences from a wide range of material evidence – from the design and structure of a Norman castle, for example, or the imagery employed in contemporary portraits of Elizabeth I and on the coinage of her reign; but these are regarded by most historians as 'extras', peripheral to their discipline. During the past thirty years the range of sources in which historians claim expertise has certainly increased. It now includes place names, landscape patterns and – for recent history – film. The fact remains, however, that the study of history has nearly always been based squarely on what the historian can read in documents or hear from informants. And ever since historical research was placed on a professional footing during Ranke's

**artefact**
Any object left over from the past.

**General Strike**
A major industrial dispute which brought virtually all of Britain's industry to a halt in May 1926. The dispute began in the mining industry but spread when other trade unions came out in support of the miners.

lifetime, the emphasis has fallen almost exclusively on the written rather than the spoken word – though oral sources, as we shall see, are now studied in methodical fashion (see Chapter 11). For the vast majority of historians, research is confined to libraries and archives.

## The written word

The reason is not just academic conservatism. From the High Middle Ages (*c.* 1000–1300) onwards, the written word survives in greater abundance than any other source for Western history. The fifteenth and sixteenth centuries witnessed not only a marked growth in record-keeping by the state and other corporate bodies but also the rapid spread of printing, which encouraged literate production of all kinds and transformed its prospects of survival. Written sources are usually precise as regards time, place and authorship, and they reveal the thoughts and actions of individual men and women as no other source can do. One has only to read an account of a society for which virtually no written records

Archival holdings are essential to historical scholarship. Not only do historians have to treat their sources carefully, they have to remember how it is that some sources made their way into the archives while others did not.
(Getty Images/Time Life Pictures)

**medieval Zimbabwe**
The medieval kingdom of Zimbabwe was a major power in southern Africa in the thirteenth to fifteenth centuries. The impressive stone ruins of its royal palace at Great Zimbabwe posed a serious challenge to those white settlers who dismissed indigenous African culture as intrinsically inferior to that of Europeans.

exist – for example Iron Age Britain or **medieval Zimbabwe** – to see how lacking in human vitality history can be when denied its principal source material. Moreover, the written word has always served many different purposes – information, propaganda, personal communication, private reflection and creative release – all of which may have relevance for the historian. The interpretation of texts serving a variety of functions from an age whose habits of mind differed sharply from our own calls for critical abilities of a very high order. Written sources are at the same time the most rewarding and (in most cases) the most plentiful. Small wonder, then, that historians seldom look elsewhere.

The use of written materials as the principal historical source is complicated by the fact that historians communicate their findings through the same medium. Both in their choice of research topic and in their finished work, historians are influenced to a greater or lesser extent by what their predecessors have written, accepting much of the evidence they uncovered and, rather more selectively, the interpretations they put upon it. But when we read the work of a historian we stand at one remove from the original sources of the period in question – and further away still if that historian has been content to rely on the writings of other historians. The first test by which any historical work must be judged is how far its interpretation of the past is consistent with all the available evidence; when new sources are discovered or old ones are read in a new light, even the most prestigious book may end on the scrapheap. In a very real sense the modern discipline of history rests not on what has been handed down by earlier historians, but on a constant reassessment of the original sources. It is for this reason that historians regard the original sources as *primary*. Everything that they and their predecessors have written about the past counts as a *secondary* source. Most of this book is concerned with secondary sources – with how historians formulate problems and reach conclusions, and how we as readers should evaluate their work. But first it is necessary to examine the raw materials a little more closely.

## 'Primary' and 'secondary' sources

The distinction between primary and secondary sources, fundamental though it is to historical research, is rather less clear-cut than it might appear at first sight, and the precise demarcation varies among different authorities. By 'original sources' is meant evidence **contemporary** with the event or thought to which it refers. But how far should our definition of 'contemporary' be stretched? No one would quibble about a conversation reported a week or even a month after it took place, but what about the version of the same episode in an autobiography composed twenty years later? And how should we categorize an account of a riot written shortly afterwards, but by someone who was not present and relied entirely on hearsay? Although some purists regard the testimony of anyone who was not an eye-witness as a secondary source,[1] it makes better sense to apply a broad definition but to recognize at the same time that some sources are more 'primary' than others. The historian will usually prefer those sources that are closest in time and place to the events in question. But sources more remote from the action have their own significance. The historian is often as much interested in what contemporaries *thought* was happening as in what actually happened: **British reactions to the French Revolution**, for example, had a profound influence on the climate of politics in this country, and from this point of view the often garbled reports of events in Paris which circulated in Britain at the time are an indispensable source. As this example suggests, to speak of a source as 'primary' implies no judgement of its reliability or freedom from bias. Many primary sources are inaccurate, muddled, based on hearsay or intended to mislead, and (as the next chapter will show) it is a vital part of the historian's work to scrutinize the source for distortions of this kind. The distinction between primary and secondary is further complicated by the fact that sometimes primary and secondary material appear in the same work. **Medieval chroniclers** usually began with an account of world history from the Creation to the life of Christ, based on well-known authorities; but what modern historians value them most for is the entries which they recorded year by year concerning current events. Equally a work can be primary in one context and secondary in another: **Macaulay's *History of England*** (1848–55) is a secondary source whose reputation has been much undermined by modern research; but for anyone studying the political and historical assumptions of the early Victorian élite, Macaulay's book, in its day a bestseller, is a significant primary source. These

**contemporary**
Literally 'at the same time as'. In historical terminology it usually refers to events or people from the period being studied.

**British reactions to the French Revolution**
When the French Revolution broke out in 1789 opinion in Britain was initially supportive. However, it quickly became implacably hostile as events in France descended into rule by violence and terror. A small group of political radicals, however, remained consistently supportive of the Revolution. These two responses continue to be mirrored in the attitudes of British historians of the period.

**medieval chroniclers**
Medieval chronicles were written narratives, often skilfully crafted into a highly readable form. We do not know how much research went into their writing, though they were often consulted by later chroniclers and writers.

**Macaulay's *History of England***
Although called a *History of England*, Macaulay's work in fact concentrates almost entirely on the important constitutional changes following the overthrow of King James II in 1688 and the accession of the first Hanoverian king, George I, in 1714.

examples might suggest what is often assumed, that 'historical documents' are the formal, dignified records of the past. It is true that records of this kind are more likely to endure, but the term should carry the widest possible reference. Every day all of us create what are potentially historical documents – financial accounts, private correspondence, even shopping lists. Whether they actually become historical documents depends on whether they survive and whether they are used as primary evidence by scholars of the future.

In order to make sense of the vast mass of surviving primary sources, the first requirement is some system of classification. Two types are in common use. The first draws a distinction between the published – which in the modern period has usually meant printed – and the unpublished or manuscript source. The second emphasizes instead the authorship of the sources, drawing a distinction between those produced by governments and those produced by corporations, associations or private individuals. Each of these methods lends itself to the precision required by the cataloguer, and bibliographies published by historians at the end of their works are normally arranged along these lines. But the criteria that historians actually apply in the course of their research, although related to these two types of classification, are rather less cut and dried. In the historian's hierarchy of sources those that carry most weight are the ones that arise directly from everyday business or social intercourse, leaving open the task of interpretation. In every recent age men and women have sought to make sense of their times, and to interpret the pattern of events through books, **broadsheets** and newspapers. Such statements offer valuable insights into the mentality of the age, but for the historian they are no substitute for the direct, day-to-day evidence of thought and action provided by the letter, the diary and the **memorandum**: these are the 'records' of history *par excellence*. Historians wish to be as nearly as possible observers of the events in question; they do not want to deliver themselves into the hands of a narrator or commentator. The most revealing source is that which was written with no thought for posterity. **Marc Bloch** called this 'the evidence of witnesses in spite of themselves';[2] it has all the fascination of eavesdropping.

**broadsheets**
A broadsheet was a form of early newspaper designed to be pinned up in a public place.

**memorandum**
An internal message or note sent within an office or institution. Memoranda from government offices can give a very detailed picture of the development of policy.

**Marc Bloch (1886–1944)**
French medievalist historian. He was one of the founders of the *Annales* school, which sought to link the study of history with an in-depth appreciation of the role of geography and other disciplines. He also wrote a perceptive study of *The Historian's Craft*. During the Second World War he fought in the French resistance, but was captured and shot shortly before the D-Day landings.

Vincenz of Beauvais, medieval polyhistorian. Although medieval chroniclers did consult documents and were sometimes able to speak with some of the major figures they wrote about, their priority was to provide a lively narrative. The historical discipline of measured analysis of source material was a much later, nineteenth-century development. (Photo: akg-images, London)

# II

## Narratives and memoirs

We begin, however, with primary sources written for the benefit of posterity. These tend to be the most accessible because their survival was seldom left to chance. Often they have a literary quality that makes them a pleasure to read. They provide a ready-made chronology, a coherent selection of events, and a strong sense of period atmosphere. Their drawback is that they recount only what people found worthy of note about their own age – which may not be what interests us today. Prior to the Rankean revolution in the nineteenth century it was on primary sources of this kind that historians tended to rely. For Roman history they turned to Caesar, Tacitus and Suetonius, while medievalists drew on the **Anglo-Saxon Chronicle** and the works of men such as **Matthew Paris** in the thirteenth century and **Jean Froissart** in the fourteenth. Nor do modern historians disparage these narrative sources. They owe their continuing importance to the fact that

**Anglo-Saxon Chronicle**
A detailed yearly chronicle of major events in Anglo-Saxon England compiled by monks at different monasteries and abbeys and brought together on the orders of King Alfred the Great. It was long thought to be an objective

they survive from periods which have left only a limited amount of record sources. In the Middle Ages most of the early chronicles were written by monks without personal experience of public affairs, but increasingly from the twelfth century they were joined by **secular clergy** who had served the king in responsible positions and could to some extent record political history from the inside. **Gerald of Wales** was a royal chaplain who became acquainted with Henry II towards the end of his reign in the 1180s. The following passage well conveys the restless energy of one of England's most remarkable kings:

> **Henry II,** king of England, was a man of reddish, freckled complexion with a large round head, grey eyes which glowed fiercely and grew bloodshot in anger, a fiery countenance and a harsh, cracked voice. His neck was somewhat thrust forward from his shoulders, his chest was broad and square, his arms strong and powerful. His frame was stocky with a pronounced tendency to corpulence, due rather to nature than to indulgence, which he tempered by exercise. . . .
> In times of war, which frequently threatened, he gave himself scarcely a modicum of quiet to deal with those matters of business which were left over, and in times of peace he allowed himself neither tranquility nor repose. He was addicted to the chase beyond measure; at crack of dawn he was off on horseback, traversing waste lands, penetrating forests and climbing the mountain-tops, and so he passed restless days. At evening on his return he was rarely seen to sit down either before or after supper. After such great and wearisome exertions he would wear out the whole court by continual standing.[3]

The autobiography is essentially a modern variant of the chronicle, with the personality of the author brought to the front of the stage. Invented by the self-conscious Italians of the Renaissance,[4] this form is favoured by artists, writers and perhaps most of all by politicians. Their fascination derives from the fact that they are the recollections of an insider. Indeed they often provide the only available first-hand account, because in all countries recent government records are closed to public inspection (see p. 77); in Britain former Cabinet ministers, when writing their memoirs, are permitted to consult official papers relating to their term of office, though they may not cite or quote from them. But the author's purpose is less to offer an objective account than to justify his or her actions in retrospect and to provide evidence for the defence before the bar of history. Autobiographies may be very revealing of mentality and values, but as a record of events they are often inaccurate and selective to the point of distortion. The historian of the **Suez Crisis** of 1956 who could use no other source than the third volume of Sir Anthony Eden's memoirs (*Full Circle*, 1960) would be in an unenviable position.

The eighteenth century understood the term 'memoirs' in a rather different sense: it denoted a personal chronicle written by someone in public life and intended for publication only after – sometimes long after – his or her death; its purpose was to record facts and opinions which it would have been indiscreet or dangerous to make known at the time, and it therefore makes much more exciting reading than the usually bland and evasive political autobiography. The master of this genre was the **Duc de Saint-Simon**, whose ambition was to leave what has been aptly called 'a minority or dissenting report'[5] on the Versailles of Louis XIV and Louis XV; his *Memoirs*, written in a superb prose style, cover the years from 1691 to 1723. His nearest English rival was Lord Hervey, a favourite of George II's Queen Caroline, who composed a malicious picture of palace intrigue between 1727 and 1737.[6]

At the same time it would be a mistake to think of the published memoir as an upper-class preserve. In Britain by the mid-nineteenth century it had become a recognized means of expression for the literate artisan as well. As David Vincent has shown, autobiographies were written in order to convey the humanity of the working man (and, more rarely, the working woman), and also to challenge common misconceptions about working-class life. The pride and resentment are evident in the opening lines of the radical **Thomas Hardy**'s autobiography, published in 1832:

> As every man whose actions, from whatever cause, have acquired publicity, is sure, in many things, to be misrepresented, such a man has an undoubted right, nay, it becomes his duty, to leave to posterity a true record of the real motives that influenced his conduct. The following Memoir, therefore, requires no apology, and none is offered.[7]

Over one hundred and forty such works have survived from the period 1790–1850 alone.

known as Angevins, from their native Anjou in France). Henry is best known for his disastrous feud with Archbishop Thomas à Becket, but he also instituted major reforms in the legal system.

**Suez Crisis**
A major international crisis in 1956 which ended in the humiliation of the imperial powers, Britain and France. President Nasser of Egypt seized control of the Suez Canal, which was owned by the Franco-British Suez Canal Company. The British Prime Minister Anthony Eden denounced Nasser's action and Britain and France, in secret alliance with Israel, launched a military invasion of Egypt. Although going well on the ground, the invasion was halted in the face of international condemnation and bitter controversy in Britain. The crisis forced Eden to resign.

**Louis de Rouvroy, Duke of Saint-Simon (1675–1755)**
Saint-Simon played an active role in the politics of the French court after the death of Louis XIV but never attained the heights of influence he had hoped for. He died in penury in 1755. Not to be confused with his more radically minded descendant Claude

Henri, Count of Saint-
Simon (1760–1825),
generally regarded as the
founder of French
socialism.

**Thomas Hardy
(1752–1832)**
Scottish radical. He was
accused and acquitted of
high treason in 1794,
during the wars with
Revolutionary France. Not
to be confused with the
novelist of the same name.

**census reports**
The census has been held
in Britain at regular ten-
year intervals ever since
1801 except for 1941,
when the demands of war
made it impossible. Census
reports include detailed
commentary as well as
statistical tables, which
makes them peculiarly
useful to social historians.

**royal commissions**
A committee of inquiry set
up at the command of the
monarch (i.e. of the
government) to
investigate an issue.
Commissions take
evidence from witnesses
and then produce detailed
reports. Both the
transcriptions of
questioning of witnesses
and the reports are usually
published.

*Hansard*
Named after its founder,
Thomas Hansard
(1776–1833), this is the
name given to the daily

# Official papers and newspapers

The chronicles and memoirs which people write for future generations are, of course, only a small minority of what is published
in any period. Most publications are issued with little thought for
posterity; they are rather intended to inform, influence, mislead
or entertain contemporaries. The invention of printing in the fifteenth century greatly facilitated the dissemination of such
writings, while the growth of literacy among the laity increased
the demand for them. Governments were quick to profit from the
revolution in communications, and by the nineteenth century
statements of policy, propaganda and digests of information on
trade, revenue and expenditure were flowing from the official
presses. In Britain perhaps the most impressive of these publications were the **census reports** published every ten years from
1801, and the reports of **royal commissions** set up from the 1830s
onwards to take evidence and make recommendations on major
social problems such as public health and conditions of work.
Another official publication of great interest is that of the reports
of parliamentary proceedings. Thomas **Hansard** began publication of the debates in the Lords and Commons as a private
venture in 1812 (though not quite the first of its kind). The series
assumed its modern format in 1909, when the government,
through His Majesty's Stationery Office, took it over; first-
person, **verbatim** reporting became the rule. Few other sources
convey so well the public face of political discourse.

But the most important published primary source for the historian is the press, which in Britain has a continuous history
dating back to the early eighteenth century, the first daily newspaper having been founded in 1702. Newspapers have a threefold
value. In the first place, they record the political and social views
which made most impact at the time; indeed the earliest newspapers, which had developed out of the vigorous tradition of
pamphleteering during the Civil War and **Commonwealth**
(1642–60), contained little else and are remembered now for the
brilliant polemics of Addison, Steele and Swift. To this day the
leaders and correspondence columns of the great London dailies
offer the best entry into the current state of **establishment opinion**
– provided due allowance is made for the editorial bias of the
paper in question. Secondly, newspapers provide a day-to-day

record of events. During the nineteenth century this function began to be filled much more fully, particularly when the development of the electric telegraph in the 1850s enabled journalists in distant postings to **file their copy** home as soon as it was written. W.H. Russell of *The Times* was one of the first to take advantage of this revolution in communications. His celebrated dispatches from the **Crimea** during the war of 1854–6, which provided shocking evidence of the disarray of the British forces, had a major impact on public opinion at home and still make compelling reading.[8] As sources of straight reporting, newspapers are likely to become even more valuable to historians in the future. For despite the vast archives that governments and corporations continue to amass, important decisions are increasingly communicated by telephone and e-mail rather than by letter, and information obtained informally by journalists at the time may provide the only contemporary written record of what has taken place. Lastly, newspapers from time to time present the results of more thorough enquiries into issues which lie beyond the scope of routine news reporting. The founder of this tradition was Henry Mayhew, an **impecunious** writer briefly employed by the *Morning Chronicle* in 1849–50. As 'Special Correspondent for the Metropolis' he wrote a series of articles exposing social conditions among the London poor in the aftermath of the great cholera epidemic of 1849, which later formed the basis of his book *London Labour and the London Poor* (1851). Few investigative journalists since then have equalled Mayhew in the thoroughness of his research or in his impact on contemporary opinion.[9]

## Literature as historical source material

There is one other kind of source intended for the eyes of contemporaries (and often for posterity too) that historians have to consider, though it is rather a special case: this is creative literature. Novels and plays cannot, of course, be treated as factual reports, however great the element of autobiography or social observation may be. Nor, needless to say, do historical novels – or Shakespeare's history plays for that matter – carry any authority as historical statements about the periods to which they refer. But all creative literature offers insights into the social and intellectual

written reports on proceedings in parliament. In its early versions, the *Parliamentary History* wrote in reported speech ('He said he would…') and sometimes described the scene in the chamber rather than reproducing the exact word. The development of shorthand enabled reporters to reproduce the exact words spoken.

**verbatim**
Reported word for word.

**Commonwealth**
From 1649 to 1654 England was ruled as a republic, known as the Commonwealth, and from 1654 to 1659 as a Protectorate under Oliver Cromwell. The constitutional and political uncertainty of the period saw the production of a huge number of pamphlets laying out conflicting political and religious theories about the direction in which the country ought to move.

**establishment opinion**
'The Establishment' was a term originally coined by young satirists and radical writers in the 1960s to denote all those persons, institutions and attitudes which do well out of the status quo and wish therefore to preserve it.

**file their copy**
'To file copy' is a journalistic term for submitting the text of an article.

**Crimea**
The Crimean War (1854–6), in which Britain fought alongside France and Turkey against Russia, was marked by serious administrative inefficiency and incompetence in British military administration. As a result, the figures who emerged with most credit from the war were those, like the journalist William Howard Russell or the nursing administrator Florence Nightingale, who exposed the shortcomings, and the ordinary British soldier who suffered from them.

**impecunious**
Poor, short of money.

**Chaucer**
Geoffrey Chaucer (1340–1400?), English poet and author of *The Canterbury Tales*. The tales cover a wide range of subjects and social classes, and are therefore heavily used by historians of the late Middle Ages.

**condition of England question**
A phrase used by the 1840s to denote the questions surrounding the problems of poverty, squalor and relations between the rich and the poor.

milieu in which the writer lived, and often vivid descriptions of the physical setting as well. The success of an author is often attributable to the way in which he or she articulates the values and preoccupations of literary contemporaries. So it makes good sense to cite **Chaucer** as a spokesman for the attitudes of the fourteenth-century laity to abuses in the Church, or Dickens as evidence of the frame of mind in which middle-class Victorians considered the '**condition of England**' **question**.

# III

## Record sources: memos, minutes and official correspondence

Because newspapers, official publications and parliamentary speeches are composed mostly with a view to their impact on contemporary opinion, historians attach greater weight to them than to the chronicles and memoirs written with the requirements of posterity in mind. But the very fact of publication sets a limit on the value of all these sources. They contain only what was considered to be fit for public consumption – what governments were prepared to reveal, what journalists could elicit from tight-lipped informants, what editors thought would gratify their readers, or MPs their constituents. In each case there is a controlling purpose which may limit, distort or falsify what is said. The historian who wishes, in Ranke's phrase, 'to show how things actually were' (see pp. 7–8) must go behind the published word, and that is why the greatest advances in modern historical knowledge have been based on research into 'records' – confidential documents such as letters, minutes and diaries. It is in these forms that men and women record their decisions, discussions and sometimes their innermost thoughts, unmindful of the eyes of future historians. Time and again, historians have found that a careful study of the record sources reveals a picture very different from the confident generalizations of contemporary observers. In nineteenth-century England the medical writer William Acton declared that respectable women experienced no sexual feelings of any kind, and his view has been much cited as evidence of Victorian repression; only when the letters and diaries between spouses were examined did it become clear that a much wider range of sexual responses existed among married women.[10] Whether the question at issue is the motives of the participants in the English Civil War, or the impact of the Industrial Revolution on standards of living, or the volume of the Atlantic slave trade, there is no substitute for the painstaking accumulation of evidence from the record sources of the period.

In most countries the largest single body of unpublished records is that belonging to the state, and since Ranke's day more research has been devoted to government archives than to any other kind of source. In the West the oldest surviving state archives took shape during the twelfth century, which saw a marked advance in the sophistication of government organization all over Europe. In England a continuous series of revenue records – the Pipe Rolls of the Exchequer – extends back to 1155, and the records of the royal courts (King's Bench and Common Pleas) to 1194. The beginning of systematic record-keeping can be dated precisely to 1199. In that year King John's chancellor, Hubert Walter, began the practice of making copies on parchment rolls of all the more important letters dispatched from **Chancery** in the king's name. Even after the emergence of other departments in the thirteenth and fourteenth centuries, the Chancery remained the nerve centre of royal administration, and its enrolments are the most important archival source for the Middle Ages in England.

**Chancery**
The royal secretariat in medieval times, administered by the King's Chancellor.

## The records of bureaucracy

During the period 1450–1550 the medieval system was superseded by a more bureaucratic administrative structure controlled by the Privy Council. The most powerful single official within this structure was the king's secretary (later called the secretary of state), and from the reign of Henry VIII his records, known as the State Papers, become the most rewarding source for the policies and actions of the government. In contrast to Chancery records the State Papers, to quote Galbraith,

> are not the routine products of an office, but the intimate and miscellaneous correspondence of an official whose duties knew no fixed limits.... The veil that separates us from character and personality in the Middle Ages is torn aside.[11]

Among the State Papers for 1536 there survives this letter summoning an unfortunate priest from Leicestershire to an interrogation, probably in connection with treason; the menacing tone is unmistakable:

> I commend me unto you. Letting you wit the King's pleasure and commandment is that, all excuses and delays set apart, ye shall incontinently upon the sight hereof repair unto me wheresoever I shall chance to be, the specialties whereof ye shall know at your coming. Without failing thus to do, as ye will answer at your peril. From the Rolls, the 8th day of July. **Thomas Crumwell** [*sic*].[12]

**Thomas Cromwell (c. 1485–1540)**
Secretary successively to Cardinal Wolsey and to King Henry VIII. Cromwell oversaw the dissolution of the monasteries, which involved rigorous examination of the internal affairs of monasteries, convents and abbeys.

It is this category of document that proliferated in the following centuries, as additional secretaries of state were appointed to run new departments that could keep abreast of the expanding scope of government. By the nineteenth century each department of state was keeping a systematic record of letters and papers received, copies of letters sent out and memoranda circulating within the department. At the apex of this complex bureaucratic structure stands the Cabinet. For the first two hundred years of its existence, its deliberations were entirely 'off the record', but since 1916 the Cabinet Secretariat has kept minutes of the Cabinet's weekly meetings and prepared papers for its use.

Another aspect of the enlargement of government under the Tudors was the beginning of routine diplomacy conducted by resident ambassadors. The Italian states set the pattern in the 1480s and 1490s; other countries soon followed, and England's diplomatic network had taken shape by the 1520s. The Venetian ambassador who, in the course of twelve months in 1503–4, sent back from Rome 472 dispatches was more industrious than most,[13] but regular reporting home was from the start an essential part of the ambassador's duties. These reports not only document the conduct of foreign policy more fully than ever before; they also record the diplomat's appraisal of the court and country to which he was accredited. Ranke relied on them heavily for both political and diplomatic history, and there have been many historians since whose expertise is almost entirely limited to diplomatic documents. By the late nineteenth century – often thought of as the 'golden age' of diplomatic history – the documentary record is so full that the historian can reconstruct every stage in a diplomatic initiative from the first tentative proposal of a ministry official to the completed report on the negotiations.

## Church records

Two other types of record share the official character of central government records. In the first place, during the Middle Ages the Church wielded as much, if not more, authority than the state, and in most European countries it retained many of its powers in the secular sphere until the early nineteenth century. Its history is fully documented by the immense quantity of Church records that are available to historians today, many of them still virtually untouched. Royal charters granting land and privileges to the Church have been preserved from the early Middle Ages, and copious records document the efficiency of **episcopal** and monastic administration. The records of the **Church courts** are more interesting than might seem likely at first glance, because so many moral misdemeanours of ordinary people came within their jurisdiction. In sixteenth- and early seventeenth-century England, for example, when the established Church's position *vis-à-vis* the Puritan sects was under threat, strenuous efforts were made through the Church courts to discipline the **laity**, and the records of these courts are therefore an important source for the social historian, particularly as regards sexual misdemeanours and sexual defamation.[14] The Church courts also retained jurisdiction over wills in England until 1858, and from Elizabeth I's reign onwards they insisted on detailed inventories of all movable property, which can now tell the historian a great deal about wealth, status and standards of living.

**episcopal**
Pertaining to bishops.

**Church courts**
Church courts dealt with offences against canon (i.e. Church) law, rather than civil offences, which were dealt with in the king's courts. Church courts often dealt with cases of sexual immorality.

**laity**
'Lay' people, i.e. those who are not members of the clergy.

## Local government and private firms

Secondly, there are the records of local government. During the thirteenth century in England lords of the manor began to follow the king's example and keep records – and particularly judicial records since they had legal jurisdiction over their tenants and servants. One result is that changes in landholding are relatively well documented for rich and poor alike. The first Justices of the Peace were commissioned by the Crown in the fourteenth century, and under the Tudors they were saddled with a mounting load of responsibility – for matters as various as policing, poor relief, wage regulation and military recruitment. Much of this burden was discharged during quarter sessions held at three-monthly intervals in each county, and recorded by a clerk of the peace.

This remained the basis of local government in England until the modern system of county and borough councils was established during the nineteenth century. Until that time a high proportion of local records are legal: the same individuals – whether lords of the manor or Justices of the Peace – were charged with judicial as well as administrative duties. Of all public records, the court records of everyday and often trivial disputes and misdemeanours shed most light on the wider society beyond the small world of government.

Church and state are the oldest record-keeping institutions in Western society. But from the fifteenth century onwards the historian can supplement them with an ever-increasing volume of records generated by private corporations and associations – guilds, universities, trade unions, political parties and pressure groups. Prior to the nineteenth century those that survive in the greatest number are the estate records of landed families, many of which endured over several centuries: their deeds, account books, maps and business correspondence are indispensable material for agrarian historians. Another source within this general category which has attracted much attention – from historians of the Industrial Revolution especially – comprises the records of businesses and firms. For example, the papers of the Stockport textile manufacturer Samuel Oldknow were discovered quite by chance in a disused mill in 1921; covering the period 1782–1812, they provide vivid documentation for the transition from the domestic to the factory system of production.[15] Many companies today have cash-books, inventories and ledgers dating back to the same period or earlier; the historian of England's brewing industry recalls,

> The family continuity in the industry has been such that in most cases
> I found myself working on the letters and the accounts of the
> ancestors of the present owners and managers of the concerns,
> reading their records on the same site where they had brewed in the
> eighteenth century.[16]

The records he examined included those of such well-known names as Whitbread, Charrington and Truman.

# IV

## Private papers

As a general rule, those activities which leave most evidence behind are *organized* activities, and especially those controlled by bodies which have a life-span beyond the careers of the individuals who happen to staff them at any one time – whether they be governments, religious bodies or businesses. For the greater part of recorded history, literate people have probably done most of their writing in the course of their professional or official duties. Nevertheless, there survives a vast mass of written material that has been set down by men and women as private individuals, outside the office or the counting house. Much the largest proportion is accounted for by private correspondence. Among the earliest and most intimate is that between a successful fourteenth-century merchant of Prato (a Tuscan cloth town) and his wife. For eighteen years (1382–1400) pressure of business kept Francesco Datini away from home in Florence and Pisa, and twice a week he wrote to Margherita, and she almost as often to him. On Datini's instructions, most of these letters, along with his extensive business correspondence, were preserved after his death in his house at Prato. The result is a unique chronicle of a medieval marriage. Something of the strain that frequent separations imposed on the marriage is conveyed in this extract from a letter by Margherita in 1389:

> As to your staying away from here until Thursday, you can do as you please, being our master – which is a fine office, but should be used with discretion ... I am fully disposed to live together, as God wills ... and I am in the right, and you will not change it by shouting. Methinks it is not needful to send me a message every Wednesday, to say you will be here on Sunday, for I trow on every Friday, you repent. It would suffice to tell me on Saturday that I could buy something more at the market: for then at least we would fare well on Sundays.[17]

There are no other sources that bring to life so clearly the family and social relationships of people in the past. Without private correspondence the biographer must be content with the public or business life – which indeed is all that medieval biographies can usually attain. One of the main reasons why it is possible to give a relatively full account of the private lives of the Victorians is that an efficient and frequent postal service enabled them to conduct a voluminous correspondence: an upper-class woman whose marriage took her away from her own family might write more than four hundred letters in a single year.[18] This pattern remained common until the spread of the telephone after the First World War. But private letters are an essential source for historians of politics as well. This is because government records are more concerned with decisions and their implementation than with the motives of the people who made them. The private correspondence of public figures reveals much that is scarcely hinted at in the official record. It is the 522 volumes of the Duke of Newcastle's papers (supported by many other private collections), rather than the State Papers or the proceedings of the House of Commons, that underpin L.B. Namier's classic analyses of electoral and parliamentary management in the mid-eighteenth century.[19] The nineteenth and early twentieth centuries were the great age of personal correspondence, when close colleagues in public life wrote to each other daily. Much of this correspondence by-passed official channels and was intended to be seen by none but the recipient. Some politicians confided to a remarkable degree in friends who were without any formal position in politics at all. For three of the years (1912–15) during which he was Prime Minister, **H.H. Asquith** wrote once or twice a day to a young lady called Venetia Stanley. In these letters he could frankly express all his political anxieties and frustrations (as well as many more trivial reflections), confident that his remarks would go no further. Here, in a letter of March 1915, is his assessment of Winston Churchill, then First Lord of the Admiralty:

**H.H. Asquith (1858–1928)**
Liberal Prime Minister 1908–16.

> As you know, like you, I am really fond of him; but I regard his future with many misgivings. . . . He will never get to the top in English politics, with all his wonderful gifts; to speak with the tongue of men & angels, and to spend laborious days & nights in administration, is no good, if a man does not inspire trust.[20]

## Diaries

Private letters are associated with another source which is in some ways even more revealing of personality and opinion – the diary. Diary-keeping began in the sixteenth century and soon became a common literary accomplishment among the educated, especially in England, which in **John Evelyn** and **Samuel Pepys** produced two of the greatest masters of the art. Unlike the chronicler or annalist, the diarist is as much preoccupied with his own subjective response as with the external events that he has witnessed. The considerations that induce someone to devote several hours each week to keeping up a diary are anything but frivolous. For creative writers the diary satisfies the compulsion to observe and reflect, free of the constraints imposed by the formal requirements of the novel, poem or play. Of politicians it is sometimes assumed that a diary serves as little more than an *aide-mémoire* to be drawn on when the time comes to compose an autobiography. But for most political diarists this is a secondary consideration compared with the release from the intense pressures of life in the public eye that a diary affords. The diary which **Gladstone** kept from 1825 to 1896 has almost the character of a confessional: the record of daily engagements and political commentaries is broken up by long passages of painful self-analysis, an unremitting quest for purity of soul.[21] No historian who has not read the diary can hope to understand the personality of this giant among Victorian statesmen. In the case of the Labour politician, **Hugh Dalton**, diary-writing seems to have filled a psychological need directly related to his political performance. As Ben Pimlott explains, the diary, which spans the years 1916 to 1960, acted both as a 'soundingboard for ideas' and as a safety-valve for Dalton's 'very strong instinct towards political self-destructiveness', being fullest for those times when he was consumed by feelings of resentment or irritation against his closest political associates.[22]

For the historian of twentieth-century politics, letters and diaries are of particular significance, despite the almost limitless volume of official records. In the course of the last two generations ministers and civil servants have tended to become more discreet in their official correspondence. During the nineteenth century such correspondence was occasionally published by authority, for example in the **Blue Books** laid by British ministers before Parliament; but this was usually done almost immediately, for pressing propaganda reasons, and the published dispatches had in some cases been composed with that express purpose. In the 1920s, however, the select publication of official records grew out of all proportion, as governments strove to excuse themselves, and blame others, for responsibility for the First World War, often

**John Evelyn (1620–1706)**
Although active in politics after the Restoration, Evelyn is best known for his diary.

**Samuel Pepys (1633–1703)**
As well as keeping his celebrated diary, which includes an account of the Fire of London, Pepys was also, as Secretary to the Admiralty, a central figure in the development of British naval power.

**Gladstone**
William Ewart Gladstone (1809–98) was a towering figure in Victorian politics, serving as Prime Minister four times. His diary is a detailed account of his daily engagements, including, obscured behind a special code, his sexual practices.

**Hugh Dalton (1887–1962)**
Labour politician. As Chancellor of the Exchequer in Clement Attlee's 1945 government Dalton played a central role in the postwar nationalization of heavy industry.

**Blue Books**
Reports of Victorian parliamentary committees and commissions were published – often selling surprisingly well – and were known as Blue Books after the colour of their covers.

with scant regard for the reputation of individual officials twenty or thirty years earlier. Ministers and civil servants, especially those concerned with foreign policy, became much more inhibited in their official correspondence; what they wrote to each other privately, or recorded in their diaries, therefore gains in interest. Moreover, much that politicians *do* say in the course of their ministerial duties does not find its way into the official record. The civil servants who compile Cabinet minutes, for example, are primarily concerned with the decisions reached; the heated political arguments, which are what interests the historian most about Cabinet meetings, go largely unrecorded. **Richard Crossman**, who served as a Cabinet minister under Harold Wilson from 1964 to 1970, kept a weekly diary which was intended, as he put it, to do something towards 'lighting up the secret places of British politics', among which the Cabinet featured prominently.[23] Crossman's diary is unusual in that, almost from the outset, he envisaged its publication within a few years; his work bears comparison with 'memoirs' in the sense understood by Saint-Simon or Hervey. By contrast, the vast majority of the diaries and letters available to the historian were written without thought of a wider readership. Of all sources they are the most spontaneous and unvarnished, revealing both the calculated stratagems and the unconscious assumptions of public figures.

**Richard Crossman (1907–74)**
Labour politician. Under Harold Wilson he was Minister of Housing and the first ever Secretary of State for Health and Social Security. The posthumous publication of his diaries in 1975–9 created something of a sensation because of their revelations about the in-fighting and internal politics at the heart of Wilson's government.

# V

## Why do sources survive?

From this discussion about the different categories of source material it will be apparent that a variety of factors have contributed to the survival of so much documentation from the past. Private letters and diaries have owed their survival to the writer's desire for posthumous fame, or the family piety of the heirs, or perhaps their inertia in leaving trunks and drawers undisturbed. In the case of public records the reasons are more straightforward and more compelling: they arise from the central role of written precedent in law and administration since the High Middle Ages. To put it bluntly, governments needed an accurate record of what was due to them in taxes, dues and services, while the king's subjects cherished evidence of privileges and exemptions which had been granted to them in the past. As the royal bureaucracy grew bigger and more unwieldy, it became increasingly necessary for officials to have a record of what their predecessors had done. As the practice of diplomacy became more formalized from the fifteenth century onwards, ministers could review the earlier relations of their governments with foreign powers and be briefed on their obligations and entitlements under foreign treaties. What was true of governments applied *mutatis mutandis* to other corporate bodies such as the Church, or the great trading companies and financial houses. The only way in which institutions with this sort of permanence could have a 'memory' was if a careful record of their transactions was preserved.

**mutatis mutandis**
(Latin) 'Those things needing to be changed having been changed'. In other words, when due allowance has been made for differences.

But practical motives are not everything. Written documents are also fragile, and the fact that they have weathered the hazards of fire, flood and sheer neglect in such profusion also requires explanation. Continuity of government and of basic law and order are vital. Throughout most of Europe the fabric of literate civilization has endured without a break since the early Middle Ages. Within Europe the distribution of the surviving documentation is largely explained by the incidence of warfare and revolutionary upheaval. It is because England has had little of either that English medieval public records are so plentiful. Last but not least, the growth of historical consciousness itself has had important consequences in minimizing the destruction of documents once they have ceased to be of practical use. Here the Renaissance was the turning point. Curiosity about classical antiquity bred an **antiquarian** mentality which valued the relics of the past for their own sake – hence the beginning of both archaeology and the systematic conservation of manuscripts and books. It is the combination of these factors that accounts for the uniquely rich documentation for the history of Western society and distinguishes it from the other great literate cultures of China, India and the Muslim world, where the survival of written sources has been much more patchy.

**antiquarian**
Valuing historical material for its curiosity or aesthetic value without considering it within its wider historical context.

## Conservation and publication

Only relatively recently, however, has it become a reasonably simple matter to locate the sources and secure access to them. Without the coming of age of historical studies in the mid-nineteenth century and the growing political awareness of the need to preserve the raw materials of a national past, historians today would face a much more daunting prospect. Their task is easiest in the case of published sources. In England there is a good chance that the researcher, assisted by bibliographies and catalogues, will find what he or she wants in one of the great 'copyright' libraries, which by Act of Parliament are entitled to a free copy of every book and pamphlet published in the United Kingdom; the most complete is the British Library (until 1973 the British Museum), whose entitlement dates back to 1757 and has been rigorously enforced since the 1840s. But what of the unpublished sources? The conservation of public and private documents, many of them written with no thought for the requirements of storage and reference, presents much greater problems.

**copyright libraries**
The others are Cambridge University Library, the Bodleian Library, Oxford, the National Libraries of Wales and Scotland, and the Library of Trinity College, Dublin.

In some cases the problems have been partially solved by publication. An immense effort was devoted to this task during the nineteenth century, when the historical value of records gained common acceptance for the first time. The pattern was set by the *Monumenta Germaniae Historica* series, which began publication with government support in 1826 under the direction of the best historians of the day; by the 1860s most of the raw materials for medieval German history were in print.[24] Other countries quickly followed suit, including Britain, where the equivalent Rolls Series began to appear in 1858. The original promoters of these projects intended to publish *all* the extant primary sources. Even for the medieval period this was an ambitious goal; for later, more lavishly documented periods it was an obvious impossibility. In the late nineteenth century, therefore, attention was increasingly switched to the publication of 'calendars', or full summaries of the records. Calendars are an immense help to the researcher, but only because they indicate which documents are relevant to his or her purpose; they are no substitute for perusal of the originals. There is therefore no evading the need to spend long and often tedious hours reading primary sources in manuscript.

## Archives

The historian's task is in most countries greatly eased by an elaborate archive service. But this is a relatively recent development, and the survival of documents from the remote past has often

When the French Revolution broke out in 1789, many villagers took the opportunity to attack the châteaux of their local landowners and destroy all documents recording the feudal taxes and services they owed. Many other documents went up in smoke at the same time, a major blow to future historians of French history.
(Mary Evans Picture Library)

owed more to luck than good management. Many archival collections have perished by accident: the Whitehall fire of 1619 destroyed many of the Privy Council papers, and the fire that swept the Palace of Westminster in 1834 took with it most of the records belonging to the House of Commons. Other holdings have been deliberately destroyed for political reasons: a prominent feature of the agrarian revolts which broke out in the French countryside in July 1789 was the burning of manorial archives that authorized the exaction of heavy dues from the peasantry.[25] In Africa during the 1960s departing colonial officials sometimes destroyed their files for fear that sensitive material would fall into the hands of their African successors.

In England, as elsewhere in Europe, the conservation of archives by the state dates back to the twelfth century. But until the nineteenth century each department of government retained its own archives. They were housed all over London in a variety of buildings, many of them highly unsuitable. Throughout the seventeenth and eighteenth centuries the Chancery records in the Tower were kept above the Ordnance Board's gunpowder stores,[26] while other repositories were exposed to the ravages of damp and rodents. These conditions not only frustrated private litigants (and the occasional historian) wishing to track down precedents but were also an embarrassment to the government itself: it was not unknown for the original of an important treaty to elude the most diligent search.[27] The mid-nineteenth century was a period of reform in this as in so many other spheres of administration. The Public Record Office was set up by Act of Parliament in 1838, and within twenty years it had gained custody of all the main classes of government record. Without that reorganization the immense progress made in the study of English medieval history – the greatest achievement of British historians in the late nineteenth and early twentieth centuries – would scarcely have been possible. Today the Public Record Office is the largest archive in the world (with over 100 miles of shelving) and offers probably the most up-to-date facilities to be found anywhere. In the course of the nineteenth century the archives of most other European countries were reorganized and made available to researchers. A comparable process has taken place in the new states of Asia and Africa which won independence between the 1940s and 1970s. The consolidation of the records of colonial administration into a national archive has been one of the first tasks undertaken in pursuit of a properly documented national past.

As the interests of historians have been enlarged to cover social and economic themes (see Chapter 5), the conservation and organization of local records have been increasingly taken in hand. This has been a formidable undertaking which has won scant public recognition. Under legislation passed in 1963 every county in England and Wales is required to maintain a county record office whose job is to gather together the different categories of local record – quarter sessions, parish, borough and manorial records, etc. Many of the record offices originated in local initiatives taken before the Second World War, and they have extended their search well beyond the semi-official categories to include the records of businesses, estates and associations. Today the holdings of all the county record offices almost certainly exceed those of the Public Record Office. Local and regional studies have become a practicable proposition for professional historians for the first time.

## Restrictions on access

Nowhere, however, have historians been granted complete freedom of access to public records. If historians were allowed to inspect files as soon as they had ceased to be in current use, they would be reading material that was only a few years old. All governments, whatever their political complexion, depend on a measure of confidentiality, and they tend to interpret this requirement very rigorously. Civil servants expect to be reasonably secure in the knowledge that what they set down officially shall not be publicly discussed in the foreseeable future. In Britain the 'closed period' laid down for public records varied considerably according to the department of origin until it was standardized at fifty years in 1958. Nine years later, after a vigorous campaign by historians, this period was reduced to thirty years. France followed suit in 1970, but in some countries, for example, Italy, fifty years is still the rule. Everywhere governments do not hesitate to withhold indefinitely documents that relate to particularly sensitive episodes – for example **the Irish crisis of 1916–22** and the **abdication** of 1936 in Britain, and in France several issues that arose during the **decline of the Third Republic in the late 1930s**. In the United States the Freedom of Information Act of 1975 allows both historians and the general public much wider access, but elsewhere the reduction of the closed period to thirty years is probably as far as the liberalization of access to public records is likely to go. Clearly this has major implications for the study of contemporary history, where historians are forced to rely much more than they would like on what was made public at the time, or what has been disclosed retrospectively in memoirs and diaries.

Yet, however galling these restrictions may seem, government archives are at least centralized and accessible. The same broadly

**Irish crisis of 1916–22**
The Easter Rising in Dublin in 1916 against British rule in Ireland triggered a long period of guerrilla warfare between the Irish Republican Army (IRA) and the British security forces, which culminated in the establishment of the Irish Free State in 1922.

**abdication**
The accession of King Edward VIII in 1936 proved problematic because of objections to his proposed marriage to Mrs Wallis Simpson, an American woman soon to divorce her second husband. Rather than give up Mrs Simpson, the King decided to abdicate in favour of his brother the Duke of York, who thus became King George VI.

**decline of Third Republic in 1930s**
In the 1930s France went through a period of internal conflict, strikes and political crisis that at times seemed to mirror contemporary Spain's descent into civil war. The divisions in French society came into the open when the country fell to the Germans in May 1940.

**Robert Cecil, Viscount Cranbourne and Earl of Salisbury (1563–1612)**
Son of Queen Elizabeth I's minister, Sir William Cecil, Robert Cecil served as Secretary of State under both Elizabeth and James I. Hatfield House is the Cecil family home.

applies to local public records. The case is entirely different with records in private hands. These are widely dispersed and subject to varying – and sometimes perverse – conditions of access; and while governments have usually acknowledged the need for some kind of archive conservation, however rudimentary, family and business records, which may serve no practical function, have often been completely neglected. Nor can the historian whose interest is confined to official documents afford to ignore these private collections. Until the Cabinet Secretariat laid down firm guidelines after 1916, it was common for retiring ministers and officials to keep official papers in their possession; from the sixteenth century onwards, a steady flow of State Papers passed out of public custody in this way,[28] and to this day most of the State Papers dating from **Robert Cecil**'s tenure of office (1596–1612) are at Hatfield House.

In most European countries one of the functions of the national libraries that were set up during the nineteenth century has been to secure possession of the most valuable private manuscript collections. Britain's national library dates back to the foundation of the British Museum in 1753. Of the Museum's foundation manuscript collections, the most important from the historian's point of view is that of Sir Robert Cotton, the early seventeenth-century collector and antiquarian; this numbered among its treasures a great many State Papers, one version of the Anglo-Saxon Chronicle, and two of the four surviving 'exemplifications' of Magna Carta (i.e. copies made at the time of the agreement between King John and the barons in 1215). Purchases and bequests since then have made the British Library far and away the largest repository of historical manuscripts in this country outside the Public Record Office. Even so, the number of important documents held elsewhere is incalculable. Many private collections have been given or loaned indefinitely to public libraries, or to the county record offices. But many more remain in the hands of private individuals, companies and associations. For over a hundred years the Historical Manuscripts Commission has promoted the care of manuscripts privately held in Britain and located their whereabouts, but there is still scope for the historian with a nose for detective work. Several of the collections of private papers on which Namier relied for his studies in eighteenth-century English politics were discovered during what he called his 'cross-country paper-chases'.[29]

## Unearthing source material

The position is worst in the case of the personal and ephemeral materials in the hands of ordinary people – the account books of small businesses, the minute books of local clubs, everyday personal correspondence and the like. Neither the local record offices nor the Historical Manuscripts Commission cast their net as widely as this, yet the recovery of everyday documentation is important if historians are ever to make good their oft-stated aspiration to treat the masses and not just their masters. This is a task for historians with a local focus everywhere, but it is seldom energetically pursued. Since people are usually unaware that they hold material that might be historically significant, historians cannot wait for documents to be brought forward; they need to engage in propaganda and go out in search of them. The Manchester Studies Unit of Manchester Metropolitan University (then the Manchester Polytechnic) began an adventurous programme of archive retrieval in 1975. Appeals for material appeared in the local press and on radio, and a field officer was appointed who approached likely holders of papers and organized house-to-house canvassing in selected neighbourhoods: the results were rewarding.[30]

It might be supposed that a clear division of labour exists between archivists and historians, with the former locating the materials and the latter putting them to use. These examples show that historians cannot in practice leave the task of tracking down documentation to others. The first step in any programme of historical research, then, is to establish the full extent of the sources. Considerable perseverance and ingenuity may be required even at this early stage.

### Roman historians

Roman history poses a problem for the historian because we are so heavily dependent on the accounts of Roman historians about whose sources we know very little. Julius Caesar (100–44 BC) wrote detailed accounts of his campaigns in Gaul and against his political rival Pompey which are generally regarded as valuable but heavily one-sided. Cornelius Tacitus (AD 55–120) seems to have used his access to senatorial records to write his histories of the early years of the empire. Tacitus took a gloomy view of the growth of imperial power, but without access to his own sources we have no yardstick against which to check his version of events. Gaius Suetonius (AD 69–140) wrote a series of short sketches of the first twelve Roman Emperors which became the model for biographical writing, but his habit of recording accurate detail alongside gossip and hearsay, without any attempt to distinguish between the two, makes him a particularly problematic source.

## Satire as a source

Satire is a potent but difficult source for historians. It dates very quickly and is often full of allusions and references to people and events which have sunk into obscurity. Its reliance on irony, in which the writer says the opposite of what he means, can mislead the unwary student. It is also easy to fall into the trap of assuming wrongly that the satirists' views were universally held. There was a thriving market in eighteenth-century England for satirical journals, like *The Tatler* and *The Spectator*. Jonathan Swift's famous *Gulliver's Travels* was originally a scathing satire on Whig politics and society, though it has survived as a fantasy tale for children in a way Swift could never have anticipated.

## 'Namierism'

Sir Lewis Namier (1888–1960) was a historian of eighteenth-century politics who developed a new approach to political history through exhaustive documentary study. His 1929 work *The Structure of Politics at the Accession of George III* was based upon the accumulation of biographical details of every single MP and member of the House of Lords in 1760. This comprehensive approach to the study of institutions is properly known as *prosopography*. He adopted a similarly exhaustive approach to his study of the Duke of Newcastle (Prime Minister 1754–6 and 1757–62), whom he once said he felt he knew better than he knew his own wife. Namier's work led to the setting up of the multi-volume *History of Parliament*, which contains detailed studies of individual MPs and constituencies.

## Further reading

J.J. **Bagley**, *Historical Interpretation*, vol. I: *Sources of English Medieval History, 1066–1840*, Penguin, 1965.

J.J. Bagley, *Historical Interpretation*, vol. II: *Sources of English History, 1540 to the Present Day*, Penguin, 1971.

David Knowles, *Great Historical Enterprises*, Nelson, 1963.

Elizabeth Hallam & Michael Roper, 'The capital and the records of the nation: seven centuries of housing the public records in London', *The London Journal*, IV, 1978.

V.H. Galbraith, *The Making of Domesday Book*, Oxford UP, 1964.

Andrew McDonald, 'Public records and the modern historian', *Twentieth-Century British History*, I, 1990.

L.J. Butler & A. Gorst (eds), *Modern British History*, I.B. Tauris, 1997.

## Notes

1  Louis Gottschalk, *Understanding History: a Primer of Historical Method*, Knopf, 1950, pp. 53–5.

2  Marc Bloch, *The Historian's Craft*, Manchester University Press, 1954, p. 61.

3  Extract from Gerald of Wales, *Expugnatio Hibernica*, translated from the Latin in D.C. Douglas and G.W. Greenaway (eds), *English Historical Documents, 1042–1189*, Eyre & Spottiswoode, 1953, p. 386.

4  The best example is the autobiography of Pope Pius II, composed in the late 1460s. See Leona C. Gabel (ed.), *Memoirs of a Renaissance Pope: the Commentaries of Pius II*, Allen & Unwin, 1960.

5  D.W. Brogan, introduction to Lucy Norton (ed.), *Historical Memoirs of the Duc de Saint-Simon*, vol. I, Hamish Hamilton, 1967, p. xix.

6  Romney Sedgwick (ed.), *Lord Hervey's Memoirs*, William Kimber, 1952.

7  Quoted in David Vincent, *Bread, Knowledge and Freedom: a Study of Nineteenth-Century Working-Class Autobiography*, Methuen, 1981, p. 26.

8  See Kellow Chesney, *Crimean War Reader*, Severn House, 1975.

9  E.P. Thompson and Eileen Yeo (eds), *The Unknown Mayhew: Selections from the Morning Chronicle, 1849–50*, Penguin, 1973.

10  Peter Gay, *The Bourgeois Experience: Victoria to Freud*, vol. II, *The Tender Passion*, Oxford University Press, 1986; John Tosh, *A Man's Place: Masculinity and the Middle-Class Home in Victorian England*, Yale University Press, 1999, ch. 3.

11  V.H. Galbraith, *An Introduction to the Use of the Public Records*, Oxford University Press, 1934, pp. 54–5.

12  Thomas Cromwell to John Harding, 8 July 1536, quoted in G.R. Elton, *Policy and Police*, Cambridge University Press, 1972, pp. 342–3.

13  Garrett Mattingly, *Renaissance Diplomacy*, Cape, 1962, pp. 110, 306.

14  See, for example, Laura Gowing, *Domestic Dangers: Women's Words and Sex in Early Modern London*, Oxford University Press, 1996.

15  George Unwin, *Samuel Oldknow and the Arkwrights*, Manchester University Press, 1924.

16  Peter Matthias, *The Brewing Industry in England, 1700–1830*, Cambridge University Press, 1959, p. xii.

17  Monna Margherita to Francesco di Marco Datini, 29 August 1389, translated and quoted in Iris Origo, *The Merchant of Prato*, Cape, 1957, p. 166.

18  Pat Jalland, *Women, Marriage and Politics, 1860–1914*, Oxford University Press, 1988, pp. 3–4.

19  L.B. Namier, *The Structure of Politics at the Accession of George III*, Macmillan, 1929, and *England in the Age of the American Revolution*, Macmillan, 1930.

20  H.H. Asquith, *Letters to Venetia Stanley*, M. and E. Brock (eds), Oxford University Press, 1982, p. 508.

21  M.R.D. Foot and H.C.G. Matthew (eds), *The Gladstone Diaries*, Oxford University Press, in progress.

22  Ben Pimlott, 'Hugh Dalton's diaries', *The Listener*, 17 July 1980. An edited version of the diaries was published by LSE in association with Jonathan Cape in two volumes in 1986.

23  Richard Crossman, *The Diaries of a Cabinet Minister*, vol. I, Hamish Hamilton and Cape, 1975, p. 12.

24  David Knowles, *Great Historical Enterprises*, Nelson, 1963, pp. 65–97.

25  Georges Lefebvre, *The Great Fear of 1789*, New Left Books, 1973, pp. 100–21.

26  Elizabeth M. Hallam and Michael Roper, 'The capital and the records of the nation: seven centuries of housing the public records in London', *The London Journal*, **IV**, 1978, pp. 74–5.

27  R.B. Wernham, 'The public records in the sixteenth and seventeenth centuries', in Levi Fox (ed.), *English Historical Scholarship in the Sixteenth and Seventeenth Centuries*, Oxford University Press, 1956, pp. 21–2.

28 *Ibid.*, pp. 20–3.

29 Julia Namier, *Lewis Namier: a Biography*, Oxford University Press, 1971, p. 282.

30 Audrey Linkman and Bill Williams, 'Recovering the people's past: the archive rescue programme of Manchester studies', *History Workshop Journal*, **VIII**, 1979, pp. 111–26.

CHAPTER FOUR

# Using the sources

Having tracked the source material down, how should the
historian set about using it? This chapter looks at different
approaches that historians adopt: some start out with a specific set
of questions, some follow whatever line of enquiry the sources
themselves throw up. It draws a distinction between the source
critic, who analyzes source material in great detail, and the
historian, who does this too but puts the sources in the context of
a wider knowledge of the period to which they relate. Sources have
to be analyzed for forgery, the author's bias has to be detected and
taken account of, and historians need to know how to spot when
material has been removed from the record or covered up.
Sometimes, however, the most revealing approach is when the
historian reads between the lines to draw out the hidden
assumptions and beliefs the author was hardly aware of showing.

If the historian's business is to construct interpretations of the
past from its surviving remains, then the implications of the
vast and varied array of documentary sources described in the
previous chapter are daunting. Who can hope to become an authority on even one country during a narrowly defined time-span
when so much spadework has to be done before the task of synthesis can be attempted? If by 'authority' we mean total mastery
of the sources, the short answer is: only the historian of remote
and thinly documented **epochs**. It is, for example, not beyond the
capacity of a dedicated scholar to master all the written materials
that survive from the early Norman period in England. The **vicissitudes** of time have drastically reduced their number, and those

**epoch**
Period, era.

**vicissitudes**
Changes in fortune.

that survive – especially record sources – tend towards the terse and economical. For any later period, however, the ideal is unattainable. From the **High Middle Ages** onwards more and more was committed to paper or parchment, with ever-increasing prospects of survival to our own day. Since the beginning of the twentieth century the rate of increase has surged ahead at break-neck speed. Between 1913 and 1938 the number of dispatches and papers received annually by the British Foreign Office increased from some 68,000 to 224,000.[1] Additions to the Public Record Office at present fill approximately 1 mile of shelving a year.[2] Amid this documentary surfeit, where does the historian begin?

**High Middle Ages**
Term usually applied to the eleventh and twelfth centuries, often taken to mark the climax of medieval society and culture.

# I

## Different approaches to using source material

Ultimately the principles governing the direction of original research can be reduced to two. According to the first, the historian takes one source or group of sources that falls within his or her general area of interest – say the records of a particular court or a body of diplomatic correspondence – and extracts whatever is of value, allowing the content of the source to determine the nature of the enquiry. Recalling his first experience of the French Revolutionary archives, Richard Cobb describes the delights offered by a source-oriented approach:

> More and more I enjoyed the excitement of research and the acquisition of material, often on quite peripheral subjects, as ends in themselves. I allowed myself to be deflected down unexpected channels, by the chance discovery of a bulky *dossier* – it might be the love letters of a *guillotiné*, or intercepted correspondence from London, or the account-books and samples of a commercial traveller in cotton, or the fate of the English colony in Paris, or eyewitness accounts of the September Massacres or of one of the *journées*.[3]

*guillotiné*
Someone who was executed by guillotine during the French Revolution.

The second, or problem-oriented, approach is the exact opposite. A specific historical question is formulated, usually prompted by a reading of the secondary authorities, and the relevant primary sources are then studied; the bearing that these sources may have on other issues is ignored, the researcher proceeding as directly as possible to the point where he or she can present some

*journées*
Literally 'days'. The term was applied to moments of particular drama during the French Revolution.

conclusions. Each method encounters snags. The source-oriented approach, although appropriate for a newly discovered source, may yield only an incoherent jumble of data. The problem-oriented approach sounds like common sense and probably corresponds to most people's idea of research. But it is often difficult to tell in advance what sources *are* relevant. As will be shown later, the most improbable sources are sometimes found to be illuminating, while the obvious ones may lead the historian into too close an identification with the concerns of the organization that produced them. Moreover, for any topic in Western nineteenth- or twentieth-century history, however circumscribed by time or place, the sources are so unwieldy that further selection can hardly be avoided, and with it the risk of leaving vital evidence untouched.

In practice neither of these approaches is usually pursued to the complete exclusion of the other, but the balance struck between them varies a good deal. Some historians begin their careers with a narrowly defined project based on a limited range of sources; others are let loose on a major archive with only the vaguest of briefs. The former is on the whole the more common, because of the pressure to produce quick results that is imposed by the **Ph.D.** degree – the formal apprenticeship served by most academic historians. A great deal of research – probably the larger part – consists not in ferreting out new sources but in turning to well-known materials with new questions in mind. Yet too single-minded a preoccupation with a narrow set of issues may lead to evidence being taken out of context and misinterpreted – 'source-mining' as one critic has called it.[4] It is vital, therefore, that the relationship between the historian and his or her sources is one of give and take. Many historians have had the experience of setting out with one set of questions, only to find that the sources which they had supposed would furnish the answers instead directed their research on to quite a different path. Emmanuel Le Roy Ladurie first turned to the land-tax registers of rural Languedoc with a view to documenting the birth of capitalism in that region; he found himself instead investigating its social structure in the broadest sense, and in particular the impact of **demographic** change:

> Mine was the classic misadventure; I had wanted to master a source
> in order to confirm my youthful convictions, but it was finally the

**Ph.D.**
Doctor of Philosophy. This is usually obtained after three years of detailed archival study resulting in the production of a thesis – a carefully argued case presented in the form of a short book.

**demographic**
Concerning changes in population.

source that mastered me by imposing its own rhythms, its own chronology, and its own particular truth.[5]

At the very least there must be a readiness to modify the original objective in the light of the questions which arise directly from the sources. Without this flexibility historians risk imposing on their evidence and failing to tap its full potential. The true master of the craft is someone whose sense of what questions can profitably be asked has been sharpened by a lifetime's exposure to the sources in all their variety. Mastery of all the sources must remain the ideal, however improbable its complete accomplishment may be.

## Analyzing sources

The reason why the ideal remains for the most part unattainable is not only that the sources are so numerous but also that each of them requires so much careful appraisal. For the primary sources are not an open book, offering instant answers. They may not be what they seem to be; they may signify very much more than is immediately apparent; they may be couched in obscure and anti-quated forms which are meaningless to the untutored eye. Before the historian can properly assess the significance of a document, he or she needs to find out how, when and why it came into being. This requires the application of both supporting knowledge and sceptical intelligence. 'Records', it has been said, 'like the little children of long ago, only speak when they are spoken to, and they will not talk to strangers'.[6] Nor, it might be added, will they be very forthcoming to anyone in a tearing hurry. Even for the experienced historian with green fingers, research in the primary sources is time-consuming; for the novice it can be painfully slow.

Historians have long been aware of the value of primary sources – and not merely the more accessible sources of a narra-tive kind. A surprising number of medieval chroniclers showed a keen interest in the great state documents of the day and repro-duced them in their writings. William Camden, the leading English historian in Shakespeare's generation, was granted access to the State Papers in order to write a history of Elizabeth I's reign. But scholarly source criticism is a much more recent devel-opment. It was largely beyond the historians of the Renaissance, for all their sophistication. Camden, for example, regarded his

**Benedictine**
Of the monastic Order of
St Benedict.

record sources as 'infallible testimonies'.[7] Many of the technical advances which underpin modern source criticism were made during the seventeenth century – notably by the great **Benedictine** scholar Jean Mabillon. But their application was at first confined to monastic history and the lives of the saints, and historians continued to live in a different world from that of the source critic (*érudit*). Edward Gibbon, the greatest historian of the eighteenth century, drew heavily on the findings of the *érudits* in his *Decline and Fall of the Roman Empire* (1776–88), but he did not emulate their methods.

The introduction of a critical approach to the sources into mainstream history-writing was Ranke's most important achievement. He owed his early fame and promotion to a merciless exposé of Guicciardini's faults as a scholar. His appetite for archival research was truly prodigious. And through his seminar at the University of Berlin he brought into being a new breed of academic historians trained in the critical evaluation of primary sources – and especially the many archival sources that were being

The English historian Edward Gibbon (1737–94) said that the idea for writing his famous account of the *Decline and Fall of the Roman Empire* came to him while sitting one evening in the ruins of the forum in Rome. Gibbon started with one major question – what caused such a mighty empire to collapse? – and he embarked on his reading of the historical records with that question always in view. His conclusion, that it was due in large part to the debilitating effects of Christianity, was in line with the radical thinking of the Enlightenment but created a storm of public controversy. (Bridgeman Art Library/Private Collection)

opened to research for the first time during the nineteenth century. It was with pardonable exaggeration that **Lord Acton** saluted Ranke as 'the real originator of the heroic study of records'.[8] Ranke won acceptance for the idea that the evaluation of sources and the writing of history must be kept in the same hands. The spread of Rankean method to Britain came comparatively late; it was primarily due to William Stubbs, whose reputation rested not only on his studies of English constitutional history but also on his scrupulous editing of medieval historical texts. To this day, what Marc Bloch called 'the struggle with documents' is one of the things which distinguishes the professional historian from the amateur.[9]

**Lord Acton (1834–1902)** British historian, Regius (i.e. royal) Professor of Modern History at Cambridge. Acton was formidably learned, and an obsessive note-taker. He edited the multi-volume *Cambridge Modern History* but never got round to writing a major work of history. It was he who wrote in a letter that 'power tends to corrupt and absolute power corrupts absolutely.'

# II

## Is it authentic?

The first step in evaluating a document is to test its authenticity; this is sometimes known as *external* criticism. Are the author, the place and the date of writing what they purport to be? These questions are particularly relevant in the case of legal documents such as charters, wills and contracts, on which a great deal could depend in terms of wealth, status and privilege. During the Middle Ages many royal and ecclesiastical charters were forged, either to replace genuine ones which had been lost or to lay claim to rights and privileges never in fact granted. The **Donation of Constantine**, an eighth-century document which purported to confer temporal power over Italy on Pope Sylvester I and his successors, was one of the most famous of these forgeries. Documents of this kind might be termed 'historical forgeries', and detecting them may tell us a great deal about the society that produced them. But there is also the modern forgery to be considered. Any recently discovered document of great moment is open to the suspicion that it was forged by somebody who intended to make a great deal of money or to run rings round the most eminent scholars of the day. The Vinland Map did just that. In 1959 an anonymous benefactor of Yale University paid a large sum for the map in the belief that it dated from the mid-fifteenth century; since the map clearly showed the north-eastern coast of North America ('Vinland'), the implication was that the earlier

**Donation of Constantine** A document purporting to show that the medieval papacy's immense political power had originally been granted by the Emperor Constantine the Great (*c.* 274–337). The Italian scholar Lorenzo Valla exposed it as a forgery by showing that its wording was not consistent with other Latin documents from the same period but reflected more recent patterns of usage.

Viking discoveries were not unknown in Europe at the time when Columbus was planning his first voyage across the Atlantic. Several experts had committed themselves to the hilt in favour of the map's authenticity before it was exposed beyond reasonable doubt as a forgery in 1974.

Once suspicions are aroused, the historian will pose a number of key questions. First, there is the issue of provenance; can the document be traced back to the office or person who is supposed to have produced it, or could it have been planted? In the case of great finds that suddenly materialize from nowhere, this is a particularly significant question. Secondly, the content of the document needs to be examined for consistency with known facts. Given our knowledge of the period, do the claims made in the document or the sentiments uttered seem at all likely? If the document contradicts what can be substantiated by other primary evidence of unimpeachable authenticity, then forgery is strongly indicated. Thirdly, the form of the document may yield vital clues. The historian who deals mostly in handwritten documents needs to be something of a **palaeographer** in order to decide whether the script is right for the period and place specified, and something of a **philologist** to evaluate the style and language of a suspect text. (It was philological tests that clinched Lorenzo Valla's case against the Donation of Constantine as early as 1439.) More specifically, official documents usually conform to a particular ordering of subject matter and a set of stereotyped verbal formulae, the hallmarks of the institution that issued them. *Diplomatic* is the name given to the study of these technicalities of form. Lastly, historians can call on the help of technical specialists to examine the materials used in the production of the document. Chemical testing can determine the age of parchment, paper and ink; the hand of the Vinland Map forger was betrayed by microphobe analysis of the ink, which revealed a substantial percentage of an artificial pigment unknown before about 1920.[10]

It would be misleading, however, to suggest that historians are constantly uncovering forgeries, or that they methodically test the authenticity of every document that comes their way. This procedure is certainly appropriate to certain branches of medieval history, where much may depend on a single charter of uncertain provenance. But for most historians – and especially the modern historian – there is little prospect of a brilliant detective coup.

**palaeographer**
One who studies ancient writings.

**philologist**
One who studies the development of language.

Their time is more likely to be spent perusing an extended sequence of letters or memoranda, recording humdrum day-to-day transactions, which would scarcely be in anyone's interest to forge. And in the case of public records under proper archival care the possibility of forgery is pretty remote.

For the medievalist some of these skills of detection have another application – to help in preparing an authentic edition out of the several corrupt variants that survive today. Before the invention of printing in the fifteenth century, the only means whereby books could be circulated was by frequent copying by hand; for most of the Middle Ages the *scriptoria* of the monasteries and cathedrals were the main centres of book production. Inevitably errors crept into the copying, and they increased as each copy was used as the basis of another. Where the original (or 'autograph') does not survive, which is frequently the case with important medieval texts, the historian is often confronted by alarming discrepancies among the available versions. This is the unsatisfactory form in which some of the major chroniclers of the medieval period have come down to us. However, close comparison of the texts – especially their scripts and the discrepancies of wording – enables the historian to establish the relationship between the surviving versions and to reconstruct a much closer approximation to the wording of the original. The preparation of a correct text is an important part of a medievalist's work, requiring a command of palaeography and philology. It is made easier now that the texts, which may be held by widely scattered libraries, can be photographed and examined alongside each other.

**scriptoria (*sing. scriptorium*)**
The writing rooms of a monastery, where documents were written and copied out.

# III

## Understanding the text

The authentication of a document and – where applicable – cleansing the text of corruptions are only preliminaries. The second and usually much more demanding stage is *internal* criticism, that is the interpretation of the document's content. Granted that author, date and place of writing are as they seem, what do we make of the words in front of us? At one level this is a question of meaning. This involves more than simply translating from a foreign or archaic language, difficult though that may be for the novice trying to make sense of medieval Latin in abbreviated form. The historian requires not merely linguistic fluency but a command of the historical context that will show what the words actually refer to. Domesday Book is a classic example of the difficulties that can arise here. It is a record of land use and the distribution of wealth in the English shires in 1086, before the institutions of the Anglo-Saxons (and the Danes) had been much altered by Norman rule; but it was compiled by clerks from Normandy whose everyday language was French and who described what they had seen and heard in Latin. Small wonder that it is not always clear, for example, to what form of land tenure the term *manerium* (usually 'manor') refers.[11] Nor are our problems solved if we stick to documents written in English. For language itself is a product of history. Old words, especially the more technical ones, pass out of currency, while others acquire a new significance. We have to be on our guard against reading modern meanings into the past. In the case of the more culturally sophisticated sources, such as contemporary histories or treatises on political theory, different levels of meaning may have been embedded in the same text, and this becomes a major task of interpretation. In coming to terms with the instability of language, historians have been influenced by recent developments in literary studies, especially the Postmodernist preoccupation with theories of language (see Chapter 7).

## Is it reliable?

Once historians have become immersed in the sources of their period and have mastered its characteristic turns of phrase and the appropriate technical vocabulary, questions of meaning tend to worry them less often. But the content of a document prompts a further, much more insistent question: is it reliable? No source can be used for historical reconstruction until some estimate of its standing as historical evidence has been made. This question is beyond the scope of any **ancillary** technique such as palaeography or diplomatic. Answering it calls instead for a knowledge of historical context and an insight into human nature. Here historians come into their own.

**ancillary**
Subsidiary, giving help to.

Where a document takes the form of a report of what has been seen, heard or said, we need to ask whether the writer was in a position to give a faithful account. Was he or she actually present, and in a tranquil and attentive frame of mind? If the information was learned at second hand, was it anything more than gossip? The reliability of a medieval monastic chronicler largely depended on how often his cloister was frequented by men of rank and power.[12] Did the writer put pen to paper immediately, or after the sharpness of his or her memory had blurred? (A point worth bearing in mind when reading a diary.) In reports of oral proceedings, a great deal may turn on the exact form of words used, yet prior to the spread of shorthand in the seventeenth century there was no means of making a verbatim transcript. The earliest mechanical means of recording speech – the phonograph – was not invented until 1877. It is extraordinarily difficult to know exactly what a statesman said in a given speech: if he wrote it out in advance he may well have departed from his text; and press reporters, usually armed with only a pencil and note-pad, are inevitably selective and inaccurate, as can be seen by comparing

The National Archives at Kew house all government records since the Norman Conquest. They were moved from a central London location in the 1970s. Until 2004 the archives were known as the Public Record Office. (M Square Visions/ Photographers Direct)

**episcopate**
The rank of bishop.

**Henry III**
King Henry III (1207–72) inherited problems with the English barons from his father, King John. Opposition to Henry was led by Simon de Montfort and Stephen Langton, Archbishop of Catherbury, and led eventually to the summoning in 1265 of the earliest parliament in English history.

**corporate privileges**
The privileges of particular groups, especially the barons.

**heresy**
Deviation from orthodox religious belief, as opposed to *infidels* (the unfaithful), who hold to a different religious belief entirely. Heresy was punishable by death in medieval Church courts.

**Ashanti**
A West African kingdom in modern-day Ghana. It was a major power in the region until the arrival of the British in the late nineteenth century. Britain annexed the Ashanti kingdom in 1901.

**polygamy**
The system whereby one man is allowed more than one wife. Although clearly in evidence in the Old Testament, it has always been severely condemned by the mainstream Christian churches.

the reports given by different newspapers of the same speech. In the case of speeches in Parliament a reliable verbatim record can be read, but even this dates back only to the reform of *Hansard* in 1909.

## What influenced the author?

What most affects the reliability of a source, however, is the intention and prejudices of the writer. Narratives intended for posterity, on which a general impression of the period tends to be based, are particularly suspect. The distortions to which autobiography is subject in this respect are too obvious for comment. Medieval chroniclers were often extremely partisan as between one ruler and another, or as between Church and state: Gerald of Wales's increasing antipathy towards Henry II was due to the king's repeated veto on his promotion to the **episcopate**; Matthew Paris's treatment of the disputes between **Henry III** and the English barons was slanted by his identification with virtually all forms of **corporate privilege** in their dealings with king or pope.[13] Chroniclers were often influenced too by the prejudices characteristic of educated people of their time – a revulsion against **heresy**, or a distaste for lawyers and money-lenders. Culture-bound assumptions and stereotypes shared by virtually all literate people of the day call for particularly careful appraisal. For the historian of pre-literate societies such as those of tropical Africa in the nineteenth century, the contemporary accounts of European travellers are a source of major importance, but nearly all of them were coloured by racism and sensationalism: judicial execution (as in **Ashanti**) appeared as 'human sacrifice', and **polygamy** was presented as a licence for sexual excess. Nor does creative literature have a special dispensation in this respect. Novelists, playwrights and poets have as many prejudices as anyone else, and these have to be allowed for when citing their work as historical evidence. E.M. Forster's *A Passage to India* (1924) is, among other things, a marvellously convincing and very unflattering portrayal of the **British Raj** at district level, but some account must surely be taken of Forster's own alienation from the kind of **stiff-upper-lip** public school man who controlled the administration in India.

The attraction of record sources – of 'witnesses in spite of themselves' (see p. 62) – on the other hand, is that through them the historian can observe or infer the sequence of day-to-day events, free from the controlling purpose of a narrator. But this is merely to eliminate one of the more obvious kinds of distortion. For however spontaneous or authoritative the source, very few forms of writing arise solely from a desire to convey the unvarnished truth. Even in the case of a diary composed without thought of publication, the writer may be bolstering his or her self-esteem and rationalizing motives. A document that appears to be a straightforward report of something seen, heard or said may well be slanted – either unconsciously, as an expression of deep-seated prejudice, or deliberately, from a wish to please or influence the recipient. The ambassador in his dispatches home may convey a greater impression of bustle and initiative on his own part than is actually the case; and he may censor his impressions of the government to which he is **accredited** in order to fit them to the policies and preconceptions of his superiors. Historians today are much more sceptical than they used to be about the claims to objectivity of the great Victorian enquirers into the 'social problem': they recognize that the selection of evidence was often distorted to fit middle-class stereotypes about the poor and to promote the implementation of pet remedies.

## The uses of bias

Once bias has been detected, however, the offending document need not be consigned to the scrap-heap. The bias itself is likely to be historically significant. In the case of a public figure it may account for a consistent misreading of certain people or situations, with disastrous effects on policy. In published documents with a wide circulation, bias may explain an important shift in public opinion. The reports of nineteenth-century Royal Commissions are a case in point. Newspapers provide other examples: the war reports of the many British dailies which were opposed to Asquith's government in 1915–16 are not a reliable guide to what was happening on the front, but they certainly help to explain why the Prime Minister's reputation at home declined so severely.[14] Autobiographies are notorious for their errors of recall and their special pleading. But in their very subjectivity often lies their greatest value, since the pattern that the writer makes of his or her own life is a cultural as much as a personal

**British Raj**
British imperial rule in India.

**stiff-upper-lip**
The attitude of stoicism and formality which was traditionally inculcated at British public shools in order to teach boys to hide their emotions, especially in the face of pain or adversity.

**accredited**
Ambassadors are sent by the government of their own country and accredited – attached – to the government of another.

construct, and it also illuminates the frame of mind in which not only the book was written but the life itself was led. Even the most tainted sources can assist in the reconstruction of the past.

## Reading sources in their context

As described so far, the evaluation of historical evidence may not seem to be unlike the cross-examination of witnesses in a court of law: in both cases the point is to test the reliability of the testimony. But the courtroom analogy is misleading if it suggests that primary sources are always evaluated in this way. One of the most illuminating ways into the past is to focus on a specific source and to reconstruct how it came into being by all available means – through textual analysis, related documents from the same source, contemporary comment and so on – as V.H. Galbraith did to great effect in the case of Domesday Book.[15] This is in effect the procedure now adopted by historians of ideas. Traditionally their subject was studied to reveal the pedigree of key concepts such as parliamentary sovereignty or the freedom of the individual through a canon of great theorists down the ages. This had the unfortunate effect of implying that the great texts were addressing 'our' issues and thus obscured the contemporary significance of the sources themselves. But the first task of the historian is to treat these works like any other document of the time and to read them, as far as possible, in the specific intellectual and social contexts in which they were written. This means having regard to both the specific genre – or *discourse* – to which the work belonged and its relation to other genres with which readers of the time would have been familiar. Recent scholars such as Quentin Skinner and J.G.A. Pocock have pointed out that what contemporaries made of, say, *Leviathan* (1651) almost certainly differed from what Thomas Hobbes himself meant to convey.[16] Context is at least as important as text in coming to terms with an original thinker in the past.

## The hidden problems of public records

The courtroom analogy is no more helpful in understanding how public records are analyzed. Traditionally the staple diet of researchers, public records have most often been studied from one of two standpoints. First, how did the institution that generated the records evolve over time, and what was its function in the **body politic**? And second, how were specific policies formulated and executed? In this context reliability is hardly the issue, for the records are studied not as *reports* (i.e. testimonies of events 'out there') but as parts of a *process* (be it administrative, judicial or policy-making) which is itself the subject of enquiry. They are as much the creation of an institution as an individual and therefore need to be examined in the context of that institution – its vested interests, its administrative routine, and its record-keeping procedures; any records to do with law or public finance call for technical knowledge of a particularly demanding kind. Considered apart from the series to which they belong, the records of public institutions no longer extant are almost certain to be misinterpreted. Thus the records of the Public Record Office should be used in the first instance 'not as a lucky bag that may produce evidence on almost anything, but for what they really are, *viz.* the systematic record of personal government developing into national government'.[17]

> **body politic**
> A metaphor for the state. The analogy of the composition and operation of a state with the working of a body was often used in political literature in Tudor and Stuart times.

To understand the full significance of these records the historian must if possible study them in their original groupings (a principle on the whole respected in the Public Record Office) rather than in the rearrangement of some tidy-minded archivist. And ideally they should be studied in their entirety. Unfortunately public record-keeping in England before about 1700 was patchy. Medieval Chancery records are basically copies of the government's out-letters, with very few of the letters that it was constantly receiving from its subjects. Conversely, Tudor State Papers are largely confined to incoming correspondence, and only a small proportion of the out-letters survive in private manuscript collections; it is therefore difficult to be sure how policies were executed, or what pressures contributed to their genesis. This deficiency in the record-keeping of the secretaries of state was not rectified until after the Restoration.[18] But, whenever possible, historians try to study the documents in series, and in their entirety, in order to minimize the danger of misinterpreting a particular item out of context.

## Gaps in the record

A knowledge of administrative and archival procedures is also vital if the historian is to be alert to one particularly serious cause of distortion in the surviving record – the deliberate removal of evidence. While the planting of a forgery in the official record presents major difficulties, it may be a comparatively easy matter to suppress an embarrassing or incriminating document. In the State Papers, for example, almost all the letters to and from **Lord Chancellor Jeffreys** for the reign of James II are missing. Since Jeffreys himself died in the Tower in 1689 after the Revolution, it has been surmised that the papers were removed by some person who had changed sides at the critical moment and stood to gain by suppressing his connection with the infamous judge of the 'Bloody Assizes'.[19] In Britain today the centralization of most government record-keeping at the Public Record Office – achieved in the mid-nineteenth century – is an effective check on this kind of tampering, but it is still possible for the responsible official to ensure that a sensitive document never leaves the department in which it was produced. Since total preservation is manifestly impracticable, there is a recognized procedure for destroying ephemeral material judged to be of no historical interest, and this is open to abuse.[20] For example, a number of Colonial Office files relating to Palestine in the late 1940s have been destroyed, presumably in order to cast a veil over British actions during the turbulent last phase of the Mandate administration; it is also likely that crucial British documents relating to the Suez Crisis of 1956 were destroyed or removed immediately.[21] No doubt there have been instances of unauthorized censorship which are proof against detection, but the historian familiar with the administrative procedures of the department in question is a great deal less likely to be duped.

**Lord Chancellor Jeffreys (1648–89)**
George Jeffreys was a zealous and deeply unpopular judge under Charles II and James II. He became notorious for the 'Bloody Assizes' in the West Country, when he sentenced 300 people to death for taking part in the Duke of Monmouth's failed rebellion of 1685.

## Officially published records

While some records have been carefully removed from the historian's reach, others have been pushed into the limelight. In several fields of modern history, collections of records published soon after the time of writing can be consulted. It is important that these collections should not be accorded special weight just because they are so accessible. They nearly always represent a selection, whose publication was intended to further some practical end, usually of a short-term political nature. The well-known series of *State Trials* was for a long time accepted as a reliable record of some of the major English criminal proceedings since the sixteenth century. But the first four volumes were promoted in 1719 by a group of propagandists in the Whig cause: as a source for the great political trials of the Stuart period they are therefore distinctly suspect.[22] During the nineteenth century the publication – often on a massive scale – of a politician's correspondence was often considered by his family and followers to be a fitting memorial, but there was usually an element of censorship so that the less savoury episodes were suppressed and the reputation of living persons protected or enhanced. Governments of the same period regarded the publication of select diplomatic correspondence (for example in the British Blue Books) as a legitimate means of building up public support for their policies; some of the 'dispatches' were composed for this very purpose. In all these cases the historian will obviously prefer to go to the originals. If these are not available, the published versions must be scrutinized carefully, and as much as possible must be found out from other sources about the circumstances in which they were compiled.

# IV

## Weighing sources against each other

It will be clear, then, that historical research is not a matter of identifying *the* authoritative source and then exploiting it for all it is worth, for the majority of sources are in some way inaccurate, incomplete or tainted by prejudice and self-interest. The procedure is rather to amass as many pieces of evidence as possible from a wide range of sources – preferably from *all* the sources that have a bearing on the problem in hand. In this way the inaccuracies and distortions of particular sources are more likely to be revealed, and the inferences drawn by the historian can be corroborated. Each type of source possesses certain strengths and weaknesses; considered together, and compared one against the other, there is at least a chance that they will reveal the true facts – or something very close to them.

This is why mastery of a variety of sources is one of the hallmarks of historical scholarship – an exacting one which is by no means always attained. One of the reasons why biography is often disparaged by academic historians is that too many biographers have studied only the private papers left by their subject, instead of weighing these against the papers of colleagues and acquaintances and (where relevant) the public records for the period. Ranke himself has been criticized for relying too heavily on the dispatches of the Venetian ambassadors in some of his writings on the sixteenth century. Observant and conscientious as most of them were, the ambassadors saw matters very much from the point of view of the governing élite. They were also foreigners, free from local political loyalties, it is true, but lacking a real feel for the culture of the country to which they were accredited.[23] The need for primary evidence from 'insiders' as well as 'outsiders' is an important guideline for historical research, with wide ramifications. The failings of Western writers on African history before the 1960s could be summed up by saying that they relied on the testimony of the European explorer, missionary and administrator, without seriously seeking out African sources.[24] In the case of the Middle East comparable distortions arise from drawing exclusively on what Edward Said has called 'Orientalist' discourse – the testimony of Western travellers and 'experts' whose stereotyped representations effectively silenced the indigenous peoples of the region.[25] Carroll Smith-Rosenberg recalls that when she started out in nineteenth-century American women's history, she found herself portraying women as victims because she had stuck to the well-thumbed educational and theological works which men wrote for and about women; her angle of vision was transformed when she uncovered the letters and diaries of ordinary women which documented the active consciousness of the 'insider'.[26]

**Gorbachev era**
Under communist rule access to state archives in the Soviet Union was virtually impossible. Under Mikhail Gorbachev archives were opened to scholars as part of his policy of *glasnost* (openness).

Tough standards now tend to be expected of historians regarding the range of sources they use. In the history of international relations, for example, it is a golden rule that both sides of a diplomatic conversation must be studied before one can be certain what the subject of the conversation was and which side put its case more effectively; this is why the inaccessibility of the Soviet archives prior to the **Gorbachev era** was so frustrating for Western historians of the origins of the Second World War. For historians of government policy in twentieth-century Britain, the temptation may be to confine research to the public records, because these survive in such profusion, and their number is increased every year as more records become available for the first time under the thirty-year rule (see p. 81). But this method is hardly conducive to a balanced interpretation. The public records tend to give too much prominence to administrative considerations (thus reflecting the principal interest of the civil servants who wrote most of them) and to reveal much less about the political pressures to which ministers responded; hence the importance of extending the search to the press and *Hansard*, private letters and diaries, political memoirs, and – for recent history – to first-hand oral evidence.[27]

## Hidden traces in the records

The examples just discussed – international relations and government policy – are topics for which there exists primary source material in abundance. In each case there is a well-defined body of documents in public custody, with numerous ancillary sources to corroborate and amplify the evidence. But there are many historical topics which are much less well served, either because little evidence has survived or because what interests us today did not interest contemporaries and was therefore not recorded. If historians are to go beyond the immediate concerns of those who created their sources, they have to learn how to interpret them more obliquely. There are two principal ways of doing so. In the first place, many sources are valued for information which the writers were scarcely aware they were setting down and which was incidental to the purpose of their testimony. This is because people unconsciously convey on paper clues about their attitudes, assumptions and manner of life which may be intensely interesting to historians. A given document may therefore be useful in a variety of ways, depending on the questions asked of it – sometimes questions that would never have occurred to the writer or to people of the time. This, of course, is one reason why beginning research with clearly defined questions rather than simply going where the documents lead can be so rewarding: it may reveal evidence where none was thought to exist. From this point of view, the word 'source' is perhaps somewhat inapposite: if the metaphor is interpreted literally, a 'source' can contribute evidence to only one 'stream' of knowledge. It has even been suggested that the term should be abandoned altogether in favour of 'trace' or 'track'.[28]

## Unwitting evidence

This flair for turning evidence to new uses is one of the distinctive contributions of recent historical method. It has been most fully displayed by historians who have moved beyond the well-lit paths of mainstream political history to fields such as social and cultural history, for which explicit source material is more difficult to come by. A case in point is the religious beliefs of ordinary people in Reformation England. Although the switches of doctrinal allegiance among the élite are relatively well recorded, evidence is very sparse for the rest of the population. But Margaret Spufford in her study of three Cambridgeshire villages has used the unlikely evidence of wills to show how religious affiliation changed. Every will began with a **dedicatory clause**, which allows some inference to be drawn concerning the doctrinal preference of the testator or the scribe. From a study of these clauses, Spufford shows how by the early seventeenth century personal faith in the **mediation of Christ** – the hallmark of Protestant belief – had made deep inroads among the local people.[29] It was, of course, no part of the testators' intentions to furnish evidence of their religious beliefs; they were concerned only to ensure that their worldly goods were disposed of in accordance with their wishes. But historians alert to the unwitting testimony of the sources can go beyond the intentions of those who created them.

Legal history arouses relatively little interest among historians at present, but court records are probably the single most important source we have for the social history of the medieval and early modern periods, when the vast majority of the population was illiterate and therefore generated no records of its own. Emmanuel Le Roy Ladurie's *Montaillou* (1978) is a classic illustration of this point. In the Vatican library there survives the greater part of the Register recording an **Inquisition** carried out between 1318 and 1325 by Jacques Fournier, bishop of Pamiers. Of the 114 people accused of heresy, twenty-five came from Montaillou, a village in the Pyrenees of no more than 250 inhab-

**dedicatory clause**
The opening section of a will, which dedicates the testator's soul to the care of Almighty God.

**mediation of Christ**
Catholic theology teaches that the believer needs the agency of the Church in order to go to heaven after death. Protestants believe that the death of Jesus Christ on the cross provides all the mediation between God and mankind that is needed, and that a believer need only believe in Christ in order to enter into heaven.

**Inquisition**
Officially known as the Holy Office, this was the Catholic Church's legal department charged with investigating accusations of heresy.

When the Cathar heresy took hold in southern France in the thirteenth century the Church sent the Inquisition to stamp it out. Centuries later the French historian Emmanuel Le Roy Ladurie used the Inquisitors' records to build up a remarkably detailed picture of the intimate lives of the inhabitants of the little mountain village of Montaillou. Le Roy Ladurie was reading the records with very different priorities from those of the men who originally compiled them.
(Paul Shawcross/ Photographers Direct)

**Maigret**
The painstaking fictional detective created by the Belgian crime writer Georges Simenon (1903–89).

itants. They were quizzed on their beliefs, their circle of friends (especially the heretical ones) and their moral conduct. The bishop saw to it that the lengthy statements made in his court were meticulously recorded and checked by the witnesses themselves; and since he was also a tireless interrogator and a stickler for detail – 'a sort of compulsive **Maigret**'[30] – the result is an extraordinarily vivid and revealing document. With the help of supporting evidence, Le Roy Ladurie has been able to reconstruct the everyday life of the peasants of Montaillou – their social relationships, their religious and magical observances, and not just their attitudes to sex but much of their actual sex life. As Le Roy Ladurie puts it, the high concentration of **Cathar** heretics in Montaillou 'provides an opportunity for the study not of Catharism itself – that is not my subject – but of the mental outlook of the country people'.[31] When historians distance themselves from the contemporary significance of a document in this way, its reliability may be of only marginal significance: what counts is the incidental detail. In eighteenth-century France it was the practice for unmarried pregnant women to make statements

**Cathar**

A form of religious heresy that spread rapidly in south-western France in the thirteenth century. Also known as Albigensianism, from its centre in the town of Albi. It held that, since man's true home is in heaven, the world must be evil. It was seen as a major doctrinal and political threat both by the papacy and by the kings of France, and was finally crushed by the Inquisition and by a ruthless military campaign known as the Albigensian Crusade.

to the magistrate in order to pin responsibility on their seducers and salvage something of their reputations. Richard Cobb carried out a study of fifty-four such statements made at Lyon in 1790–2, and as he points out, the identity of the seducers is a trivial issue compared with the light that is shed on the sexual mores of the urban poor, their conditions of work and leisure, and the popular morality of the day.[32] It is studies such as these that demonstrate the full force of Marc Bloch's injunction to his fellow historians to study 'the evidence of witnesses in spite of themselves' (see p. 62).

## Working backwards from the sources

The second oblique method of exploiting historical evidence is much more controversial, and it was also propounded by Marc Bloch. Bloch wanted to reconstruct French rural society in the Middle Ages. The documents for the period contain a great deal of information but little sense of how the details fit together to form an overall picture. Such a picture emerges only in the eighteenth century, when French agrarian life was systematically described by agronomists and by commissions of inquiry, and when accurate local maps began to appear in large numbers. Bloch maintained that only someone familiar with the structure of French rural society as it was revealed in the eighteenth century could make sense of the medieval data. He did not, of course, assume that nothing had changed in the meantime; his point was rather that in this kind of situation the historian should carefully work back by stages from what is known in order to make sense of the fragmentary and incoherent evidence for earlier periods.

> The historian, especially the agrarian historian, is perpetually at the mercy of his documents; most of the time he or she must read history backwards if he or she hopes to break the secret cypher of the past.[33]

This approach, known as the *regressive* method, is much used in African history, where the documentary sources for pre-colonial society are of poor quality. In his book *The Tio Kingdom* (1973), for example, Jan Vansina draws on his own ethnographic fieldwork in the 1960s to shed light on the observations of European visitors to the kingdom in the 1880s, who mentioned many indigenous features without understanding their meaning or their place in the social structure. It would otherwise have been quite impossible to make any sense of Tio society as a whole on the eve of the European takeover. The regressive method is certainly a second-best which contravenes the usual rules for evaluating primary sources, but if applied sensitively with an eye for change it produces revealing results.

# V

## Methodology and instinct

In approaching the sources, the historian is anything but a passive observer. The relevant evidence has to be sought after in fairly out-of-the-way and improbable places. Ingenuity and flair are required to grasp the full range of uses to which a single source may be put. Of each type of evidence the historian has to ask how and why it came into being, and what its real import is. Divergent sources have to be weighed against each other, forgeries and gaps explained. No document, however authoritative, is beyond question; the evidence must, in E.P. Thompson's telling phrase, 'be interrogated by minds trained in a discipline of attentive disbelief'.[34] Perhaps these precepts hardly merit the name of method, if that suggests the deliberate application of a set sequence of scientific procedures for verifying the evidence. Innumerable handbooks of historical method have, it is true, been written for the guidance of research students since Ranke's time, and on the continent and in the United States formal instruction in research techniques has long been part of the postgraduate historian's training.[35] Britain, on the other hand, has until recently been the home of the 'green fingers' approach to source criticism. G.M. Young, an eminent historian of the inter-war period, declared that his aim was to read in a period until he could hear its people speak. He was later echoed by Richard Cobb:

> The most gifted researchers show a willingness to *listen* to the wording of the document, to be governed by its every phrase and murmur ... so as to *hear* what is actually being said, in what accent and with what tone.[36]

This suggests not so much a method as an attitude of mind – an instinct almost – which can only be acquired by trial and error.

But to argue further, as Cobb has done, that the principles of historical enquiry defy definition altogether is a mystification.[37]

In practice, unfavourable notice of a secondary work often turns on the author's failure to apply this or that test to the evidence. Admittedly, the rules cannot be reduced to a formula, and the exact procedures vary according to the type of evidence; but much of what the experienced scholar does almost without thinking can be described – as I have tried to do here – in terms that are comprehensible to the uninitiated. When spelt out in this way, historical method may seem to amount to little more than the obvious lessons of common sense. But it is common sense applied very much more systematically and sceptically than is usually the case in everyday life, supported by a secure grasp of historical context and, in many instances, a high degree of technical knowledge. It is by these taxing standards that historical research demands to be judged.

## Bishop Stubbs' *Select Charters* and the British constitution

The work of the nineteenth-century British historian Bishop William Stubbs (1829–1901) is an example of the application of scholarly historical research to contemporary concerns. Stubbs was Regius Professor of Modern History at Oxford, and later Bishop of Chester and of Oxford. His compilation of medieval charters and his three-volume *Constitutional History of England* were drawn up to show through exhaustive documentary evidence the antiquity – and therefore the legitimacy – of English legal and political institutions. His work is therefore as important nowadays for what it reveals about the Victorian mentality as it is for understanding the period Stubbs was actually studying.

## Orientalism

In the eighteenth century European scholars developed a keen interest in the history and culture of the 'Orient', a concept they applied to an area ranging from North Africa and the Middle East through the Indian subcontinent to China and Japan. In his 1978 book *Orientalism* the literary scholar Edward Said argued that this interest in fact reflected the Europeans' sense of their own superiority over what they saw as a romanticized and 'mysterious' East.

## British rule in Palestine

Palestine, roughly equivalent to modern-day Israel and Jordan, was a province of the Turkish Ottoman Empire until after the First World War, when the British took the area over, under mandate from the League of Nations. However, the British were also bound by their undertaking under the 1917 Balfour Declaration to establish a homeland in Palestine for the Jewish people. Palestinian resistance to Jewish immigration grew steadily through the 1930s. After the Second World War and the Holocaust, increasing demands for large-scale Jewish settlement in Palestine enjoyed considerable international support. Jewish terrorist groups, Irgun and the Stern Gang, launched a series of bomb attacks on British troops and administration buildings. British attempts to create some sort of bi-national Arab–Jewish state failed, and in 1947 the United Nations agreed to partition Palestine between Jews and Arabs. Britain handed the mandate back to the UN in 1948, and the UN immediately declared the Jewish state of Israel.

## Further reading

Marc Bloch, *The Historian's Craft*, Manchester UP, 1954.

G. Kitson Clark, *The Critical Historian*, Heinemann, 1967.

G.R. Elton, *The Practice of History*, Sydney UP, 1967.

Jacques Barzun & Henry F. Graff, *The Modern Researcher*, 3rd edn, Harcourt Brace Jovanovich, 1977.

John Fines, *Reading Historical Documents: a Manual for Students*, Blackwell, 1988.

V.H. Galbraith, *An Introduction to the Study of History*, Watts, 1964.

Jacques Le Goff & Pierre Nora (eds), *Constructing the Past: Essays in Historical Methodology*, Cambridge UP, 1985.

Stephen Davies, *Empiricism and History*, Palgrave 2003.

## Notes

1 Anthony P. Adamthwaite, *The Making of the Second World War*, Allen & Unwin, 1977, p. 20.

2 Elizabeth M. Hallam and Michael Roper, 'The capital and the records

of the nation: seven centuries of housing the public records in London', *The London Journal*, IV, 1978, p. 91.

3 Richard Cobb, *A Second Identity: Essays on France and French History*, Oxford University Press, 1969, p. 15.

4 J.H. Hexter, *On Historians*, Allen Lane, 1979, p. 241. The label is rather unfairly pinned on Christopher Hill.

5 Emmanuel Le Roy Ladurie, *The Peasants of Languedoc*, Illinois University Press, 1974, p. 4.

6 C.R. Cheney, *Medieval Texts and Studies*, Oxford University Press, 1973, p. 8.

7 William Camden, Preface to *Britannia* (1586), as quoted in J.R. Hale (ed.), *The Evolution of British Historiography*, Macmillan, 1967, p. 15.

8 Lord Acton, *Lectures on Modern History*, Fontana, 1960: first published in 1906, p. 22.

9 Marc Bloch, *The Historian's Craft*, Manchester University Press, 1954, p. 86.

10 Helen Wallis and others, 'The strange case of the Vinland Map: a symposium', *Geographical Journal*, CXL, 1974, pp. 183–214.

11 Bloch, *The Historian's Craft*, p. 165; J.J. Bagley, *Historical Interpretation*, vol. I: *Sources of English Medieval History, 1066–1540*, Penguin, 1965, pp. 24, 29–30.

12 See, for example, the impressive list of informants and contacts in Richard Vaughan, *Matthew Paris*, Cambridge University Press, 1958, pp. 11–18.

13 Antonia Gransden, *Historical Writing in England, c. 550 to c. 1307*, Routledge & Kegan Paul, 1974, pp. 242–5, 367–72.

14 Stephen Koss, *Asquith*, Allen Lane, 1976, pp. 181–2, 217.

15 V.H. Galbraith, *The Making of Domesday Book*, Oxford University Press, 1964. This approach is commended in T.G. Ashplant and Adrian Wilson, 'Present-centred history and the problem of historical knowledge', *Historical Journal*, XXXI, 1988, pp. 253–74.

16 Quentin Skinner, 'Meaning and understanding in the history of ideas', *History and Theory*, VIII, 1969, pp. 3–53, and J.G.A. Pocock, *Politics, Language and Time*, Methuen, 1972, especially ch. 1.

17 V.H. Galbraith, *Studies in the Public Records*, Nelson, 1948, p. 6.

18 G.R. Elton, *England, 1200–1640*, The Sources of History, 1969, pp. 41, 70–3.

19 G.W. Keeton, *Lord Chancellor Jeffreys and the Stuart Cause*, Macdonald, 1965, p. 23.

20 Michael Roper, 'Public records and the policy process in the twentieth century', *Public Administration*, LV, 1977, pp. 153–68.

21 Colin Holmes, 'Government files and privileged access', *Social History*, **VI**, 1981, p. 342.

22 G. Kitson Clark, *The Critical Historian*, Heinemann, 1967, pp. 92–6, 109–14.

23 Herbert Butterfield, *Man on His Past*, Cambridge University Press, 1955, p. 90.

24 J.D. Fage (ed.), *Africa Discovers Her Past*, Oxford University Press, 1970.

25 Edward W. Said, *Orientalism*, Routledge & Kegan Paul, 1978.

26 Carroll Smith-Rosenberg, *Disorderly Conduct: Visions of Gender in Victorian America*, Oxford University Press, 1986, pp. 25–7.

27 For a fuller discussion, with examples, see Alan Booth and Sean Glynn, 'The public records and recent British economic historiography', *Economic History Review*, 2nd series, **XXXII**, 1979, pp. 303–15.

28 G.J. Renier, *History: Its Purpose and Method*, Allen & Unwin, 1950, pp. 96–105.

29 Margaret Spufford, *Contrasting Communities: English Villagers in the Sixteenth and Seventeenth Centuries*, Cambridge University Press, 1974, pp. 320–44.

30 Emmanuel Le Roy Ladurie, *Montaillou: Cathars and Catholics in a French Village, 1294–1324*, Penguin, 1980, p. xiii.

31 *Ibid.*, p. 231.

32 Richard Cobb, 'A view on the street', in his *A Sense of Place*, Duckworth, 1975, pp. 79–135.

33 Marc Bloch, *French Rural History*, Routledge & Kegan Paul, 1966, p. xxviii.

34 E.P. Thompson, *The Poverty of Theory*, Merlin Press, 1978, pp. 220–1.

35 The classic work is C.V. Langlois and C. Seignobos, *Introduction to the Study of History*, Greenwood, 1979; first published in 1898. Louis Gottschalk, *Understanding History: A Primer of Historical Method*, Knopf, 1950, and Jacques Barzun and Henry F. Graff, *The Modern Researcher*, Harcourt Brace Jovanovich, 3rd edn, 1977, are to be preferred as more up-to-date statements.

36 Richard Cobb, *Modern French History in Britain*, Oxford University Press, 1974, p. 14.

37 Richard Cobb, 'Becoming a historian', in his *A Sense of Place*, pp. 47–8. See also Jacques Barzun, *Clio and the Doctors*, Chicago University Press, 1974, p. 90.

# CHAPTER FIVE

# The themes of mainstream history

Much of the history students encounter is concerned with political events, but that is far from the limit of the historian's interest or concerns. This chapter looks at how historians have widened their range since the heyday of Victorian constitutional history, to look at the role of economic factors in historical events, and to look at how history can contribute to an understanding of the development of society itself.

**early modern**
'Early modern' is usually taken to mean the period from the Renaissance to the French and Industrial Revolutions, equating roughly to the Tudor, Stuart and Hanoverian periods in English history.

Both the immense variety of primary sources discussed in Chapter 3 and the laborious methods of evaluation outlined in Chapter 4 severely limit the extent to which historians can claim competence in their subject. Their expertise is usually confined to a particular period: scholars are labelled as, for example, 'medievalists', '**early modernists**' or 'contemporary historians', and in practice the period for which they have a sound grasp of the sources is likely to be limited still further – to a century perhaps in the case of a medievalist, and often no more than a decade in the case of a specialist in the nineteenth or twentieth centuries. Nearly always, too, these periods are studied in relation to one country or region only. The specialist in the English Revolution of the seventeenth century, for example, would naturally be interested in those countries of Western Europe which, like France and the Netherlands, experienced their own crises at the same time, but his or her knowledge of them would probably not be founded on anything more than a reading of the secondary literature – and regrettably in many cases only the literature in

English and one other European language. Those historians with first-hand research experience in more than one country or period are a small minority.

In addition to the specialization of time and place, there is also the specialization of theme. Of course in any epoch of the past all aspects of human thought, activity and achievement have a claim on the historian's attention, but they cannot all be studied at once, unless the horizon of research is drastically confined to a single locality (an approach that is discussed below, pp. 139–40). For historians who wish to maintain a national or regional focus, concentration on one theme or strand immediately reduces the volume of essential primary sources to more manageable proportions. Which theme is pursued in research may owe much to personal considerations – a particular enthusiasm or eccentricity. But whereas modern historical scholarship achieves a more or less steady output for all the periods and countries which are reasonably well documented, its choice of theme is much more subject to changing fashion. The claims of social relevance, the development of new techniques of research and the theoretical insights of other disciplines all influence historians in determining which aspects of the past should enjoy research priority. For these reasons, choice of theme gives a much clearer indication of the actual content of historical enquiry than does choice of period or country. This chapter examines the three most popular traditional categories – political history, economic history and social history. More recent additions, notably cultural history, will be considered later (see Chapter 10).

# I

## The dominance of political history

*Political history* is conventionally defined as the study of all those aspects of the past that have to do with the formal organization of power in society, which for the majority of human societies in recorded history means the state. It includes the institutional organization of the state, the competition of factions and parties for control over the state, the policies enforced by the state, and the relations between states. To many people, the scope of history would appear to be exhausted by these topics. The syllabuses taught in British schools until very recently, publishers' lists of bestsellers and television programmes all convey the impression that if political history is not the only kind of history, it is much the most important. Historians themselves, however, are by no means of one mind on this point. The reason why political history merits its status as the senior branch is not because it is intrinsically more significant than any other – though naturally advocates of political history claim that it is[1] – but because it enjoys much the longest pedigree. While political history has been written and read continuously since ancient times, other branches have developed as permanent additions to the repertory only during the past hundred years.

The reasons for this traditional dominance are clear enough. Historically the state itself has been much more closely associated with the writing of history than with any other literary activity. On the one hand, those who exercised political power or aspired to it looked to the past for guidance as to how best to achieve their ends. At the same time, political élites had an interest in promoting for public consumption a version of history which legitimized their own position in the body politic, either by emphasizing their past achievements or by demonstrating the antiquity of the constitution under which they held office. Moreover, political history has always found an avid **lay readership**. The rise and fall of statesmen and of nations or empires lends itself to dramatic treatment in the grand manner. Political power is intoxicating, and for those who cannot exercise it themselves, the next best thing is to enjoy it vicariously in the pages of a **Clarendon** or a Guicciardini. The consequences were bitterly deplored by Arthur Young, the English agronomist famous for his descriptions of the French countryside on the eve of the Revolution:

> To a mind that has the least turn after philosophical inquiry, reading modern history is generally the most tormenting employment that a man can have: one is plagued with the actions of a detestable set of men called conquerors, heroes, and great generals; and we wade through pages loaded with military details; but when you want to know the progress of agriculture, or commerce, and industry, their effect in different ages and nations on each other ... all is a blank.[2]

**lay readership**
i.e. readers outside the academic historical profession.

**Clarendon**
Edward Hyde, Earl of Clarendon (1608–74). He fought on the royalist side in the Civil War and was raised to high office at the Restoration. He is best known for his three-volume narrative *History of the Great Rebellion* (i.e. the Civil War), which he began while in exile with the Prince of Wales (later Charles II) in 1646.

## Political history in turbulent times

In fact, during the Enlightenment of the eighteenth century, a 'philosophical' turn of mind was rather more evident than Young allowed for. **Voltaire**'s historical works ranged over the whole field of culture and society, and even Gibbon did not confine himself to the dynastic and military fortunes of the Roman Empire. But the nineteenth-century revolution in historical studies greatly reinforced the traditional preoccupation with statecraft, **faction** and war. German historicism was closely associated with a school of political thought, best represented by Hegel, which endowed the concept of the state with a moral and spiritual force beyond the material interests of its subjects; it followed that the state was the main agent of historical change. Equally, the nationalism that inspired so much historical writing at this time led to an emphasis on the competition between the great powers and the struggles of submerged nationalities for political self-determination. Few historians would have quarrelled with Ranke when he wrote, 'the spirit of modern times ... operates only by political means'.[3] The Victorian historian, E.A. Freeman, put it more simply: 'History is past politics'.[4] The new emphasis on the critical study of primary sources merely confirmed the trend, since the state archives – the richest and most accessible body of source material – were first and foremost a record of policy-making and institutional growth. The new university professors in the Rankean mould were essentially political historians.

## What should political history be about?

Yet, as the definition given earlier would suggest, political history can mean many different things, and its content has been almost as varied and as subject to fashion as any other branch of history. Ranke himself was chiefly interested in how the great powers of Europe had acquired their strongly individual characters during the period between the Renaissance and the French Revolution. He looked for explanations less to the internal evolution of those states than to the unending struggle for power between them. One of Ranke's legacies, therefore, was a highly professional approach to the study of foreign policy. *Diplomatic history* has been a staple pursuit of the profession ever since, its appeal periodically reinforced as historians have responded to a public demand to

**Voltaire**
François Marie Arouet de Voltaire (1694–1778). One of the most celebrated writers of the French eighteenth-century Enlightenment. Voltaire was best known for his witty satires on contemporary manners and ideas, but he also wrote historical works, including studies of Louis XIV and of the Swedish King Charles XII, and a treatise on Newtonian physics.

**faction**
A political grouping, usually held together by patronage or personal, rather than party, loyalty.

understand the origins of the latest war. In the aftermath of the First World War especially, much of this work verged on nationalist propaganda, and it was too heavily dependent on the archives of a single country. At times diplomatic history has been reduced to scarcely more than a record of what one diplomat or foreign minister said to another, with little awareness of the wider influences which so often shape foreign policy – financial and military factors, the influence of public opinion, and so on. Nowadays the best diplomatic history deals with international relations in the most comprehensive sense, rather than the diplomacy of a particular nation. A fine example is Christopher Thorne's *Allies of a Kind* (1978), a political and strategic study of the Western powers' campaign against Japan between 1941 and 1945, based on official and private documents in the United States, Britain, the Netherlands and Australia. Other historians have breached the insularity of traditional diplomatic history by demonstrating the influence of domestic factors on foreign policy.[5]

Many of Ranke's contemporaries and followers emphasized instead the internal evolution of the European nation-states, and *constitutional history* was largely their creation. This emphasis was most pronounced in Britain, where history became an academically respectable subject during the 1860s and 1870s almost entirely on the strength of constitutional history. Its leading proponent, William Stubbs, was at pains to stress the intellectual advance that this approach represented on the kind of history that had gone before:

> The History of Institutions cannot be mastered – can scarcely be approached – without an effort. It affords little of the romantic incident or of the picturesque grouping which constitute the charm of History in general, and holds out small temptation to the mind that requires to be tempted to the study of Truth. But it has a deep value and an abiding interest to those who have the courage to work upon it ... Constitutional History has a point of view, an insight, a language of its own; it reads the exploits and characters of men by a different light from that shed by the false glare of arms, and interprets positions and facts in words that are voiceless to those who have only listened to the trumpet of fame.[6]

Its central theme was of course the evolution of Parliament, considered by the Victorians to be England's most priceless contribution to civilization and thus the appropriate focus for a national history. England's constitutional history was seen as a sequence of momentous conflicts of principle, alternating with periods of gradual change, stretching back to the early Middle Ages; it was enshrined in a succession of great state documents (Magna Carta and the like) which required disciplined textual study. For fifty years after the publication of Stubbs's three-volume *Constitutional History of England* (1873–8), constitutional history carried the greatest academic prestige in this country, and major revisionist work continues to be done to this day. In the hands of Stubbs's followers – most of them medievalists as he was – the subject was diversified to encompass two closely related specialisms: the history of law and administrative history. Legal history attracts relatively little interest today, but administrative history shows every sign of enjoying a new lease of life as historians seek to interpret the massive increase in the functions and personnel of government that has taken place in all Western societies during the twentieth century.

# II

## The problem of biography

Implicit in the approaches discussed so far is an interest in the outstanding individual – the makers of foreign policy, the statesmen who promoted or resisted constitutional change, and the leaders of revolutionary movements. Quite apart from the intrinsic importance of such people, political narrative of any kind has always owed much of its broad appeal to the fact that the lives of statesmen are more fully and vividly documented than those of any other category of people in the past. This human curiosity has been indulged by historians in the form of *biography* for as long as history has been written. It has, however, often been overlaid by intentions that are inconsistent with a strict regard for historical truth. During the Middle Ages and the Renaissance many biographies were frankly **didactic**, designed to present the subject as a model of Christian conduct or public virtue. In Victorian times the characteristic form of biography was commemorative: for the heirs and admirers of a public figure the most fitting memorial was a large-scale 'Life', based almost exclusively

**didactic**
With an overtly educational purpose.

**warts-and-all**
Honest, showing the bad points as well as the good. The term comes from a portrait of Oliver Cromwell by the painter Sir Peter Lely. Cromwell, who had one or two warts on his face, told Lely he did not want a falsely flattering portrait but wanted to be painted 'warts and all'.

**George I (1714–27)**
George was Elector of the German state of Hannover when he was offered the British throne on the death of Queen Anne in 1714. Electors were those German princes who had the right to vote for the Holy Roman Emperor.

**Lytton Strachey (1880–1932)**
British writer and member of the famous group of literary figures known from the area of London where many of them lived as the Bloomsbury group. Strachey's *Eminent Victorians* (1918) shocked many readers by taking a satirical, sarcastic approach to four revered figures from the previous century, including Florence Nightingale and General Gordon.

on the subject's own papers (many of them carefully preserved for this very purpose) and so taking the writer at his or her own valuation. Figures in the more distant past were treated hardly less reverently. Honest, 'warts-and-all' biography was practised by only a few brave spirits. The Victorian reader of biographies was therefore confronted by a gallery of worthies, whose role was to sustain a respect for the nation's political and intellectual élite.

Although biographies of this kind are still published from time to time, the grosser distortions perpetrated by nineteenth-century biographers largely belong to the past. For historians the essential requirement in a biography is that it understands the subject in his or her historical context. It must be written by someone who is not merely well grounded in the period in question but who has examined all the major collections of papers which have a bearing on the subject's life – including those of adversaries and subordinates as well as friends and family. A historical biography is, in short, a major undertaking. For her study, *George I: Elector and King* (1978), Ragnhild Hatton spent seven years in a quest which took her to the Royal Archives at Windsor Castle, the Public Record Office, the Hannover archives in West Germany, and the private papers of leading politicians in both England and Hannover. For earlier figures the volume of material is likely to be smaller, but it may be even more scattered; one of the reasons why there is hardly a single satisfactory biography of a Renaissance pope is that both their early careers and their many-sided interests as popes often ranged over the whole of Europe and are reflected in more archives than any one historian can hope to cover.

Yet even biography which meets the requirements of modern scholarship is not without its critics. Many historians believe that it has no serious place in historical study. The problem of bias cannot be lightly disposed of. Although there has been a vogue for debunking biography ever since **Lytton Strachey** exposed the human frailties of his ironically named *Eminent Victorians* (1918), anyone who devotes years to the study of one individual – something that Strachey never did – can hardly escape some identification with the subject and will inevitably look at the period to some extent through that person's eyes. Furthermore, biographical narrative encourages a simplified, linear interpretation of events. Maurice Cowling, a leading specialist in modern British political history, has argued that political events can only be understood by showing how members of the political establishment reacted on one another. 'For this purpose', he writes:

> biography is almost always misleading. Its refraction is partial in relation to the [political] system. It abstracts a man whose public action should not be abstracted. It implies linear connections between one situation and the next. In fact connections were not linear. The system was a circular relationship: a shift in one element changed the position of all the others in relation to the rest.[7]

It is hard to deny that, with the best will in the world, biography nearly always entails some distortion, but there are good grounds for not dismissing it altogether. First, Cowling's objection carries much less weight in the case of political systems where power is concentrated in one man: full-scale biographies of Hitler and Stalin are indispensable to an understanding of Nazi Germany or Soviet Russia. Secondly, at the other extreme, biographies of people who were in no way outstanding can sometimes, if the documentation is rich enough, illuminate an otherwise obscure aspect of the past: Iris Origo's *Merchant of Prato* (1957) recreates the domestic world of a fourteenth-century Tuscan merchant who was remarkable only for the pains he took to ensure that his voluminous correspondence should be preserved for posterity (see p. 73). Thirdly, it is sometimes forgotten by the detractors of biography that the critical use of primary sources requires systematic biographical research. What the authors of these sources wrote can be fairly interpreted only if their background and day-to-day circumstances are grasped: for this if for no other reason historians need to have a good biography of Gladstone, whose writings over a period of some fifty years are such an important source for nineteenth-century British political history.[8]

Lastly, and perhaps most important of all, biography is indispensable to the understanding of motive and intention. There is much dispute among historians as to how prominently matters of motive – as distinct from economic and social forces – should feature in historical explanation, and they certainly receive less emphasis now than they did in the nineteenth century; but plainly the motives of individuals have *some* part to play in explaining historical events. Once this much is conceded, the relevance of biography is obvious. The actions of an individual can be fully understood only in the light of his or her emotional make-up, temperament and prejudices. Of course in even the best-documented lives a great deal remains a matter of conjecture: the writings of public figures especially are usually coloured by self-deception as well as deliberate calculation. But the biographer who has studied the development of his or her subject from childhood to maturity is much more likely to make the right inferences. It is for this reason that during the present century biographers have increasingly stressed the private or inner lives of their subjects as well as their public careers. From this perspective the personal development of important individuals in the past is a valid subject of historical enquiry in its own right.

# III

## The fine grain of politics

It would be very misleading, however, to suggest that the practice of political history remains wedded to the categories marked out in the nineteenth century – diplomatic history, constitutional history and the lives of 'great men'. In Britain especially, reaction against the traditional forms of political history has turned on the contention that none of them directly confronts what ought to be a central issue in any study of politics, namely the acquisition and exercise of political power and the day-to-day management of political systems. From this perspective, the Stubbs tradition, with its emphasis on constitutional principles and the formal institutions of government, seems unhelpful, although the central issues of constitutional history which he raised continue to be vigorously debated.

## Sir Lewis Namier: history from the backbenches

The most influential spokesman for this reaction was L.B. Namier, whose writings on eighteenth-century England marked something of a turning point. What interested Namier was not primarily the great political issues of the time or the careers of the leading statesmen but the composition and recruitment of the political élite as revealed by the minutiae of the personal case histories of ordinary MPs. His method was essentially collective biography (for which the technical term is 'prosopography', although Namier did not use it). In *The Structure of Politics at the Accession of George III* (1929) and later works Namier asked why men sought a seat in the Commons, how they obtained one, and what considerations guided their political conduct in the House. He cut through the ideological pretensions with which politicians clothed their behaviour (aided and abetted by later historians), and neither their motives nor their methods emerged with much credit. As a result, most of the accepted picture of eighteenth-century English politics was demolished – the two-party system, the packing of the Commons with government placemen, and the assault on the constitution by the young George III. Namier's approach was quickly taken up by historians working on other periods, and towards the end of his life he enshrined it in the officially sponsored *History of Parliament*, which will eventually comprise biographies of everyone who sat in the House of Commons between 1485 and 1901.[9]

## The psychology of politics

If Namier's approach to political history seems limited, it at least had the merit of correcting the distorting effects of the 'great man' school of history. It also happened to be rather appropriate to mid-eighteenth-century English politics, which were particularly faction-ridden and barren of major issues of principle. In the work of several more recent historians, however, can be found an even narrower focus, applied to other periods in British history when issues of principle were of much greater moment. According to this approach, what really matters is 'High Politics' – that is, the manoeuvring for power and influence among the few dozen individuals who controlled the political system.[10] An extreme instance is the work of A.B. Cooke and John Vincent, who justify their treatment of the Irish Home Rule crisis of 1885–86 – a crisis with extra-parliamentary dimensions if ever there was one – in these terms:

> Explanations of Westminster should centre not on its being at the top of a coherently organized pyramid of power whose bottom layer was the people, but on its character as a highly specialized community, like the City or Whitehall, whose primary interest was inevitably in its own very private institutional life.[11]

## The limitations of political history

Such an approach, in which the analysis of motive and manoeuvre is allowed full play, makes for a fascinating study in the psychology of political conflict. But it illuminates the surface only. As soon as it is conceded that politics is not only about personalities but also about the clash of competing economic interests and rival ideologies, then the wider society outside the rarified atmosphere of court or parliament becomes critically important. This is self-evident in the case of periods of revolutionary change, when the political system broke down as a result of changes in the structure of economy or society. In more stable political situations the dimensions of class and ideology may not be so clearly articulated, but they are present nonetheless, and any analysis of political trends beyond the short term demands that they be understood. At the very least, historians have to be aware of the social and economic background of the political élite and the role of public opinion. Namier himself was not as deficient in this respect as has sometimes been supposed. The effect of his obsession with the 'small men' of politics was to reveal the eighteenth-century House of Commons as a microcosm of the landed and moneyed society of the day; but at the same time he was largely indifferent to the evidence which extra-parliamentary agitation afforded of more deep-seated changes in politics and society. Because of the way in which politics in our own time is habitually presented as an enclosed world with its own rituals and conventions, political historians are particularly prone to apply too narrow a definition to their subject. More than any other branch of history, political history depends for its vitality on a close involvement with its intellectual neighbours, and particularly with the fields of economic and social history.

# IV

## History beyond the élite

Each of the categories described so far was already a well-established part of the scholarly scene by the end of the nineteenth century. Modern research in these fields has therefore been built on a foundation of inherited methods and inherited findings. But the result of these strengths in nineteenth-century historiography was that the subject was almost exclusively confined to the activities of individuals and narrowly defined élites. During the twentieth century, however, much the most significant enlargement in the scope of historical studies has been the shift of interest from the individual to the mass – from the drama of public events in which individual achievement and failure were most evident to the underlying structural changes which over the centuries have transformed the lot of ordinary men and women.

It is hardly an exaggeration to say that economic and social history, which exemplify this shift, did not exist for Ranke's generation. By the late nineteenth century, however, Western Europe and the United States were emerging from a major economic and social transformation which historical study as then practised was

One of the most significant ideas to come out of the French Revolution was the concept of the nation as a focus for group identity, instead of loyalty to a dynastic ruler. Nationalism was often linked to liberalism, although it was also taken up by illiberal conservatives. Nineteenth-century Europe saw a number of revolutionary nationalist risings, although Italy and Germany, the two main examples of nineteenth-century states established along nationalist lines, both owed their existence more to the manoeuvres of statesmen than they did to revolutionaries. The nation-state was at the heart of President Woodrow Wilson's policy of national self-determination at the Paris Peace Conference of 1919. (Mary Evans Picture Library)

manifestly incapable of explaining. Although Marx's thought has been rigorously applied to historical research in the West on a large scale only during the past fifty years (see Chapter 8), his emphasis on the historical significance of the means of production and of relations between classes had already gained wide currency among politically literate people by the early twentieth century. Moreover, the effect of the rise of organized labour and the mass socialist parties was to push issues of economic and social reform more insistently onto the centre of the political stage than ever before. Developments in the early twentieth century pointed in the same general direction. For many, the First World War dealt a fatal blow to the ideal of the nation-state, whose rise had been the great theme of nineteenth-century **historiography**, while the recurrent slumps and depressions in the world economy confirmed the need for a more systematic grasp of economic history.

Around the turn of the century the narrowly political focus of academic history came under increasing attack from historians themselves. Manifestos calling for a new and broader approach were launched in several countries – most self-consciously in the United States, where they sailed under the flag of the 'New History'. In Britain the connection between historical study and current social issues was particularly evident in the careers of **Sidney and Beatrice Webb**, social reformers and historians of the British labour movement; economic history featured from the start in the curriculum of the London School of Economics, which they founded in 1895.

## Learning from other subjects: the *Annales* school

However, it was in France that the implications of broadening history's scope were most fully worked out. This was the achievement of Marc Bloch, a medievalist, and Lucien Febvre, a specialist in the sixteenth century, whose followers today probably command greater international prestige in the academic world than any other school. In 1929 Bloch and Febvre founded a historical journal called *Annales d'histoire sociale et économique*, usually known simply as *Annales*.[12] In the first issue they demanded of their colleagues not just a broader approach but an awareness of what they could learn from other disciplines, especially the social sciences – economics, sociology, social psy-

**historiography**
The study of the writing of history, although sometimes also used to denote the range of historians' writings on a particular theme.

**Sidney (1859–1947) and Beatrice (1858–1943) Webb**
British social historians and reformers, prominent in the 1910s and 1920s. They took a leading role in the socialist Fabian Society and in the trade union movement. Convinced of the importance of social and economic history, they published a *History of Trade Unionism* and in 1895 they helped to found the London School of Economics.

chology and geography (a particularly strong enthusiasm of the *Annales* historians). While conceding that the practitioners of these disciplines were primarily concerned with contemporary problems, Bloch and Febvre maintained that only with their help could historians become aware of the full range of significant questions which they could put to their sources. And whereas earlier reformers had called for an inter-disciplinary method, it was systematically put into practice by the *Annales* historians in a formidable corpus of publications, of which Marc Bloch's *Feudal Society* (1940) is probably the best known outside France. From this basic premise, historians of the *Annales* school have continued to broaden and refine the content and methodology of history, with the result that many of the new directions which the discipline has taken in the past thirty years owe much to their contribution. At the same time, the principal apologists of the *Annales* school heaped considerable scorn on the traditional pursuits of political narrative and individual biography – a reaction which was shared by many economic and social historians in Britain: in Tawney's words, politics was 'the squalid scaffolding of more serious matters'.[13]

# V

## Economic history

In this new intellectual climate, *economic history* was the first specialism to gain recognition. By 1914 it had emerged as a sharply defined area of study in several countries, including Britain. The relevance of economic history to contemporary problems largely explains its head-start over other contenders; indeed, in many universities, especially in America, economic history was studied not as part of general history but in conjunction with economics, a discipline whose own claims to academic respectability had only just won general recognition by the end of the nineteenth century. Both in Britain and on the continent, much of the pioneer work concerned the economic policies of the state – an approach which required the minimum adaptation on the part of historians schooled in political history. But this was clearly an inadequate base on which to come to grips with the historical phenomenon of industrialization, which from the start loomed large on the agenda of economic historians everywhere. It resulted in a special emphasis on Britain, the first country to experience an industrial revolution, and attracted continental as much as British historians. Their work was particularly strong on local studies of particular industries, such as Lancashire cotton textiles or Yorkshire woollens, and it highlighted individual initiative and technical innovation. A pale reflection of this approach is still to be seen in those old-fashioned textbooks which chronicle Britain's Industrial Revolution as a sequence of inventions made in the late eighteenth century.

## Gaps in the economic record

Today economic historians can fairly claim that their subject matter embraces every aspect of economic life in the past, which is to say all those activities that have to do with production, exchange and consumption. But the character and haphazard distribution of the primary sources place severe limits on the periods and places whose economic history can be reconstructed in the round – far more serious than in the case of political history. The urge to gather information about the contemporary economy, which consumes so much energy and money today, dates back no further than the seventeenth century at the earliest, and it was only during the nineteenth century that either government departments or private bodies pursued their enquiries at all systematically. For their knowledge of earlier periods, historians depend on laboriously collating the records kept by individuals and institutions of their own financial transactions, and the survival of these records is very much a matter of chance. In England's case manorial estate records survive in considerable numbers from the thirteenth century, especially those belonging to the Church, which changed hands less frequently than estates in secular ownership and which commanded higher standards of literacy.[14] But the only major documentary archive of a medieval English trading firm which has come down to us is the papers of the Cely family, who were prominent in the export of wool to the Low Countries in the 1470s and 1480s.[15] Not until the eighteenth century do commercial records become really plentiful. Public records have, of course, proved more durable, but the government's curiosity about the economic activities of its subjects was almost entirely confined to those which it taxed. Thus, although the main features of England's export trade from the late thirteenth century emerge clearly enough from the customs records,[16] we know frustratingly little about the country's internal trade, which went virtually untaxed. For the Middle Ages, and for much of the early modern period too, the range of economic questions which historians can answer with any degree of confidence is drastically limited by the **paucity** of the evidence.

**paucity**
Scarcity.

## The difficult interplay of economic and political history

In many ways economic history offers about the biggest contrast to political history that can be imagined. Its chronology is quite different. It often makes light of differences of political culture and national tradition, particularly in studies of the modern global economy. And it gives minimal scope to personality and motive, the classic preoccupations of historians; instead 'impersonal' forces such as inflation or investment tend to hold the centre of the stage in economic history. Furthermore, economic historians delight in undermining the bedrock assumptions of their non-specialist colleagues – most provocatively in several works which deny that Britain experienced an industrial revolution at all.[17] For all these reasons many political historians would prefer to hold economic history at arm's length. But in practice their own agenda has been influenced by the findings of economic history in very positive ways. For example, the financial predicament of Tudor governments – and the political difficulties with Parliament that these brought in their train – cannot be grasped without an understanding of the great inflation of the sixteenth century.[18] Similarly, interpretations of the origins of the Boer War, which broke out in 1899 between Britain and the gold-rich Transvaal, have been modified in the light of precise information about the vicissitudes of the international gold standard at that time.[19]

## Business history

Two trends stand out in current writing on modern economic history, though they do not, of course, define its entire scope. The first one is business history – the systematic study of individual firms on the basis of their business records. The source materials are usually manageable, and firms that allow access to them sometimes foot the bill for research as well. Whether or not the historian identifies with the values of capitalist entrepreneurship, what comes out the best from these studies is a keener under-standing of the mechanisms of economic expansion, often at a critical juncture in the history of an industry. This is certainly true of Charles Wilson's path-breaking *History of Unilever* (1954), which, by tracing the history of the British and Dutch parent companies from the 1850s onwards, showed how the manufac-turing of soap and margarine grew to its massive modern proportions. The implications of research in business history can be wider still. How far the beginning of Britain's economic decline in the period 1870–1914 was caused by a failure of entrepreneur-ship is a major issue on which business historians have much to contribute.[20]

## History of the macro-economy

Business history may be regarded as economic history on the ground. The second approach, by contrast, seeks to explain the dynamics of growth or decline for an entire economy. This is quite simply the biggest issue in economics today, both for professional economists and for the lay public; and since it has been present in a recognizably modern form since the onset of industrialization two hundred years ago, it is hardly surprising that historians should be interested too. But in seeking to contribute to a wider debate they have been compelled to sharpen their analytical tools. The older economic histories such as J.H. Clapham's *Economic History of Modern Britain* (1926–38) were essentially descriptive: they reconstructed the economic life of a particular period, some-times in vivid detail, but in explaining how one phase gave way to the next they showed little interest in the actual mechanisms of economic change. The current debates are very largely about those mechanisms, and they are conducted in the context of the highly sophisticated theoretical work on growth that economists have been carrying out since the 1950s. If historians are to do justice to their material in this area, they have to be much more versed in the competing theoretical explanations than they used to be; and since the testing of these theories depends on the accurate measurement of indices of growth, historians must become quantifiers. As will be discussed in Chapter 9, more and more economic historians since the 1960s have been becoming essentially quantitative historians, for whom both questions and methods of research are increasingly set by economic theory rather than history. In this field the breaking down of those interdisciplinary barriers which the *Annales* school called for half a century ago has been more complete than in any other.

# VI

## What is social history?

*Social history* is less self-evident in its identity and scope than any of the categories discussed so far. It is only in the past thirty years that any measure of agreement has emerged among social historians as to what their subject is really about. Until that time the term 'social history' was understood in three quite distinct ways, each one marginal to the interests of historians in general, and it was regarded (in Britain at least) as no more than a very junior partner of economic history. There was, first, the history of social problems such as poverty, ignorance, insanity and disease. Historians focused less on the experience of people afflicted by these conditions than on the 'problem' that they posed to society as a whole; they studied the reforming efforts of private **philanthropy**, as seen in charitable institutions such as schools, orphanages and hospitals, and the increasingly effective intervention of the state in the social field from the mid-nineteenth century onwards. The limitations of this genre of social history can be illustrated in the case of Ivy Pinchbeck and Margaret Hewitt's two-volume study, *Children in English Society* (1969, 1973); they document in detail the achievements of organized charity and government concern over a period of four hundred years, but the recipients of all this care and attention are only occasionally heard, while children who were not in need are entirely absent from their account.

Social history meant, secondly, the history of everyday life in the home, the workplace and the community. As **G.M. Trevelyan** put it, 'Social history might be defined negatively as the history of

**philanthropy**
Charitable work.

**G.M. Trevelyan**
George Macaulay Trevelyan (1876–1962). British historian, great-nephew of the celebrated historian Thomas Babington Macaulay. A prolific writer, he is best known for his popular *English Social History*, which reflected a wartime regret for the passing of a more stable society.

a people with the politics left out'.[21] His *English Social History* (1944), for long a standard work, took little account of economics either, and much of it reads like a catch-all for the miscellaneous topics which did not fit into his earlier (and largely political) *History of England* (1926); there is much descriptive detail, but little coherence of theme. Much of this kind of writing has an **elegiac** tone: a regret for the passing of the pre-industrial order, when everyday life was on a human scale and geared to natural rhythms, and a revulsion from the anomie and ugliness of modern urban living.

**elegiac**
Lyrical, poetic evocation of times past.

## 'History from below': the history of labour

Lastly, there was the history of the common people, or working classes, who were almost entirely absent from political history, and who featured in economic history only in an inert and undifferentiated way as 'labour' or 'consumers'. In Britain this kind of social history was from the end of the nineteenth century dominated by historians sympathetic to the labour movement. Although often passionately committed to the workers' cause, their writings were hardly affected by Marxist influence at all. Their main concern was to furnish the British labour movement with a collective historical identity, and they sought it not through a new theoretical framework (for which Marxism was of course well suited) but in the historical experience of the working class itself during the preceding century – the material and social deprivation, the tradition of self-help, and the struggles for improved wages and conditions of employment. For G.D.H. Cole, the leading British labour historian during the 1930s and 1940s, nothing seemed more important than that 'as the working class grows towards the full exercise of power, it should look back as well as forward, and shape its policy in the light of its own historic experience'.[22] Labour history tended to live in a world of its own, with only a limited impact on those not involved in the labour movement. Yet precisely because of this political context, labour history continues to be written – if under new labels such as 'history from below' or 'people's history'. Initially it represented the strongest strand within the History Workshop movement, which emerged during the 1970s as a forum of academic and community historians, based at

Ruskin College, Oxford (itself closely associated with the trade union movement).

## Women's history

Now, however, History Workshop gives as much if not greater prominence to a more recent strand of oppositional history: women's history. During the early 1970s women's history emerged as an aspect of **Women's Liberation**. The target of feminist historians' indignation was as much labour history as conventional political history, since the workers who organized in trade unions or relaxed in pubs and clubs were typically assumed to be male without question. Since then an immense amount of historical reclamation has been achieved: of women as workers in factories and mines; as political activists in **Owenism** and **Chartism** – not to mention the campaigns for the suffrage; as wives and mothers; and as precursors of the caring professions.[23] It is with regard to the family that the impact of women's history

**Women's Liberation**
A pioneering feminist movement of the late 1960s and 1970s, often shortened to 'Women's Lib'. It was associated with an angry and assertive style of campaigning against inequality and injustice towards women.

**Owenism**
Robert Owen (1771–1858) was a Welsh industrialist whose experiments in running his spinning mill at New Lanark in Scotland along humanitarian and co-operative lines led him to found the Grand National Consolidated Trades' Union to represent the entire skilled working class. The union was killed off in 1834 when a group of farm labourers at Tolpuddle in Dorset was transported to Australia for swearing an oath of loyalty to it. However, Owen's ideals were revived ten years later by a group of trade unionists in Rochdale, Lancashire, who founded the first Co-Operative movement, in which all members would sink their subscription into a central fund, which would be used to maintain a Co-Operative shop which could sell goods to members at lower prices than elsewhere. Co-Op shops are still found on the high street nowadays. (Chris Gibson/ Photographers Direct)

**Chartism**
A working-class political movement in the 1830s and 1840s. It derived its name from the People's Charter, drawn up in 1838, which laid out a comprehensive set of proposals for the reform of Parliament.

**'angel mother'**
The image, often found in Victorian literature and popular culture, of a mother who is at once beautiful, caring, dutiful and obedient.

on social history in general has been greatest. Historians in the 1960s had engaged in a rather narrow debate about household size and levels of fertility.[24] The new focus on women drew attention to the internal dynamics of the family in terms of power, nurture and dependence. Uncovering the reality behind the ornamental 'angel mother' of Victorian family piety, for instance, has also made it necessary to revise our picture of the domestic life of men and children.[25] As a result of this and other work, the whole realm of the private – as distinct from the public world of conventional history – is being brought within the scope of historical understanding.

## History and social structure

But none of the approaches mentioned so far entirely explains why social history, for so long the poor relation, now enjoys such prominence. What has happened in recent years is that its subject matter has been redefined in a much more ambitious manner. Social history now aspires to offer nothing less than the history of social structure. The notion of 'social structure' is a sociological abstraction of a conveniently indeterminate kind which can be – and has been – clothed in any number of theoretical garbs. But what it essentially means is the sum of the social relationships between the many different groups in society. Under the influence of Marxist thought, class has had the lion's share of attention, but it is by no means the only kind of group to be considered: there are also the cross-cutting ties of age, gender, race and occupation.

Social structure may seem to be a static, timeless concept, partly because it has been treated in this way in the writings of many sociologists. But it need not be so, and historians tend naturally to adopt a more dynamic approach. As Keith Wrightson, a leading social historian of early modern England, puts it:

> Society is a process. It is never static. Even its most apparently stable structures are the expression of an equilibrium between dynamic forces. For the social historian the most challenging of tasks is that of recapturing that process, while at the same time discerning long-term shifts in social organization, in social relations and in the meanings and evaluations with which social relationships are infused.[26]

Against the background of a durable social structure, those individuals or groups who move up or down are often particularly significant, and social mobility has been much studied by historians. Beyond a certain point, social mobility is incompatible with the maintenance of the existing structure and a new form of society may emerge, as happened most fundamentally during the Industrial Revolution. Urbanization, in particular, needs to be studied not just in its economic aspects but also as a process of social change, including the assimilation of immigrants, the emergence of new forms of social stratification, and the hardening distinction between work and leisure; important work along these lines has been pioneered in America, and urban history is now a significant specialism in Britain too.[27] The analysis of social structure and social change can have major implications for economic and political history, and social historians in recent years have staked out large claims in these areas. The long drawn-out '**gentry controversy**' was mainly a dispute about the connection between changing social structure and political conflict in England during the hundred years before the Civil War.[28] The origins of the Industrial Revolution are now sought not only in economic and geographical factors but also in the social structure of eighteenth-century England – especially the 'open aristocracy' with a two-way flow of men and wealth into and out of its ranks.[29] At this point, social history begins to approximate to the 'history of society' in its broadest sense, which, it has been argued, is its proper domain.[30]

Much of the earlier, less ambitious social history is relevant to this new concern, provided its terms of reference are revised. The new social historians include many who started within the more limited horizons of one or other of the established categories. **E.P. Thompson**, the best-known social historian during the 1960s and 1970s, had his roots deep in the labour history tradition, but in *The Making of the English Working Class* (1963) he stepped outside it; the growth of a working-class awareness during the Industrial Revolution is placed in the widest possible context, including religion, leisure and popular culture, as well as the factory system and the origins of trade unionism; and, so far from politics being 'left out', the presence of the state is both constant and menacing, as an instrument of class control.

**gentry controversy**

A long-running argument in academic circles about the development of social change in early seventeenth-century England and its bearing on the origins of the English Civil War. The argument was over whether the lesser landowning class (the gentry) was 'rising' in social and economic status at the expense of the older landed aristocracy, or whether the opposite was true. The argument raged for many years and was a staple feature of undergraduate essays; however, since it is not easy to come up with a clear-cut definition of 'gentry' and 'aristocracy', or exactly what is meant by a class 'rising', no clear conclusion was ever reached.

**E.P. Thompson (1924–93)**

British Marxist historian. Thompson was also active in socialist politics. His *Making of the English Working Class* was the first attempt to tell the story of the development of a distinctive working-class culture and identity in the late eighteenth and early nineteenth century.

## Social history: the challenge of methodology

As social history has raised its sights, so its research techniques have become more demanding. There is probably no other field whose primary sources are so varied, so widely dispersed, and so uneven in quality. The vast majority of extant historical records were, after all, created by large corporate institutions, such as government, Church and business. While this suits the political historian well enough, and up to a point the economic historian too, it poses major problems for the social historian. The limited scope of the earlier social history is partly explained by the tendency of historians to take the line of least resistance and follow the trail through the records of institutions with an avowedly 'social' function – schools, hospitals, trade unions and the like; the result was all too often work of a narrowly institutional character. But the new social history demands a great deal more. Social groups do not leave corporate records. Their composition and their place in the social structure have to be reconstructed from a broad range of sources composed for quite different and usually much more mundane reasons. Some idea of the effort required can be grasped from Lawrence Stone's *The Crisis of the Aristocracy, 1558–1641* (1965). His conclusions are based primarily on the estate records and personal correspondence of the families concerned, some of it on public deposit in libraries and county record offices, but much of it still in the **muniment rooms** of stately homes; in addition he draws on the records of lawsuits and of correspondence with the government in the Public Record Office, contemporary literary sources, and a vast array of local and family histories compiled over the past two centuries or so.

An even greater problem is posed by the mass of the population which lived outside the charmed circle of literacy. Their conditions and opinions became the subject of systematic social surveys only during the nineteenth century. Until then the picture that we form of the lower classes is inevitably dominated by those activities which brought down on them the attention of the authorities: litigation, sedition and – most of all – common crime and offences against Church discipline. At times of popular discontent this attention was particularly intrusive, and whole areas of society which normally remain 'invisible' may be illuminated by legal and police records. The riots which periodically broke out in

**muniment room**
A fireproof room for storing historical and legal documents.

eighteenth-century London are a case in point.[31] Equally, fear of revolution may intensify official surveillance of lower-class activities, as in England during the Napoleonic Wars: 'But for spies, **narks** and letter-copiers, the history of the English working class would be unknown', wrote E.P. Thompson with only a little over-statement.[32] Such opportunities are all the more precious because at other times information about the common people is usually much thinner. Court records are still useful, but in more settled conditions judicial activity was less intense, and it is therefore much more difficult to build up the profile of a local community. Before any generalization can be made with confidence, a vast quantity of court records has to be sifted, usually in conjunction with other sources such as manorial records, tax registers, wills and the records of charitable institutions. In Britain, as in other countries, there is almost limitless scope for further work along these lines.

**nark**
(old slang) A police informer.

# VII

## The dangers of tunnel vision

Historians and their writings are commonly classified according to one of the categories described in this chapter. It is probably inevitable that this should be so. In all branches of knowledge most advances are made by specialists working on a narrow front, and the basic threefold division of political, economic and social history at least corresponds to recognizable areas of thought and behaviour. The problem is that no human activity can be pigeon-holed in this way without denying some of its dimensions: political conflict is often an expression of fundamental material differences, the pace of economic change is likely to be conditioned by the rigidity or suppleness of the social structure, and so on. Historians who specialize in one branch of history risk attributing too much to one kind of factor in their explanations of historical change. Economic history that does not look beyond the factors of production, political history confined to a Namierite perspective, international history which reflects only the small change of diplomacy – all these are instances of what J.H. Hexter has aptly termed 'tunnel vision'.[33] Social history has already moved quite far away from its large-scale ambitions of twenty years ago. Keith Wrightson complains of 'the enclosure of English social history', by which he means the limitation of its potential by narrow periodization and by compartmentalization into sub-disciplines such as popular culture or crime, lacking in integration.[34] Tunnel vision is an occupational disease of historians (as of other scholars), and it is intensified among those who are set on applying the theories and techniques of the social sciences – usually economics or sociology.

One might expect that these deficiencies would be made good by survey works – those general syntheses that seek to draw together the research findings of a large number of specialists into a coherent whole. The performance of historians in this respect has often been woefully inadequate. Traditionally the writing of such works was placed in the hands of political historians on the grounds that political history constituted the 'core' of the subject. The results were sometimes bizarre. As recently as 1960, the volume in the **Oxford History of England series** for the period 1760–1815 was almost entirely composed of political narrative; only a tenth of the book was devoted to economic change, although no theme during the period has greater significance than the onset of the Industrial Revolution.[35] Nowadays a much more even-handed coverage is usually found in survey works, and political historians no longer hog the show. But surveys that achieve a real integration are still very much the exception.[36] The conventional division between 'politics', 'economics' and 'society' is often rigidly adhered to in the structure of these books, because historians who approach their own research with 'tunnel vision' are conditioned to think in this way when they attempt a bird's-eye view.

**Oxford History of England series**
A multi-volume history of England which began to appear in the 1930s under the editorship of Sir George Clark. Originally intended to be a definitive survey, the volumes nowadays seem dated and very much of their time. The series received a fillip when A.J.P. Taylor's lively and provocative volume on *English History 1914–45* was added to the series in 1965.

## The quest for 'total' history

In historical research there are therefore compelling reasons in favour of avoiding thematic specialization. The influence of the *Annales* historians has been particularly salutary here. The appeal of the founders was not so much for new specialisms – although they were certainly attacking the excessive ascendancy of political history in France at the time – as for an end to compartmentalization: the direction of research must be determined not by the label attached to the historian or by the character of the chosen body of sources but by the intellectual requirements of a specified historical problem. The ultimate aim of the historian was to recapture human life in all its variety or – in the phrase that has since become the rallying cry of the *Annales* school – to write 'total history' (*histoire totale* or *histoire intégrale*). The fulfilment of this ideal has often been credited to Fernand Braudel, Febvre's successor as editor of *Annales* and *doyen* of the historical profession in France. In *The Mediterranean and the Mediterranean World in the Age of Philip II* (1947) Braudel treated every dimension of his vast subject in brilliantly evocative detail: the physical and human geography of the region, its economic and social life, its political structures, and the Mediterranean policies of Philip II and his rivals. The book is probably the finest achievement of the *Annales* school, but it still falls short of 'total history' because – as many critics have pointed out[37] – the different approaches are not integrated with each other: the political narrative which forms the third and concluding section of the book is largely detached from the geographical and economic panorama in the first two parts.

## Achieving synthesis through the history of a locality

Braudel's experience suggests that the ideal of 'total history' cannot be realized on so vast a stage as the Mediterranean. It is scarcely more practicable for a single country. If all the sources are to be mastered and a full integration of theme to be achieved, the geographical limits of the enquiry must be drastically narrowed. Paradoxically, therefore, 'total history' turns out in practice to mean *local history*. Traditionally local history was the preserve of amateurs whose horizons were limited by their local loyalties and their social position in the community (usually **squire** or **parson**); their work was much stronger on antiquarian detail than on interpretation, and was largely ignored in academic circles. In the past forty years, however, local history has been increasingly taken up by professional historians because of the opportunity it offers of straddling the conventional demarcations between specialisms. The *Annales* historians were among the first to practise the new kind of local history. Le Roy Ladurie's work on rural Languedoc between the fifteenth and eighteenth

**squire**
A local landowner, typically a member of the gentry with a knighthood or minor title.

**parson**
A vicar, often owing his position to the patronage of the local squire. Squire and parson were usually the leading figures in any village community.

century exemplifies the strength of the *Annales* approach; he summed up the subject of his first book, *The Peasants of Languedoc* (1966), as

> the long-term movements of an economy and of a society – base and superstructure, material life and cultural life, sociological evolution and collective psychology, the whole within the framework of a rural world which remained very largely traditional in nature.[38]

In Britain the emphasis has been not so much on regions as on individual towns and villages, where the historian can become familiar with every inch of the ground as well as every page of documentation. But the aspiration towards 'total history' is comparable. As W.G. Hoskins put it,

> The local historian is in a way like the old-fashioned G.P. of English medical history, now a fading memory confined to the more elderly among us, who treated Man as a whole.[39]

Even at the local level, the attainment of a true 'total history' still presents immense difficulties, and only a handful of works have brought it off. But the many local histories that have travelled some way along this road have nevertheless acted as a powerful solvent of the rigidities to which conventional specialists working on a larger canvas are so prone. For political historians particularly, local history serves as a reminder that their subject is about not only the central institutions of the state but also the assertion of authority over ordinary people; politics is likely to be interpreted less as an enclosed arena than as the sphere in which conflicts between opposing interests in society are fought out. Thus, as a result of the many county studies undertaken in recent years, historians now have a more sophisticated understanding of the inter-relationship between religious, economic and political factors in the origins of the English Civil War.[40] That local history enjoys such high standing among present-day historians probably offers the best assurance that the traditional boundaries between specialisms will not be permitted to stand in the way of a thematically integrated view of the past.

# Arthur Young (1741–1820)

English writer and agriculturalist, author of detailed accounts of tours through the agricultural areas of England, Ireland and France. He visited France each year between 1787 and 1790, and his accounts therefore provide historians with an invaluable account, from an intelligent and informed outside observer, of the state of French rural society on the eve of the Revolution.

# Hegelian Dialectic

Georg Wilhelm Friedrich Hegel (1770–1831). The leading German philosopher of the early nineteenth century. He argued that human events in history were determined by the operation of *dialectic* – the clash of opposing forces or ideas out of which emerged a *synthesis*, which would in its turn be challenged by an opposing *antithesis*. Hegel believed that this process would lead eventually to a state of harmony based upon Christian ethics and morality; Karl Marx, who was much influenced by Hegel, 'turned him on his head' by divorcing Hegel's ideas from their Christian framework and applying the dialectic model to the clash of class interests throughout history, leading ultimately to control of economy and society by the working class.

# Tudor Inflation

Across sixteenth-century Europe there developed a steady and alarming rise in prices which caused considerable hardship. The reasons for the inflation were not clear to contemporaries, who blamed anything from human greed to the enclosure of common land to graze sheep. The English government of Edward VI responded by debasing the coinage in order to put more money into circulation, but this simply led people to put their prices up still higher. Historians long thought the inflation was caused by the influx of gold and silver bullion from the Americas, but nowadays it is thought to be a result of the huge rise in population during the period.

## Further reading

David Cannadine (ed.), *What Is History Today?*, Palgrave, 2003.

Stefan Berger, Heiko Feldner & Kevin Passmore (eds), *Writing History: Theory and Practice*, Arnold, 2003.

Peter Burke (ed.), *New Perspectives on Historical Writing*, Polity Press, 1991.

Anna Green & Kathleen Troup (eds), *The Houses of History: a Critical Reader in Twentieth-Century History and Theory*, Manchester UP, 1999.

George G. Iggers, *New Directions in European Historiography*, Wesleyan UP, 1975.

Lawrence Stone, *The Past and the Present Revisited*, Routledge, 1987.

Carlo M. Cipolla, *Between History and Economics: an Introduction to Economic History*, Blackwell, 1991.

Miles Fairburn, *Social History: Problems, Strategies and Methods*, Routledge, 1999.

Peter Burke, *The French Historical Revolution: the Annales School 1929–89*, Polity Press, 1990.

Fernand Braudel, *On History*, Weidenfeld & Nicolson, 1980.

## Notes

1  For example, S.T. Bindoff, 'Political history', in H.P.R. Finberg (ed.), *Approaches to History*, Routledge & Kegan Paul, 1962, and G.R. Elton, *Political History*, Allen Lane, 1970, pp. 57–72.

2  Arthur Young writing from Florence in 1789, quoted in J.R. Hale (ed.), *The Evolution of British Historiography*, Macmillan, 1967, p. 35.

3  Leopold von Ranke, *History of Servia*, 1828, quoted in Theodore H. von Laue, *Leopold Ranke: the Formative Years*, Princeton University Press, 1950, p. 56.

4  Edward A. Freeman, *The Methods of Historical Study*, Macmillan, 1886, p. 44.

5  E.g. Paul Kennedy, *The Rise of the Anglo-German Antagonism 1860–1914*, Allen & Unwin, 1980.

6  William Stubbs, *The Constitutional History of England*, vol. I, Oxford University Press, 1880, p. v.

7  Maurice Cowling, *The Impact of Labour, 1920–1924*, Cambridge University Press, 1971, p. 6.

8 Derek Beales, *History and Biography*, Cambridge University Press, 1981.

9 Sir Lewis Namier and John Brooke, *The House of Commons 1754–1790*, 3 vols, HMSO, 1964, marked the first stage in this massive enterprise.

10 The concept of 'High Politics' is expounded in Cowling, *The Impact of Labour*, pp. 3–12.

11 A.B. Cooke and John Vincent, *The Governing Passion: Cabinet Government and Party Politics in Britain, 1885–86*, Harvester, 1974, p. 22.

12 The journal was renamed *Annales: économies, sociétés, civilisations* in 1946.

13 R.H. Tawney, obituary of George Unwin (1925), quoted in N.B. Harte (ed.), *The Study of Economic History*, Frank Cass, 1971, p. xxvi.

14 See the helpful discussion in J.Z. Titow, *English Rural Society, 1200–1350*, Allen & Unwin, 1969.

15 Alison Hanham (ed.), *The Cely Letters 1472–1488*, Oxford University Press, 1975.

16 See, for example, E.M. Carus-Wilson and O.P. Coleman, *England's Export Trade 1275–1547*, Oxford University Press, 1963.

17 R.C. Floud and D. McCloskey (eds), *The Economic History of Britain since 1700*, 2 vols, Cambridge University Press, 1981.

18 R.B. Outhwaite, *Inflation in Tudor and Early Stuart England*, 2nd edn, Macmillan, 1982.

19 J.J. Van-Helten, 'Empire and high finance: South Africa and the international gold standard, 1890–1914', *Journal of African History*, XXIII, 1982, pp. 529–48.

20 For a review of the literature, see P.L. Payne, *British Entrepreneurship in the Nineteenth Century*, Macmillan, 1974.

21 G.M. Trevelyan, *English Social History*, Longman, 1944, p. vii. An almost identical definition is given in G.J. Renier, *History: Its Purpose and Method*, Allen & Unwin, 1950, p. 72.

22 G.D.H. Cole, *A Short History of the British Working-Class Movement, 1789–1947*, Allen & Unwin, 1948, pp. v–vi.

23 Two studies stand out from a growing body of fine literature: Barbara Taylor, *Eve and the New Jerusalem: Socialism and Feminism in the Nineteenth Century*, Virago, 1983; and Anne Summers, *Angels and Citizens: British Women as Military Nurses 1854–1914*, Routledge & Kegan Paul, 1988.

24 Peter Laslett and Richard Wall (eds), *Household and Family in Past Time*, Cambridge University Press, 1972.

25 John Tosh, *A Man's Place: Masculinity and the Middle-Class Home in Victorian England*, Yale University Press, 1999.

26 Keith Wrightson, *English Society 1580–1680*, Hutchinson, 1982, p. 12.

27 See Stephan Thernstrom, 'Reflections on the new urban history', *Daedalus*, C, 1971, pp. 359–75. For British developments, see H.J. Dyos, *Exploring the Urban Past*, Cambridge University Press, 1982.

28 For a review of the literature, see Lawrence Stone, *The Causes of the English Revolution, 1529–1642*, Routledge & Kegan Paul, 1972.

29 Harold Perkin, *The Origins of Modern English Society, 1780–1880*, Routledge & Kegan Paul, 1969.

30 E.J. Hobsbawm, 'From social history to the history of society', *Daedalus*, C, 1971, pp. 20–45.

31 See, for example, George Rudé, *Paris and London in the Eighteenth Century: Studies in Popular Protest*, Fontana, 1970. For a critical review, see Joanna Innes and John Styles, 'The crime wave: recent writing on crime and criminal justice in eighteenth-century England', *Journal of British Studies*, XXV, 1986, pp. 380–435.

32 E.P. Thompson, *Writing by Candlelight*, Merlin Press, 1980, p. 126.

33 J.H. Hexter, *Reappraisals in History*, Longman, 1961, pp. 194–5.

34 Keith Wrightson, 'The enclosure of English social history', in Adrian Wilson (ed.), *Rethinking Social History: English Society 1570–1920 and its Interpretation*, Manchester University Press, 1993, pp. 59–77.

35 58 out of 573 pages in J. Steven Watson, *The Reign of George III, 1760–1815*, Oxford University Press, 1960.

36 Two striking exceptions are J.R. Hale, *Renaissance Europe, 1480–1520*, Fontana, 1971, and Jacques Le Goff, *Medieval Civilization 400–1500*, Blackwell, 1988.

37 See especially, J.H. Hexter, *On Historians*, Collins, 1979, pp. 132–40.

38 Emmanuel Le Roy Ladurie, *The Peasants of Languedoc*, University of Illinois Press, 1974, p. 289.

39 W.G. Hoskins, *English Local History: the Past and the Future*, Leicester University Press, 1966, p. 21.

40 For a fuller discussion of this point, see R.C. Richardson, *The Debate on the English Revolution Revisited*, Routledge, 1988, ch. 7.

# CHAPTER SIX

# Writing and interpretation

Most students' experience of historical writing is limited to producing essays or assignments, addressing questions and problems set by others for assessment purposes. Historians, however, are usually able to set their own questions of the material they have unearthed, and can plan and design their work as they choose. How, then, does the historian turn research into historical writing? And what role does the historian's interpretation play in the process?

The previous chapter was intended to indicate the main categories of enquiry which confine the task of original research to manageable proportions; but inevitably it strayed into a consideration of the contribution that each approach has made to historical knowledge, and in so doing glanced over a vital intervening stage in the historian's work – the ordering of the material in written form. The application of critical method to the primary sources along the lines described in Chapter 4 generally results in the validation of a large number of facts about the past with a bearing on one particular issue, or a group of related issues, but the significance of this material can only be fully grasped when the individual items are related to each other in a coherent exposition. There is nothing obvious or predetermined about the way in which the pieces fit together, and the feat is usually accomplished only as a result of much trial and error. Many historians who have a flair for working on primary sources find the process of composition excruciatingly laborious and frustrating. The temptation is to continue amassing material so that the time of reckoning can be put off indefinitely.

# I

## Do historians *need* to write history?

One school of opinion maintains that historical writing is of no real significance anyway. The intense excitement that such historians experience in contemplating the original documents has led them to the position that the only historical education worth the name is the study of primary sources – preferably in their original state, but failing that in reliable editions. One of the austerest proponents of this view was V.H. Galbraith, a distinguished medievalist who was **Regius Professor** at Oxford in the 1950s. Almost all his published work was devoted to elucidating particular documents and placing them in their historical context – notably **Domesday Book** and the chronicles of St Albans Abbey; he never wrote the broad interpretative work on fourteenth-century England for which he was uniquely qualified. As he put it:

> What really matters in the long run is not so much what we write about history now, or what others have written, as the original sources themselves. . . . The power of unlimited inspiration to successive generations lies in the original sources.[1]

There is a certain logic about this purist position. It will evoke a sympathetic response in all those historians whose research is source-oriented rather than problem-oriented (see p. 9), many of whom find it extraordinarily difficult to determine when, if ever, the time for synthesis has arrived. In history, more than most other disciplines, undirected immersion in the raw materials has an intellectual justification. Exposure to original sources ought to feature in any programme of historical study, and it is entirely proper that scholarly reputations should continue to be founded on the editing of these materials. But as a general prescription Galbraith's rejection of conventional historical writing is completely misplaced. It would of course entail an abdication from all history's claims to social relevance, which require that historians communicate what they have learned to a wider audience. But it would be hardly less disastrous even supposing that these claims

**Regius Professor**
A 'royal' professor appointed by the crown. Regius professorships were introduced in the eighteenth century as a means of extending a degree of government control into the universities of Oxford and Cambridge.

**Domesday Book**
The famous survey of land tenure in England undertaken on the orders of King William I in 1086.

to relevance could be refuted. For it is in the act of writing that historians make sense of their research experience and bring into focus whatever insights into the past they have gained. Much scientific writing takes the form of a report expressing findings which are entirely clear in the scientist's mind before he or she puts pen to paper. It is highly doubtful whether any historical writing proceeds in the same way. The reality of any historical conjuncture as revealed in the sources is so complex, and sometimes so contradictory, that only the discipline of seeking to express it in continuous prose with a beginning and an end enables the researcher to grasp the connections between one area of historical experience and another. Many historians have remarked on this creative aspect of historical writing, which is what can make it no less exhilarating than the detective work in the archives.[2] Historical writing is essential to historical understanding, and those who shrink from undertaking it are something less than historians.

# II

## The forms of historical writing

Historical writing is characterized by a wide range of literary forms. The three basic techniques of description, narrative and analysis can be combined in many different ways, and every project poses afresh the problem of how they should be deployed. This lack of clear guidelines is partly a reflection of the great diversity of the historian's subject matter: there could not possibly be one literary form suited to the presentation of every aspect of the human past. But it is much more the result of the different and sometimes contradictory purposes behind historical writing, and above all of the tension which lies at the heart of all historical enquiry between the desire to *re-create* the past and the urge to *interpret* it. A rough and ready explanation for the variety of historical writing is that narrative and description address the first requirement, while analysis attempts to grapple with the second.

## History as description

That the re-creation of the past – 'the reconstruction of the historical moment in all its fullness, concreteness and complexity'[3] – is more than a purely intellectual task is plain to see from its most characteristic literary form: *description*. Here historians are striving to create in their readers the illusion of direct experience, by evoking an atmosphere or setting a scene. A great many run-of-the-mill historical works testify to the fact that this effect is not achieved by mastery of the sources alone. It requires imaginative powers and an eye for detail not unlike those of the novelist or poet. This analogy would have been taken for granted by the great nineteenth-century masters of historical description such as Macaulay and Carlyle, who were much influenced by contemporary creative writers and took immense pains with their style. Modern historians are less self-consciously 'literary', but they too are capable of remarkably evocative descriptive writing – witness Braudel's panorama of the Mediterranean environment in the sixteenth century.[4] Whatever else they may be, such historians are artists, and there are too few of them.

## History as narrative

Braudel's work is unusual today for the prominence which it accords to description. For effective – indeed indispensable – as such writing is, it cannot express the historian's primary concern with the passage of time. Its role has therefore always been subordinated to the main technique of the re-creative historian: *narrative*. In most European languages the word for 'history' is the same as that used for 'story' (French, *histoire*; Italian, *storia*; German, *Geschichte*). Narrative too is a form the historian shares with the creative writer – especially the novelist and the epic poet – and it explains much of the appeal that history has traditionally enjoyed with the reading public. Like other forms of story-telling, historical narrative can entertain through its ability to create suspense and arouse powerful emotions. But narrative is also the historian's basic technique for conveying what it felt like to observe or participate in past events. The forms of narrative which achieve the effect of re-creation most successfully are those that approximate most nearly to the sense of time that we experience in our own lives: whether from hour to hour, as in an account of a battle, or from day to day, as in an account of a political crisis, or over a natural life-span, as in a biography. The great exponents of recreative history have always been masters of dramatic and vividly evocative narrative. Modern classics of narrative history include **Steven Runciman**'s *History of the Crusades* (three volumes, 1951–4) and **C.V. Wedgwood**'s two books on the reign of Charles I, *The King's Peace* (1955) and *The King's War* (1958). In works of this quality we can see the virtues of historical narrative fully exemplified: exact chronology, the role of chance and contingency, the play of irony, and perhaps most of all the true complexity of events in which the participants so often foundered. In a phrase that sums up the aspirations of the historicist tradition, Wedgwood defined her obligation to the people of the past as being 'to restore their immediacy of experience'.[5] **Simon Schama**'s highly readable bestseller, *Citizens* (1989), aimed to achieve a similar effect with regard to the French Revolution.

# III

## Historical causes and consequences

But the historian is of course engaged in very much more than an exercise in resurrection. It would be entirely consistent with this objective to treat events in the past as isolated and arbitrary, but the historian does not in fact treat them in this way. Historical writing is based on the presupposition that particular events are connected with what happened before, with contemporary developments in other fields, and with what came afterwards; they are conceived, in short, as part of a historical process. Those events which in retrospect appear to have been phases in a continuing sequence are deemed specially significant by the historian. The questions 'What happened?' and 'What were conditions like at such-and-such a time?' are preliminary – if indispensable – to asking 'Why did it happen?' and 'What were its results?' Historical writing based on these priorities may be said to have begun with the 'philosophic' historians of the Enlightenment. During the nineteenth century it drew further impetus from the great historical sociologists – de Tocqueville, Marx and **Weber** – who sought to explain the origins of the economic and political

**Steven Runciman**
Runciman (1903–2000) was a medievalist specializing in the history of Byzantium and the Byzantine Church. His monumental three-volume *History of the Crusades* weaves together numerous strands into a rich and complex narrative. Runciman was one of the first popular writers to give due attention to the role of the Byzantines in the Crusades.

**C.V. Wedgwood**
Dame Veronica Wedgwood (1910–97) was a popular historian of the English Civil Wars. Her *The King's Peace* and *The King's War* are vivid narratives, written from a viewpoint sympathetic to, if not always condoning, King Charles I.

**Simon Schama (1945–)**
Schama, a pupil of the Cambridge historian J.H. Plumb, wrote acclaimed works on the Netherlands in the seventeenth and eighteenth centuries before coming to general attention with *Citizens*, a highly readable but critical narrative account of the French Revolution written for the bicentennial celebrations in 1989. Schama went on to present a hugely popular television *History of Britain* for the BBC.

**Weber**
Max Weber (1864–1920).
German political
philosopher. Although, like
Marx, Weber stressed the
importance of class in
determining the
development of society,
he put forward a much
more complex and
sophisticated analysis of
what social class actually
consists of. In particular he
stressed the importance of
social status, which might
not equate to strict class
categories and can change
over time.

transformations of their own day. Questions of cause and conse-quence have been at the heart of many of the most heated historical controversies in recent times.

Asking the question 'Why?' may simply mean asking why an individual took a particular decision. Historians have always given close attention to the study of motive, both because of the traditional prominence of biography in historical studies and because the motives of the great are at least partially reflected in their surviving papers. Diplomatic history is particularly prone to dwell on the intentions and tactics of ministers and diplomats. But even in this limited setting the question 'Why?' is less simple than it looks. However honest and coherent statements of inten-tion may be, they are unlikely to tell the whole story. Every culture and every social grouping has its unspoken assumptions – those nostrums and values that 'go without saying' and yet may deeply affect behaviour. In order to take account of this dimen-sion, the historian must be well versed in the intellectual and cultural context of the period studied, and quick to pick up tell-tale hints of this context in the documents. With regard to the origins of the First World War, for instance, James Joll has called attention to the morbid fear of revolution and the fashionable doctrine of the survival of the fittest as underlying features of the European political mind; and he points out that in moments of crisis such as July 1914 policy-makers were most likely to fall back on their unspoken assumptions, acting in too great a panic to make a considered appraisal of their predicament.[6]

## Beyond human motivation: latent causes, long-term consequences

However, the really significant questions in history do not turn on the conduct of individuals but concern major events and collective transitions that cannot possibly be explained by the sum total of human intentions. This is because underneath the *manifest* history of stated intention and conscious (if unspoken) preoccu-pation there lies a *latent* history of processes which contemporaries were only dimly aware of, such as changes in demography, economic structure or deep values.[7] The Victorians saw in the abolition of slavery in the 1830s a famous victory for humanitarianism, as exemplified in the campaigning zeal of men such as William Wilberforce. In retrospect we can see how the legislation of 1833 was also brought about by the declining fortunes of the Caribbean slave economy and the shift towards an industrialized society in Britain itself.[8] Because historians can look at a society in motion through time, they can register the influence of such factors. But the historical actors themselves could not possibly have a full grasp of all the structural constraints under which they were operating.

Nor could they anticipate the *outcome* of their actions. Like causes, consequences cannot simply be read off from the stated motives of the protagonists, for the simple reason that latent or structural factors so often come between intention and outcome. As E.H. Carr pointed out, our notion of the facts of history must be broad enough to include 'the social forces which produce from the actions of individuals results often at variance with, and sometimes opposite to, the results which they themselves intended'.[9] To revert to the issue of slavery, the intention of the British abolitionists was certainly to confer liberty on the slaves and to improve their material conditions. But the extent of the improvement in practice varied greatly from one part of the Caribbean to another, in ways which the humanitarians had not foreseen. Moreover, other consequences unfolded which lay beyond their terms of reference altogether, notably the impact of the anti-slavery crusade on the propaganda techniques of other moral campaigns, such as those for temperance and social purity.[10] There is a sense in which, from the viewpoint of posterity, consequences are *more* significant than causes, since they usually determine the importance we accord to a given event. It is a curious fact that vastly more has been written on the causes of the English Revolution, for instance, than on its consequences: the extent to which it established a new political culture, or paved the way for more efficient forms of capitalism, is far less widely known than, say, the rise of Puritanism or the financial crises of the early Stuart monarchy.

## Multi-layered analysis

The treatment of cause and consequence makes just as heavy demands on the skill of the writer as historical re-creation does, but of a rather different kind. To convey the immediacy of lived experience calls for intricate narrative and evocative description on several different levels. To approximate to an adequate explanation of past events, on the other hand, requires analytical complexity. Causation in particular is always multiple and many-layered, owing to the manner in which different areas of human experience constantly obtrude on one another. At the very least, some distinction needs to be made between background causes and direct causes: the former operate over the long term and place the event in question on the agenda of history, so to speak; the latter put the outcome into effect, often in a distinctive shape that no one could have foreseen. Lawrence Stone has provided an effective example of a slightly more sophisticated version of this model. In his hundred-page essay, 'The causes of the English Revolution', he considers in turn the 'preconditions' which came into being in the century before 1629, the 'precipitants' (1629–39) and the 'triggers' (1640–2), and thus shows the interaction of long-term factors, such as the spread of Puritanism and the Crown's failure to acquire the instruments of autocracy, with the role of individual personalities and fortuitous events.[11]

Another way of understanding the task of historical explanation is to see any given conjuncture in the past as lying in a field where two planes intersect. One plane is vertical (or diachronic), comprising a sequence through time of earlier manifestations of this activity: in the case of the abolition of slavery this plane would be represented by the fifty years of campaigning for abolition before 1833, and by the ebb and flow of plantation profits over the same period. The other plane is the horizontal (or synchronic): that is, the impinging of quite different features of the contemporary world on the matter in hand. In the present example these might include the political momentum for reform around 1830 and the new **nostrums** of political economy. Carl Schorske likens the historian to a weaver whose craft is to produce a strong fabric of interpretation out of the warp of sequence and the woof of contemporaneity.[12]

**nostrum**
An idea, particularly one promoted zealously as a remedy for a problem.

## The limitations of historical narrative

This analytical complexity means that narrative is most unlikely to be the best vehicle for historical explanation. It was certainly the characteristic mode of Ranke and the great academic histo-

A.J.P. Taylor (1906–90) became a well-known figure through his historical writings for the popular press and his television lectures. His popularity and deliberately provocative analysis infuriated historians who did not share his attachment to narrative history as a format for historical explanation. (Topfoto/Topham/ Picturepoint)

rians of the nineteenth century, who in practice were interested in much more than 'how things actually were'. And one of the most widely read (and readable) professional historians in Britain today – A.J.P. Taylor – hardly wrote anything else. But this traditional literary technique in fact imposes severe limitations on any systematic attempt at historical explanation. The placing of events in their correct temporal sequence does not settle the relationship between them. As Tawney put it:

> Time, and the order of occurrences in time, is a clue, but no more; part of the historian's business is to substitute more significant connections for those of chronology.[13]

The problem is twofold: in the first place, narrative can take the reader up a blind alley. Because B came after A does not mean that A *caused* B, but the flow of the narrative may easily convey the impression that it did. (Logicians call this the ***post hoc propter hoc*** fallacy.) Secondly, and much more importantly, narrative imposes a drastic simplification on the treatment of cause. The

***post hoc propter hoc*** (Latin) Literally 'after this therefore because of this'. In other words the false assumption that because two events happen in sequence there must necessarily be a causal connection between them.

historical understanding of a particular occurrence proceeds by enlarging the inventory of causes, while at the same time trying to place them in some sort of pecking order. Narrative is entirely inimical to this pattern of enquiry. It can keep no more than two or three threads going at once, so that only a few causes or results will be made apparent. Moreover, these are not likely to be the most significant ones, being associated with the sequence of day-to-day events rather than long-term structural factors. This is true of the political sphere, which appears to lend itself so well to narrative and has always been the principal theme of the great narrative historians. In the case of revolutions or wars, for example, narrative historians emphasize the precipitating causes of conflict at the expense of those factors which predisposed the societies concerned to conflict.

The historiography of the First World War illustrates this point well. Taylor, the narrative historian *par excellence*, took a characteristically extreme view. 'It is the fashion nowadays', he wrote in 1969,

> to seek profound causes for great events. But perhaps the war which broke out in 1914 had no profound causes. For thirty years past, international diplomacy, the balance of power, the alliances, and the accumulation of armed might produced peace. Suddenly the situation was turned round, and the very forces which had produced the long peace now produced a great war. In much the same way, a motorist who for thirty years has been doing the right thing to avoid accidents makes a mistake one day and has a crash. In July 1914 things went wrong. The only safe explanation is that things happen because they happen.[14]

In putting forward what might be termed the minimalist position, Taylor doubtless intended to provoke, but his outlook is more prevalent than one might suppose. It is implicated in any attempt to encompass any of the great transformations in history by narrative means. Neither C.V. Wedgwood nor Simon Schama, for instance, was much interested in the structural factors predisposing England or France to revolution; they wanted to place the role of human agency and the flux of events in the foreground. Both of them were reacting against the Marxist approach to revolution, and traditional narrative suited a perspective which was fully formed before they embarked on their books. The choice of narrative must be recognized for what it is: an interpretative act, rather than an innocent attempt at story-telling.

The limitations of narrative apply still more to institutional and economic change, where there may be no identifiable protagonists whose actions and reflections can be treated as a story. No one has succeeded in representing the causes of the Industrial Revolution in narrative form. The problems are clearest of all in the case of the 'silent changes' in history[15] – those gradual transformations in mental and social experience which were reflected on the surface of events in only the most oblique manner. As the scope of historical studies has broadened in the twentieth century to include these topics, so the hold of narrative on historical writing has weakened. Few intellectual rallying cries have proved more effective than the attack by the *Annales* school on *l'histoire événementielle.*

*l'histoire événementielle* (French) i.e. events-led, as opposed to analytical or descriptive, history.

## The strengths and weaknesses of analytical history

The result is that historical writing is now very much more analytical than it was a hundred years ago. In historical analysis the main outline of events tends to be taken for granted; what is at issue is their significance and their relationship with each other. The multiple nature of causation in history demands that the narrative be suspended and that each of the relevant factors be weighed in turn, without losing sight of their connectedness and the likelihood that the configuration of each factor shifted over time.

This is certainly not the only function of analytical writing. Analysis can serve to **elucidate** the connectedness of events and processes occurring at the same time, and especially to lay bare the workings of an institution or a specific area of historical experience. In British historiography the classic instance is Namier's *Structure of Politics at the Accession of George III* (1929), a sequence of analytical essays on the various influences which determined the composition and working of the House of Commons around 1760. Structural studies of this kind are most prevalent in social and economic history, where some grasp of the totality of the social or economic system is required if the significance of particular changes is to be fairly assessed. Then there is the critical evaluation of the evidence itself, which may require a discussion about textual authenticity and the validity of factual inference, as well as a weighing up of the pros and cons of

**elucidate** to explain something complex.

alternative interpretations. It has been said of Ranke that his careful evaluation of contemporary records was seldom allowed to ruffle the surface of his stately narrative;[16] few historians would be allowed to get away with that kind of reticence today. But it is in the handling of the big explanatory issues in history that analysis most comes into its own. As historical writing becomes more geared to problem-solving, so the emphasis on analysis has increased, as a glance at any of the academic journals will show.

However, this does not mean that narrative is completely at a discount. For undiluted analytical writing raises its own problems. What it gains in intellectual clarity, it loses in historical immediacy. There is an inescapably static quality about historical analysis as if, in E.P. Thompson's much-cited metaphor, the time machine has been stopped in order to allow a more searching inspection of the engine room.[17] Namier's studies of eighteenth-century politics lay themselves open to criticism for this very reason.[18] Furthermore, explanations that seem convincing at an analytical level may prove unworkable when measured against the flux of events. The truth is that historians need to write in ways that do justice to both the manifest and the latent, both profound forces and surface events. And in practice this requires a flexible use of both analytical and narrative modes: sometimes in alternating sections, sometimes more completely fused throughout the text. This in fact is the way in which most academic historical writing is carried out today.

## Narrative and the social historian

Today's historians are learning new ways of deploying narrative. Whereas in the nineteenth century it was often treated, without much reflection, as *the* mode of historical exposition, narrative is now the subject of critical scrutiny by scholars *au fait* with literary studies. **Hayden White**, for example, has emphasized the **rhetorical** choices made by every historian who resorts to narrative and has identified some of the principal rhetorical stratagems found in their work (see p. 197).[19] Historians tend to be much more self-conscious and critical in their use of narrative than they used to be. In particular, the traditional association with political events is now much less evident. Social historians, in a reversal of

**rhetorical**
Rhetoric is the art of speaking or writing in order to persuade. It relies on skilful use of devices, such as 'rhetorical questions' (whose answers are deemed so obvious that they do not need to be stated), at least as much as on the actual qualities of the argument itself.

**Hayden White**
American literary theorist. His views on the artificiality of constructed narrative build heavily on the work of Jacques Derrida (1930–2004) and the deconstructionist school, which held that text and language itself is replete with the hidden assumptions and prejudices of the author and of his or her cultural background.

their practice a generation ago, now favour narrative as a means of conveying how the social structures, life cycles and cultural values that they analyze in abstract terms were experienced by actual people. But instead of constructing a narrative for society as a whole, they compose exemplary or illustrative stories, perhaps best termed 'micronarratives'.[20] Richard J. Evans has written a study of crime and punishment in nineteenth-century Germany in which each chapter begins with an individual story as a way into the theme that follows; appropriately he calls his book *Tales from the German Underworld* (1998). In a classic of this new genre, Natalie Zemon Davis recounts the tale of a peasant in the French Basque country who lived as the husband of an abandoned wife for three years during the 1550s, until the real husband turned up and the impostor was exposed and executed. *The Return of Martin Guerre* (1983) is an absorbing story, also made into a film, but for Davis the case 'leads us into the hidden world of peasant sentiment and aspiration', shedding light for example on whether people 'cared as much about truth as about property'.[21] Lawrence Stone was somewhat premature when he spoke in 1979 of a 'revival of narrative', but the last two decades have confirmed that historians are indeed breathing new life into the most traditional form of historical writing.[22]

# IV

## Writing up research: the academic monograph

These problems of choice of form are usually confronted for the first time by the practising historian in the form of the monograph – that is, the writing up of a piece of original research, initially as a thesis for a higher degree and then as a book or an article in one of the learned journals. In this kind of writing the complexities of the evidence are likely to be displayed in the text, and the statements made there validated by meticulous footnote references to the appropriate documents. Many monographs are highly technical and are hardly accessible to anyone but fellow specialists. And, since the essence of the monograph is that it is based on primary rather than secondary sources, its scope is likely to be very restricted. This is particularly so in the case of a young scholar presenting the results of three or four years' Ph.D. research. Although in a technical sense such works are 'an original contribution to knowledge' (as required under the regulations for higher degrees), their significance is often slight. The pressure to complete an acceptable thesis within a few years in order to secure an academic job often causes the researcher to play safe by focusing on a well-defined body of sources never previously studied – or at any rate not with the same historical problem in mind. Lucien Febvre caustically observed the tendency for most historical works to be written by people who 'simply set out to show that they know and respect the rules of their profession'.[23] That is doubtless an unavoidable consequence of the professionalization of history. At the same time, arresting results do from time to time emerge from post-graduate research: one thinks, for example, of Michael Anderson's *Family Structure in Nineteenth-Century Lancashire* (1971), still a mine of demographic information on the working class, or Linda Colley's major reinterpretation of early **Hanoverian Toryism**, *In Defiance of* **Oligarchy** (1982). The prospects for the apprentice are best in new fields of research: the progress of African history during the past forty years has been marked by a string of major Ph.D. theses which have mapped out entirely new terrain.[24] At the very least, the Ph.D. provides a training in the conduct of research and the writing of monographs, and it is by these means that the stock of properly validated historical knowledge is extended.

## Taking the broader view

Yet if historians confined their writings to those topics for which they have mastered the primary sources, historical knowledge would be so fragmented as to be meaningless. Making sense of the past means explaining those events and processes that appear sig-nificant with the passage of time and that are inevitably defined in terms which are broader than any researcher can encompass by his or her own unaided efforts: the origins of the English Civil War rather than the policies of **Archbishop Laud**, the social con-sequences of the Industrial Revolution rather than the decline of the handloom weavers of the West Riding, the Scramble for Africa rather than the **Fashoda Crisis**. It must be obvious that an understanding of topics of this complexity is not attained by the

**Hanoverian Toryism**
In 1714 the protestant Elector of the German state of Hannover was invited to take the British throne as King George I in order to forestall the succession of the Catholic claimant, Prince James Edward Stuart. The Tory Party was so tainted by its association with the Stuarts that for years historians trained in the Namier school of history treated it as a tiny fringe group of marginal importance. Linda Colley's Ph.D. research showed that the Tories were a much more substantial and significant group than had previously been supposed.

**oligarchy**
Rule by a relatively small, enclosed class. The term is often used in connection with the domination by the Whigs of the political life of eighteenth-century Britain.

mere accumulation of detailed researches. In Marc Bloch's words, 'The microscope is a marvellous instrument for research; but a heap of microscopic slides does not constitute a work of art'.[25] When historians step back to take an overview of one of these topics, they face much more acute problems of interpretation – of combining many strands into a coherent account, of determining the weight of this factor or that. And even after a lifetime of research in the relevant primary sources, which may allow them to be discriminating in the use they make of other scholars, they will still have to take much of their work on trust.

## The grand sweep of history

These difficulties are compounded when the historian steps still further away from the moorings of his or her first-hand research and attempts a comprehensive survey of an entire epoch. If a monograph is a secondary source, the survey can fairly be described as a 'tertiary' source, since the writer is inevitably placed in the position of making emphatic statements about topics based on no more than a reading of the standard secondary authorities. Nitpicking criticism by the specialists whose fields have been trespassed upon is the inevitable result. Works of this kind will be much more vulnerable to the vagaries of fashion, and their judgements will be overtaken by new research much more quickly than those of the narrowly conceived monograph. The academic standing of the synthesis by a single hand is further compromised by the sad truth that many are not true syntheses at all but textbooks which for ease of reference summarize the state of knowledge in a rigidly compartmentalized and mechanical fashion. Some historians, conscious that their claims to professional expertise are most convincingly demonstrated in the evaluation of primary sources, feel instinctively that this is no work for 'real scholars'.[26] Others have sought to meet the demand for surveys by participating in collaborative histories. The prototype was the *Cambridge Modern History*, planned under the supervision of Lord Acton in 1896 and covering European history since the mid-fifteenth century in twelve volumes, each composed of national and thematic chapters by the leading authorities. Since then collaborative histories have proliferated. Yet, invaluable though they may be as concise statements of specialist knowledge, such compilations evade the issue. However

**Archbishop Laud**
William Laud (1573–1645). Archbishop of Canterbury under King Charles I. Laud was a controversial choice, suspected of wanting to reintroduce Catholic practices into the Church of England and, even more controversially, into the Scottish Kirk. Scottish resistance to Laud's religious policies precipitated the crisis that developed into the English Civil War. Laud was arrested and impeached in 1641, and finally executed by order of Parliament.

**Fashoda Crisis, 1899**
A diplomatic crisis between Britain and France over control of the southern Sudan which for a time threatened to push the two countries into war. A British military expedition which had conquered the northern Sudan encountered a much smaller French exploratory mission, which tried unsuccessfully to claim the country for France.

like-minded the contributors and however forceful the editor, a consistency of approach cannot be attained, and the themes which cut across the specialist concerns of the contributors are completely omitted.

The wide-ranging survey by a single historian fulfils several vital functions. First, it is at its best a fertile source of new questions. Unremitting primary research, with its necessary but obsessive attention to detail, can lead to a certain intellectual blinkering: 'the dust of archives blots out ideas', as Acton rather unkindly put it.[27] The historian who takes time off from the records to survey an extended period is much more likely to detect new patterns and new correlations which can later be tested in detailed research. E.J. Hobsbawm's *Age of Revolution* (1962), still unsurpassed as a survey of Europe from 1789 to 1848 under the twin impact of the French Revolution and the Industrial Revolution, positively bristles with arresting juxtapositions which no historian confined to a single country could have entertained. Asa Briggs, by shifting the usual periodization of British history in his *Age of Improvement 1783–1867* (1959), achieved a comparable effect. In a new field where major issues of interpretation have scarcely been formulated, this kind of stock-taking can yield rich dividends, particularly when there is a tendency to proceed initially by the accumulation of case studies. This has been notably true of the history of mentalities and the history of the colonial impact on Africa, to take just two examples. The dangers of fragmentation are obvious. There must come a point when the historian considers the individual cases together, so that a new landscape of continuity, change and contradiction can be discerned and a new agenda laid out. A.G. Hopkins's pioneering *Economic History of West Africa* (1973) was just such a synthesis, and for more than a decade it influenced the direction of research in that region.

Secondly, the grand survey is the principal means by which historians fulfil their obligations to the wider public. Popular interest in the writings of academic historians is by no means confined to survey works – witness the success of Garrett Mattingly's *The Defeat of the Spanish Armada* (1959) or Emmanuel Le Roy Ladurie's *Montaillou* (1976). But the appeal of these two books is primarily of a re-creative kind. If historians are to succeed in communicating their understanding of historical change and of the connectedness of past and present, then it is through the ambitious overview that they will do it. Many historians, intent on preserving their academic standing at all costs, are unduly oppressed by the dangers of superficiality and outright error, and there is much snobbish disparagement of those who write for the general reader. But it is not impossible to combine sound scholarship with a lay appeal. *Haute vulgarisation*, as Hobsbawm describes his own highly distinguished ventures in this field,[28] is a necessary skill of the historian.

*Haute vulgarisation* (French) i.e. making popular from on high. A play on the association of 'haute' (high) with such exclusive pursuits as *haute cuisine* or *haute couture*.

## The march of history

Lastly, the large-scale synthesis raises questions of historical explanation which are profoundly important in their own right and which are beyond the scope of anything less ambitious. History is a 'progressive' subject in the sense that few people contemplating the past with the benefit of hindsight can fail to ask themselves in what direction events were moving. This question is not a matter of metaphysical speculation but rather a recognition that fundamental areas of human experience are subject to cumulative change over time. The issue may be evaded in studies confined to a short time-span, but it is central to any attempt to make sense of a whole era: can one detect increasing occupational specialization, or enlargement of social scale, or an expansion in the scope of government, or greater freedom of belief and expression – or any of these trends in reverse? Alternatively, to adopt a less incremental view of the historical process, a given period may be seen rather in terms of discontinuity and disjuncture, where new circumstances force a break with the inherited tendencies of the past. That is the implication, for example, of using the label 'the **New Imperialism**' to refer to European expansion towards the end of the nineteenth century.[29] Consideration of an extended period raises problems of historical interpretation of a different – and surely more significant – order than those which crop up in the study of a well-defined episode.

**New Imperialism** Historians have seen the drive for European overseas expansion in the late nineteenth century as marking a distinctively assertive phase in the development of empire, different from the slower and more piecemeal expansion of previous decades. The 1880s and 1890s have therefore been termed the period of 'New Imperialism'.

## Historical synthesis

The historian's perspective is equally enriched by syntheses which range widely over space as well as time, because these open up the possibility of the comparative method. No society in the past should be viewed in isolation, not only because hardly any of the societies that historians have studied were isolated in reality but also because many of their most significant features prevailed over a wide area at the same time: think of **feudal tenure** in early medieval Europe, or **plantation slavery** in the New World in the seventeenth and eighteenth centuries, or **absolute monarchy** in eighteenth-century Europe. A comparison of the countries involved enables us to separate the essential from the particular and to weight our explanations accordingly. In *White Supremacy* (1981), for example, George M. Fredrickson compares the development of race relations in America and South Africa from the arrival of the first white settlers in the seventeenth century until the ascendancy of the ideology of **segregation** in the twentieth century. In so doing he exposes the particularities of each society more clearly; white supremacy turns out to be not a 'seed planted by the first settlers that was destined to grow at a steady rate into a particular kind of tree' but 'a fluid, variable, and open-ended process'.[30] Why analogous societies differ in their historical experience is a problem of perennial interest which is accessible only to the synthesizer standing outside the confines of primary research.

One consequence of the immense expansion in the scope of historical enquiry which has taken place in the past hundred years is that our definition of a 'comprehensive' survey is much more demanding than that of the great nineteenth-century masters: it includes both the giddy passage of 'events' and the material and mental conditions of life which in many periods – and certainly in the pre-industrial world – changed very slowly if at all, and yet constrained what people could do or think. G.R. Elton's affirmation that 'history deals in events, not states; it investigates things that happen and not things that are'[31] is a questionable half-truth. How surface and background – or events and 'structure' – are related is central to any understanding of historical process, as we have seen already. The large body of writing inspired by the Marxist tradition can be interpreted as one manifestation of this

**feudal tenure**
The system in medieval England whereby social position was determined by a person's relationship to the land. Land was always 'held' (hence 'tenure') from someone else, usually – though not always – a social superior. Ultimately all land was held from the Crown.

**plantation slavery**
The predominant crops grown in the southern states of the nineteenth-century United States were tobacco and cotton. The most economically efficient way to farm them was in large plantations worked by African slave labour, hence 'plantation slavery'.

**absolute monarchy**
The seventeenth- and eighteenth-century theory of government which held that all power should lie in the hands of the monarch, who was appointed by God. In theory an absolute monarch could use this power to enact laws for the well-being of the people.

**segregation**
Until the civil rights campaigns of the 1950s and 1960s strict racial segregation was imposed in the southern United States. It was enforced in South Africa through the policy of *apartheid*, introduced in 1948 and not abandoned until 1991.

concern (see Chapter 8), but it is the *Annales* school that has confronted the problem most directly, and Fernand Braudel more than anyone else. 'Is it possible', he asks,

> somehow to convey simultaneously both that conspicuous history which holds our attention by its continual and dramatic changes – and that other, submerged history, almost silent and always discreet, virtually unsuspected either by its observers or its participants, which is little touched by the obstinate erosion of time?[32]

## The plurality of social time

For Braudel the root of the difficulty lies in the conventional historian's idea of unilinear time – that is, a single time-scale characterized by continuity of historical development. Because of the historian's emphasis on the documents and the aspiration to get inside the minds of those who wrote them, this time-scale can hardly be other than a short-term one which registers the sequence of events to the exclusion of structure. Braudel's solution is to jettison unilinear time altogether and to introduce instead the 'plurality of social time'[33] – the notion that history moves on different planes or registers, which can for practical purposes be reduced to three: the long term (*la longue durée*), which reveals the fundamental conditions of material life, states of mind and above all the impact of the natural environment; the medium term, in which the forms of social, economic and political organization have their life-span; and the short term, the time of the individual and of *l'histoire événementielle*. The problem, which Braudel himself did not solve in *The Mediterranean*, is how to convey the coexistence of these different levels in a single moment of historical time – how to elucidate their interaction in a coherent exposition which incorporates different levels of narrative, description and analysis. This is an issue about which contemporary historians are much more keenly aware than their predecessors; it is perhaps the most fundamental that they face.

# V

## The qualities of a historian

What qualities does the successful practice of history call for? Outside observers have often taken an unflattering view. Probably the most famous put-down of the profession ever written was **Dr Johnson**'s:

> Great abilities are not requisite for an Historian; for in historical composition, all the greatest powers of the human mind are quiescent. He has the facts ready to hand so there is no exercise of invention. Imagination is not required in any high degree; only about as much as is used in the lower forms of poetry.[34]

This was hardly fair comment even in Johnson's day, and in the light of the development of the profession since the eighteenth century it seems even less apt. For the truth is that the facts do *not* lie ready to hand. New facts continue to be added to the body of historical knowledge, while at the same time the credentials of established facts are subject to constant reassessment; and, as Chapters 3 and 4 showed, the defective condition of the sources renders this dual enterprise far more difficult than might appear at first sight. The training of academic historians instituted in the nineteenth century was – and still is – primarily intended to disabuse them of any notion that the facts can be apprehended without effort. The qualities most emphasized in manuals of historical method are accordingly mastery of the primary sources and critical acumen in evaluating them.

But these skills can only take the historian one stage along the road. The process of interpretation and composition suggests a number of other equally essential qualities. First of all, the historian has to be able to perceive the relatedness of events and to abstract from the mountains of detail those patterns that make best sense of the past: patterns of cause and effect, patterns of periodization which justify such labels as 'Renaissance' or 'medieval', and patterns of grouping which make it meaningful to speak of a **petit bourgeoisie** in nineteenth-century France or 'rising gentry' in early seventeenth-century England. The more ambitious the scope of the enquiry, the greater the powers of abstraction and conceptualization required. The small number of really satisfying syntheses on the grand scale is

**Dr Johnson**
Samuel Johnson (1709–84). English writer and lexicographer, best known for having produced the world's first dictionary of the English language. Johnson was given to pithy comments which still lend themselves to quotation. He was the subject of an extensive biography by his friend James Boswell.

**petit bourgeoisie**
*Bourgeois* simply means 'of the town' and is therefore applied to those, principally the 'middle' classes, whose sphere of operation is urban rather than rural. However, since this ranges from the wealthy merchant and professional classes down to small shopkeepers, the term needs to be qualified. *Bourgeoisie* is usually reserved for substantial businessmen and those in the professions, while *petit bourgeois* (the 'little' bourgeoisie, sometimes rendered as 'petty bourgeois' in English) refers to shopkeepers and small businessmen.

a measure of how rare a generous endowment of these intellectual qualities is.

## Imagination

As well as an intellectual cutting edge, the historian also requires imagination. This term can easily lead to confusion in the context of historical writing. It is not intended to convey the idea of sustained creative invention, though it was evidently against this yardstick that Dr Johnson found historians wanting. The point is rather that any attempt to reconstruct the past presupposes an exercise of imagination, because the past is never completely captured in the documents which it left behind. Again and again historians encounter gaps in the record which they can fill only by being so thoroughly exposed to the surviving sources that they have a 'feel' or instinct for what might have happened. Matters of motive and mentality frequently fall into this category, and the more alien and remote the culture the greater the imaginative leap required to understand it. Those books condemned as 'dry as dust' are usually the ones in which the accumulation of detail has not been brought to life by the play of the writer's imagination.

How is the historical imagination nurtured? It helps, of course, to keep your eyes and ears (and nostrils) open to the world around you. As Richard Cobb found:

> A great deal of Paris eighteenth-century history, of Lyon nineteenth-century history can be walked, seen, and above all heard, in small restaurants, on the platform at the back of a bus, in cafés, or on the park bench.[35]

## The historian's knowledge of life

The ability to empathize with people in the past presupposes a certain self-awareness, and some historians have gone so far as to suggest that psychoanalysis might form part of the apprentice's training.[36] Breadth of experience, however, is a much more promising foundation. In the days when history-writing was largely confined to political narrative, experience of public life was widely regarded as the best training for historians; as Gibbon said of his short career as an MP:

> The eight sessions that I sat in parliament were a school of civil prudence, the first and most essential virtue of an historian.[37]

Wartime service probably deepened the insights of many twentieth-century historians of politics, diplomacy and war. But it is *variety* of experience which really tells – experience of different countries, classes and temperaments – so that the range of imaginative possibilities in the historian's mind bears some relation to the range of conditions and mentalities in the past. Unfortunately the usual career pattern of academic historians nowadays makes little allowance for this requirement. A suggestion some years ago that the best training for a historian is a trip round the world and several jobs in different walks of life may have been impracticable, but it was not meant to be flippant.[38]

It is one thing, however, to have an imaginative insight into the past, and quite another to be able to convey this to the reader. Verbal or literary skills are of considerable importance to the historian. At any time prior to the nineteenth century this would have been taken for granted. Since classical times the profession of historian had been considered by its leading exponents to be above all a literary accomplishment. History had its presiding **muse** (Clio), a secure place in the culture of the reading public, and a range of rhetorical and stylistic conventions which it was the principal task of the aspirant historian to master. All this changed with the rise of academic history. The problems which exercised the professional historians who followed in Ranke's footsteps were those of method rather than presentation. Command of the sources or 'scholarship' has often been counterposed to 'writing', to the detriment of the latter; 'Clio, once a Muse, is now more commonly seen, with a reader's ticket, verifying her references at the Public Record Office.'[39] As a result a great deal of unreadable history has been written in the last hundred years.

But good writing is more than an optional extra or a lucky bonus. It is central to the re-creative aspect of history. The insights derived from the exercise of historical imagination cannot be shared at all without a good deal of literary flair – an eye for detail, the power to evoke mood, temperament and ambience, and an illusion of suspense – qualities that are most fully developed in creative writing. History of the explanatory kind does not share so much common ground with creative literature, which may be

**muse**
In Greek mythology, the muses were the daughters of Zeus and Mnemosyne, the goddess of memory. Each presided over a particular branch of knowledge and the arts, such as music, poetry, comedy and mime. The muse of history was Clio.

In classical mythology Clio was the muse who inspired historians, just as other muses inspired poets and musicians, etc. When Clio is invoked today, the implication is that history is one of the literary arts and should be judged by aesthetic standards. (Photo: akg-images, London)

one reason why those historians who set most store by the literary claims of their discipline – G.M. Trevelyan or C.V. Wedgwood, for example – have contributed relatively little to this sphere. Close argument and the need to hedge so many statements with qualifications and caveats are not conducive to 'literary' expression. Nevertheless, the problem of combining narrative with analysis which attends any venture in historical explanation is essentially a problem of literary form. Its solution is hardly ever dictated by the material.

Set out in this way, it may be that none of the qualities or skills required of the historian seems particularly demanding. But it is rare to find all of them combined in sufficient measure in the same person. Very few historians are equally endowed in the technical, intellectual, imaginative and stylistic spheres, and despite the immense expansion of professional scholarship in recent decades, the number of fully satisfying historical works in any branch of study remains small. At the same time, the varied nature of the historian's equipment serves to reiterate another point – that history is essentially a *hybrid* discipline, combining the technical and analytical procedures of a science with the imaginative and stylistic qualities of an art.

## Alexis de Tocqueville

Alexis de Tocqueville (1805–59) was a French lawyer, historian and social commentator. His 1835 study of *Democracy in America* argued that although Americans enjoyed greater liberty than Europeans, their liberty led to oppression of the poor by the materialistic rich on a much greater scale than was to be found in the monarchies of Europe. De Tocqueville was a staunch libertarian and opponent of the centralizing tendencies of bureaucratic government; he was Foreign Minister in the short-lived second French Republic (1849–52) but refused to serve under the autocratic government of Louis Napoleon (Emperor Napoleon III from 1852). His classic study of *The Ancien Regime and the French Revolution* argued that the Revolution and the Napoleonic Empire that followed it merely continued the oppressive, centralizing tendencies of the Bourbon regime. He also taught that an oppressive regime is at its most vulnerable precisely at the moment when it begins to reform itself.

## Periods of history

It is easy to forget that historical periods are later constructs; no one at the time knew they were living in the 'ancient' world or the 'Middle' Ages. These terms also reflect the values and judgements of those who coined them. The term 'Middle Ages' was coined by scholars of the fifteenth- and sixteenth-century Renaissance to refer to what they saw as a long period of ignorance and superstition which interposed between the 'golden age' of the ancients and their own day. Periods are often defined in terms of centuries or decades – 'the eighteenth century', 'the Sixties' – or else in terms of rulers, as in 'Tudor England' or 'the Victorians', though this can be unsatisfactory: 'Victorian' attitudes can be traced up to the First World War; the reign of the first Tudor monarch, Henry VII, was not significantly different from that of his Yorkist predecessors; and the features most commonly associated with the youth culture of the Sixties can be more accurately dated from *c.* 1965 to *c.* 1975. Historians often deliberately ignore conventional periodization: Frank O'Gorman has written of the 'long eighteenth century', from the 'Glorious' Revolution of 1688 to the Reform Act of 1832, while Eric Hobsbawm has written of a 'short twentieth century', beginning with the First World War and ending with the fall of European Communism in 1989–91.

## Origins of the First World War

The causes of the First World War (1914–1918) have long proved a fruitful source of historical controversy. The wartime allies concluded that Germany was directly to blame and drew up the draconian Treaty of Versailles on that basis; German resentment at this helps to explain popular support for Hitler. By the 1960s most historians were more prepared to explain the outbreak of the war in terms of the complex interplay of political, diplomatic, military, social and personal factors. However, the German historian Professor Fritz Fischer broke this consensus by arguing that German diplomatic correspondence showed that the German government had indeed been planning for war and was largely to blame for it. The British historian A.J.P. Taylor argued provocatively that in the end the crucial factor was that each state's railway timetables were so rigid that it was impossible for even the most powerful government, once orders had been given for troops to move, *not* to invade its neighbours. Few modern historians share Taylor's extreme view, but the Fischer thesis still retains a substantial body of support.

## The abolition of slavery

The campaign against the transatlantic slave trade began among evangelical Christians in late eighteenth-century England and pioneered many of the features of modern pressure groups. The movement's most important convert was William Wilberforce, Tory MP for Hull and a close friend of the Prime Minister, William Pitt the Younger. Despite support from Pitt and the Opposition leader, Charles James Fox, it took until 1807 to persuade parliament to outlaw the slave trade, and till 1833 to abolish slavery itself. Illiterate and without skills, thrown into a job market in which they could earn only the lowest wages, many former slaves were reduced to penury.

## Further reading

**G.R. Elton**, *The Practice of History*, Fontana, 1969.

**William Lamont** (ed.), *Historical Controversies and Historians*, UCL Press, 1998.

**Peter Burke** (ed.), *New Perspectives on Historical Writing*, Polity Press, 1991.

**L.P. Curtis** (ed.), *The Historian's Workshop*, Knopf, 1970.

**Bernard Bailyn**, 'The challenge of modern historiography', *American Historical Review,* **LXXXVII**, 1982.

**W.H. Walsh**, 'Colligatory concepts in history', in Patrick Gardiner (ed.), *The Philosophy of History*, Oxford UP, 1974.

**Alun Munslow**, *Deconstructing History*, Routledge, 1997.

**Hayden White**, *Metahistory: the Historical Imagination in Nineteenth-Century Europe*, Johns Hopkins UP, 1973.

## Notes

1 V.H. Galbraith, *An Introduction to the Study of History*, C. Watts, 1964, p. 80.

2 See, for example, E.H. Carr, *What is History?*, Penguin, 1964, pp. 28–9, and J.G.A. Pocock, 'Working on ideas in time', in L.P. Curtis (ed.), *The Historian's Workshop*, Knopf, 1970, pp. 161, 175.

3 H. Butterfield, *History and Human Relations*, Collins, 1951, p. 237.

4 Fernand Braudel, *The Mediterranean and the Mediterranean World in the Age of Philip II*, Collins, 1972.

5 C.V. Wedgwood, *The King's Peace 1637–1641*, Collins, 1955, p. 16.

6 James Joll, 'The unspoken assumptions', in H.W. Koch (ed.), *The Origins of the First World War*, Macmillan, 1972.

7 For an excellent discussion of this notion, see Bernard Bailyn, 'The challenge of modern historiography', *American Historical Review*, **LXXXVII**, 1982, pp. 1–24.

8 The classic statement of this viewpoint is Eric Williams, *Capitalism and Slavery*, University of North Carolina Press, 1944.

9 Carr, *What is History?* p. 52.

10 Christine Bolt and Seymour Drescher (eds), *Anti-Slavery, Religion and Reform*, Dawson, 1980 (especially the essay by Brian Harrison).

11 Lawrence Stone, *The Causes of the English Revolution 1529–1642*, Routledge & Kegan Paul, 1972, ch. 3.

12  Carl E. Schorske, *Fin-de-Siècle Vienna: Politics and Culture*, Weidenfeld & Nicolson, 1980, p. xxii.

13  R.H. Tawney, *History and Society*, Routledge & Kegan Paul, 1978, p. 54.

14  A.J.P. Taylor, *War by Time-table: How the First World War Began*, Macdonald, 1969, p. 45.

15  R.W. Southern, *The Making of the Middle Ages*, Hutchinson, 1953, pp. 14–15.

16  Agatha Ramm, 'Leopold von Ranke', in John Cannon (ed.), *The Historian at Work*, Allen & Unwin, 1980, p. 37.

17  E.P. Thompson, *The Poverty of Theory*, Merlin Press, 1978, p. 85.

18  H. Butterfield, *George III and the Historians*, Collins, 1957.

19  Hayden White, *Metahistory*, Johns Hopkins University Press, 1973.

20  Peter Burke, 'History of events and the revival of narrative', in P. Burke (ed.), *New Perspectives on Historical Writing*, Polity Press, 1991, p. 241.

21  Natalie Zemon Davis, *The Return of Martin Guerre*, Penguin, 1985, pp. 4, viii.

22  Lawrence Stone, 'The revival of narrative' (1979), reprinted in his *The Past and the Present Revisited*, Routledge & Kegan Paul, 1987.

23  Lucien Febvre, 'A new kind of history', 1949, translated in Peter Burke (ed.), *A New Kind of History*, Routledge & Kegan Paul, 1973, p. 38.

24  For example, Andrew Roberts, *A History of the Bemba*, Longman, 1973; Jeff Guy, *The Destruction of the Zulu Kingdom*, Longman, 1979.

25  Marc Bloch in Annales, 1932, quoted in R.R. Davies, 'Marc Bloch', *History*, **LII**, 1967, p. 273.

26  See, for example, F.M. Powicke, *Modern Historians and the Study of History*, Odhams, 1955, p. 202.

27  Quoted in H. Butterfield, *Man on His Past*, Cambridge University Press, 1955, p. 91.

28  E.J. Hobsbawm, *The Age of Revolution: Europe 1789–1848*, Cardinal, 1973, p. 11.

29  See, for example, C.C. Eldridge (ed.), *British Imperialism in the Nineteenth Century*, Macmillan, 1984.

30  George M. Fredrickson, *White Supremacy: a Comparative Study in American and South African History*, Oxford University Press, 1981, p. xviii.

31  G.R. Elton, *The Practice of History*, Fontana, 1969, p. 22.

32  Braudel, *The Mediterranean*, vol. I, p. 16.

33  Fernand Braudel, 'History and the social sciences: *la longue durée*', 1958, reprinted in his *On History*, Weidenfeld & Nicolson, 1980, p. 26.

34  R.W. Chapman (ed.), *Boswell's Life of Johnson*, Oxford University Press, 1953, p. 304.

35  Richard Cobb, *A Second Identity*, Oxford University Press, 1969, pp. 19–20.

36  H. Stuart Hughes, *History as Art and as Science*, Chicago University Press, 1964, pp. 65–6.

37  M.M. Reese (ed.), *Gibbon's Autobiography*, Routledge & Kegan Paul, 1970, p. 99.

38  Theodore Zeldin, 'After Braudel', *The Listener*, 5 November 1981, p. 542.

39  Galbraith, *Introduction*, p. 4.

# CHAPTER SEVEN

# The limits of historical knowledge

Historians make many claims for their subject, but can any historical account amount in fact to anything more than its author's personal take on the past? This chapter looks at the debate surrounding the essential nature of historical work and therefore, to some extent, its value. The positivist position sees history as a form of science, in which historians amass facts from hard evidence and draw valid conclusions; the idealists on the other hand stress that the incomplete and imperfect nature of the historical record obliges the historian to employ a considerable degree of human intuition and imagination. Challenging both positions are the Postmodernists, who point to the highly subjective values and assumptions latent not just in the historical record but in the very language that historians use to express their ideas. Does this mean that objective historical accounts are an impossibility, and if so, what is the student to make of a philosophy that questions history's very existence as a subject?

The earlier chapters of this book were essentially descriptive. They were intended to show how historians go about their work – their guiding assumptions, their handling of the evidence and their presentation of conclusions. The point has now been reached where some fundamental questions about the nature of historical enquiry can be posed: how securely based is our knowledge of the past? Can the facts of history be taken as given? What authority should be attached to attempts at historical explanation? Can historians be objective? Answers to these questions have taken widely divergent forms and have

History publishing is a huge business, with thousands of new titles appearing every year. Does this mean that we are closer to the truth about the past, or does it just mean that there are as many histories as there are people prepared to write them?

(© James Leynse/CORBIS)

occasioned intense debate, much of it fuelled by criticisms from outside the ranks of historians. The profession is deeply divided about the status of its findings. At one extreme there are those such as G.R. Elton who maintain that humility in the face of the evidence and training in the technicalities of research have steadily enlarged the stock of certain historical knowledge; notwithstanding the arguments which the professionals take such delight in, history is a cumulative discipline.[1] At the other extreme, Theodore Zeldin holds that all he (or any historian) can offer his readers is his personal vision of the past, and the materials out of which they in turn can fashion a personal vision that corresponds to their own aspirations and sympathies: 'everyone has the right to find his own perspective'.[2] Although the weight of opinion among academic historians inclines towards Elton's position, every viewpoint between the two extremes finds adherents within the profession. Historians are in a state of confusion about what exactly they are up to – a confusion not usually apparent in the confident manner with which they often pronounce on major problems of interpretation.

# I

## Is history a science?

To ask such questions about history or any other branch of learning is to enter the terrain of philosophy, since what is at issue is the nature of knowledge itself; and the status of historical knowledge has been hotly contested among philosophers since the Renaissance. Most working historians – even those disposed to reflect on the nature of their craft – take little account of these debates, believing with some justification that they often obscure rather than clarify the issues.[3] But the intense disagreement that divides historians reflects a tradition of keen debate among philosophers. During the nineteenth century two sharply opposed positions crystallized around the question of whether history was a science; as recently as the 1960s, when E.H. Carr created such a stir, this was still the key **epistemological** issue in history. In our own day the ground of debate has shifted to the nature of language and the extent of its bearing on the real world, past and present. Both these debates – the scientific and the linguistic – will now be examined in turn.

**epistemological**
Relating to theory of knowledge, how we know things.

The central question in the debate about history and science has always been whether humankind should be studied in the same way as other natural phenomena. Those who answer this question in the affirmative are committed to the methodological unity of all forms of disciplined enquiry into the human and natural order. They argue that history employs the same procedures as the natural sciences and that its findings should be judged by scientific standards. They may differ as to how far history has in fact fulfilled these requirements, but they are agreed that historical knowledge is valid only in so far as it conforms to scientific method. During the twentieth century conceptions of the nature of science have been radically modified, but the nineteenth-century view was straightforward enough. The basis of all scientific knowledge was the meticulous observation of reality by the **disinterested**, 'passive' observer, and the outcome of repeated observations of the same phenomenon was a generalization or 'law' that fitted all the known facts and explained the regularity observed. The assumption of this, the 'inductive' or 'empirical' method, was that generalizations flowed logically from the data, and that scientists approached

**disinterested**
Neutral, objective. Not to be confused with 'uninterested'.

their task without preconceptions and without moral involvement.

## Positivism: induction from facts

As a result of its immense strides in both pure and applied work, science enjoyed unrivalled prestige during the nineteenth century. If its methods unlocked the secrets of the natural world, might they not prove the key to understanding society and culture? *Positivism* is the name given to the philosophy of knowledge which expresses this approach in its classic, nineteenth-century form. Its implications for the practice of history are clear. The historian's first duty is to accumulate factual knowledge about the past – facts that are verified by applying critical method to the primary sources; those facts will in turn determine how the past should be explained or interpreted. In this process the beliefs and values of historians are irrelevant; their sole concern is with the facts and the generalizations to which they logically lead. Auguste Comte, the most influential positivist philosopher of the nineteenth century, believed that historians would in due course uncover the 'laws' of historical development. Full-blown professions of positivist faith are still made occasionally,[4] but nowadays a watered-down version is preferred. Latter-day positivists maintain that the study of history cannot generate its own laws; rather, the essence of historical explanation lies in the correct application of generalizations derived from other disciplines supposedly based on scientific method such as economics, sociology and psychology.

## Idealism: intuition and empathy

The second position, which corresponds to the school of philosophy known as *idealism*, rejects the fundamental assumption of positivism. According to this view, human events must be carefully distinguished from natural events because the identity between the enquirer and his or her subject matter opens the way to a fuller understanding than anything that the natural scientist can aspire to. Whereas natural events can only be understood from the outside, human events have an essential 'inside' dimension composed of the intentions, feelings and mentality of the actors. Once the enquirer strays into this realm the inductive method is of limited use. The reality of past events must instead be apprehended by an imaginative identification with the people of the past, which depends on intuition and empathy – qualities that have no place in the classical view of scientific method. According to idealists, therefore, historical knowledge is inherently subjective, and the truths that it uncovers are more akin to truth in the artist's sense than the scientist's. Furthermore, historians are concerned with the individual, unique event. The generalizations of the social sciences are not applicable to the study of the past, nor does history yield any generalizations or laws of its own.

This outlook came naturally to the nineteenth-century proponents of historicism (see Chapter 1) with their demand that every age be understood in its own terms and their practical emphasis on political narrative made up of the actions and intentions of 'great men'. Ranke's fame as the champion of rigorous source criticism has sometimes been allowed to obscure the emphasis that he laid on contemplation and imagination: 'after the labour of criticism', he insisted, 'intuition is required'.[5] In the English-speaking world the most original and sophisticated exponent of the idealist position has been the philosopher and historian R.G. Collingwood. In his posthumously published *The Idea of History* (1946), he maintained that all history is essentially the history of thought, and that the historian's task is to re-enact in his own mind the thoughts and intentions of individuals in the past. Collingwood's influence is evident in the case of present-day opponents of 'scientific' theory such as Zeldin, who deplores the tendency for history to become 'a coffee-house in which to discuss the findings of other disciplines in time perspective' and pleads for a history concerned with individuals and their emotions.[6] Conversely, history's scientific pretensions tend to be taken much more seriously by historians of collective behaviour – voting or consumption for example – because in these spheres regularities are evident which can sometimes form the basis of firm and significant generalizations.

But the implications of the unresolved clash between positivism and idealism go much further than the distinction between traditional political history and the more recent fields of economic and social history. They help to explain why there is so much disagreement among historians about the nature of virtually every aspect of their work from primary source evaluation through to the finished work of interpretation.

# II

## An incomplete and tainted record

Much of the professional self-esteem of the new breed of academic historians in the nineteenth century was based on the rigorous techniques that they had perfected for the location and criticism of primary sources. The canons they established have governed the practice of historians ever since, so that the whole edifice of modern historical knowledge is founded on the painstaking evaluation of original documents. But the injunction 'Be true to your sources' is less straightforward than it looks, and sceptics have seized on a number of problem areas. First, the primary sources available to the historian are an *incomplete* record, not only because so much has perished by accident or design but in a more fundamental sense because a great deal that happened left no material trace whatever. This is particularly true of mental processes, both conscious and unconscious. No historical character, however prominent and articulate, has ever set down more than a tiny proportion of his or her thoughts and assumptions; and often some of the most influential beliefs are those that are taken for granted and therefore are not discussed in the documents. In the second place, the sources are *tainted* by the less than pure intentions of their authors and – more insidiously – by their confinement within the assumptions of men and women in that time and place. 'The so-called "sources" of history record only such facts as appeared sufficiently interesting to record';[7] or, more polemically, the historical record is forever rigged in favour of the ruling class, which at all times has created the vast majority of the surviving sources. In some Marxist circles this contention has led to an absolute scepticism about the possibility of knowledge of the past, and history has been put on the intellectual scrap-heap (see p. 240).

There is an element of truth in both these criticisms, but those who push them to extremes betray an ignorance of how historians actually work. What a researcher can learn from a set of documents is not confined to its explicit meaning; that meaning is first of all scrutinized for bias and then used as the basis for inference. When properly applied, the critical method enables the historian to make allowances for both deliberate distortion and the unthinking reflexes of the writer – to extract meaning 'against the grain of the documentation', in Raphael Samuel's useful phrase.[8] Much of the criticism directed against historical method rests on the common misconception that primary sources are the testimonies of witnesses – who like all witnesses are fallible but in this instance are not available for cross-examination. Yet, as was shown in Chapter 4, a great deal of the historian's documentation is made up of record sources which themselves constitute the event or process under investigation: historians interested, say, in the character of Gladstone or the administrative machinery of the medieval Chancery are not dependent on contemporary reports and impressions (interesting though these may be); they can base their accounts on the private correspondence and diaries of Gladstone himself, or on the records generated in the course of the Chancery's day-to-day business. Moreover, much of the importance attached to primary sources derives not from the intentions of the writer but from information which was incidental to his or her purpose and yet may provide a flash of insight into an otherwise inaccessible aspect of the past. The historian, in short, is not confined by the categories of thought in which the documents were composed.[9]

## A profusion of records

But there is a third and more formidable difficulty in the notion that historians simply follow where the documents lead, and this turns on the *profusion* of the available sources. These sources may, it is true, represent a very incomplete record; yet for all but very remote periods and places they survive in completely unmanageable quantities. This is a problem that has been confronted only during the present century. Nineteenth-century historians, especially those of a positivist turn of mind such as Lord Acton, believed that finality in historical writing would be attained when primary research had brought to light a complete assemblage of the facts; many of these facts might seem obscure and trivial, but they would all tell in the end. These writers were blinded to the limitations of their method by the very narrow way in which they conceived both the content of history and a primary source: when Acton at the end of the century wrote, 'nearly all the evidence that will ever appear is accessible now',[10] he was referring only to the great collections of state records. Since Acton's day the subject matter of history has been vastly enlarged, and the significance of whole bodies of source material whose existence nineteenth-century historians were scarcely aware of has been established. Faced with the virtually limitless content that history could in theory embrace, modern historians have been compelled to subject the notion of historical 'fact' to severe scrutiny.

## What are facts?

Objection is sometimes made to the idea of 'facts' in history on the grounds that they rest on inadequate standards of proof: most of what pass for the 'facts' of history actually depend on inference. Historians read between the lines, or they work out what really happened from several contradictory indications, or they may do no more than establish that the writer was probably telling the truth. But in none of these cases can the historian observe the facts in the way that a physicist can. Historians generally have little time for this kind of critique. Formal proof may be beyond their reach; what matters is the validity of the inferences. In practice historians spend a good deal of time disputing and refining the inferences that can be legitimately drawn from the sources, and the facts of history can be said to rest on inferences whose validity is widely accepted by expert opinion. Who, they ask with some justice, could reasonably ask for more?

Historians are much more troubled by the implications of the apparently limitless number of facts about the past which can be verified in this way. If the entire past of humankind falls within the historian's scope, then every fact about that past may be said to have some claim on our attention. But historians do not proceed on this assumption – not even the specialist in some limited aspect of a well-defined period. There is in practice no limit to the number of facts that have a bearing on such a problem, and the historian who resolved to be guided solely by the facts would never reach any conclusion. The common-sense idea (and the central tenet of positivism) that historians efface themselves in front of the facts 'out there' is therefore an illusion. The facts are not given, they are selected. Despite appearances they are never left to speak for themselves. However detailed a historical narrative may be, and however committed its author to the re-creation of the past, it never springs from the sources ready-made; many events are omitted as trivial, and those that do find a place in the narrative tend to be seen through the eyes of one particular participant or a small group. Analytical history, in which the writer's intention is to abstract the factors with greatest explanatory power, is more obviously selective. Historical writing of all kinds is determined as much by what it leaves out as by what it puts in. That is why it makes sense to distinguish with E.H. Carr between the facts of the past and the facts of history. The former are limitless and in their entirety unknowable; the latter represent a selection made by successive historians for the purpose of historical reconstruction and explanation:

> The facts of history cannot be purely objective, since they become facts of history only in virtue of the significance attached to them by the historian.[11]

## The selection and rejection of facts

If historical facts are selected, it is important to identify the criteria employed in selecting them. Are there commonly shared principles, or is it a matter of personal whim? One answer, much favoured since Ranke's day, is that historians are concerned to reveal the essence of the events under consideration. Namier expressed this idea metaphorically:

> The function of the historian is akin to that of the painter and not of the photographic camera; to discover and set forth, to single out and stress that which is of the nature of the thing, and not to reproduce indiscriminately all that meets the eye.[12]

But this amounts to little more than a restatement of the original question, for how is the 'nature of the thing' to be determined? It makes for less confusion if it is admitted outright that the standards of significance applied by the historian are defined by the nature of the historical problem that he or she is seeking to solve. As M.M. Postan put it:

**facets**
Features, characteristics.

**canons**
Rules, laws.

The facts of history, even those which in historical parlance figure as 'hard and fast', are no more than relevances: **facets** of past phenomena which happen to relate to the preoccupations of historical inquirers at the time of their inquiries.

As new historical facts are accepted into the **canon**, so old ones pass out of currency except, as Postan mischievously remarks, in textbooks which are full of 'ex-facts'.[13]

There is an element of rhetorical exaggeration about this view. Historical knowledge abounds in facts such as the Great Fire of London or the execution of Charles I whose status is for all practical purposes unassailable, and critics such as Elton have seized on this point to discredit the distinction between the facts of the past and the facts of history, which they feel introduces a dangerous element of subjectivity.[14] But, as anyone who has sampled the work of professional historians knows, historical writing is never composed entirely, or even principally, of these unassailable facts. The decision whether to include this set of facts rather than that is closely affected by the purpose that informs the historian's work.

Clearly, then, much depends on the kind of questions that the historian has in mind at the outset of research. As was discussed in Chapter 4, there is something to be said for selecting a rich and previously untapped vein of source material and being guided by whatever questions it throws up (see pp. 89–90). The difficulty with this method is that nobody actually approaches the sources with a completely open mind – the grounding in the standard secondary literature which precedes any research will see to that. Even if no specific questions have been formulated, the researcher will study the sources with certain assumptions that are only too likely to be an unthinking reflection of current orthodoxy, and the result will be merely a clarification of detail or a modification of emphasis within the prevailing framework of interpretation.

## Historical hypotheses

Significant advances in historical understanding are more likely to be achieved when a historian puts forward a clearly formulated hypothesis which can be tested against the evidence. The answers may not correspond to the hypothesis, which must then be discarded or modified, but merely to ask new questions has the important effect of alerting historians to unfamiliar aspects of familiar problems and to unsuspected data in well-worked sources. Consider, for example, the origins of the English Civil War. Nineteenth-century historians approached this as a problem of competing political and religious ideologies, and they selected accordingly from the great mass of surviving information about early seventeenth-century England. From the 1930s onwards an increasing number of scholars sought to test a Marxist approach to the conflict, and as a result new material which related to the economic fortunes of the gentry, the aristocracy and the urban bourgeoisie became critically important. More recently several historians have employed a 'Namierite' approach in which the constitutional and military conflicts are seen as the expression of rivalry between political · factions: hence the networks of patronage and the intrigues at court are now coming more into play.[15] The point is not that the Marxist or Namierite position amounts to a rounded explanation of the war but rather that each hypothesis has brought into focus certain previously neglected factors which will have a bearing on any future interpretation. Marc Bloch, whose own work proceeded on the basis of hypotheses, put the issue clearly:

> Every historical research supposes that the inquiry has a direction at the very first step. In the beginning, there must be the guiding spirit. Mere passive observation, even supposing such a thing were possible, has never contributed anything productive to any science.[16]

## A new understanding of the nature of science

Significantly, scientists today would themselves mostly agree. The positivist theory still dominates the lay person's view of science, but it no longer carries much conviction among the scientific community. Inductive thought and passive observation have ceased to be regarded as the hallmarks of scientific method. Rather, all observation whether of the natural or the human world is selective and therefore presupposes a hypothesis or theory, however incoherent it may be. In **Karl Popper**'s influential view, scientific knowledge consists not of laws but of the best available hypotheses; it is provisional rather than certain knowledge. Our understanding advances through the formulation of new

**Karl Popper (1902–94)** British scientist and philosopher. Popper rejected induction as a basis for science and argued that the proper role of scientific observation was to refute existing theories rather than to try to confirm them.

hypotheses that go beyond the evidence currently available and must be tested against further observation, which will either refute or corroborate the hypothesis. And because hypotheses go beyond the evidence, they necessarily involve a flash of insight or an imaginative leap, often the bolder the better. Scientific method, then, is a dialogue between hypothesis and attempted refutation, or between creative and critical thought.[17] To historians this is a much more congenial definition of science than the one it has replaced.

## The importance of imagination

But although history and the natural sciences may converge in some of their fundamental methodological assumptions, important differences remain. In the first place, far greater play is allowed to the imagination in history. It is by no means confined to the formulation of hypotheses but permeates the historian's thinking. Historians are not, after all, only concerned to explain the past; they also seek to reconstruct or re-create it – to show how life was experienced as well as how it may be understood – and this requires an imaginative engagement with the mentality and atmosphere of the past. In maintaining that all history is the history of thought, Collingwood unduly confined the scope of the subject. But it is certainly true that the evaluation of documentary sources depends on a reconstruction of the thought behind them; before anything else can be achieved, the historian must first try to enter the mental world of those who created the sources.

Furthermore, although idealists from Ranke to Collingwood have placed an exaggerated emphasis on 'unique' events, individuals are certainly a legitimate and necessary object of historical study, and the variety and unpredictability of individual behaviour (as opposed to the regularities of mass behaviour) demand qualities of empathy and intuition in the enquirer as well as logical and critical skills. And whereas scientists can often create their own data by experiment, historians are time and again confronted by gaps in the evidence which they can make good only by developing a sensitivity as to what might have happened, derived from an imagined picture that has taken shape in the course of becoming immersed in the surviving documentation. In all these ways imagination is vital to the historian. It not only generates fruitful hypotheses; it is also deployed in the reconstruction of past events and situations by which those hypotheses are tested.

## The impossibility of consensus

The second and even more critical distinction to be made between history and the natural sciences is that the standing of explanations put forward by historians is very much inferior to that of scientific explanation. It may be that scientific explanations are no more than provisional hypotheses, but they are for the most part hypotheses on which all people qualified to judge are in agreement; they may be superseded one day, but for the time being they represent the nearest possible approximation to the truth and are commonly recognized as such. In matters of historical explanation, on the other hand, a scholarly consensus scarcely exists. The known facts may not be in doubt, but how to interpret or explain them is a matter of endless debate, as my example of the English Civil War illustrated. The 'faction hypothesis' has not superseded the 'class-conflict hypothesis' or the 'ideology hypothesis'; all are very much alive and receive varying emphasis from different historians.

The reason for this diversity of opinion lies in the complex texture of historical change. We saw in Chapter 6 how both individual and collective behaviour are influenced by an immense range of contrasting factors. What needs stressing here is that each historical situation is unique in the sense that the exact configuration of causal factors is unrepeatable. It might be argued, for instance, that the reasons why the European powers withdrew from most of their African colonies during the 1950s and 1960s were common to some thirty-odd different territories. But this would be valid only as a very broad-brush statement. The respective strength of the colonial power and the nationalist movement varied from one country to another according to its value to the metropolis, its experience of social change, the size of the resident European community, and so on.[18] In practice, therefore, each situation has to be investigated afresh, with the strong possibility of different findings, and as a result the basis for a comprehensive theory of historical causation simply does not exist.

## A multiplicity of hypotheses

Perhaps this would not matter if certainty was attainable in explaining *particular* events. But this more modest objective eludes historians as well. The problem here is that the evidence is never sufficiently full and unambiguous to place a causal interpretation beyond doubt. This is true of even the best-documented events. In a case like the origins of the First World War, the sources provide ample evidence of the motives of the protagonists, the sequence of diplomatic moves, the state of public opinion, the upward spiral of the arms race, the relative economic strength of all the nations involved, and so on. But what the evidence alone cannot do is tell us the *relative* import-ance of all these varied factors, or present a comprehensive picture of how they interacted with each other.[19] In many instances the sources do not directly address the central issues of historical explanation at all. Some of the influences on human conduct such as the natural environment or the neurotic and irrational are apprehended subconsciously; others may be experi-enced directly but not disclosed in the sources. Questions of historical explanation cannot, therefore, be resolved solely by ref-erence to the evidence. Historians are also guided by their intuitive sense of what was possible in a given historical context, by their reading of human nature, and by the claims of intellec-tual coherence. In each of these areas they are unlikely to concur. As a result several different hypotheses can hold the field at any one time. **Burckhardt** frankly acknowledged the problem in the Preface to his *Civilization of the Renaissance in Italy* (1860):

**Burckhardt**
Jakob Burckhardt (1818–1897). Swiss historian credited with having coined the term Renaissance (French: 'rebirth') to describe the cultural changes and revival of classical form in fifteenth-century Italy.

> In the wide ocean upon which we venture, the possible ways and directions are many; and the same studies which have served for this work might easily, in other hands, not only receive a wholly different treatment and application, but lead also to essentially different conclusions.[20]

The area of knowledge beyond dispute is both smaller and much less significant in history than it is in the natural sciences. This is a crucial limitation which is not properly confronted by present-day champions of 'objectivity' in history.[21]

# III

## The historian as selector

This comparison between history and natural sciences is perhaps somewhat contrived, given that the assumptions most people make about the standing of scientific knowledge are an outdated residue of nineteenth-century positivism; scientific knowledge is in reality less certain and less objective than is commonly supposed. But what the comparison does bring out is the extent to which our knowledge of the past depends on choices freely exercised by the historian. The common-sense notion that the business of historians is simply to uncover the past and display what they have found will not stand up. The essence of historical enquiry is *selection* – of 'relevant' sources, of 'historical' facts and of 'significant' interpretations. At every stage both the direction and the destination of the enquiry are determined as much by the enquirer as by the data. Clearly, the rigid segregation of fact and value demanded by the positivists is unworkable in history. In this sense, historical knowledge is not, and cannot be, 'objective' (that is, **empirically** derived in its entirety from the object of the enquiry). This does not mean, as sceptics might suppose, that it is therefore arbitrary or illusory. But it does follow that the assumptions and attitudes of historians themselves have to be carefully assessed before we can come to any conclusion about the real status of historical knowledge.

**empiricism**
Reasoning from experiment and experience, rather than from theoretical principles. Although strict scientific experimentation is a form of empiricism, so too is decution based on ill-defined 'common sense', which can lend empiricism an ambiguous intellectual status.

## The historian in context

Up to a point those standards can be seen as the property of the individual historian. The experience of research is a personal and often very private one, and no two historians will share the same imaginative response to their material. As Richard Cobb put it, 'the writing of history is one of the fullest and most rewarding expressions of an individual personality'.[22] But however rarefied the atmosphere that historians breathe, they are, like everyone else, affected by the assumptions and values of their own society. It is more illuminating to see historical interpretation as moulded by social rather than individual experience. And because social values change, it follows that historical interpretation is subject to constant revision. What one age finds worthy of note in the past may well be different from what previous ages found worthy. This principle can be illustrated many times over within the relatively short span of time since the emergence of the academic profession of history. For Ranke and his contemporaries the sovereign nation-states which dominated the Europe of their day seemed the climax of the historical process; the state was the principal agent of historical change, and human destiny was largely determined by the shifting balance of power between states. This world-view was seriously eroded by the First World War: after 1919, against the background of optimism engendered by the **League of Nations**, history-teaching in Britain tended to stress rather the growth of internationalism over the centuries. More recently, the way in which historians study the world beyond Europe and the United States has been transformed in the light of the changes they have lived through. Fifty years ago the history of Africa was still treated as an aspect of the expansion of Europe, in which the indigenous peoples scarcely featured except as the object of white policies and attitudes. Today the perspective is very different. African history exists in its own right, embracing both the pre-colonial past and the African experience of – and response to – colonial rule, and stressing the continuities of African historical development, which had previously been completely obscured by the stress on the European occupation. And those continuities have already been reassessed: whereas in the 1960s historians of Africa were mainly concerned with placing African nationalism in a historical perspective of pre-colonial state formation and resistance to colonial rule, they are now, after thirty years' disillusionment with the fruits of independence, preoccupied with the historical antecedents of Africa's deepening poverty. Twice in the course of a single lifetime the standards of significance applied by historians to the African past have been substantially revised.

However, to say that history is rewritten by each generation (or decade) is only part of the truth – and positively misleading if it suggests the replacement of one consensus by another. In the case of history written during the High Middle Ages or the Renaissance it might be appropriate to speak of a scholarly consensus, since historians and their audience were drawn from a very restricted sector of society, and at this distance in time the differences between historians seem much less significant than the

**League of Nations**
The international organization set up at the end of the First World War to settle international disputes without recourse to war. It inspired enormous levels of optimism, especially in Britain, in its early years.

values they held in common. But the attainment of universal literacy and the extension of education in Western society in this century mean that historical writing now reflects a much wider range of values and assumptions. The towering political personalities of the past such as Oliver Cromwell or Napoleon Bonaparte are interpreted in widely divergent ways by professional historians as well as lay people, partly according to their own political values.[23] Liberal or conservative historians such as **Peter Laslett** tend to conceive of social relations in pre-industrial England as reciprocal, while radically inclined historians such as E.P. Thompson see them as exploitative.[24] **Michael Howard** has made public confession of a bias which is widely shared – a bias in favour of a liberal political order in which alone the historian has been permitted to work without censorship.[25] Many other historians, however, would set a higher value on material progress or equality in social relations than on freedom of thought and expression. Historical interpretation is a matter of value judgements, moulded to a greater or lesser degree by moral and political attitudes. At the turn of the century Acton's successor at Cambridge, J.B. Bury, looked forward to the dawn of scientific history with these words: 'Though there be many schools of political philosophy, there will no longer be divers schools of history.'[26] It would be nearer the truth to say that for as long as there are many schools of political philosophy there will be divers schools of history. Paradoxically there is an element of present-mindedness about all historical enquiry.

**Peter Laslett (1915–2001)**
British historian. He pioneered the study of the history of the English family. His ground-breaking work of social history *The World We Have Lost* overturned many common assumptions about everyday life in early modern England.

**Sir Michael Howard (1922–)**
British military historian, Regius Professor of Modern History at Oxford 1980–89.

## The search for origins

The problem, of course, is to determine at what point present-mindedness conflicts with the historian's aspiration to be true to the past. The conflict is clearest in the case of those writers who ransack the past for material to fuel a particular ideology, or who falsify it in support of a political programme, as Nazi historians did under the Third Reich and supporters of Holocaust denial do today. Such works are propaganda, not history, and it is usually clear to the professional – and sometimes the lay person – that evidence has been suppressed or manufactured. Among historians themselves present-mindedness commonly takes two forms. The first is an interest in the historical origins of the modern world, or some particularly salient feature of it – say the nuclear family household or parliamentary democracy. In itself this is a positive response to the claims of social relevance, and it has the merit of providing a clear principle of selection leading to an intelligible picture of the past. But it also carries risks of superficiality and distortion. The problem with seeking the historical antecedents of some characteristically 'modern' feature is that the outcome can so easily seem to be predetermined, instead of being the result of complex historical processes. Abstracting one strand of development to be traced back to its origins too often means an indifference to historical context; the further back the enquiry proceeds, the more likely will a stress on linear descent obscure the contemporary significance of the institution or convention in question. Thus the Whig historians of the nineteenth century completely misunderstood the structure of medieval English government because of their obsessive interest in the origins of Parliament. A comparable criticism has been levelled at recent work on the medieval and early modern history of family relations and sexuality.[27] As Butterfield put it in *The Whig Interpretation of History* (1931) – probably the most influential polemic ever written against present-minded history – 'the study of the past with one eye, so to speak, upon the present is the source of all sins and sophistries in history, starting with the simplest of them, the anachronism'.[28] 'Whig' history exhibits a tendency to underestimate the differences between past and present – to project modern ways of thought backwards in time and to discount those aspects of past experience which are alien to modern ideas. In this way it reduces history's social value, which derives largely from its being a storehouse of past experiences contrasted to our own.

## A voice for the oppressed

Today a second variant of present-minded history (or 'presentism') is much more prevalent. This is the history written out of political commitment to a social group that has previously been marginalized by the prevalent historiography. As explained in Chapter 1, effective political action in the present requires an articulate social memory, and to supply this has been one of the main objectives of black historians and women's historians in

Britain and the United States. It is said that the purpose of these radical histories is not just to uncover what was previously 'hidden from history'[29] but to demonstrate historical experience of a predetermined kind – in this case oppression and resistance – to the exclusion of material that fits less neatly with the political programme of the writer. Thus the complicity of West African societies in the transatlantic slave trade may be omitted, or the sexual conservatism of much nineteenth-century feminism. When ethnic particularism or gender loyalty provides the decisive impetus for research, the differences between 'then' and 'now' may be downplayed in the cause of forging an identity across the ages, while no serious effort may be made to understand the experience of other groups with a part in the story. The way is then open for a reactive historiography marked by a more explicit and hard-nosed defence of the established order than that which existed before.

## 'Everyman his own historian'

If the outcome of historical enquiry is so heavily conditioned by the preferences of the enquirer and can so easily be altered by the intervention of another enquirer, how can it merit any credibility as a serious contribution to knowledge? If fact and value are inextricably tied together, how can a distinction be drawn between sound and unsound history? Between the two World Wars it was the fashion in some quarters to concede most, if not all, of the sceptics' case. Historical interpretation, these historians averred, should be considered true only in relation to the needs of the age in which it was written. With the phrase 'Everyman his own historian',[30] the American scholar Carl M. Becker renounced the aspirations to definitive history that had characterized the profession since Ranke. More recently the case has been succinctly put by Gordon Connell-Smith and Howell Lloyd:

> History is not 'the past', nor yet the surviving past. It is a
> reconstruction of certain parts of the past (from surviving evidence)
> which in some way have had relevance for the present circumstances
> of the historian who reconstructed them.[31]

## The unattainability of the past

The implications of this position are disturbing. Not surprisingly historians are reluctant to allow their discipline's claim to academic respectability to be so lightly abandoned. Over the past thirty years the orthodox response to relativism has been to make what is essentially a restatement of historicism. Historians, the argument goes, must renounce any standards or priorities external to the age they are studying. Their aim is to understand the past in its own terms, or in **Elton's** words 'to understand a given problem from the inside'.[32] Historians should be steeped in the values of the age and should attempt to see events from the standpoint of those who participated in them. Only then will they be true to their material and their vocation. But this claim to speak with the voice of the past will not bear inspection. On the face of it, historians may appear to be strikingly successful in assimilating the values of those they write about: diplomatic historians usually accept the ethics of *raison d'état* which have governed the conduct of international relations in Europe since the Renaissance, and the historian of a political movement may well be able to achieve an empathy with the outlook and aspirations of its members. However, as soon as historians cast their net more widely to embrace an entire society, 'the standards of the age' becomes a question-begging phrase. Whose standards should be adopted – those of the rich or the poor, the colonized or the colonizers, Protestant or Catholic? It is a fallacy to suppose that historians who renounce all claim to 'relevance' thereby ensure the objectivity of their work. In practice their writing is exposed to two dangers. On the one hand they may find themselves confined by the priorities and assumptions of those who created the sources; on the other, the end-product is quite likely to be influenced – if only unconsciously – by their own values, which are difficult to make allowances for because they are undeclared. Elton's work illustrates both these tendencies: his Tudor England is seen through the spectacles of the authoritarian paternalist bureaucracy whose records Elton knew so intimately and whose outlook was evidently congenial to his own conservative convictions.[33] Re-creative history is a legitimate pursuit, but it is a mistake to suppose that it can ever be completely realized, or that it carries the promise of objective knowledge about the past.

**Elton**

Sir Geoffrey Elton (1921–94) first made his name with a detailed study, based on his Ph.D. thesis, of what he called *The Tudor Revolution in Government*. He held that Thomas Cromwell had instituted such a strikingly modern system of bureaucracy at Henry VIII's court that it amounted in effect to an administrative revolution. However, Elton was sometimes accused of seeing everything in Tudor England as if it related to bureaucratic administration.

## History and hindsight

There is another serious difficulty encountered by the strictly historicist approach. We can never recapture the authentic flavour of a historical moment as it was experienced by people at the time because we, unlike them, know what happened next; and the significance which we accord to a particular incident is inescapably conditioned by that knowledge. This is one of the most telling objections that can be made against Collingwood's idea that historians re-enact the thought of individuals in the past. Like it or not, the historian approaches the past with a superior vision conferred by hindsight. Some historians do their best to renounce this superior vision by confining their research to a few years or even months of history for which they can give a blow-by-blow account with a minimum of selection or interpretation, but the total divestment of hindsight is not intellectually possible. Besides, should not hindsight be viewed as an asset to be exploited rather than a disability to be overcome? It is precisely our position in time relative to the subject of our enquiry that enables us to make sense of the past – to identify conditioning factors of which the historical participants were unaware, and to see consequences for what they were rather than what they were intended to be. Strictly interpreted, 'history for its own sake' would entail surrendering most of what makes the subject worth pursuing at all, without achieving the desired goal of complete detachment. The problems of historical objectivity cannot be evaded by a retreat into the past for the past's sake.

# IV

## The challenge of Postmodernism

So far this evaluation of historical enquiry has implied a hierarchy of approaches in which Positivist science stands as the ultimate yardstick of intellectual rigour. Scientific method is here viewed as the only means of gaining direct knowledge of reality, past or present. The procedures of historicism offer a scarcely tenable defence, and to the extent that they fall short of scientific method must be deemed inferior. This debate has been running for as long as history has been seriously studied, and it shows no sign of being resolved. However, in the past two decades the hand of the sceptics has been strengthened by a major intellectual shift within the humanities which has rejected historicism as the basis for history and all other text-based disciplines. This is Postmodernism. Its hallmark is the prioritization of language over experience, leading to outright scepticism as to the human capacity to observe and interpret the external world, and especially the *human* world. The implications of Postmodernism for the standing of historical work are potentially serious and must be addressed with some care.

## The tyranny of language

Modern theories of language stand in a tradition first laid out by Ferdinand de Saussure at the beginning of the twentieth century. Saussure declared that, far from being a neutral and passive medium of expression, language is governed by its own internal structure. The relationship between a word and the object or idea it denotes – or between 'signifier' and 'signified' in Saussure's terminology – is in the last resort arbitrary. No two languages have an identical match between words and things; certain patterns of thought or observation which are possible in one language are beyond the resources of another. From this Saussure drew the conclusion that language is non-referential – that speech and writing should be understood as a linguistic structure governed by its own laws, not as a reflection of reality: language is not a window on the world but a structure that determines our perception of the world. This way of understanding language has the immediate effect of downgrading the status of the writer: if the structure of the language is so constraining, the meaning of a text will have as much to do with the formal properties of the language as with the intentions of the writer, and perhaps more. Any notion that writers can accurately convey 'their' meaning to their readers falls to the ground. In a much-quoted phrase Roland Barthes spoke of 'the death of the author'.[34] One might equally speak of the death of the textual critic in the traditional sense, since those who interpret texts have as little autonomy as those who wrote them. There can be no objective historical method standing outside the text, only an interpretative point of address fashioned from the linguistic resources available to the interpreter. The historian (or literary critic) does not speak from a privileged vantage point.

However, it is simplistic to speak of the 'language' of any society in the singular, if by this we mean to suggest a common structure and uniform conventions. Any language is a complex system of meanings – a multiple code in which words often signify different meanings to different audiences; indeed the power of language partly resides in the unintended layers of meaning it conveys. The kind of textual analysis in which the immediate or 'surface' meaning is set aside in favour of the less obvious is called in Postmodern circles '**deconstruction**' – a term coined by Jacques Derrida. Deconstruction covers a bewildering mass of daring and dissonant readings. If Saussure's severance of signifier from signified is treated as an absolute principle, there is after all no limit to the range of permitted readings. The creative approach to interpreting texts – playful, ironic and subversive by turns – is a hallmark of Postmodern scholarship.[35]

## Intertextuality: text and context

For most exponents of the linguistic turn, however, some limit is placed on the freedom with which we can 'read' texts by the constraints of 'intertextuality'. According to this perspective, the texts of the past should not be viewed in isolation, because no text has ever been composed in isolation. All writers employ a language that has already served purposes similar to their own, and their audience may interpret what they write with reference to yet other conventions of language use. At any given time the world of texts is composed of diverse forms of production, each with its own cultural rationale, conceptual categories and patterns of usage. Each text belongs, in short, to a 'discourse' or body of language practice. Today the term 'discourse' is best known in the distinctive twist given to it by French philosopher **Michel Foucault**. For him 'discourse' meant not just a pattern of language use but a form of 'power/knowledge', pointing to the way in which people are confined within the regulatory scope of specific discourses. He showed how new, more restrictive discourses of madness, punishment and sexuality became established in Western Europe between 1750 and 1850, challenging the conventional interpretation of this period as one of social and intellectual progress.[36] Foucault was unusual among the founding fathers of Postmodernism in conveying a strong sense of period. But as used

**deconstructionists**
Also known as constructionists, the literary forebears of historical Postmodernists. Inspired by the French literary scholar Jacques Derrida, they stressed the importance of analyzing not just the wording of a text but the hidden assumptions and social or moral values within its vocabulary, even questioning whether text actually denotes what its words theoretically mean.

**Michel Foucault (1926–84)**
French philosopher and social historian. Foucault's studies of restrictive or oppressive institutions, such as nineteenth-century hospitals, prisons and mental asylums, has led to a new understanding of the power relationship between the individual and the state.

by most literary scholars, discourse and 'intertextuality' have a tendency to float free of any anchorage in the 'real' world, thus bearing out Derrida's celebrated aphorism, 'there is nothing outside the text'.[37]

## Relativism: nothing is certain

Analyzing discourse, like all the critical procedures associated with modern linguistics, is founded on relativism. Its champions dismiss the idea that language reflects reality as the representational fallacy. Language, they assert, is inherently unstable, variable in its meanings over time, and contested in its own time. If accepted at face value, that indeterminacy is fatal to traditional notions of historical enquiry. It becomes meaningless to attempt a distinction between the events of the past and the discourse in which they are represented; as Raphael Samuel put it in a neat summary of Roland Barthes, history becomes 'a parade of signifiers masquerading as a collection of facts'.[38] As we saw in Chapter 4, historians certainly do not regard their primary sources as infallible, and they are accustomed to reading them against the grain for implicit meanings. But underlying their scholarly practice is the belief that the sources can yield up some, at least, of the meaning they held for those who wrote and read them originally. That is **anathema** to the deconstructionist, for whom no amount of technical expertise can remove the subjectivity and indeterminacy inherent in the reading of texts. Deconstructionists offer us instead the pleasure of finding any meanings we like, provided we do not claim authority for any of them. No amount of scholarship can give us a privileged vantage point. All that is available to us is a free interaction between reader and text, in which there are no approved procedures and no court of appeal. To claim any more is naïvety or – in the more intemperate Postmodernist statements – a deception practised on the innocent reader.

**anathema**
Completely unacceptable. The term comes from the Roman Catholic Church, where it is used to denote ideas and beliefs that are entirely incompatible with Catholic doctrine.

## The negation of history

Because historians claim vastly more than this, every aspect of their practice is open to challenge by Postmodernism. Once the validity of the historical method of interpreting texts is undermined, all the procedures erected on that foundation are called into question. The Rankean project of re-creating the past collapses, because it depends on a privileged, 'authentic' reading of the primary sources. In place of historical explanation, Postmodernist history can only offer intertextuality, which deals in discursive relations between texts, not causal relations between events; historical explanation is dismissed as no more than a chimera to comfort those who cannot face a world without meaning.[39] The conventional actors of history fare no better. If the author is dead, so too is the unified historical subject, whether conceived of as an individual or as a collectivity (such as class or nation): according to the Postmodernist view, identity is constructed by language – fractured and unstable because it is the focus of competing discourses. Perhaps most important of all, deconstructing the individuals and groups who have been the traditional actors in history means that history no longer has a big story to tell. The nation, the working class, even the idea of progress, all dissolve into discursive constructions. Continuity and evolution are rejected in favour of discontinuity, as for example in Foucault's conception of four unconnected historical epochs (or 'epistemes') since the sixteenth century.[40] Postmodernists are generally scathing about the 'grand narratives' or 'metanarratives' of historians – such as the rise of capitalism or the growth of free thought and toleration. The most they will concede is that the past can be arranged into a multiplicity of stories, just as individual texts are open to a plurality of readings.

A reappraisal as radical as this has major implications for how we understand the activity of being a historian. Postmodernists have brought two important perspectives to bear on this. First, they emphasize that historical writing is a form of literary production which, like any other genre, operates within certain rhetorical conventions. In his very influential *Metahistory* (1973), Hayden White analyzes these conventions in aesthetic terms and classifies historical writing according to twelve stylistic permutations and four underlying '**tropes**'. The specifics of this elaborate analysis are less important than White's theoretical conclusion, that the character of any work of history is determined not so much by the author's scholarship or ideology as by the **aesthetic** choices that he or she makes (usually unconsciously) at the outset of the enquiry and that inform the discursive strategies of the text.

**trope**
A metaphor or figure of speech.

**aesthetic**
Artistic or relating to art or beauty.

With its privileging of the aesthetic over the ideological, this is a somewhat purist position. Postmodernism is currently more strongly identified with a second perspective, in which the historian is seen as the vector of a range of political positions rooted in the here and now. Because the documentary residue of the past is open to so many readings, and because historians employ language which is ideologically tainted, history-writing is never innocent. There being no shape to history, historians cannot reconstruct and delineate it from outside. The stories they tell, and the human subjects they write about, are merely subjective preference, drawn from an infinity of possible strategies. Historians are embedded in the messy reality they seek to represent, and hence always bear its ideological imprint. They may do no more than replicate the dominant or 'hegemonic' ideology; alternatively, they may identify with one of a number of radical or subversive ideologies; but all are equally rooted in the politics of today. From this angle all versions of history are 'presentist', not just the politically committed ones. In Keith Jenkins's phrase, history becomes 'a discursive practice that enables present-minded people(s) to go to the past, there to delve around and reorganise it appropriately to their needs'.[41] Since those needs are diverse, and even mutually exclusive, there can be no community of historians and no dialogue between those who hold to different perspectives. Thirty years ago, E.H. Carr represented the limits of scepticism in the historical profession when he acknowledged the dialogue between present and past which animates any work of history. Postmodernists take a big step closer to relativism by accepting – even celebrating – a plurality of concurrent interpretations, all equally valid (or invalid). 'One must face the fact', writes Hayden White, 'that, when it comes to the historical record, there are no grounds to be found in the record itself for preferring one way of construing its meaning rather than another'.[42] Historians, it is said, do not uncover the past; they invent it. And the time-honoured distinction between fact and fiction is blurred.

**hegemonic**
Dominant, exercising power over a region or domain.

# V

## Postmodernism in its context

How should historians respond to this onslaught? One task for which they are well equipped is to place Postmodernism itself in historical context. This means recognizing that it is located in a particular cultural moment. As the name implies, Postmodernism is a reactive phenomenon. 'Modernism' denotes the core beliefs which underpinned the evolution of modern industrial societies from the mid-nineteenth to the mid-twentieth century, especially the belief in progress and faith in the efficacy of disciplined, rational enquiry. In throwing them over, Postmodernists signal their desire for the new and for their emancipation from the previous generation. But the appeal of Postmodernism is best explained by its resonance with some of the defining tendencies in contemporary thought. For some time now the view has gained currency that much that the West has traditionally stood for has come to a dead end: its global supremacy is in decline, its technological flair has become a liability (as in the arms race), and its much-vaunted monopoly of reason is held to be irrelevant to an increasing range of human problems, from the understanding of the psyche to the care of the environment. The Holocaust, instead of being treated as an aberration, is now taken to be a grimly ironical commentary on the conventional equation of progress with Western civilization. There is widespread disillusion with the previously uncontested virtues of scientific method. Postmodernism is the theoretical stance which best illustrates these tendencies. By calling into question the possibility of objective enquiry, it undermines the authority of science. By denying shape and purpose to history, it distances us from all that we find hardest to face in our past – as well as that in which we used to take pride. If, as Postmodernism asserts, history really has no meaning, it follows that we must become fully responsible for finding meaning in our own lives, bleak and demanding though the task may be. History as traditionally conceived becomes not only impractical but irrelevant.

## The precursors of Postmodernism

This is not the first time that the credentials of history as a serious discipline have been called into question. The emphasis placed by Postmodernists on the indeterminacy of language and the pervading tone of cultural pessimism are very contemporary, but their denial of historical truth has a very familiar ring about it. In the era of religious wars in Europe in the sixteenth and seventeenth centuries, historians were dismissed by philosophers as credulous impostors, and their much-vaunted sources written off as unreliable. The nineteenth-century historicists, despite their more rigorous standards of scholarship, were soon being attacked by relativists who argued that absolute historical truth was a chimera. In fact there have been sceptics for as long as history has been written. Doubts about the status of the 'real', and our ability to apprehend it in the past or the present, have been part of the Western philosophical tradition since the ancient Greeks. Historians themselves have participated in these debates. Postmodernism is less of a novelty than its proponents sometimes claim.

## History adapts

Nor is the relationship between history and Postmodernism quite so antagonistic as my account so far implies. It may be, as some Postmodernists argue, that the Rankean documentary ideal is finished and that history as we know it is destined for the scrap-heap.[43] But what this gloomy prognosis overlooks is that historians are already in the process of assimilating aspects of the Postmodernist perspective. As has so often been the case in the past, root-and-branch critiques of the discipline have a tendency to attack a **straw man**. Historians have always shown a capacity to engage with critics of the truth claims of their discipline and to take on board some of their arguments. They are not nearly so committed to the unified historical subject as some critics have supposed; it is now rare for scholarly writers to structure a book around 'the nation' or 'the working class' without carefully analyzing the changing and contested significance of these labels.[44] Equally, many of the 'grand narratives' of Western history – such as the Whig interpretation of English history or the Industrial

**straw man**

An old term for an idea or body that is not as strong as it looks.

Revolution – have been subjected to much more devastating attack by empirically minded historians than they have by Postmodernists.[45]

Historical writing has also been directly influenced by the linguistic turn in the humanities. Recognizing the structural constraints which language may impose on its users has proved a particularly helpful insight. Gareth Stedman Jones proved as much in his reassessment of Chartism in *Languages of Class* (1983). The failure of the Chartists to sustain a mass campaign for popular democratic rights after the middle-class agenda had been met in the **Reform Act** of 1832 has been explained in various ways by historians. Stedman Jones concludes that the movement essentially failed because its politics was constituted by a discourse inherited from the past which was inappropriate to a rapidly changing political landscape. It is a powerful (though not undisputed) case for 'an analysis of Chartism which assigns some autonomous weight to the language within which it was conceived'.[46] Historians are also sympathetic to the notion that texts embody more than one level of meaning, and that the implicit or unconscious meaning may be what gives the text its power. In late nineteenth-century Britain, for example, the popular language of the New Imperialism was obviously about nationalism and racism; but with its stress on 'manliness' and 'character' it also carried a heavy charge of masculine insecurity, which arose from changes in women's position in the family and the workplace. When politicians used that language, they both reflected and intensified an uncertain sense of manhood, almost certainly without meaning to.[47] Determining the discourse to which a particular text belongs, and its relation to other relevant discourses, is a task that goes beyond the procedures of source criticism as traditionally understood. As a result, historians now tend to be more sensitive to the counter-currents of meaning in their sources, pushing Marc Bloch's well-known aphorism about 'witnesses in spite of themselves' in a new and rewarding direction.

**Reform Act**
The pioneering measure of parliamentary reform, which was finally passed into law in 1832. Historians point out that its provisions were relatively modest but that its symbolic importance was immense.

## Language and cultural hegemony

Equally, the Postmodern critique of historical writing has met with some positive responses among historians. In particular, White's dissection of the literary conventions embedded in historical narrative has resulted in a renewed awareness of historical writing as a literary form and a greater readiness to experiment.[48] Even more promising, the Postmodern deconstruction of discourse as a form of cultural power has made it harder to ignore the fact that history-writing itself can be an expression of cultural hegemony, and this in turn has opened up opportunities for radical contestation by groups previously excluded from the record. Edward Said's interest in how language is formed and how a subject is constituted has gone hand in hand with his investigation of the Arab and the Palestinian in Western discourse; his path-breaking *Orientalism* (1976) proved to be a turning point in the emergence of a post-colonial or multi-cultural history. Feminists, in their ambition to penetrate the limitations of 'man-made language', have acknowledged a comparable debt to the linguistic turn.[49] These instances go some way to support the Postmodernists' contention that their perspective holds out the prospect of democratic empowerment. When to that is added the pervasive influence of language-led theory on the development of cultural history in recent years (as discussed in Chapter 10), it is clear that the encounter between Postmodernism and more traditional theories of history has been quite fruitful.

# VI

## The limitations of Postmodernism

However, there is a limit beyond which most historians will not go in embracing Postmodernism. Many welcome a greater sophistication in interpreting texts and a heightened awareness of the cultural significance of historical writing. But few are prepared to join in a rejection of the truth claims of history as usually practised. Confronted by the full force of the deconstructionist critique, historians tend to be confirmed in their preference for experience and observation over first principles. In theory an impeccable case can be made for the proposition that all human language is self-referential rather than representational. But daily life tells us that language works extremely well in many situations where meaning is clearly communicated and correctly inferred. On any other assumption human interaction would break down completely. If language demonstrably serves these practical func-

tions in the present, there is no reason why it should not be understood in a similar spirit when preserved in documents dating from
the past. Of course there is an *element* of indeterminacy about all
language; the lapse of time serves to increase it, and a three
hundred-year-old text straddling two or three discourses may be
very difficult to pin down. Historians frequently acknowledge
that they cannot fathom all the levels of meaning contained in
their documents. But to maintain that *no* text from the past can
be read as an accurate reflection of something outside itself flies
in the face of common experience. In a set of trade figures or a
census return the relation between text and reality is palpable
(which is not to say that it is necessarily accurate). A carefully
considered literary production such as an autobiography or a **political tract** disguised as a sermon presents much more complex
problems, but it is still important to recognize that their authors
were attempting a real engagement with their readers, and to get
as close as we can to the spirit of that engagement.

It is at this point that historians invoke the discipline of historical context. The meanings that link words and things are not
arbitrary and infinite but follow conventions created by real
culture and real social relations. The task of scholarship is to
identify these conventions in their historical specificity and to
take full account of them in interpreting the sources. Whereas
exponents of the linguistic approach treat 'context' as meaning
*other texts* only, with the further complication that they too invite
a variety of readings, historians insist that texts should be set in
the full context of their time. That means taking seriously not just
the resources of the language but the identity and background of
the author, the conditions of production of texts, the intended
readership, the cultural attitudes of the time, and the social
relations that enveloped writer and readers. Every text is socially
situated in specific historical conditions; in the useful phrase of
Gabrielle Spiegel, there is a 'social logic of the text' which is open
to demonstration by historical enquiry.[50] So, for example, my
reading of the language of late nineteenth-century imperialism
can be taken seriously because the strains in gender relations at
that time are very well documented, and because the cultural
identification of empire with masculinity bore some relation to
imperial realities. No doubt deconstruction could yield other
interpretations, more elegant and intriguing than this; but unless

**political tract**
A tract is a small booklet,
larger than a pamphlet but
smaller than a book, which
puts across an argued
case. Tracts were widely
used in the nineteenth
century by church and
religious reform groups,
but there were plenty of
political tracts as well.

they have a firm anchorage in historical context, they amount to an imposition by the critic on the text. Respect for the historicity of the sources is fundamental to the historical project; the point at which it is breached is where historians part company with the deconstructionists. Historians do not claim that in all cases their method can uncover every dimension of textual meaning; in order for historical work to be done, it is sufficient to demonstrate that *some* of the original meaning can be reclaimed, so that we can look beyond discourse to the material and social world in which the texts were created. The verification of historical events and the discipline of historical context mean that historians can distinguish between what happened in history and the discourse in which it is represented.

## The need for historical explanation

Historians are no more willing to jettison the truth claims of the accounts which they themselves construct. It is one thing to acknowledge the rhetorical aspects of historical writing but quite another to treat it as only – or largely – rhetoric. Historical narratives are certainly moulded by the historian's aesthetic sense, but they are not inventions: some, like the major revolutionary upheavals, arise partly from the consciousness of those who lived through them; others fall into shape through the benefit of historical hindsight. The stories we tell ourselves about the past may not be completely coherent or completely convincing, but they are rooted in the fact that human beings not only believe them but *enact* them on the assumption that social action is a continuum through past, present and future. The task of historical explanation is similarly one that cannot be shirked. It represents not an escape from the real world, as the bleaker versions of Postmodernism insist, but an essential application of reason, based on patterns of cause and consequence which go beyond the confined domain of intertextuality. As for the **emancipatory** potential of competing narratives, this amounts to little if the ambitions of each identity group are confined to producing a history which is 'true' only for its own members. Real empowerment comes from writing history which carries conviction beyond one's own community, and this means conforming to the scholarly procedures which historians of all communities respect. That,

**emancipatory**
Liberating.

rather than the consolation prize of a permissive relativism, has been the objective of most 'multi-cultural' historians. Despite the pessimism of some conservative commentators,[51] pluralism does not necessarily mean **relativism**.

The nub of the Postmodernist critique is that historicism is dead and should be abandoned as a serious intellectual endeavour. In fending off this attack, historians point out not only that the weaknesses of historical enquiry have been grossly exaggerated but that a broadly historicist stance towards the past is culturally indispensable. It is a precondition of critical social thought about the present and the future. As Joyce Appleby, Lynn Hunt and Margaret Jacob put it, 'Rejecting all meta-narratives cannot make sense, because narratives and meta-narratives are the kinds of stories that make action in the world possible'.[52] A consciousness of the past as 'other', a set of coherent narratives linking past and present and an explanatory mode of historical writing are all practical necessities. If the ambition to know the past is completely surrendered, we shall never be able to determine how the present came to be. The social function of history is not to be so lightly abandoned.

**relativism**
The idea that all codes of values or ethics are equivalent and exist in relation to their context; it is therefore not possible to say that any one of them is in any sense 'better' than any other.

# VII

## Theoretical objections, practical answers

In questioning the credentials of historical knowledge, Postmodernism has breathed fresh life into a strand of scepticism which stretches back to the Renaissance. The fallibility (or 'indeterminacy') of the sources, the gap between validated facts and the explanations that endow them with meaning, and the personal and political investment that historians bring to their work, have long been hostages to fortune. Positivism condemned them as damning departures from scientific rigour; Postmodernism subsumes them in a larger refutation of rational enquiry. Whether viewed from a positivist or a Postmodern standpoint, the epistemological credentials of history do not look impressive. Primarily this is because abstract theories are best tested in carefully controlled conditions, whereas history is a hybrid discipline which defies simple pigeon-holing. The divergent and sometimes contradictory objectives which historians pursue are what gives the subject its distinctive character, but they also lay it open to theoretical attack.

Though some historians still seek refuge in an untenable empiricism,[53] the more thoughtful defenders of the discipline concede that it is open to major theoretical objections. Commentators such as Appleby, Hunt and Jacob, or Richard J. Evans know that historical knowledge always involves an encounter between present and past in which the present may weigh too heavily on the past. They know that the sources do not 'speak' directly, that facts are selected, not given, that historical explanation depends on the application of hindsight, and that every historical account is in some sense moulded by the aesthetic and political preferences of the writer. Their defence rests on the contention that, while *in theory* these features may invalidate historical work, *in practice* they can be – and are – confined to manageable proportions. History is neither an exemplar of realism nor a victim to relativism. It occupies a middle ground in which scholarly procedures are upheld in order to keep the avenues of enquiry as close to the 'real' and as far removed from the 'relative' as possible.[54] Historians are members of a profession one of whose principal functions is to enforce standards of scholarship and to restrain waywardness of interpretation. Peer-group scrutiny operates as a powerful mechanism for ensuring that within the area of enquiry they find significant, historians are as true as they can be to the surviving evidence of the past.

## The historian's safeguards: self-awareness and **peer review**

**peer review**
Academic work is usually scrutinized in detail by other academics in a process known as peer review.

**polemic**
An angry and impassioned argument.

Three requirements stand out in this respect. First, the historian should scrutinize his or her own assumptions and values in order to see how they relate to the enquiry in hand. One of the attractions of E.P. Thompson is that he made no secret of his sympathies – even acknowledging that one chapter in *The Making of the English Working Class* was **polemic**.[55] This kind of awareness is particularly important in the case of those historians who have no particular axe to grind but can all too easily be the unconscious vector of values taken for granted by people of their own background. That is one reason why, as emphasized by Zeldin, self-knowledge is a desirable trait among historians (see p. 165) – and also why the confessional mode of historical writing should be welcomed, at least in the author's preface or introduction. Secondly, the risk of assimilating findings to expectations is reduced if the direction imparted to the enquiry is cast in the form of an explicit hypothesis, to be accepted, rejected or modified in the light of the evidence – with the author always the first to try to pick holes in his or her interpretation. The appropriate conduct for historians is not to avoid social relevance but to be fully aware of why they are attracted to their particular slice of history and to show as much respect for contrary as for supporting evidence. It is sometimes forgotten by non-practising critics that much of the excitement of historical research comes from finding results which were *not* anticipated and pushing one's thesis into a new direction. Thirdly and above all, historians must submit their work to the discipline of historical context. The case against 'presentism' and deconstructionism is that they remove events and personalities from their real time and place, forcing them into a conceptual framework which would have meant nothing to the age in question. In fact historians have much less excuse for falling into this trap than they used to. The enlargement of the scope of historical studies during the past fifty years, and the way in which the best historical syntheses reflect this enlargement, means that historians today should have a much better-developed sense of context than their predecessors did; peer review operates particularly effectively in this area.

Respect for these three injunctions does much to limit the amount of distortion in historical writing. It does not, however, put an end to debate and disagreement. It would be wrong to suppose that if all historians could only attain a high degree of self-awareness, make their working hypotheses explicit and maintain a scrupulous respect for historical context they would then concur in their historical judgements. Nobody can become completely dispassionate about his or her own assumptions or those of earlier ages; the evidence can usually be read in support of conflicting hypotheses; and, since the sources never recapture a past situation in its entirety, the sense of historical context depends also on an imaginative flair that will vary according to the insight and experience of the individual scholar. The nature of historical enquiry is such that, however rigorously professional the approach, there will always be a plurality of interpretation. That should be counted as a strength rather than a weakness. For advances in historical knowledge arise as much from the play of debate between rival interpretations as from the efforts of the individual scholar. And the same debates which enliven the historical profession are intimately connected with the alternative visions we hold of our society in the present and the future. If history was uncontested, it would fail to provide the materials for critical debate on the social issues of the day. Plurality of historical interpretation is an essential – if underestimated – prerequisite for a mature democratic politics. The past will never be placed beyond controversy; nor should it be.

## Inductive reasoning

Historians have to achieve a balance between *deductive* and *inductive* reasoning. Deductive reasoning is employed when the conclusion is entirely supported by the information on which it is based, known as the *premise*. Thus, if the premises are a) that all cats are vertebrates and b) that Toby is a cat, we can safely *deduce* that Toby is a vertebrate; indeed no other deduction is possible. Deductive reasoning is well illustrated in the methods adopted by the fictional detective Sherlock Holmes, who once remarked that, when all other possibilities have been eliminated, what is left, *however unlikely*, must be the solution. The point of the italics is that many people allow their expectations, drawn from everyday experience, to influence their interpretation of data. This is *inductive reasoning*. For example, a visitor to London who saw a host of red buses and black taxis might, understandably but still wrongly, conclude that all London buses are red and all London taxis are black. Mathematicians rely entirely on deductive reasoning and can be impatient of scientists' tendency to slip into the inductive; for historians, with their often patchy and incomplete evidence, the temptation to rely too much on purely inductive reasoning is even stronger. Every time a historian generalizes from a single incident or example he or she is employing inductive reasoning, which further evidence might well show to be mistaken.

## Holocaust denial

In the closing stages of the Second World War, allied armies overran German concentration camps and uncovered evidence of

the Nazis' policy of exterminating Jews, Gypsies and other
groups. However, a move also got under way fuelled by extreme
right-wing and anti-semitic groups in different countries to deny
that the Holocaust had ever happened. A characteristic approach
of Holocaust denial is to adopt an outwardly respectable,
academic manner and to appear to subject the evidence for the
Holocaust to careful and objective scrutiny. For example, it is
often pointed out that no document has survived with Hitler's
signature on it ordering the murder of Jews. From this it is
argued, implausibly, that Hitler can have known nothing of the
Holocaust. Holocaust denial is based upon the systematic
suppression or distortion of the evidence. In 2000 the right-wing
British writer David Irving sued Penguin Books for claiming he
was anti-semitic and a Holocaust denier. Irving lost his case when
it emerged in court that his work was riddled with selective
quotation and even falsification of historical evidence.

## Whig history

The Whigs were a political group that dominated British politics
in the eighteenth and nineteenth centuries. Whiggery developed
out of the parliamentary side in the English Civil War and
retained a strong attachment to the rights and privileges of
Parliament, whose virtues, the Whigs believed, could be explained
by a particular reading of English history. The Whigs interpreted
it as a long battle with the Crown for the restoration of the
ancient rights of Parliament, which they fondly believed had been
enjoyed in Anglo-Saxon times but lost at the time of the Norman
Conquest. Historians have long since shown the Whig version of
events to be myth, but the general theme of progress towards a
pinnacle in the present day remained very popular. Herbert
Butterfield attacked Whig history for looking at medieval or
Tudor institutions in entirely modern terms and not taking the
contemporary context into account; left-wing historians have
rejected Whig history for its over-confident, patriotic tone. The
general Whig tendency, however, to see modern conditions or
attitudes as the peak of perfection and then to look to the past to
see how we attained it, is by no means confined to constitutional
history and can be found in such diverse fields as women's history
or the history of science and medicine.

## Further reading

E.H. Carr, *What is History?* Penguin, 1961

G.R. Elton, *The Practice of History*, Sydney UP, 1967

W.H. Walsh, *An Introduction to Philosophy of History*, 3rd edn, Hutchinson, 1967

Richard Evans, *In Defence of History*, Granta, 1997

Ludmilla Jordanova, *History in Practice*, Arnold, 2000

R.G. Collingwood, *The Idea of History*, Oxford UP, 1946

Keith Jenkins, *The Postmodern History Reader*, Routledge, 1997

Keith Jenkins, *On 'What Is History?'*, Routledge, 1995

Beverley Southgate, *Postmodernism in History*, Routledge, 2003

Willie Thompson, *Postmodernism and History*, Palgrave, 2004

Hayden White, *The Content of the Form*, Johns Hopkins UP, 1987

Joyce Appleby, Lynn Hunt & Margaret Jacob, *Telling the Truth about History*, Norton, 1997

Gertrude Himmelfarb, *On Looking into the Abyss*, Knopf, 1994

## Notes

1  G.R. Elton, *The Practice of History*, Fontana, 1969.

2  Theodore Zeldin, 'Ourselves as we see us', *Times Literary Supplement*, 31 December 1982. See also his article, 'After Braudel', *The Listener*, 5 November 1981.

3  See, for example, Elton, *The Practice of History*, pp. vii–viii.

4  Lee Benson, *Toward the Scientific Study of History*, Lippincott, 1972.

5  L. von Ranke, quoted in Peter Novick, *That Noble Dream: the 'Objectivity Question' and the American Historical Profession*, Cambridge University Press, 1988, p. 28.

6  Zeldin, 'After Braudel'. See also his article, 'Social and total history', *Journal of Social History*, **X**, 1976, pp. 237–45.

7  K.R. Popper, *The Open Society and its Enemies*, vol. 2, 5th edn, Routledge & Kegan Paul, 1966, p. 265.

8  Raphael Samuel (ed.), *People's History and Socialist Theory*, Routledge & Kegan Paul, 1981, editor's introduction, p. xlv.

9  E.H. Carr, *What is History?* Penguin, 1964, p. 16, rather surprisingly falls into this error.

10 Lord Acton, letter to the contributors to the *Cambridge Modern History*, 1896, reprinted in Fritz Stern (ed.), *Varieties of History*, 2nd edn, Macmillan, 1970, p. 247.

11 Carr, *What is History?* p. 120.

12 L.B. Namier, *Avenues of History*, Hamish Hamilton, 1952, p. 8.

13 M.M. Postan, *Fact and Relevance*, Cambridge University Press, 1970, p. 51.

14 Elton, *The Practice of History*, pp. 74–82.

15 See R.C. Richardson, *The Debate on the English Revolution Revisited*, Routledge, 1988.

16 Marc Bloch, *The Historian's Craft*, Manchester University Press, 1954, p. 65.

17 Popper's views are lucidly expounded in Bryan Magee, *Popper*, Fontana, 1973.

18 R.F. Holland, *European Decolonization 1918–81*, Macmillan, 1985.

19 James Joll, *The Origins of the First World War*, Longman, 1984.

20 Jakob Burckhardt, *The Civilization of the Renaissance in Italy*, Phaidon, 1960, p. 1.

21 This is particularly true of Elton, *Practice of History*.

22 Richard Cobb, *A Second Identity*, Oxford University Press, 1969, p. 47. See also Zeldin's comments in the same vein in *France 1848–1945*, Vol. I, Oxford University Press, 1973, p. 7.

23 See, for example, Pieter Geyl, *Napoleon: For and Against*, 2nd edn, Cape, 1964.

24 Compare, for example, Peter Laslett, *The World We Have Lost*, 2nd edn, Methuen, 1971, with E.P. Thompson, *Whigs and Hunters*, Penguin, 1977.

25 Michael Howard, *The Lessons of History*, Oxford University Press, 1981, p. 21.

26 J.B. Bury, 'The science of history', 1902, reprinted in Stern, *Varieties of History*, p. 215.

27 Adrian Wilson, 'The infancy of the history of childhood: an appraisal of Philippe Ariès', *History and Theory*, XIX, 1980, pp. 132–53.

28 H. Butterfield, *The Whig Interpretation of History*, Penguin, 1973, p. 30.

29 Cf. Sheila Rowbotham, *Hidden from History*, Pluto Press, 1973.

30 Cited in J.H. Hexter, *On Historians*, Collins, 1979, p. 15.

31 Gordon Connell-Smith and Howell A. Lloyd, *The Relevance of History*, Heinemann, 1972, p. 41.

32 Elton, *Practice of History*, p. 31.

33 Elton's conservative convictions are most clearly set out in his two inaugural lectures, 'The future of the past' (1968) and 'The history of England' (1984), reprinted in his *Return to Essentials*, Cambridge University Press, 1991.

34 Roland Barthes, *Image, Music, Text*, Fontana, 1977, pp. 42–8.

35 The textual theories that have grown up in the wake of Saussure are usefully set out in Raman Selden, Peter Widdowson and Peter Brookes, *A Reader's Guide to Contemporary Literary Theory*, 4th edn, Prentice Hall, 1997.

36 For a good introduction, see P. Rabinow (ed.), *The Foucault Reader*, Penguin, 1991.

37 Jacques Derrida, *Of Grammatology*, Johns Hopkins University Press, 1976, p. 158.

38 Raphael Samuel, 'Reading the Signs', *History Workshop Journal*, **32**, 1991, p. 93.

39 Hayden White, *The Content of the Form*, Johns Hopkins University Press, 1987, p. 72.

40 Michel Foucault, *The Archaeology of Knowledge*, Tavistock, 1972.

41 Keith Jenkins, *Re-Thinking History*, Routledge, 1991, p. 68.

42 Hayden White, quoted in Novick, *That Noble Dream*, p. 601.

43 See, for example, Alun Munslow, *Deconstructing History*, Routledge, 1997; Keith Jenkins, *On 'What Is History?'*, Routledge, 1995.

44 Linda Colley, *Britons: Forging the Nation, 1707–1837*, Yale University Press, 1992, is a good example of a highly critical analysis uninfluenced by Postmodernism.

45 For attacks on the Whig interpretation of history, see J.C.D. Clark, *English Society 1688–1832: Ideology, Social Structure and Political Practice during the Ancien Régime*, Cambridge University Press, 1985, and Conrad Russell, *The Causes of the English Civil War*, Oxford University Press, 1990. For attacks on the concept of the Industrial Revolution, see R. Floud and D. McCloskey (eds), *The Economic History of Britain since 1700*, 2 vols, Cambridge University Press, 1981.

46 Gareth Stedman Jones, *Languages of Class: Studies in English Working Class History 1832–1982*, Cambridge University Press, 1983, p. 107.

47 H. John Field, *Toward a Programme of Imperial Life*, Clio Press, 1982; John Tosh, 'What should historians do with masculinity: reflections on nineteenth-century Britain', *History Workshop Journal*, 38, 1994, pp. 179–202.

48 For a review of these trends, see Peter Burke (ed.), *New Perspectives on Historical Writing*, Polity Press, 1991.

49 See, for example, Joan Scott, *Gender and the Politics of History*, Columbia University Press, 1988.

50 Gabrielle M. Spiegel, 'History, historicism, and the social logic of the text', *Speculum*, **LXV** (1990), pp. 59–86.

51 Gertrude Himmelfarb, *On Looking Into the Abyss*, Knopf, 1994.

52 Joyce Appleby, Lynn Hunt and Margaret Jacob, *Telling the Truth About History*, Norton, 1994, p. 236.

53 Elton, *Return to Essentials*; Arthur Marwick, 'Two approaches to historical study: the metaphysical (including "Postmodernism") and the historical', *Journal of Contemporary History*, **XXX**, 1995, pp. 5–35.

54 Appleby, Hunt and Jacob, *Telling the Truth About History*; Richard J. Evans, *In Defence of History*, Granta, 1997.

55 E.P. Thompson, *The Making of the English Working Class*, revised edn, Penguin, 1968, p. 916.

# CHAPTER EIGHT

# History and social theory

What role should theory play in the work of a historian? Some approach history from the point of view of a committed Marxist or feminist and find that the application of social theory helps to make sense of a past that might otherwise defy analysis. However, others see such theorizing as dangerous, twisting the facts to fit the theory. This chapter considers the relationship between history and different social theories and suggests that Marxism and feminism might have rather more to offer the historian than their detractors have allowed for.

## Hypothesis and theory

I suggested in the previous chapter that one of the ways in which historians can guard against unconsciously assimilating their interpretations of the past to their own bias is by formulating hypotheses to be tested against the available evidence. Such a hypothesis may be no more than a provisional explanation suggested to the historian by a reading of the relevant secondary authorities and exclusive to the historical problem in hand. But a closer inspection often reveals a more elevated parentage. A hypothesis is not just a preliminary assessment of a particular historical conjuncture in its own terms; it usually reflects certain assumptions about the nature of society and the nature of culture; in other words, historical hypotheses amount to an application of *theory*. In many disciplines theory represents the abstracting of generalizations (sometimes laws) from an accumulation of research findings. Historians hardly ever use the term in this sense. Theory for them usually means the framework of interpretation which gives impetus to an enquiry and influences its outcome. Historians sharply differ about the legitimacy of this procedure. Some are strongly committed to a particular theoretical orientation; some acknowledge the stimulus that a theoretical point of departure can offer, while resisting any imposition of theory on the historical evidence; others regard any use of theory as an insidious encroachment on the autonomy of history as a discipline.

The current practice of history is strongly influenced by two quite distinct bodies of theory. The more recent addresses the problem of meaning and representation. Traditionally historians have relied on their techniques of source criticism in order to capture the meanings which people in the past have given to their experience. Yet the more remote and alienating the experience, the more inadequate that methodology becomes. As the scope of cultural history has broadened, historians have increasingly acknowledged the insights of other disciplines – psychoanalysis, literary theory and above all **cultural anthropology**. Chapter 10 will examine more fully the problems of interpreting cultural meaning and the debt which many historians now acknowledge towards these disciplines. The second body of theory is concerned with the nature of society – its structure, its persistence and its eventual evolution into a different structure. It comprises an extraordinarily rich intellectual tradition, going back at least to the Enlightenment. In practice no historian seeking to understand the major changes in the pre-modern and modern world can afford to ignore social theory. That is the main reason why Marxism has been so influential and why it continues to be drawn on by historians when the political future of Communism looks so unpromising. In this chapter I first review the general debate about the merits and demerits of social theory; I then examine Marxism and its application in some detail, and conclude with the growing contribution of gender theory to historical explanation.

**cultural anthropology**
The study of the cultural meanings by which people live in society (usually small-scale societies).

# I

## The need for abstract theory

Broadly speaking, social theories arise from the problems presented by three aspects of historical explanation. There is first the difficulty of grasping the inter-relatedness of every dimension of human experience at a given time. For most historians up to the end of the nineteenth century this was not in practice a major problem, since their interest tended to be confined to political and constitutional history; accordingly some notion of the body politic was all the conceptual equipment they required. But during the twentieth century the enlargement in the scope of historical enquiry and in the volume of evidence, together with the pressures towards thematic specialization, have demanded an ever greater capacity to think in terms of abstractions. We saw in Chapter 5 how easily historians fall into the trap of seeing the past as compartmentalized into 'political', 'economic', 'intellectual' and 'social' history, and how the idea of 'total history' arose as a corrective (see p. 138). But total history is unattainable without some concept of how the component aspects of human experience are linked together to form a whole – some theory of the structure of human society in its widest sense. Most concepts of this kind depend heavily on analogies with the physical world. Society has been variously conceived as an organism, a mechanism and a structure. Each of these metaphors represents an attempt to go beyond the crude notion that any one sphere determines the rest, and to express the reciprocal or mutually reinforcing relationship between the main categories of human action and thought.

## Identifying the motor of historical change

The second problem which invites the application of theory is that of historical change. Historians spend most of their time explaining change – or its absence. This dominant preoccupation inevitably raises the question of whether the major transitions in history display common characteristics. Is historical change driven by a motor, and if so what does the motor consist of? More specifically, does industrialization require adherence to one particular path of economic development? Can one identify in history the essential components of a revolutionary situation? In framing their hypotheses in particular instances historians are often influenced by the attractions of this kind of theory – for example the idea that **demography** holds the key[1] or that the most durable changes in society arise from the **gradualist** reforms conceded by **paternalistic** ruling classes rather than from revolutionary demands articulated from below.[2]

## Seeking the meaning of history

Thirdly, and most ambitiously, there are the theories which seek to explain not merely *how* historical change takes place but the direction in which all change is moving; these theories are concerned to interpret human destiny by ascribing a meaning to history. Medieval writers conceived history as a linear transition from the Creation to the Last Judgement, controlled by Divine Providence. By the eighteenth century that view had been secularized as the idea of progress: history was interpreted as a story of material and intellectual improvement whose outcome in the future would be the triumph of reason and human happiness. Modified versions of that outlook continued to have a powerful hold in the nineteenth century: on the continent history meant the rise of national identities and their political expression in the nation-state; for the Whig historians of England it meant the growth of constitutional liberties. Full-blown professions of faith in progress may be rare today,[3] given the trail of destruction which has marked the history of the [twentieth] century; but theories of progressive change still underpin many historical interpretations in the economic and social sphere, as is shown by the frequency with which historians reach for such words as 'industrialization' and 'modernization'.

## The rejection of theory

Although these three types of historical theory are analytically distinct, they all share an interest in moving from the particular to the general in an effort to make sense of the subject as a whole. It might be supposed that this is a natural progression, shared by all branches of knowledge. A great many historians, however, reject the use of theory completely. They see two possible grounds for doing so. The first argument concedes that there may be patterns

**demography**
The study of the growth and development of population.

**gradualist**
Proceeding slowly, making very gradual progress.

**paternalistic**
Instituting changes and reforms from 'on high', i.e. carried out by those in authority for those below them, rather than introduced by the beneficiaries themselves.

and regularities in history but maintains that they are not accessible to disciplined enquiry. It is hard enough to provide an entirely
convincing explanation of any one event in history, but to link
them in a series or within an overarching category places the
enquirer at an intolerable distance from the verifiable facts. As
Peter Mathias (here acting as **devil's advocate**) concedes:

> The bounty of the past provides individual instances in plenty to
> support virtually any general proposition. It is only too easy to beat
> history over the head with the blunt instrument of a hypothesis and
> leave an impression.[4]

**devil's advocate**
One who deliberately sets
out to put the opposite
case for the purposes of
debate. The term comes
from the process whereby
the Vatican used to decide
on proposals for creating a
new saint, where the
devil's advocate presented
the case against the
candidate.

On this view, theoretical history is speculative history and should
be left to philosophers and prophets.[5]

The possibility that theory will 'take over' from the facts is certainly not to be made light of. The gaps in the surviving historical
record, and especially the lack of clinching evidence in matters of
causation, leave a great deal of scope for mere supposition and
wishful thinking. At the same time, the range of evidence bearing
on many historical problems is so large that selection is unavoidable – and the principles governing that selection may prejudice
the result of the enquiry. The record of recent centuries is so voluminous and varied that contradictory results can be obtained
simply by asking different questions. In the context of American
history Aileen Kraditor puts this point as follows:

> If one historian asks, 'Do the sources provide evidence of militant
> struggles among workers and slaves?' the sources will reply,
> 'Certainly'. And if another asks, 'Do the sources provide evidence of
> widespread **acquiescence** in the established order among the American
> population throughout the past two centuries?' the sources will reply,
> 'Of course'.[6]

**acquiescence**
Acceptance.

Almost any theory can be 'proved' by marshalling an impressive
collection of individual instances to fit the desired pattern.

## Safeguards against excessive theorizing

Theory-oriented history is certainly prone to these dangers – but
so too, it must be recognized, is the work of many historians who
reject theory and remain blissfully unaware of the assumptions
and values which inform their own selection and interpretation of
evidence. The way forward is not to retreat into an untenable

empiricism but to apply much higher standards to the testing of theory. Wishful thinking is more likely to be controlled by historians who approach their enquiries with explicit hypotheses than by those who try to follow where the sources lead. When selection of the evidence cannot be avoided, it must be a representative selection which will reveal both contrary and supporting indicators. A given theory may account for *part* of the evidence relating to the problem in hand, but that is not enough; it must be compatible with the weight of the evidence overall. In Kraditor's words, 'the data omitted must not be essential to the understanding of the data included'.[7] All this assumes a certain detachment on the part of historians towards their theories, and a readiness to change tack in the lack of evidence. But where these controls are neglected, the profession as a whole is vigilant in their defence. Historians are seldom happier than when citing contrary evidence and alternative interpretations to cast doubt on the work of their colleagues – especially those who seem to have a bee in their bonnet. Moreover, a great deal of historical synthesis consists of comparing the merits of competing theories in order to determine which, if any, illuminates the problem under discussion. The speculative tendencies in theoretical history do not go unchecked for long.

# II

## Is theory relevant to historical enquiry?

The second and more challenging line of attack questions the legitimacy of theory-making in history on the grounds that it denies the very essence of the discipline. Human culture, the argument goes, is so richly diverse that we can only understand man in specific epochs and locations: 'He remains an irreducible subject, the one non-object in the world'.[8] Models of human behaviour are therefore a delusion. The business of the historian is to reconstruct events and situations in their unique individuality, and on their own terms; their interpretations apply only to particular sets of circumstances. Nothing is to be gained from comparing historical situations separated by time or space – indeed a great deal will be lost, since the result can only be to obscure the essentials of each. In David Thomson's words, 'The historical attitude, by definition, is hostile to system-making'.[9] This view has a distinguished pedigree. It captures the essence of historicism as expounded in the nineteenth century. Ranke's injunction that historians should study the past 'to show how things actually were' was intended primarily as an antidote to the great evolutionary schemes of the Enlightenment historians and the followers of Hegel. His narrative style was hostile to abstraction and generalization and well suited to conveying the particularity of events. The classical historicist position is inimical both to comprehensive theories of social structure and to theories of social change, while its demand that every age should be evaluated in its own terms is difficult to reconcile with any view of history as progress towards a desirable goal.

## The dangers of determinism

These grounds for rejecting theories of history are closely related to another argument which has often been given heavy emphasis: that theory denies not only the 'uniqueness' of events but also the dignity of the individual and the power of human agency. Traditional narrative shorn of any explanatory framework gives maximum scope to the play of personality, whereas a concern with recurrent or typical aspects of social structure and social change elevates abstraction at the expense of real living individuals. Worst of all from this viewpoint are theories of the third kind, whose insidious effect is to confer an inevitability on the historical process which individuals are powerless to change, now or in the future; all theories of history, the argument goes, have determinist elements, and determinism is a denial of human freedom.[10] The polar opposite of determinism is the rejection of any meaning in history beyond the play of the contingent and the unforeseen – a view held by many historians in the mainstream of the discipline. A.J.P. Taylor delighted in informing his readers that the only lesson taught by the study of the past is the incoherence and unpredictability of human affairs: history is a chapter of accidents and blunders.[11]

Lastly, the traditionalists recoil from one of the main practical consequences of writing theory-oriented history, which is to place history in a dependent relationship with the social sciences. Theory-minded historians, they maintain, do not develop their own models but apply the theoretical findings of sociology, social anthropology and economics – disciplines whose focus is on the present not the past, and who are interested in history only as a testing ground for their own theories. Theoretical historians simply play into their hands and undermine the autonomy of their own discipline. Historians ought to be vigilant about threats to the distinctiveness of their calling, whether from within or without. Elton goes further: in its undiluted form, history offers the surest antidote against the system-builders among the social scientists who proffer pat solutions to complex human problems.[12]

## The conservatism of historians

Elton's view suggests one explanation as to why the historical profession has been so strongly averse to theory, and that is its conservatism. The study of history has attracted more than its fair share of conservatives concerned to invoke the sanction of the past in defence of institutions threatened by radical reform, or quite simply to find a mental escape from the disorienting impact of rapid social change around them. The true conservative, lacking a vision of progress, distrusts theories of the meaning of history as the rhetoric of the **Utopian** Left and is alarmed by the notion of a general model of social change which might be employed to push through undesirable projects of social engineering in the future. But the research methods of historians themselves have also acted as a strong antidote to theory. As M.M. Postan put it, the

> critical attitude to **minutiae** has become in the end a powerful agent of selection. It now attracts to history persons of a cautious and painstaking disposition, not necessarily endowed with any aptitude for theoretical synthesis.[13]

In fact a great deal of the opposition to theory is born of prejudice. The negative tendencies which the traditionalists have identified are certainly there and if allowed free rein would lead to the damaging consequences which alarm them so much; but as any examination of the better examples of theoretical history will show, these tendencies do not go unchecked, and the outcome is an enrichment rather than an impoverishment of historical understanding.

**Utopian**
Unrealistically idealistic. The term comes from Sir Thomas More's book *Utopia*, which imagines a perfect but unattainable society. 'Utopia', derived from the Greek u-topos, means 'no such place'.

**minutiae**
Very small details.

## The need to generalize

Consider, first of all, the contention that theory detracts from the uniqueness of historical events. Historians have in fact never written of events as though they were entirely unique, because it is impossible to do so. The very language which historians employ imposes a classification on their material and implies comparisons beyond their immediate field of interest. The only reason why scholars can use the phrase 'feudal tenure' of a particular relationship between lord and tenant, or the word 'revolution' of a major political upheaval, is because they share with their readers a common notion of what those words mean, based on a recognition that the world would be incomprehensible if we did not all the time subsume particular instances into general categories. The point was clearly made by E.E. Evans-Pritchard, the leading figure in the last generation of British social anthropologists, who advocated a cordial relationship between history and the social sciences:

> Events lose much, even all, of their meaning if they are not seen as having some degree of regularity and constancy, as belonging to a certain type of event, all instances of which have many features in common. King John's struggle with his barons is meaningful only when the relations of the barons to Henry I, Stephen, Henry II, and Richard are also known; and also when the relations between the kings and barons in other countries with feudal institutions are known; in other words, where the struggle is seen as a phenomenon typical of, or common to, societies of a certain kind.[14]

But if the use of generalizing concepts alerts us to regularities in the material, it also exposes those aspects which resist categorization and which give the event or situation its unique qualities. The contention of the theoretical historian is that if these comparisons are implicit in any historical analysis worth the name, then there is everything to be gained in clarity of thought by making them explicit – by constructing, for example, a model of feudal society or of revolutionary change.

## Is history concerned with individuals?

Equally, the claim that history is the rightful province of the individual looks dangerously misleading on closer inspection.

Historians are compelled at every turn to classify people into groups, whether by nationality, religion, occupation or class. This is because it is these larger identities which confer significance on them as social beings. And what these groups have in common is a tendency to think and act in certain ways, to the point where their response can be predicted. No two individuals are ever entirely alike, but how they behave in certain roles (e.g. as consumers of foodstuffs or as adherents of a particular creed) may follow a highly regular pattern. The emphasis that historians place on group activity is not, therefore, a denial of human individuality but simply a recognition that what the individual does in common with others usually has far greater impact, historically, than anything else he or she does. Furthermore, the cumulative effect of the actions which a particular group takes in pursuit of its objectives is to *institutionalize* that behaviour – that is, to entrench it in such a way that the options open to individuals thereafter are constrained or (to use a useful sociological term) *structured*. This is not the same as saying that people's actions are determined: certain patterns of behaviour may be strongly indicated, but they can be rejected or modified by the resolve of a new generation to break out of the mould. No one has expressed the tension between human agency and social structuring more lucidly than Philip Abrams, who significantly combined the professions of historian and sociologist:

> The two-sidedness of society, the fact that social action is both something we choose to do and something we have to do, is inseparably bound up with the further fact that whatever reality society has is an historical reality, a reality in time. When we refer to the two-sidedness of society we are referring to the ways in which, in time, actions become institutions and institutions are in turn changed by action. Taking and selling prisoners becomes the institution of slavery. Offering one's services to a soldier in return for his protection becomes feudalism. Organizing the control of an enlarged labour force on the basis of standardized rules becomes bureaucracy. And slavery, feudalism and bureaucracy become the fixed, external settings in which struggles for prosperity or survival or freedom are then pursued. By substituting cash payments for labour services the lord and peasant jointly embark on the dismantling of the feudal order their great-grandparents had constructed.[15]

The best theories – and I will argue shortly that Marxism is one of these – owe their appeal precisely to the fact that they acknowledge and seek to elucidate the reciprocal relationship of action and structure. Theory does not devalue the individual; it seeks rather to explain the constraints which limit people's freedom and frustrate their intentions, and in doing so it uncovers patterns in history. By contrast, the historian who maintains an exclusive focus on the thoughts and actions of individuals (as diplomatic historians all too often do) is likely to find no shape and to see instead only a chaotic sequence of accident and blunder.

## Lessons from social science

As for the threatened submergence of history by the social sciences, there are strong reasons why historians should – in the first instance at least – avail themselves of imported theory. The social sciences are by definition concerned with what people do in aggregates rather than as individuals; and since their range embraces entire societies, social scientists have from the outset needed theory in order to engage with their subject matter at all. Economists since **Adam Smith** in the late eighteenth century and sociologists since **Auguste Comte** in the mid-nineteenth century have regarded explicit theory as a prerequisite for interpreting their data, and as a result a body of sophisticated theoretical knowledge has been built up in both disciplines, and latterly in social anthropology too. The use made by historians of these theories is simply an acknowledgement that the social sciences have a head start. In fact history has always been influenced by theorists from without, Smith and Comte being cases in point. But it is only in the past forty years that historians have begun to take the measure of the full range and versatility of social science theory.

There are two real problems here. One is that much social science theory, especially in economics, is intended to explain quite restricted fields of activity, often in a somewhat artificially detached way, and the result of applying this theory to historical work may be to intensify the 'tunnel vision' to which historians specializing in a particular branch are anyway so prone (see p. 137). The other problem concerns the alleged indifference to history of the social sciences. This charge is not without foundation. Many theories, for example that of the free-market economy, are based on the premise of equilibrium, which strikes

**Adam Smith (1723–90)**
Scottish economist. Smith is the most important of the eighteenth-century neo-classical school of economic theory; his 1776 work *The Wealth of Nations* is generally credited with having invented the modern study of economics. Smith held that economies are governed by a 'hidden hand' of market forces and therefore thrive best when government regulation and interference are kept to a minimum.

**Auguste Comte (1798–1857)**
French political philosopher and founder of the positivist school. Positivism aims to integrate the different branches of knowledge into a coherent whole.

JOHN LILBURNE ON THE PILLORY.

John Lilburne, political agitator and English leader of the Levellers. Here, he appeals to a crowd as he stands at a pillory. (Mary Evans Picture Library)

**ahistorical**
In breach of the rules of the historical discipline, e.g. by dealing with historical events out of context, or even in the wrong context.

historians as a profoundly **ahistorical** way of conceiving society – a denial of the trajectories of change and adjustment which are present in every case; and other theories (such as the modernization theory so prevalent in American sociology) which purport to embrace a historical dimension are based on a naïve antithesis between 'traditional' and 'modern' at odds with any sense of process in history. Certainly much of the borrowing by historians from the social sciences has been shallow and uncritical, and it has too readily assumed that theory is somehow value-free and objective, whereas it is the subject of sharp ideological differences among social scientists themselves.[16] But neither of these objections is a reason for avoiding theory; they suggest only that historians should be discriminating about what they take on board. In fact the theories whose influence on recent historians has been particularly pervasive are those which seek to encompass social structure or social change as a whole, and of these theories the most influential are derived from the great social thinkers of the nineteenth century, who had a profound sense of history – Max Weber and above all Karl Marx. But the real answer to the traditionalists' fear of absorption by the social sciences is that these theories are not tablets from Heaven to be inscribed on the historical record. They should be seen rather as a point of departure. The result of historical work will be to modify them, probably quite drastically, and to erect in their place theories which represent a genuine cross-fertilization between history and social science. Both sides can only benefit from that outcome.

# III

## The case against Marxist history

The way is now open for a discussion in which the Marxist interpretation of history can be assessed in the context of the dangers and opportunities that attend any venture in theoretical history. The dangers in this case are familiar enough: Marx's detractors have made such play with some of the less attractive tendencies in his thought that, to all except the fairly restricted number of people who have read Marx himself or academic commentaries on his writings, he is associated with a bleak determinism and an utter cynicism about human nature. On this reading, the central tenets of Marxism go something like this. 'History is subject to the inexorable control of economic forces, which move all human societies along the road to socialism through the same stages, capitalism being the stage currently occupied by most of humankind. At all times material self-interest has been the mainspring of human behaviour, regardless of the motives people have actually professed. Classes represent the collective expression of this self-interest, and all history is therefore nothing more than the history of class conflict. Ideology, art and culture are merely a mirror of this fundamental identification, having no historical dynamic of their own. The individual is the product of his or her own age and class and however talented and forceful is powerless to affect the course of history; it is the masses who make history, but even they only do so according to a predetermined pattern.' At one time or another in the hundred years that have elapsed since Marx's death, each of these propositions has been subscribed to by Marxists, but all of them represent a crude simplification of what he actually wrote. Marx's thought was developed over some thirty years of research and reflection, and the resulting corpus of theory is far more complex and subtle than the **shibboleths** of 'vulgar' Marxism allow.

**shibboleth**
(Hebrew) A derogatory term for a slogan or catchphrase.

## The basis of Marxist theory

Marx began with the fundamental premise that what distinguishes people from animals is their ability to produce their means of subsistence. In the struggle to satisfy their physiological and material needs, men and women have developed progressively more efficient means of exploiting their environment (or mastering nature, as Marx would have put it). To the question 'what is history about?' Marx answered that it was about the growth of human productive power, and he looked forward to the time when the basic needs of all people would be amply satisfied: only then would humanity find self-fulfilment and achieve its full potential in every sphere. In maintaining that the only true, objective view of the historical process was rooted in the material conditions of life, Marx sharply distinguished himself from the main currents of nineteenth-century historiography with their choice of nationalism, freedom or religion as the defining themes of history. It is entirely appropriate that Marx's view should be referred to as 'historical materialism', a term coined by his life-long collaborator and intellectual heir, Friedrich Engels. From this basic perspective, first sketched in *The German Ideology* (1846), Marx never wavered. For the rest of his life much of his effort was devoted to working out its implications for the interpretation of social structure, the stages of social evolution, and the nature of social change.

## Marx's analysis of society

Marx conceived of society as comprising three constituent levels. Underlying all else are the *forces of production* (or productive forces): that is, the tools, techniques and raw materials together with the labour power that realizes their productive potential. The forces of production have certain implications for the *relations of production* (or productive relations) by which Marx meant the division of labour and the forms of cooperation and subordination required to sustain production – in other words the economic structure of society. This structure in turn forms a base or foundation on which is built the *superstructure*, composed of legal and political institutions and their supporting ideology. The most succinct summary of Marx's view of social structure appears in the preface to his *A Contribution to the Critique of Political Economy* (1859):

> In the social production of their existence, men inevitably enter into definite relations, which are independent of their will, namely relations of production appropriate to a given stage in the development of their material forces of production. The totality of these relations of production constitutes the economic structure of society, the real foundation, on which arises a legal and political superstructure and to which correspond definite forms of social consciousness. The mode of production of material life conditions the general process of social, political and intellectual life. It is not the consciousness of men that determines their existence, but their social existence that determines their consciousness.[17]

## A determinist model?

However, this is not the crudely deterministic model that it has so often been taken to be. In the first place, the forces of production are by no means confined to the instruments of production and the brawn of the workers. Technical ingenuity and scientific knowledge (on which the further development of the forces of production so clearly depended by Marx's day) are also included: full allowance is made for human creativity, without which we would remain slaves of the natural world around us. Secondly, although it clearly follows from Marx's view that politics and ideology – the traditional preoccupations of the historian – can only be understood in relation to the economic base, Marx also allowed for influences in the reverse direction. For example, no system of economic relations can become established without a prior framework of property rights and legal obligations; that is to say, the superstructure does not just reflect the relations of production but has an enabling function as well. The three-tier model thus allows for reciprocal influences.[18] And thirdly, Marx did not suggest that all non-economic activities were determined by the base. It is arguable whether artistic creation should be included in the superstructure at all. But even those spheres that belong unequivocally to the superstructure are not *exclusively* determined by the base. Both political institutions and religion have their own dynamic, as Marx and Engels acknowledged in their own historical writings, and in the short term especially economic factors may be of subsidiary importance in accounting for events; as Braudel observes, Marx was essentially a theorist of *la longue durée* (see p. 163).[19] It is probably closer to the spirit of Marx's thought to see the economic structure as setting limiting conditions rather than determining the elements of the superstructure in all their particularity. Engels was most emphatic on this point. As he wrote to a correspondent some years after Marx's death:

> According to the materialistic conception of history, the *ultimately* determining element in history is the production and reproduction of real life.
>
> More than this neither Marx nor I has ever asserted. Hence if somebody twists this into saying that the economic element is the *only* determining one he transforms that proposition into a meaningless, abstract, senseless phrase. The economic situation is the basis, but the various elements of the superstructure . . . also exercise their influence upon the course of the historical struggles and in many cases preponderate in determining their *form*.[20]

Clearly the base/superstructure metaphor lends itself to a deterministic interpretation, and several of Marx's utterances can be so interpreted, but his *oeuvre* as a whole does not suggest that he saw it in such stark terms.

**oeuvre**
(French) An author's complete works.

## Marx's analysis of history

One of the best-known features of Marx's thought is his periodization of history. He distinguished three historical epochs down to his own day, each moulded by a progressively more advanced mode of production. These were Ancient Society (Greece and Rome), Feudal Society, which emerged after the fall of the Roman Empire, and Capitalist (or 'modern bourgeois') Society, which had first come into being in England in the seventeenth century and had since triumphed elsewhere in Europe, particularly as a consequence of the French Revolution. What gave political edge to the periodization was Marx's conviction that Capitalist Society must in due course give way to Socialist Society and the complete self-fulfilment of humankind; indeed when he first sketched the scheme in 1846 he believed the advent of socialism to be imminent. Marx maintained that his periodization was the outcome of his historical enquiries rather than of dogmatic theorizing, and that is borne out by the changes and qualifications he made in the light of fuller research. He later posited an additional mode of production in the form of Germanic Society, contemporaneous with Ancient Society and one of the sources of Feudal Society.[21] He placed Asia in a distinct category from Europe: according to Marx, the Asiatic mode of production had an inadequate internal dynamic of historical change, and capitalism (and thus ultimately socialism) could be established in the Orient only as a result of colonialism. And in the Russian case, he retreated from his earlier view that full-scale capitalism was the indispensable prerequisite of socialism, forty years before the Russian Revolution. Marx reproved those critics who

> must metamorphose my historical sketch of the genesis of capitalism in Western Europe into a historic-philosophic theory of the general path every people is fated to tread, whatever the historical circumstances in which it finds itself.[22]

In short, Marx did not lay down a single evolutionary path which all human societies are predetermined to follow exactly.

## Dialectic in production as the motor of social change

Such a rigid periodization would have ill consorted with Marx's view of social change, the richest and most suggestive part of his theory of history. Marx summed up his interpretation in the passage which immediately follows the extract from the 1859 preface quoted earlier:

> At a certain stage of development, the material productive forces of society come into conflict with the existing relations of production or – this merely expresses the same thing in legal terms – with the property relations within the framework of which they have operated hitherto. From forms of development of the productive forces these relations turn into their fetters. Then begins an era of social revolution. The changes in the economic foundation lead sooner or later to the transformation of the whole immense superstructure.[23]

Marx believed that the contradiction or *dialectic* between the forces of production and the relations of production was the principal determinant of long-term historical change: each mode of production contains within it the seeds of its successor. Thus, to take an example on which he held emphatic views, the English Revolution of the seventeenth century occurred because the forces of production characteristic of capitalism had reached the point where their further development was held back by the feudal property relations sanctioned by the early Stuart monarchy; the outcome of the revolution was a remodelling of the relations of production which cleared the way for the Industrial Revolution a hundred years later.

## Class conflict

This rather abstract conception of historical change is made visible in the form of *class conflict*. Marx identified classes not according to wealth, status or education – the usual criteria employed in his day – but quite specifically in terms of their role in the productive process. The division of labour which has characterized every mode of production since Ancient Society results in the creation of classes whose true interests are mutually antagonistic. Each successive stage has had its dominant class and has also harboured the class destined to overthrow it. Thus Marx ascribed the English Revolution to the urban bourgeoisie, who were developing the new capitalist forces of production, just as he expected socialism to be achieved in his own day by the new factory proletariat spawned by industrial capitalism. It is class conflict expressing the contradictions within society that drives history in a forward direction. This is not to say that the masses are the makers of history. Although Marx believed that humanity's prospects for a better future lay in the hands of the **proletariat,** his interpretation confined the masses to an **ancillary** role in earlier history; he was only too well aware that the world in which he lived was essentially the creation of the bourgeoisie, whom Marx both admired and reviled for what they had achieved.

Marx's conception of class is the point at which his view of the role of human agency in history can be assessed. Class is defined in structural terms according to its relation to the means of production, but Marx knew that for a class to be effective politically requires a *consciousness* of their class in its members. The long-term trajectory of change may be determined by the dialectic

**proletariat**
The industrial working class. The term passed into general use after it was popularized in the writings of Karl Marx.

between the forces and relations of production, but the timing and the precise form of the transition from one stage to the next depend on the awareness and capacity for action of real human beings. Indeed, Marx's entire career was devoted to equipping the proletariat of his time with an understanding of the material forces at work in their own society so that they would know when and how to act against the capitalist system. People are the victims of material forces, but in the right conditions they have the opportunity to be agents of historical change. That paradox lies at the centre of Marx's view of history. As he wrote in his finest piece of contemporary history, 'The eighteenth Brumaire of Louis Bonaparte' (1852):

> Men make their own history, but they do not make it just as they please; they do not make it under circumstances chosen by themselves, but under circumstances directly encountered, given, and transmitted from the past.[24]

How Marx understood the reciprocal relationship of action and circumstances is never made clear, but what he claimed to have done was to reveal the long-term structural factors which render certain historical developments inevitable in the long run. These are, so to speak, the defining limits within which the actions of men and women, whether as individuals or as groups, have their scope.

# IV

## Marx's critique of historians

What were the implications of Marx's theories for the actual writing of history? As we have seen, these theories lend themselves to a simplified rigid schema, and this was the form in which they were expounded by many of the first Marxists, whose primary interest was in the political struggle and who were content with an unequivocal determinism which pointed towards a proletarian revolution in the near future. The founders of historical materialism were not in sympathy with this approach. As Engels remarked in 1890:

> Too many of the younger Germans simply make use of the phrase 'historical materialism' (and *everything* can be turned into a phrase)

only in order to get their own relatively scanty historical knowledge – for economic history is still in its swaddling clothes! – constructed into a neat system as quickly as possible, and they then deem themselves something very tremendous.[25]

Marx was emphatic that his theory was a guide to study, not a substitute for it:

> Viewed apart from real history, these abstractions have in themselves no value whatsoever. They can only serve to facilitate the arrangement of historical material, to indicate the sequence of its separate strata. But they by no means afford a recipe or schema, as does philosophy, for neatly trimming the epochs of history. On the contrary, our difficulties begin only when we set about the observation and the arrangement – the real depiction – of our historical material, whether of a past epoch or of the present.[26]

What Marx rejected was not historical study as such but the method employed by the leading historians of his day. Their error, he maintained, lay in taking at face value what the historical actors said about their motives and aspirations; in so doing, Ranke and his imitators imprisoned themselves within the dominant ideology of the age in question, which was merely a cloak for the real material interests of the dominant class. 'Objective' history – that is, the dialectic of forces and relations of production – was accessible through research into the economic structure of past societies without reference to the subjective utterances of historical personalities:

> Just as one does not judge an individual by what he thinks about himself, so one cannot judge such a period of transformation [i.e. a social revolution] by its consciousness, but, on the contrary, this consciousness must be explained from the contradictions of material life, from the conflict existing between the social forces of production and the relations of production.[27]

At the same time, Marx never developed a clear methodology of history. His own historical writings veered from the compelling political narrative of 'The eighteenth Brumaire' (1852) to the abstract economic analysis of the first volume of *Capital* (1867). And there remain ambiguities in his conception of both the forces and the relations of production, as well as the connection between base and superstructure. So historians working within the Marxist tradition have had plenty of interpretative work to do.

## The impact of Marxism

During the generation after Marx's death in 1883, historical materialism began to have a pervasive though somewhat blurred effect on the climate of intellectual opinion, as his major writings were translated into other European languages and socialist parties of a Marxist persuasion sprang up. Marxism was certainly one of the main currents contributing to the emergence of economic history as a distinct field of enquiry (see pp. 125–6). As J.H. Clapham – no friend of socialism – conceded in 1929, 'Marxism, by attraction and repulsion, has perhaps done more to make men think about economic history and inquire into it than any other teaching'.[28] But the content and method of the Marxist interpretation took longer to make an impact. It first affected the practice of professional historians on a significant scale in the Soviet Union, where, from the Bolshevik takeover until Stalin's clampdown in 1931–2, historical research and debate within a Marxist framework were very lively.[29] The subjection of historical work to a strict party line in Russia coincided with the emergence of Marxism as a powerful intellectual stimulus in the West. This was prompted by the obvious crisis in capitalism as a result of the **Great Crash of 1929** and the apparent bankruptcy of liberal democracy in the face of Fascism. But although important pioneer work in Marxist history was done in Britain and elsewhere during the 1930s, it was mostly achieved by active members of the Communist Party, who were viewed with suspicion by most historians and received little academic preferment. Since the 1950s, however, Marxist approaches to history have been much more widely influential – and with historians who have no connection with the Communist Party and in many cases are not politically active at all. Many of the acknowledged leaders of the profession such as Christopher Hill and E.J. Hobsbawm write from a Marxist perspective. Hobsbawm himself put the case fairly in 1978 when he wrote:

> It is probably impossible today for any non-Marxist historian not to discuss either Marx or the work of some Marxist historian in the course of his or her normal business as a historian.[30]

Why is it that a historical interpretation which originated as a revolutionary critique of contemporary society and which is open to dogmatic abuse commands so much attention among scholars?

**Great Crash of 1929**
The disastrous fall in prices on the New York Stock Exchange on 24 October 1929, which ended the prosperity of the 1920s and ushered in the worldwide economic depression of the 1930s. Also known as the Wall Street Crash.

The reason can hardly be any longer the central role accorded by
Marxism to economic history, since the majority of economic historians (particularly in Britain and the United States) are
non-Marxist. Nor can the appeal of Marxism be attributed to the
attractions of an 'underdog' view of history: although the Marxist
approach gives great weight to the role of the masses at certain
historical conjunctures, it does not offer a worm's-eye view of
history, nor is it concerned to celebrate the heroism of earlier generations of proletarians. The real reason for Marxism's strong
appeal is that it answers so well to the historian's need for theory
– and in all three of the areas where theory is least dispensable.

## The usefulness of Marxist social analysis

Through the base/superstructure model Marxism offers a particularly useful way of conceiving the totality of social relations in
any given society. It is not just that the political, social, economic
and technological all have their place; in a full-scale Marxist
analysis these familiar distinctions lose their force. Social and
economic history become inseparable, and the study of politics is
saved from becoming the minute reconstruction of the antics of
professional politicians in their own arena, to which it can so
easily be restricted by the specialist (see p. 124). The appeal of
'total history' as practised by the *Annales* school also rests on its
opposition to compartmentalization, but Braudel and his followers have conspicuously failed to develop a satisfactory model
for integrating political history with the environmental and demographic studies which provide the backbone of their work (see
pp. 162–3). In this respect at least, it must be counted as inferior
to Marxist history with its emphasis on the reciprocal interaction
between the productive forces, the relations of production and the
superstructure. It is no accident that Hobsbawm, one of the finest
writers of the broad historical survey today, is a Marxist with a
profound grasp of the master's own writings.[31]

It is the same reciprocal interaction which saves Marxism from
the ahistorical error so common in other theories of regarding
social equilibrium as the norm. Marxist historians hold as a fundamental premise that all societies contain both stabilizing
elements and disruptive elements (or contradictions), and that historical change occurs when the latter burst out of the existing

social framework and through a process of struggle achieve a new order. Historians have found the notion of the dialectic to be an invaluable tool in analyzing social change of varying intensity, from the barely perceptible movement within a stable social formation to periods of revolutionary ferment.

## History as progress?

Marxism's claim to find a direction in the whole historical process is the most difficult part of its appeal to assess. Marxist historians today are certainly not much given to writing in terms of grand evolutionary schemes, and it is likely that only a minority are interested in the light their enquiries might shed on the prospect of a classless society mapped out by Marx for the future. But there can be little doubt that Marxism is today the principal legatee of the view of history as progress. The notion that the major social conflicts in history issue in change for the better exerts a powerful appeal, clearly present in one of Christopher Hill's most unequivocally Marxist statements on the English Civil War:

> A victory for Charles I and his gang could only have meant the economic stagnation of England, the stabilization of a backward feudal society in a commercial age, and have necessitated an even bloodier struggle for liberation later. The Parliamentarians thought they were fighting God's battles. They were certainly fighting those of posterity, throwing off an intolerable **incubus** to further advance.[32]

**incubus**
(Latin) Originally a demon who possessed and deformed unborn children in the womb, hence a major hindrance or encumbrance.

Adherence to the Marxist framework can have the effect of conferring on quite limited enquiries a significance which arises from their place in a grand historical process.

## Divisions within Marxism: culturalism v. economism

Response to the strong pull exerted by Marxism's theoretical range does not, however, mean that historians practising in the Marxist tradition are confined within an orthodoxy. What is striking about the growth of Marxist historiography during the past thirty years or so, especially in Britain, is its diversity. As familiarity with Marx's writing has spread, so historians have responded to the different and quite contradictory strands in his *oeuvre*, reflected in a major divide in recent Marxist scholarship between what insiders call 'culturalism' and 'economism'. This divide is best illustrated by reaction to the most widely read work of Marxist history ever written in this country – E.P. Thompson's *The Making of the English Working Class* (see p. 135). The central theme of the book is how, in reaction to proletarianization and political repression, the English labouring classes developed a new consciousness so that by 1830 they had achieved a collective identity as a working class and the capacity for collective political action: that consciousness was not the automatic by-product of the factory system but was the outcome of reflection on experience in the light of a vigorous native radical tradition. The book is thus 'a study in an active process, which owes as much to agency as to conditioning'.[33] Thompson himself maintains that his book was true to Marx's recognition that men do, in some measure, 'make their own history'. His critics argued that Thompson underestimated the force of the qualification added by Marx to that statement. They pointed out that in omitting any detailed discussion of the transition from one mode of production to another, Thompson failed to acknowledge the rootedness of class in economic relations and therefore exaggerated the role of collective agency; because Thompson was lax in his theory, he became trapped within the subjective experience of his protagonists.[34] Thompson was unrepentant; he reaffirmed the need to hold theory and experience in some kind of balance and to interpret Marxism as an evolving and flexible tradition rather than a closed system,[35] and such is the power of his own historical writing that 'culturalism' – or 'socialist humanism' as Thompson preferred to call it[36] – is likely to coexist with 'economism' within the Marxist fold for the foreseeable future.

## The working class and Marxist theory

*The Making of the English Working Class* expresses another marked tendency within British Marxist historiography, and that is its interest in the history of popular movements, almost regardless their efficacy. One of the criticisms which can be made of Marxism, as of other goal-oriented interpretations of history, is that it distorts our understanding of the past by concentrating unduly on those people and movements which were on the side of

**handloom weavers**
Those who wove cloth on individual looms usually operated within the worker's home under the old 'domestic' system of textile production which preceded the introduction of factory production. Handloom weavers were eventually forced out of the market by competition from factories, so they are often used by historians as an indication of the impact of the new methods of production in the early nineteenth century.

**Diggers**
A seventeenth-century radical group led by Gerrard Winstanley who established a series of self-supporting communal settlements in Surrey in 1649, at the end of the English Civil War. Regarded by Cromwell and Fairfax as dangerous subversives, the Diggers were suppressed by the army the following year.

**Ranters**
The name given to various groups of extreme religious radicals in the years following the end of the English Civil War. Strongly opposed to any form of laws or control, the Ranters went far beyond the norms even of radical religious practice by going naked, swearing and blaspheming from the pulpit, and indulging in public fornication. They

'progress'. But Thompson's emphasis falls less on the new factory workforce, which was the nucleus of the organized working class of the future, than on the casualties of the Industrial Revolution – people such as the **handloom weavers** whose means of livelihood was destroyed by the factory system. This tendency is even more pronounced in the work of Christopher Hill on the seventeenth century. In works such as *The World Turned Upside Down* (1972), his attention shifted more and more from the 'bourgeois' revolution which succeeded to the 'revolt within the Revolution'[37] – to the socialism and libertarianism of sects such as the **Diggers** and **Ranters** which were born before their time and were completely suppressed by the victors in the Civil War. But this emphasis is no antiquarian indulgence on Hill's part. His contention is that today we are living in a society in which the radical ideas of the sects have a practical socialist relevance – that by rediscovering a lost tradition we can learn from their ideas and experience; at the end of *The World Turned Upside Down* we are urged to be 'doers not talkers only'.[38] In the same spirit – though less plausibly – Thompson suggests that the lost popular causes of the English Industrial Revolution may yield insights which can be acted upon today; if not in England then in the Third World, where industrialization is still in its infancy.[39]

## Marxism and the state

Yet for all the fascination held by popular movements, Marxist history is not just 'history from below' (and neither Thompson nor Hill ever suggested that it is). Struggles between classes are ultimately resolved at the political level, and it is through control of the state that new dispositions of class power are sustained. In fact it can be argued, though it is not very fashionable to do so, that 'history from above' is just as important a perspective for Marxist historians. The results are more interesting than might seem likely at first sight. For the state cannot just be written off as the political arm of whichever class happens to enjoy hegemony at the time: that is a 'vulgar' Marxist simplification. The interpretation most favoured today is that the state's historic role is to defend the common and long-term interests of the dominant class – and more particularly to promote the conditions in which the mode of production on which that hegemony is based can be reproduced into the next generation. In doing this the state may often find itself in conflict with the urgent short-term interests of particular sections within the ruling class. Thus Perry Anderson argues in his *Lineages of the Absolute State* (1974) that the antagonism often shown towards sections of the aristocracy by the absolutist monarchies of seventeenth- and eighteenth-century Europe must not obscure the fact that these regimes were deeply committed to the maintenance of feudal relations, and especially private landed property. A further development of the same idea is the notion that state power depends not only on control of the instruments of coercion but also on a certain legitimacy in the minds of the ruled; since that legitimacy will not be acknowledged if the state acts exclusively and nakedly in the interests of one class, there has to be some sensitivity to the common good and to principles of natural justice; the likely alternatives would be class conflict and sedition on a scale which might imperil the continuance of the dominant mode of production. For this reason the state has usually displayed a certain autonomy *vis-à-vis* the class it primarily represents, but how much autonomy should in practice be allowed to the state is understandably a source of considerable tension in class-dominated societies. Far from making political history redundant, then, a Marxist perspective requires a very careful analysis of the pressures to which the state has responded and which have often resulted in the implementation of varied and contradictory policies within the life-span of a single social formation. Thus in the area of history most burdened by the weight of conventional scholarship Marxist historiography contributes fresh and stimulating insights.

## The illusion of scientific precision

All the same a fair assessment of the Marxist theory of history is not made easier by the inflated claims advanced by Marx himself. The successive transformations of the mode of production could, he asserted, be 'determined with the precision of natural science',[40] and this view was fully endorsed by official **historiography in the Soviet bloc**. Like so many students of society in the nineteenth century, Marx was dazzled by the apparent successes of natural science. In directing attention at

were suppressed by the authorities, though it is not clear from the necessarily sensationalist accounts how widespread their activity and influence actually was.

*vis-à-vis*
(French) With regard to.

**historiography in the Soviet bloc**
The writing of history in the Soviet Union was closely controlled by the state to ensure that it adhered to Communist orthodoxy. Until the reforms introduced by Mikhail Gorbachev, General Secretary of the Communist Party between 1985 and 1990, Soviet archives were closed to all but officially approved historians, which in effect excluded any foreign scholars.

240

the material forces in history – rather than ideology or motive – Marx believed that he could overcome the subjectivity inherent in all mainstream history-writing. Yet even if it is accepted that long-term historical change *does* arise from the development of the productive process, scientific precision remains an illusory goal, for that process must necessarily be studied by reference to the records and other writings of people whose perceptions of the material world around them were distorted by non-materialist considerations. Penetration beyond the professed meaning of the sources to their 'real' meaning is very much a matter of flair and judgement rather than watertight logical demonstration. Confining the search for causes to materialist factors does not free the Marxist from the difficulties which attend any venture in historical explanation – the gaps in the record and the failure of the evidence to yield clear and unequivocal connections of cause and consequence.

## The structuralist rejection of historical method

For the Marxist there are two possible responses to this unsatisfactory state of affairs. The first is to place theory on an elevated pedestal where it is untouched by the mundane world of empirical evidence: the deeper structures which underlie both the past and the present cannot be grasped by assembling all the facts but can be apprehended only by those in possession of the correct theory. This was the position adopted by the influential 'structuralist' school of Marxism, led by the French philosopher Louis Althusser. Correct theory is derived from a correct reading of Marx's mature works, especially *Capital*, in a form which practically amounts to a denial of human agency in history. A renunciation of the empirical method is defended (in the teeth of Marx's statements to the contrary) on the grounds that all historical documentation is tainted by the structure of thought and language prevalent at the time of writing: the 'real' facts of history are beyond our reach, and the distorted images we have of the past are an irrelevance.[41] Naturally enough historians react strongly against this dismissal of the premises on which their discipline is founded, and it is not difficult to puncture Althusser's case. Historians do not rely exclusively on written texts; they also exploit material artefacts which yield evidence about the past

*Capital*
Marx's major work of economic analysis, first published in 1867. It was originally intended to be a three-part work, but only the first part was ever published in full. It contains Marx's analysis of the development of capitalism out of the feudal and primitive economies which had preceded it and his argument that capitalism, as an inherently exploitative system, would inevitably implode, leading to the establishment of a socialist system.

independently of language and its associations. And – more centrally – the whole critical apparatus deployed by historians on written sources is designed to penetrate the mental categories of the writer and the culture in which he or she wrote, and by piecing together widely disparate evidence to arrive at a perception of the period which was beyond the reach of any contemporary.[42] Even among Marxist ideologues the Althusserian fashion is decidedly on the wane. It has had very little influence on the practice of history or on the view taken of it by the wider public.

## The dangers of Marxist reductionism

The second response is to acknowledge, without overstating, the limitations which the nature of historical enquiry imposes on the aspiration to be 'scientific', and to participate in a common enterprise with historians of other persuasions. Broadly speaking this is the course pursued by Hill, Hobsbawm, Thompson and most Marxist historians writing in Britain today. This entails engaging seriously with the criticism most often levelled at theory-oriented history, and Marxism especially, that it is 'reductionist'. By reductionism is meant the *a priori* selection of one level of reality as fundamental, and the interpretation of everything else in terms of that one level. Perhaps the biggest weakness of Marxist theory is that it does not recognize the strength of associations which men and women enter into for reasons which have nothing to do with production. It is not difficult to argue that identification by religion, race or nationality has been at least as important over the long term as identification by class. These loyalties cannot simply be dismissed as 'false consciousness' promoted by the ruling class to blind the lower orders to their real condition of exploitation; it is much more likely that they satisfy a fundamental human need. Like other social theorists Marx could not help being unduly influenced by what was observable in his own day when advancing his universalist claims. Class identification and class conflict were characteristic features of the industrializing societies of Germany, France and Britain in which Marx passed all his life, but they were much less pronounced in earlier periods, and historians of pre-industrial societies have great difficulty in applying Marxist theory in a comprehensive fashion.

*a priori*
(Latin) Following logically from the previous point.

After the fall of the Berlin Wall in November 1989 popular insurrection overturned Communist governments across Eastern Europe. Some held that Marxism itself had been discredited; graffiti on this statue of Marx and Engels in Dresden, in East Germany, has them declaring 'We are not guilty', a view shared by many who saw the Soviet dictatorship as a perversion of Marxism. Not everyone agreed, however, and many statues of Marx and Engels, like those of Lenin, were overturned and smashed. (Alamy/ICP)

Significantly, Hill's work on seventeenth-century England has shown a progressively stronger tendency to treat religious persuasion as an independent variable.[43] Marxism holds many insights for the history of the Middle Ages and the early modern period, but it is not an adequate vehicle for a 'total history' of pre-industrial societies in Europe – and still less in Asia and Africa.

# V

## Marxism and the fall of Communism

The extended treatment I have given to the Marxist theory of history may seem to some readers like a self-indulgent surrender to an outmoded radicalism. Has not Marxism now been placed on the scrap-heap with the reduction of the world's Marxist governments to a tiny handful and the collapse of international Communism since 1989? Even before that date a group of self-styled 'revisionists' was setting out to turn back the Marxist tide and to topple the ascendancy of Hill, Thompson and Hobsbawm

– 'that cohort of scholars whose minds were formed in the matrix of **inter-war Marxism**', as one of the revisionists remarked.[44] The conservatives' distrust of Marxism has certainly had full rein during the past fifteen years.

It is too early to tell what the long-term intellectual consequences of the sea-change of 1989–92 will be, but two reasons suggest that Marxism will not be quickly written off. First, most Marxist historians were not very interested in how their work might bear on the political present and future, preferring to minimize the links between Marx's theory of history and his theory of revolutionary politics. Secondly, no amount of political adversity today can alter the fact that, quantitatively and qualitatively, Marxism has had a completely exceptional impact on the writing of history. No other theory can match its range and sophistication. For as long as historians recognize the need for theory, they will be drawn to the Marxist tradition.

## Alternative theoretical models

The grounds for that prediction will become clear as we consider the comparative lack of theoretical development in other kinds of history. Marxism has of course encountered strong opposition from many British historians, but not on the whole *theoretical* opposition. When conservatives have rejected the categories of historical materialism, they have done so by appealing to the central importance of other historical forces, such as the rule of law, the nation-state or the Church as community.[45] These concerns lead to a different focus, but they do not by and large generate a theorized history. The surviving historical record is so top-heavy with their concerns that conservatives can adopt a beguiling empiricism in their work. From this perspective, theory is the desperate recourse of those who are struggling to come in from the margins; historians who deal with the world as it is, rather than as it might be, do not need to embrace theory. One of the few exceptions has been the use of modernization theory by economic historians explaining the global transition to industrialized urban societies since the eighteenth century, and this never became very popular outside the United States.[46]

Theories of history therefore tend to be the province of the Left. Until the 1970s the hegemony of Marxism in Left circles was

**inter-war Marxism**
In the period between the two World Wars, the success of the Russian Revolution and the development of the world's first Communist state caught the imagination of many around the world, especially those increasingly disillusioned with the liberal democracies and repelled by the rise of Fascism. There therefore developed an extensive network of Communist sympathizers who were committed to spreading Communism to their own countries. Some took the opportunity to fight on the Republican side in the Spanish Civil War (1936–39); some of the most committed went on to spy for the Soviet Union after the Second World War.

such that rival theories tended to be advanced *within* the Marxist tradition, as already explained in relation to historians such as E.P. Thompson. More recently other theories have begun to take shape outside Marxism, though usually influenced by it. One focus for such thinking has been race and ethnicity. Under the umbrella of '**post-colonialism**' a number of writers have begun to advance a framework for understanding the modern world which deconstructs the traditional nation-state in terms of inter-dependence, ethnic diversity, racial '**othering**' and global inequality, and work along these lines will certainly grow in the next few years.[47] Another logical development would be a 'green' history, in which conceptualization and periodization would be organized round environmental issues; but there is little sign of that as yet.

## Gender history

The tendency to push theory in new directions is clearest at present in the elaboration of *gender* as a structuring principle fundamental to all historical analysis. The impetus here came from the growing awareness during the 1980s that an effective Left politics needed a new social base, and from changes in feminist thinking specifically. As we saw earlier, feminist historians were initially intent on finding a usable past by documenting women's historical experience and achievements (see pp. 5–6 and 133–4). For all its success in laying bare what had previously been concealed or denied, this kind of women's history had considerable limitations. It set out to recover a distinctive women's world – a 'herstory' – in opposition to mainstream history, but with no effective strategy for changing it (and in some instances with little interest in doing so). For some time it was unclear whether women's history would become one among several intellectual strands in the women's liberation movement, or a potentially transforming dimension of academic history. Developments during the 1980s and 1990s suggest the latter.

## Moving on from 'women's history'

As a mature historical practice women's history is today characterized by three principles which together open the way for a comprehensive historical theory. In the first place, 'woman' is

**post-colonialism**
The school of historical analysis which looks at the history of European imperialism from a more critical standpoint. An important feature of post-colonialist study is the central role it accords to the indigenous history and culture of colonized peoples.

**'othering'**
The process whereby a group or people establishing a sense of their own identity creates a hostile image of a second group which embodies all the characteristics and features the first group most dislikes and fears. The way in which the British constructed a hostile image of the French during the eighteenth century is a good example, but 'othering' the indigenous people was a common feature of European imperialism as well.

no longer seen as a single undifferentiated social category. Class, race and cultural beliefs about sexual difference have all had an immense influence on how women are perceived – and also how they perceive themselves – and most historical work relates to specific groups rather than womanhood in general; even when histories of women are attempted, social and cultural distinctions are central to the enterprise.[48] Secondly, just as the category of 'woman' has been disaggregated, so too has the notion of a uniform and constant oppression by men. The term 'patriarchy' has been criticized as implying that sexual difference is *the* fundamental principle of stratification in human society, present in all periods and thus 'outside' history; by explaining everything, it explains nothing. 'Patriarchy' can still usefully be used to indicate sexual hierarchy in the household, particularly where men control a form of domestic production, as they did in pre-industrial Europe. But the record of the past shows immense variety in the extent of oppression, resistance, accommodation and convergence in relations between men and women, and the task of the historian is to explain this variation

In the late 1960s and early 1970s the Women's Liberation movement led to the development of a feminist approach to history which sought to bring out the contribution of women and the many ways in which they were held down by the male-dominated societies of the past.
(CORBIS/Bettmann)

rather than submerge it in a universal principle of sexual oppression.[49] Thirdly and most important of all, women's history has increasingly taken the history of men within its scope: not men in their traditional appearance of genderless autonomous beings but men seen in relation to the other half of humanity. This means that men are considered historically as sons and husbands, while in the public sphere men's exclusion of women becomes a matter for investigation, instead of being taken for granted. As Jane Lewis has put it,

> our understanding of the sex/gender system can never hope to be complete until we have a deliberate attempt to understand the total fabric of men's worlds and the construction of masculinity.[50]

This approach has probably done more than any other to qualify earlier notions of patriarchy. Viewing both sexes in relation to each other tends to highlight variations of time and place at the expense of enduring structures. Feminist-inspired history has moved decisively from consciousness-raising to explanation.[51]

## Gender history and relations between the sexes

The history of gender represents a theoretically informed attempt to bring the two sexes and their complex relations into our picture of the past and in so doing to modify the writing of *all* history. It is by no means the only current within women's history, but it holds out the greatest promise for the discipline as a whole. In current usage 'gender' means the social organization of sexual difference. It embodies the assumption that most of what passes for natural (or God-given) sexual difference is in fact socially and culturally constructed and must therefore be understood as the outcome of historical process. (Of course it is that very confusion between nature and culture that has given stratification by gender such staying power and has caused it to escape notice in much of the historical record.) The focus of gender history is less on the predicament of one sex than on the whole field of relations between the sexes. And this field includes not just the obvious points of contact such as marriage and sex but all social relations and all political institutions, which, on this view, are in varying degrees structured by gender: by the exclusion of women, by the polarization of masculine and feminine attributes, and so on. Men are no less constructed by gender than women are. Both men's social power and their 'masculine' qualities can only be apprehended as aspects of a gender system: neither 'natural' nor constant, but defined by a shifting relation to the feminine. This perspective underlies recent writing on the tortuous evolution of the term 'manliness' since the early modern period, and the best work on the history of the family.[52] Because both sexes can only be correctly understood in relational terms, the history of gender is conceptually equipped to attain a fully comprehensive social reach; and on this basis it has the potential to offer a theory of social structure and of historical change.

## Gender history and Marxist theory

Comparisons with Marxist history are illuminating. Gender history has experienced the same tension between the demands of historical explanation and the politics of emancipation as the history of class has done. With its potential for a comprehensive social analysis, gender history also promises at the very least to make good some of the deficiencies of Marxist theory. Marxist historians are second to none in analyzing production, but their theory gives much less weight to reproduction – whether viewed as a biological event or a process of socialization. This is one of the strengths of the gender perspective, as recent work on women's place in the Industrial Revolution shows.[53] More broadly, gender history has the effect of collapsing the rigid distinction between the public and private spheres which has informed almost all historical writing, including Marxist work. That this distinction may have obscured the true complexity of economic and social life in the past is strongly indicated by Leonore Davidoff and Catherine Hall's *Family Fortunes* (1987), the most impressive achievement in gender history in Britain to date. Their central thesis is that in early nineteenth-century England one of the key objectives of the burgeoning business world was to support the family and domesticity – and conversely that the approved domestic traits of middle-class men (sobriety, sense of duty and so on) answered to the requirements of entrepreneurial and professional life. In work of this kind, the historical relationship of gender and class begins to be uncovered in all its intricate particularity.

## Patriarchy or production?

How that relationship should be theorized is a vexed question. Broadly speaking, feminist interpretations are aligned along a continuum between two 'purist' positions. At one end are those who treat patriarchy as the predetermining inequality, to which all other forms of social differentiation are secondary. At the other end the exact opposite is maintained by feminists concerned to keep their allies on the Left: that gender differences are an aspect of the relations of production, analytically located between the productive forces and the superstructure of society; in the more extreme versions class is held to determine gender. This divide may possibly be bridged by accepting what has been called a 'doubled vision' of the social order, embracing both gender and class, both public and private.[54] At all events understanding of these issues is more likely to be advanced by historical work than by any other discipline, which is one reason why the history of gender now receives increasing attention both within and outside the profession.

# VI

## Social theory and the 'big questions' of history

It is a common opinion among non-Marxist and non-feminist historians that the attempt to apply theory with real commitment to particular situations in the past results in a one-dimensional interpretation which distorts the true complexity of the historical process. But all historians, unless they are diehard traditionalists, concede that theory has been very productive of stimulating hypotheses. Its value, they claim, lies not in its explanatory power but in its capacity to raise interesting questions and to alert scholars to fresh source material – in a word, it has merit as a *heuristic* device. Historical research usually demonstrates that a given theory does not hold when confronted by the richness of actual experience, but in the process a new area of historical enquiry may be opened up. From this angle Marxist theory has a very good track record as a source of 'fertile error':[55] whatever its failings it has generated a great deal of historical knowledge about the connections between political process and the socio-economic structure. Much the same can be said of the

**heuristic**
Learning from discovery and experiment.

contribution of gender history to our knowledge of women and relations between the sexes. Equally it might be argued that the attempt to write comparative history has proved its worth less in revealing common patterns than in sharpening our awareness of the fundamental differences between the periods or places under discussion.

This might be termed the minimalist justification of the use of theory by historians. What it overlooks is that historical knowledge consists of more than specific conjunctures and processes in the past. Historians with their professional commitment to primary research all too easily forget that there are large-scale problems of historical interpretation which cry out for treatment: how to explain long-term processes such as the growth of industrialization or bureaucracy, and the recurrence of institutions such as feudalism or plantation slavery in widely separated societies. The broader the scope of the enquiry, the greater the need for theory which does not simply alert the historian to fresh evidence but which actually attempts to *explain* the process or pattern in question. Marxist historiography, if it has done nothing else, has at least brought some of the 'big questions' of history more insistently to the centre of the scholarly arena and has served to expose to scrutiny the unconscious models which so often inform the work of historians most resolute in their rejection of theory. The same salutary effect is now being produced by the application of theories of gender to the past.

The conscious application of social theory by historians to these broad questions is still in its infancy. It has given rise to a great deal of reductionist history by second-rate scholars anxious to prove their theoretical credentials. But in the hands of the best historians – and it is by their efforts that the enterprise should surely be judged – the awareness of context and the command of the sources ensure a proper relationship between theory and evidence. As Thompson put it, historical understanding advances by means of 'a delicate equilibrium between the synthesizing and the empiric modes, a quarrel between the model and the actuality'.[56] It is to be expected that, submitted to this discipline, social theories should be tried and found wanting, but that is no reason for renouncing their use. The business of historians is to apply theory, to refine it, and to develop new theory, always in the light of the evidence most broadly conceived. And they do so not in pursuit of the ultimate theory or 'law' which will 'solve' this or that problem of explanation but because without theory they cannot come to grips with the really significant questions in history.

## Theorists and the 'English Civil War'

Marxist history has made a particularly important contribution to the historiography of the English Civil Wars of 1642–9. In his book *The World Turned Upside Down*, the British historian Christopher Hill broke with orthodox analysis, which had concentrated on the constitutional arguments between Parliament and the Crown, to look at the explosion of radical political and religious groups the period also witnessed, such as the Levellers and Gerrard Winstanley's Diggers. Hill was not merely putting forward a version of 'history from below'; he was presenting the period as one in which constitutional and religious arguments were essentially conduits for a more fundamental conflict between classes. Other historians have responded to the relentlessly secular terms of Marxist analysis by stressing the roots of the conflict in actual religious belief, rather than viewing religion as a vehicle for non-religious issues of class control. The growth of nationalist movements in Scotland, Wales and Northern Ireland has led to a separate reappraisal of the period in British terms, in which the conflict between Crown and Parliament is seen as part of a much broader interplay of religious and constitutional issues in Ireland and Scotland, as well as England. Where the period used to be referred to simply as 'the English Civil War', it is now common to hear reference made, according to the standpoint of the speaker, to 'the English Revolution' or 'the British Civil Wars'.

## E.P. Thompson and *The Making of the English Working Class*

E.P. Thompson's 1963 *The Making of the English Working Class* won a wide popular readership for the way it brought the experiences of ordinary people to the historical forefront. It was the first systematic attempt to provide the working class as a whole, as opposed to the trade unions or the co-operative movement, with a heritage and a sense of collective identity. Thompson's book remains popular, particularly among those on the political Left, though it is admired across the political divide for the clarity of its style and for the humanity of its judgements. Thompson himself went on to become a leading figure in the Campaign for Nuclear Disarmament.

## Karl Marx and Friedrich Engels

Friedrich Engels (1820–95) was the son of a prosperous German cotton manufacturer. He acted as his father's agent in Manchester, then the centre of European cotton manufacture, and was thus able to gain a detailed understanding of the workings of the British economy and to observe at close hand the lives of the working classes, which he described in his 1844 exposé, *The Condition of the Working Classes in England*. He met Marx the same year, and the two men produced *The Communist Manifesto* in 1848, laying out the basic theory of Communism and calling on working men of all lands to unite to free themselves from oppression. After the failure of the European revolutions of 1848–9 Marx joined Engels in England and began the mammoth task of research in the British Museum Reading Room, which was to result in 1867 in his detailed critique of the capitalist system *Das Kapital* (*Capital*). Marx took a leading role in the First International, an international workers' association which, he hoped, would precipitate proletarian revolution and establish the communist order, but he was unable to prevent it from splitting into Marxist and anarchist factions. Marx died in poverty in 1883 and was buried in Highgate Cemetery in London, where his tomb is still a place of pilgrimage for socialists and Communists. Engels devoted the rest of his life to translating and editing Marx's works in order to bring them to a wider readership.

## *The eighteenth Brumaire of Louis Bonaparte*

Louis Napoleon Bonaparte (1808–73) was the third son of Napoleon I's brother Louis. He became head of the Bonaparte dynasty in 1832 on the death of Napoleon I's son, the Duke of Reichstadt. Napoleon I had come to power by means of a military *coup d'état* staged on 9 November 1799, or 18th Brumaire Year X in the revolutionary calendar then in use. Louis Napoleon sought to emulate him in two abortive *coup* attempts in 1836 and 1840, after the second of which he was imprisoned for life. He escaped to England but returned to France after the revolution of 1848 established a republic. He was elected to the new constituent assembly as a representative of the Parisian working class, and won the presidential elections of December 1848 with a huge majority. However, he soon fell into conflict with the elected assembly and resorted to ever more autocratic measures. On 2 December 1851 he sent troops to close the assembly, declared the constitution dissolved and ordered widespread arrests. A year later he declared a Second Empire with himself as the Emperor Napoleon III ('Napoleon II' having been the Duke of Reichstadt). Marx seized on this betrayal of working-class aspirations in his sardonic essay *The Eighteenth Brumaire of Louis Bonaparte* (*sic*), in which he coined the famous aphorism that when history repeats itself it does so 'the first time as tragedy, the second time as farce'. Napoleon III's subsequent career bore out Marx's cynicism: after a string of diplomatic and military failures he was overthrown after the disastrous war with Prussia of 1870–1 and ended his days as a political refugee and asylum seeker in England.

## Further reading

Mary Fulbrook, *Historical Theory*, Routledge, 2002

John Tosh (ed.), *Historians On History: an Anthology*, Longman, 2000

L.S. Feuer (ed.), *Karl Marx and Friedrich Engels: Basic Writings on Politics and Philosophy*, Fontana, 1969

Matt Perry, *Marxism and History*, Palgrave, 2002

Peter Burke, *History and Social Theory*, Polity Press, 1995

Eric Hobsbawm, *On History*, London: Abacus, 1997

E.P. Thompson, *The Poverty of Theory*, Merlin Press, 1978

Harvey J. Kaye, *The British Marxist Historians*, Polity Press, 1984

S.H. Rigby, *Marxism and History: a Critical Introduction*, Manchester UP, 1987

Laura Lee Downs, *Writing Gender History*, Arnold, 2004

Joan W. Scott, *Gender and the Politics of History*, Columbia UP, 1988

Karen Offen, Ruth R. Pierson & Jane Rendall (eds), *Writing Women's History: International Perspectives*, Indiana UP, 1991

# Notes

1 See Emmanuel Le Roy Ladurie, *The Mind and the Method of the Historian*, Harvester, 1981, ch. 1.

2 Some such theory evidently underlies much of G.R. Elton's work, and also the 'high politics' school of historiography, discussed above, pp. 77–8.

3 A major exception is E.H. Carr, *What is History?* Penguin, 1964.

4 Peter Mathias, 'Living with the neighbours: the role of economic history', 1970, reprinted in N.B. Harte (ed.), *The Study of Economic History*, Cass, 1971, p. 380.

5 For this view, see Jacques Barzun, *Clio and the Doctors*, Chicago University Press, 1974.

6 Aileen S. Kraditor, 'American radical historians on their heritage', *Past and Present*, LVI, 1972, p. 137.

7 *Ibid.*, p. 137.

8 Paul K. Conkin, 'Intellectual history', in Charles F. Delzell (ed.), *The Future of History*, Vanderbilt University Press, 1977, pp. 129–30.

9 David Thomson, *The Aims of History*, Thames & Hudson, 1969, p. 105.

10 Isaiah Berlin, 'Historical inevitability', 1954, reprinted in Patrick Gardiner (ed.), *The Philosophy of History*, Oxford University Press, 1974.

11 Comments in this vein recur in Taylor's *Bismarck*, Hamish Hamilton, 1955, and *The Origins of the Second World War*, Penguin, 1964.

12 G.R. Elton, *The Practice of History*, Fontana, 1969, pp. 55–6.

13 M.M. Postan, *Fact and Relevance*, Cambridge University Press, 1971, p. 16.

14 E.E. Evans-Pritchard, 'Anthropology and history', 1961, reprinted in his *Essays in Social Anthropology*, Faber, 1962, p. 49.

15 Philip Abrams, *Historical Sociology*, Open Books, 1982, pp. 2–3.

16 See the criticism of Gareth Stedman Jones, 'From historical sociology to theoretical history', *British Journal of Sociology*, XXVII, 1976, pp. 295–305, and Tony Judt, 'A clown in regal purple: social history and the historians', *History Workshop Journal*, VII, 1979, pp. 66–94.

17 Karl Marx, *A Contribution to the Critique of Political Economy*, Lawrence & Wishart, 1971, pp. 20–1.

18 This interpretation is convincingly argued in Melvin Rader, *Marx's Interpretation of History*, Oxford University Press, 1979. For a contrary view, see G.A. Cohen, *Karl Marx's Theory of History: A Defence*, Oxford University Press, 1978.

19 Fernand Braudel, 'History and the social sciences: *la longue durée*', 1958, reprinted in his *On History*, Weidenfeld & Nicolson, 1980, p. 51.

20 Engels to J. Bloch, 21 September 1980, reprinted in Karl Marx and Friedrich Engels, *Basic Writings on Politics and Philosophy*, L.S. Feuer (ed.), Fontana, 1969, pp. 436–7.

21 Karl Marx, *Pre-Capitalist Economic Formations*, Lawrence & Wishart, 1964, especially Introduction by E.J. Hobsbawm.

22 Marx to the editorial board of *Otechestvennive Zapiski*, November 1877, reprinted in Marx and Engels, *Basic Writings*, p. 478.

23 Marx, *A Contribution*, p. 21.

24 Marx, 'The eighteenth Brumaire of Louis Bonaparte', 1852, reprinted in Marx and Engels, *Basic Writings*, p. 360.

25 Engels to C. Schmidt, 5 August 1890, reprinted in Marx and Engels, *Basic Writings*, p. 436.

26 Marx and Engels, 'The German ideology', 1846, in *Basic Writings*, p. 289.

27 Marx, *A Contribution*, p. 21.

28 J.H. Clapham, 'The study of economic history', 1929, reprinted in Harte, *Study of Economic History*, pp. 64–5.

29 John Barber, *Soviet Historians in Crisis, 1928–30*, Macmillan, 1981.

30 Eric Hobsbawm, 'The Historians' Group of the Communist Party', in Maurice Cornforth (ed.), *Rebels and their Causes*, Lawrence & Wishart, 1978, p. 39.

31 See his *Age of Revolution*, Weidenfeld & Nicolson, 1962, and his *Age of Capital*, Weidenfeld & Nicolson, 1976.

32 Christopher Hill, *The English Revolution 1640*, 3rd edn, Lawrence & Wishart, 1955, p. 43.

33 E.P. Thompson, *The Making of the English Working Class*, Penguin, 1968, p. 9.

34 See Richard Johnson, 'Thompson, Genovese and socialist-humanist history', *History Workshop Journal*, VI, 1978, pp. 79–100, and Perry Anderson, *Arguments within English Marxism*, Verso, 1980.

35 E.P. Thompson, *The Poverty of Theory*, Merlin Press, 1978, especially pp. 110–19.

36 *Ibid.*, p. 88.

37 Christopher Hill, *The World Turned Upside Down*, Penguin, 1975, p. 14.

38 *Ibid.*, p. 386.

39 Thompson, *The Making of the English Working Class*, p. 13.

40 Marx, *A Contribution*, p. 21.

41 Barry Hindess and Paul Q. Hirst, *Pre-Capitalist Modes of Production*, Routledge & Kegan Paul, 1975, pp. 308–13.

42 The classic refutation is Thompson, *The Poverty of Theory*. For a more succinct statement, see Raphael Samuel, 'History and theory', in R. Samuel (ed.), *People's History and Socialist Theory*, Routledge & Kegan Paul, 1981, pp. xl–lii.

43 Compare Hill, *English Revolution*, with his *The World Turned Upside Down*, separated by over thirty years.

44 J.C.D. Clark, *English Society 1688–1832: Ideology, Social Structure and Political Practice during the Ancien Régime*, Cambridge University Press, 1985, p. 1; and his *Revolution and Rebellion: State and Society in England in the Seventeenth and Eighteenth Centuries*, Cambridge University Press, 1986, p. 2.

45 See, for example, the work of G.R. Elton and J.C.D. Clark.

46 W.W. Rostow, *The Stages of Economic Growth*, Cambridge University Press, 1960.

47 Catherine Hall, 'Histories, empires and the post-colonial moment', in Iain Chambers and Lidia Curti (eds), *The Post-Colonial Question: Common Skies, Divided Horizons*, Routledge, 1996, pp. 65–77.

48 See, for example, Olwen Hufton, *The Prospect Before Her: a History of Western Women, 1500–1800*, HarperCollins, 1995.

49 The classic airing of the pros and cons of patriarchy is the short interventions of Sheila Rowbotham, Sally Alexander and Barbara Taylor in Raphael Samuel (ed.), *People's History and Socialist Theory*, Routledge & Kegan Paul, 1981, pp. 363–73.

50 Jane Lewis (ed.), *Labour and Love: Women's Experience of Home and Family 1850–1940*, Blackwell, 1986, editor's introduction, p. 4. See also John Tosh, 'What should historians do with masculinity? Reflections on nineteenth-century Britain', *History Workshop Journal*, 38, 1994, pp. 179–202.

51 Natalie Zemon Davis, 'Women's history' in transition: the European case', *Feminist Studies*, III, 1975–76, pp. 83–103.

52 Michael Roper and John Tosh (eds), *Manful Assertions: Masculinities in Britain since 1800*, Routledge, 1991; Leonore Davidoff and Catherine Hall, *Family Fortunes: Men and Women of the English Middle Class 1780–1850*, Hutchinson, 1987.

53 Louise Tilly and Joan Scott, *Women, Work and Family*, 2nd edn, Methuen, 1987.

54 Joan Kelly, *Women, History and Theory*, Chicago University Press, 1984, ch. 3.

55 H.R. Trevor-Roper, 'History: professional and lay', 1957, reprinted in H.L. Lloyd-Jones, V. Pearl and B. Worden (eds), *History and Imagination*, Duckworth, 1981, p. 13.

56 Thompson, *The Poverty of Theory*, p. 78.

# CHAPTER NINE

# History by numbers

Disraeli once spoke of statistics as a form of lying, but there is no denying that as statistical analysis has grown in importance, especially with the development of ever-more sophisticated information technology, no historian can ignore its importance to historical study. Statistics can give an impression of precision and accuracy, but major pitfalls await the unwary student who approaches them in a spirit of blind faith. Statistics may or may not be lies, but they are as open to bias, distortion, unsupported inferences or plain error as any other type of historical source.

The revival of interest in social theory discussed in the last chapter represents only one of the ways in which history has been influenced by the social sciences in recent years. There has also been a broadening of the technical resources of the discipline, as new types of source have been identified and new ways of exploiting familiar materials have been explored. By far the most important of these is quantitative history. Almost no branch of historical research has been unaffected, and in the case of economic and social history something approaching a transformation has taken place. Two reasons account for this development. In the first place, the fundamental shift in emphasis from the individual to the mass which occurred earlier in this century (Chapter 5) has major quantitative implications. For as long as historians concentrated on the doings of the great, they hardly needed to count. But once they became seriously interested in economic growth, social change and the history of entire communities, questions of number and proportion assumed a critical importance. Economic and social historians who turned for guidance to the social sciences had to face the fact that the quantitative element in both economics and sociology was pronounced. If historians proposed to deal with the same sort of questions as economists and sociologists, they could hardly avoid using – or at least testing – their methods. The second reason is technological. During the 1960s the computer came of age: it became cheaper and more accessible, while both the kind of data it could handle and the operations it could carry out were rapidly diversified, in ways well suited to the requirements of historical research. As a result a whole range of quantitative exercises which would have defied unaided human effort became practicable for the first time. In this chapter I consider what the scope of quantitative history is, and how far it has transformed the methodology of historical enquiry.

# I

## Quantitative history

Quantitative history is founded on the conviction that in making quantitative statements historians should take the trouble to count rather than content themselves with impressionistic estimates. Two initial examples will indicate the difference this can make. First, it is a reasonable assumption that the average height of British people has risen over the past two hundred years as nutrition and disease control have advanced. But only when Roderick Floud and his colleagues made a systematic study of the recruitment records of the Army and charitable institutions did it become clear that the long-term upward trend was put into reverse in the mid-nineteenth century, or that the overall figures for the eighteenth century conceal a yawning gap between the aristocracy and the poor; as the authors proudly pointed out, this was 'the first attempt to write the **anthropocentric** history of Britain and Ireland'.[1] My second example is drawn from a more contentious field, the Atlantic slave trade. Until recently historians had assumed that the number of Africans shipped to the New World between the fifteenth and the nineteenth centuries totalled somewhere between fifteen and twenty million. This figure was based on little more than the guesswork of nineteenth-

**anthropocentric**
concerned with the
physical measurement of
human beings.

century writers, many of them prominent in the campaign to abolish the slave trade. In his quantitative study, *The Atlantic Slave Trade: A Census* (1969), Philip Curtin concluded that the number had been markedly exaggerated. By first critically evaluating and then adding together the figures available for particular periods and areas of the trade, he showed that the total was most unlikely to have been more than ten and a half million or less than eight million. This adjustment has no bearing on the moral outrage of posterity: whatever the total, it still represents an appalling blot on the record of Western civilization. But Curtin's figures provide for the first time a solid basis for considering the effects of the trade on the societies of tropical Africa and those of the Americas.[2]

## Verifying generalizations

In the course of their work historians make quantitative statements more frequently than might at first be supposed. Obviously a question such as 'what was Charles I's revenue in 1642?' or 'how large was the Liberal vote in the general election of 1906?' invites an answer as numerically precise as the sources will allow, and the reader of a reputable secondary work would expect nothing less. But many of the broader generalizations which historians habitually make are by implication also quantitative – for example, 'the British working class was literate by 1914' or 'women married late in early modern England'. A statement of this kind may echo the observation of a thoughtful contemporary, or it may arise from a comparison of a number of well-authenticated examples. But how can we tell whether the contemporary was right, or that the examples cited are typical? Only a quantitative analysis can put these statements beyond reasonable doubt, by revealing the incidence of literacy and the range and frequency of the ages at which women actually married. Until quite recently most historians were reluctant to accept this argument. In the 1940s G.M. Trevelyan described the evidential base of his subject in these terms:

> The generalizations which are the stock-in-trade of the social
> historian must necessarily be based on a small number of particular
> instances, which are assumed to be typical, but which cannot be the
> whole of the complicated truth.[3]

The problem with this method is that the particular instances can all too easily be selected to confirm what the historian expected to find, and conviction may be lent to unwarrantable assumptions. Today the findings of the 'qualitative' historians such as Trevelyan are being increasingly modified or refined by the quantitative analysis of data systematically assembled to reflect an entire society. In this way not only is the main trend revealed but also the variations and exceptions which highlight the distinctive experience of a particular locality or group. Thus Curtin's work on the slave trade was important not only for establishing a total but also for quantifying the concentration of the trade in the eighteenth century and the exceptional losses sustained by Angola and the Niger Delta region as compared with the other catchment areas. Finally, at its most ambitious, quantitative history seeks to elucidate an entire historical process by measuring and comparing all the relevant factors: why did the population of England increase so dramatically during the eighteenth century? What effects did the construction of railways in the mid-nineteenth century have on the development of the American economy? At this point, quantitative history stakes its claim to be not simply an ancillary technique but to take over the centre ground of historical enquiry.

During the past forty years an immense scholarly effort has been invested in quantitative research, and increasingly sophisticated statistical techniques have been applied. The findings are often presented in a highly technical and inaccessible manner, as will be clear from a glance at any recent volume of the *Economic History Review* or the *Journal of Economic History*. Undoubtedly this poses a problem for non-quantitative historians, who are reluctant to take these findings on trust and yet are uncomfortably aware of the authority attached to quantitative statements of all kinds today. But no specialized knowledge is required to understand where quantitative historians get their figures from, or in broad terms the uses to which they can be put. A non-technical discussion of these issues is sufficient to indicate both the strengths and the weaknesses of the quantitative approach – what it can achieve and what it cannot.

# II

## Demographic history

The field in which a quantitative approach is most essential and where arguably it has made its greatest contribution is *demographic history*. Demography without numbers is an absurdity, so in this area the quantitative historian can fairly claim to be indispensable. Demographic history involves a great deal more than merely working out the size of a given population in the past – difficult though even that can be in the absence of reliable census data. More significant than the total is the breakdown in terms of age, gender and household size. Calculations of this kind may reveal the ratio of producers to dependants, the proportion of households with living-in servants, and other indicators of importance to the economic and social historian. The most challenging task facing the demographic historian is to determine the causes of population change over time – or the lack of it. Here the first step is to reconstruct the birth rate, the marriage rate and the death rate. Each of these 'vital' rates is in turn influenced by many different factors which lend themselves to quantification with greater or lesser ease – the incidence of contraception and abortion, the age of marriage, the illegitimacy rate, the impact of famines and epidemics, and so on. For many, the attraction of this kind of enquiry is that it uncovers patterns which relate to the whole of society, rather than just that segment of it illuminated by literary sources. In the case of pre-industrial societies, which lived so much closer to the margin of subsistence than our own, it can be argued that demography was *the* determinant of social and economic life. On these grounds demographic history is central to the kind of 'total history' written by the *Annales* school with its primary interest in the early modern period.[4]

Demographic history mainly depends on two types of source. The first lists all the members of a country or community alive at any one time. This of course is the main function of the modern census, which was invented in the Scandinavian countries in the mid-eighteenth century. In Britain a census of the whole population has been taken at ten-yearly intervals since 1801, and it is generally conceded that after 1841 (when the name of each individual was noted for the first time), errors in the totals are statistically insignificant. Other listings survive from earlier

Regular ten-year censuses in Britain started in 1801, during the Napoleonic Wars. They consititute a key resource for economic, social, local and even family historians; when the National Archives put the 1901 census returns on the web, demand for access was so great that the system immediately crashed. But how accurate are census returns? Were respondents telling the truth? Did census enumerators make mistakes? Quantitative methods cannot tell us. (CORBIS/Hulton-Deutsch Collection)

**communicants**
One who 'communicates' – i.e. takes the bread and wine of Holy Communion.

**incumbent**
A clergyman in charge of a parish.

periods – tax returns, returns of church **communicants**, declarations of political loyalty and the like. But, though comprehensive in intent, these were seldom so in practice, and the margin of error is very uncertain and inconsistent. One consequence of the relatively recent origin of census-taking is that it has proved extraordinarily difficult to establish the relationship between demographic change and the onset of industrialization in late eighteenth-century Britain. This is where the second type of source comes in – the recording in sequence of the 'vital' events in a given locality. For English history the most important source is the parish registers kept by Anglican **incumbents**, who from 1538 were required by law to record all baptisms, marriages and burials in their parishes; the system persisted until the beginning of civil registration in 1837. From a sample of parish registers E.A. Wrigley and R.S. Schofield have calculated national rates of births, marriages and deaths, and have used these to project the total population of England back from 1801 as far as the mid-sixteenth century. As a result they are able to pinpoint small variations in the growth rate much more precisely than before, and to demonstrate the preponderant influence which changes in the marriage rate had on the long-term rate of population growth.[5]

## Tracing individuals through the statistics

Wrigley and Schofield's work is an example of *aggregative* analysis, i.e. the interpretation of totals. But these same authors have applied a quite different approach to the parish registers which arises from the fact that every entry refers to named persons. The demographic history of a parish can therefore be reconstructed in terms of the growth and decline of its constituent families – or at any rate those that remained confined to a single parish. This technique, known as family reconstitution, is an example of *nominative* analysis, i.e. analysis through names rather than totals. It is immensely time-consuming: to reconstitute one parish of 1,000 persons over a period of three centuries requires about 1,500 hours, or a year's undistracted work.[6] But it has the advantage of showing patterns of fertility and mortality in much greater detail, and in a specific economic and social context. The knowledge that the birth rate was rising or the death rate declining in itself adds little to our understanding of the *causes* of population change; a good family reconstitution study may, however, show whether a rising birth rate was due, for example, to a lowering of the age of first marriage among women or to a decline in the incidence of lifelong **spinsterhood**. These findings can in turn be interpreted with reference to the conditions prevailing in the areas concerned.[7]

**spinsterhood**
The state of being an unmarried woman, commonly used for a woman who has passed the normal 'marriageable' age.

## The statistics of social structure

The second field in which quantitative methods have proved important is the history of *social structure*. There is in fact a close connection between this field and demographic history, because the same sources loom large in both. Any source which lists an entire population or records its 'vital' events offers, at least potentially, the possibility of classifying that population into social groups. This is most easily achieved in the case of groups defined by age or gender. But historians are becoming increasingly resourceful in abstracting other aspects of social structure from

demographic data. The changing size and structure of the household is a case in point. The evidence of both pre-census listings
and family reconstitution has effectively undermined the traditional notion that pre-industrial society in Western Europe was
characterized by large, complex households of the extended
family type.[8] From the mid-nineteenth century the ever-increasing
scope and precision of the questions asked in the census means
that a whole range of social issues is opened up to quantitative
analysis – occupation, status, religious affiliation, rural migration
to the towns, and so on.[9] The 'new urban history' in the United
States is largely based on the premise that the changing social
structure of a city can be reconstructed by analyzing the manuscript schedules of the US census in conjunction with other
nominative data (notably tax records, city directories and registers of births, marriages and deaths).[10]

## Parliamentary statistics

It may seem surprising that quantitative methods have much relevance to the third field to be considered here, namely *political
history*. The traditional concern of the political historian is, after
all, with 'unique' events and with the actions and motives of individual statesmen. But once the field of enquiry is broadened to
include the political system as a whole, quantitative history comes
into its own. This is most evident in the realm of electoral behaviour. Just as psephology – the study of present-day elections – is
largely a matter of juggling with numbers, so too the study of
elections in the past demands a quantitative approach.
Admittedly, for any period up to the development of opinion polls
in the 1950s the quantification of political attitudes presents
major problems (and it can be argued that it still does). But the
historian has other advantages which are denied to the modern
psephologist. Prior to the **Ballot Act of 1872** parliamentary elections in Britain were conducted in public and votes were
individually recorded. Where registers of votes can be analyzed in
conjunction with other nominative data on income, status or
religion, the way is open to firmer conclusions about the basis of
party affiliation in nineteenth-century Britain.[11]

Quantitative techniques have also been usefully applied to one
other concern of political historians – the study of political élites.

**Ballot Act, 1872**
The act which introduced
the secret ballot into
British elections. The
practice of declaring one's
vote in public had been a
way by which voters were
held accountable to the
wider community, most of
whom did not have the
vote. However, it also left
voters open to
intimidation, especially
when they were the
tenants of one or other of
the candidates, and a
secret ballot had been a
regular feature of radical
demands for a reform of
Parliament since the early
nineteenth century.

It is too easy to allow our picture of an élite – as of any social group – to be determined by a handful of well-known case histories. But in the case of a precisely defined élite such as the House of Commons, the salient biographical details of the entire membership can be assembled (see pp. 122–3). This was Namier's most important contribution to historical method. Subsequent scholars have merely subjected collective biography to more rigorous quantitative analysis. Quantitative historians have been rather more original in their studies of the political behaviour – as opposed to the background – of legislative bodies. Most modern legislatures keep a record of votes taken: the division lists of the House of Commons extend back in an unbroken sequence to 1836. These can be tabulated according to the issues and then set against the findings of collective biography to clarify the basis of support for and opposition to particular policies. Studies of this kind have proliferated in America as part of the much-vaunted 'new political history'.[12]

## Economic history

Lastly, quantitative methods have had a decisive impact on *economic* history. The reasons are obvious enough. Economics – like demography – is a highly quantitative discipline. The principal elements in an economic system – prices, incomes, production, investment, trade and credit – all lend themselves to precise measurement; indeed, they demand it if the workings of the system are to be clearly understood. From the beginning of economic history as a distinct specialism in the late nineteenth century, economic historians collected quantitative economic data, usually as one aspect of whatever research they were engaged on. It is only in the last forty years or so, however, that historians have tackled the problem of constructing extended statistical sequences, often from varied and imperfect sources, as a means of illuminating long-term economic trends. B.R. Mitchell and Phyllis Deane's *Abstract of British Historical Statistics* (1962) represents the most systematic attempt to do this for Britain so far. But it is some of the French quantitative historians who have pressed this approach furthest: the exponents of 'serial history' (*l'histoire sérielle*) aim to build up extended sequences of prices, crop yields, rents and incomes which together will enable them to construct a model for France's development during the early modern period – and ultimately Europe's as well.[13] The claims of the 'new economic history' (or 'cliometrics') in the United States are, if anything, greater, and are critically evaluated in the fifth section of this chapter.

# III

## The analysis of statistical evidence

It is sometimes imagined that the application of quantitative methods on a large scale displaces the traditional skills of the historian and calls for an entirely new breed of scholar. Nothing could be further from the truth. Statistical know-how can only be effective if it is treated as an *addition* to the historian's tool-kit and subject to the normal controls of historical method. Given the special authority which figures carry in our numerate society, the obligation to subject quantitative data to tests of reliability is at least as great as in the case of literary sources. And once the figures have been verified, their interpretation and their application to the solution of specific historical problems require the same qualities of judgement and flair as any other kind of evidence. Each of these two stages presents its own problems.

## Unreliable statistical evidence

A historian is saved an immense amount of work if he or she is lucky enough to find a set of ready-made statistics – say a table of imports and exports or a sequence of census reports. Yet the reliability of such sources must never be taken for granted. We need to know exactly how the figures were put together. Were the returns made by the man on the spot distorted by his own self-interest – like the tax collector who understated his takings and pocketed the difference? Were the figures conjured out of thin air by a deskbound official, or totted up by a subordinate who was not competent in arithmetic? Both these possibilities arise in the case of the impressive-looking statistics published by British colonial administrations in Africa, which were often based on returns made by poorly educated and underpaid chiefs. How much scope was there for errors of copying as the figures were passed on from one level of the bureaucracy to the next? Could the same item have been counted twice by different officials? Where statistics were compiled from questionnaires, as in social surveys or the census, we need to know the form in which the questions were put in order to determine the scope for confusion on the part of the respondents, and we have to consider whether the questions – on income or age, for example – were likely to elicit frank answers. Only an investigation of the circumstances of compilation, using the conventional skills of the historian, can provide the answer to these questions.

Often what interests historians is less a single set of figures than a sequence over time which enables them to plot a trend. The figures must accordingly be tested not only for their reliability but also for their *comparability*. However accurate the individual totals in such a sequence may be, they can only be regarded as a statistical sequence if they are strictly comparable – if, that is, they are measuring the same variable. It needs only a slight discrepancy in the basis of assessment to render comparisons null and void. A classification which seems clear and consistent enough on paper may be applied differently over time, or between one place and another, which is one reason why comparative criminal statistics have to be treated so cautiously. In the case of the English census, the increasing refinement of the **occupational schedule** in every count since 1841 means that it is difficult to quantify the growth and decline of specific occupations. Even the most seemingly straightforward statistical sequences may conceal pitfalls of this kind. Comprehensive commercial statistics for England date back to 1696, when the post of Inspector-General of Imports and Exports was created. But because the official table of values drawn up by the first Inspector-General was applied almost without modification until the end of the eighteenth century, during which time some prices rose while others fell, the figures as they stand cannot be used to calculate the changing balance of trade.[14] Nor do modern statistical tables necessarily pass the test of comparability. Consider, for example, the official cost-of-living index, which measures the cost of a typical 'shopping bag' against the current wage rate. In Britain the index, begun in 1914, ought to provide a reliable picture of the declining standard of living during the Depression of the 1930s. But during the inter-war period the price side of the index continued to be based on the

**occupational schedule**
The section in the census question which asks for the respondent's occupation. From broad categories of occupation in the early censuses, the categories were steadily refined, making each individual census more specific than its predecessors but making it difficult to trace developments in particular occupations over time.

same 'shopping bag', even though changing patterns of consumption meant that the weighting given to the various items (fresh vegetables, meat, clothing, etc.) in 1914 no longer corresponded with the actual make-up of the average family budget.[15]

## Compiling the statistics

Most quantitative history, however, is not based on ready-made statistics. It was only in the late seventeenth century that the advantages of a statistical approach to public issues began to be canvassed, only during the nineteenth century that the state acquired the resources of manpower and money to undertake such work, and only in the present century that statistical information has been gathered in a really comprehensive way by both government and private bodies. For most of the questions which interest historians, the likelihood is that the figures will have to be laboriously constructed from the relevant surviving materials. To construct quantitative data in such a way that valid statistical inferences can be drawn from them is no easy matter. The issues of reliability and comparability will be posed not once but many times over as the historian seeks out data from varied and scattered source materials. The classification of the data in tabular form now becomes the task of the historian; and the criteria on which that classification is based raise questions of historical judgement rather than statistical method.

Above all, the construction of statistics raises acute problems of selection. There are, it is true, quantitative enquiries whose scope is so narrowly defined that all the relevant data can be assembled: W.O. Aydelotte's quantitative collective biography of all the members who sat in the parliament of 1841–7 (the period of Sir Robert Peel's premiership leading to the split in the Tory Party over the **Corn Laws**) is a case in point.[16] But, as we have seen, one of the main attractions of the quantitative approach is the opportunity it offers for making statements not just about small élites but about whole classes or societies over long periods of time. And whereas the vast bureaucracy employed by most modern states can gather comprehensive national statistics with relative ease, no historian, however well endowed with research assistants and computer time, can hope to survey *all* the primary sources needed for a quantitative study of, say, farm size in Tudor

**Corn Laws**
The debate on the future of the Corn Laws was one of the most important political controversies of the nineteenth century. The laws, which governed the relative prices of imported and home-grown corn, had become symbols of the Tory government's attachment to the farming interest and to high import duties (known as protection) at a time of food shortages at home. When Peel, Tory Prime Minister between 1841 and 1846, decided to bow to intense popular pressure and repeal them, the ensuing controversy split the Tory Party in two. It was nearly thirty years before the party was properly back in power again.

England or personal incomes in early Victorian Britain. Modern statisticians have developed reliable techniques for taking a random sample, that is, one in which every element making up the whole has an equal chance of being included in the sample. In historical research it is often not practicable to apply these techniques to the letter, but the researcher must at least ensure that every variable is fairly represented in the sample. In one project the enumerators' returns for the 1851 census were prepared for computer analysis in order to provide answers to a number of questions about social and economic structure which fell outside the scope of the report on the census published at the time; a 2 per cent sample was chosen which comprised the total population of one in every fifteen enumeration districts (945 in all). All the census information about these 415,000 individuals was fed into the computer, with the result that historians can now get a much clearer idea about variations in education, land tenure, household composition, the size of the labour force in different businesses, and many other issues.[17]

## Incomplete statistical records

For the historian of periods earlier than the nineteenth century, the problem of selection is likely to have been partly or wholly solved by the ravages of time. But the residue that survives is still a sample of the original range of records, and it is important to recognize that it is often anything but a random sample. Some types of record are more likely to survive than others because their owners had a greater interest in their survival or better facilities for preserving them, for reasons which may introduce a manifest bias into the sample. Thus surviving business records are nearly always weighted in favour of the successful long-lasting firm, at the expense of smaller businesses which were unable to weather a crisis. Lawrence Stone was dogged by a problem of this kind in his study of the English aristocracy between 1558 and 1641. Although he had some information on all of the 382 individuals who held titles at that period, the proportion of noble families whose private papers survive in abundance never rose above one-third, and these families were mostly those of wealthy earls rather than minor barons, whose estates were more subject to disintegration or dispersal. Stone was accordingly obliged to make allowances for the fact that many of his findings were drawn from an unrepresentative sample.[18]

# IV

## Presenting statistics

Having once established that the figures are reliable, comparable and representative, the historian can set about putting the data to work. Sometimes the figures amount to an unequivocal answer to the question in hand, and all that remains is to devise the best way of presenting them clearly on the printed page – whether by table, graph, histogram, 'cake' or pyramid. Some very elementary processing may be desirable, such as the calculation needed to work out percentages or averages. The findings of economic historians in matters such as exports or production often lend themselves to straightforward exposition, known in the trade as 'descriptive statistics'; an excellent example is the forty-odd pages of tables and charts which appear at the end of E.J. Hobsbawm's economic history of Britain since 1750, *Industry and Empire* (1968). But as historians have extended the application of quantitative methods they have increasingly found that what counts is not so much the explicit meaning of the figures as the inferences that can be drawn from them.

## Drawing inferences from the data

The drawing of such inferences may be essentially a statistical operation. In the case of an extended series of export statistics, for example, the researcher may wish to abstract the long-term trend of growth or decline, the regular fluctuations of slump and boom, and the irregular fluctuations caused by war, plague and the vagaries of government policy; only the sophisticated techniques of time-series analysis will make this feasible.[19] Even more complex statistical techniques are employed by Wrigley and Schofield in their backward projection of the English population from the nineteenth to the sixteenth century: there must be few historians who can follow them through that labyrinth. From the historian's point of view, a particularly useful kind of statistical inference is the coefficient of correlation, i.e. the demonstration of a relationship between two variables. It is often important to know whether such a relationship exists and of what type – say between party affiliation and voting behaviour, or between the duration of marriage and the number of offspring. If reliable quantitative data are available for each variable, the relationship can be worked out by statistical means. The computer can be of great assistance in this kind of project. Suppose that, for every one of the five hundred members of a legislature, the researcher has assembled information under twelve headings (which might include age, education, party, constituency, income, occupation, and voting record on six different issues) and wishes to test each of these twelve variables against all the others. The working out by hand of each of these correlations would be an almost imposs-ible task; a correctly programmed computer, on the other hand, would print out the required tables in minutes.[20] The result might be that a hitherto unsuspected correlation was revealed, sug-gesting a fruitful new line of research. It is important, nevertheless, not to exaggerate the significance of a statistically verified correlation: it does not take account of the possibility of coincidence, nor will it reveal which variable influenced the other; it may be, indeed, that the two variables are determined by a third, as yet unidentified variable. On all these points, historians must fall back on their common sense and their knowledge of the period and its problems.

## Tracing the reality behind the figures

But most historians who make inferences from quantitative data do not need to use statistics at all; instead they treat the figure as an indicator or 'index' of some other, usually much less tangible phenomenon for which direct quantitative evidence is not avail-able. It is tempting to infer political attitudes from statistics of voting behaviour, or the influence of a book from its sales, or the intensity of religious belief from the returns of Easter communi-cants, but none of these inferences can be taken for granted; nor does their validity depend on statistical principles. In each case it depends on a historically informed awareness of other factors which may have affected the figures. Were voters open to corrup-tion, or responsive to personalities rather than policies? Was the book bought as an item of conspicuous consumption and put away

The taking of Holy Communion was often regarded as a significant indication of an individual's religious loyalties. In the late seventeenth century the Test Act made attendance at Anglican Communion a prerequisite for holding public office. However, it is by no means clear that all church-goers took the issue of communication so seriously: non-Anglicans were happy to take Anglican Communion occasionally in order to meet the terms of the Test Act. Attendance at Communion can be a shaky measure of piety even within the Catholic Church: before the reforms of the Council of Trent it was common even for devout Catholics to communicate only at Christmas and Easter. (CORBIS/Bettmann)

unread? Can we assume that taking Communion had the same significance for peasant congregations as it did for the clergy who compiled the returns?[21] The application of demographic data to family history has proved to be a minefield. To take just one example, it cannot be assumed without a great deal of supporting qualitative evidence that a narrow age-gap between husband and wife (as was already the case in early modern England) indicates a more affectionate and companionable marital relationship.[22] Thus, at the point where numerical data touch on a major historical question, quantitative methods in themselves often resolve nothing. As three leading proponents of quantitative history have conceded:

> Statistical manipulations merely rearrange the evidence; they do not, except on an elementary level, answer general questions, and the bearing of the findings upon the larger problems of interpretation in which historians are interested is a matter, not of arithmetic, but of logic and persuasion.[23]

Statistics may serve to reveal or clarify a particular tendency; but how we *interpret* that tendency – the significance we attach to it and the causes we adduce for it – is a matter for seasoned historical judgement, in which the historian trained exclusively in quantitative methods would be woefully deficient.

# V

## Cliometrics – the quantification of history

There is, however, one quantitative approach to history which claims to have transcended these limitations to some extent, and which has as a result generated heated controversy. Its first champions during the 1960s in the United States coined the word 'cliometrics' to distinguish their approach, and the term is now widely understood – although those who reserve judgement on its claims prefer to retain the inverted commas. 'Cliometrics' proceeds on the assumption that certain areas of human behaviour are best understood as a system in which both the variables and the relationship between them can be quantified; when the value of one variable changes, the effect which this has on the system as a whole can be calculated. The field of human behaviour most suited to this approach is economics. In fact 'cliometrics' is simply a fancy label for what is often called 'the new economic history'. It draws its inspiration from econometrics – that is, the techniques that statisticians have evolved to analyze economies of the present and to predict their future development. In proceeding from known to unknown variables the economist applies a theory of the relationship between the elements in an economic system (capital, wages, prices, etc.); when an economic theory is expressed in mathematical terms, it is known as a *model*. Econometrists are concerned to test and apply models by statistical means. For example, in input–output analysis a model is employed in order to calculate what inputs an economy (or one sector within it) requires to achieve a given production target.

## Counterfactual statistics

For those historians with the necessary training in statistics, it is easy to see the appeal of econometric methods. They hold out the prospect of filling in some of the gaps in our existing historical knowledge which are due to the patchiness of firm quantitative data about the past. And, if carried to their logical limits, they allow historians to assess the economic effect of a given policy or innovation by measuring it against what *would* have happened if the policy had not been implemented or the innovation had proved stillborn: the system can be reconstructed to accommodate a different value for one or more variables. That at least is what the most advanced 'cliometricians' would claim. In *Railroads and Economic Growth* (1964), to take the most celebrated case, R.W. Fogel sought to measure the contribution which nineteenth-century railway construction made to the US economy by constructing a hypothetical (or '**counterfactual**') model of what the American economy would have been like in 1890 if no railways had been built. He concluded that, even supposing no additional canals or roads were built, gross national product would have been only 3.1 per cent lower, and that 76 per cent of the land actually farmed in 1890 would still have been farmed. Previously most historians – including Fogel himself – had believed that the railways had had a much more dynamic effect on the American economy. Fogel maintained that counterfactual propositions are implicit in many historical judgements, and that what he had done was to expose this particular assumption as false by subjecting it to rigorous statistical testing.[24]

**counterfactual**
A process of historical hypothesis-setting popularized by Niall Ferguson in *Virtual History* (London 1997). It entails working through the implications of possibilities which existed in the past but did not actually happen as a way of reaching a fuller assessment of what did.

## The limitations of cliometrics

There are, however, several reasons why the work of the 'cliometricians' should be used with caution. To those historians who maintain that research questions should emerge from immersion in the widest possible range of primary sources, 'cliometric' history is inadmissible because its point of departure is always a clearly defined problem formulated in theoretical terms. But, as I argued in Chapter 8, there is no reason in principle why historians should not turn to theory in order to expose fresh problems or bring a new perspective to bear on familiar ones. The difficulty, of course, is that recourse to theory does not of itself confer authority on the findings; an inappropriate theory will naturally produce distorted results. This is plainly a relevant consideration in the case of the 'new economic history' because there are at least three well-established economic theories to choose from – the neo-classical, the Marxist and the Keynesian. But the objections to economic theory go farther than this. To the historian they are all suspect because they start from the premise that human beings in seeking to fulfil their material needs are governed by motives of a 'rational' profit-maximizing, cost-cutting kind. Yet often this is exactly what has to be demonstrated, not assumed: consumers may be deterred from buying in the cheapest market by calls to 'buy British' or to shun Jewish businesses; employers may pay wages over the odds or improve working conditions out of consideration for a paternalist self-image. An economic theory which explains economic behaviour in 'ideal' conditions is unlikely to do so when confronted by the social and cultural factors which obtain in a historically specific situation, and historians who insist on using such a theory on the grounds that they are interested in purely economic problems are afflicted by a particularly disabling form of 'tunnel vision'.

## Impossibility of scale

The second objection applies to those econometric studies that, like Fogel's railway study, encompass an entire economy. It is humanly impossible to construct a model which takes account of every variable; indeed, models are useful precisely because they *simplify* reality. What can reasonably be demanded of a model is that it includes every *significant* variable. But in the case of a national economy even this requirement is in practice very difficult to fulfil, and just which variables are selected for inclusion becomes a crucial question. Fogel himself has been criticized for failing to include in his model the effects of railway construction on the mobility of the workforce and on technical advances in other sectors of the economy. Equally, once one factor (railway) is removed from the model for the purposes of counterfactual analysis it is virtually impossible to take account of all the consequent changes, direct and indirect, in the other variables; they cannot all be measured, and it remains an open question whether Fogel measured the most significant ones.[25]

## Contentious assumptions

Fogel's work also raises in an acute form the third objection to 'cliometrics' – that it leans too heavily on unverifiable inferences.

Statistics itself is no more than a technique for making inferences from quantitative data, but most of them – such as the coefficient of correlation and the time-series analysis mentioned earlier – are mathematical inferences which can be demonstrated to follow from the data. The problem with 'cliometrics' is that too many of its inferences are not of this kind: they are valid only if the model on which they are founded is valid. And the danger is that the historian, instead of systematically testing the theory against the data to see if it works, takes the theory as given and uses it to construct new quantitative data. Each stage in the chain of reasoning whereby unknown quantities are constructed out of known quantities may be riddled with theoretical assumptions. This objection is clearest in the case of counterfactual models, such as Fogel's hypothetical American economy of 1890, which are by definition unverifiable; but it also applies to less virtuoso performances such as the calculation of overall levels of investment from miles of main railway line constructed. It is easy for the unwary reader to forget that the calculations of the 'cliometricians' are no firmer than the theories which underpin them.[26]

## An over-reliance on the quantifiable

The last point, which has been particularly emphasized by 'traditionalist' critics, is that 'cliometric' models tend to introduce serious if unintended bias into the selection of sources. This is because, as mathematical models, they can take account only of numerical data. Non-quantifiable variables are automatically excluded, and the result may be a badly skewed interpretation. This point is not always squarely faced by advocates of 'cliometric' history. Thus Roderick Floud writes:

> The 'new' economic historian concentrates on measurable economic phenomena, and uses economic theory linking those phenomena, specifically because he wishes to cut through the complexity of history and to concentrate on those phenomena which best explain the events he is studying.[27]

**inferences**
Conclusions or hypotheses which are derived by observers from given information.

It is precisely this equation of the measurable with the most significant phenomena that must be questioned. Some 'cliometricians' have preferred the problematical **inferences** which they make from quantitative data to the clear and emphatic evidence provided by non-quantitative sources. In their highly controversial book, *Time on the Cross* (1974), R.W. Fogel and S.L. Engerman abstracted statistical data from probate records, plantation records and census schedules, which revealed the white planters of the American South in the mid-nineteenth century as a 'rational' and humane capitalist class, and their slaves as a prosperous and well-treated workforce. By ignoring the mass of 'qualitative' evidence in personal testimonies and correspondence, they exposed themselves to a devastating counterattack from historians able to demonstrate the importance of aristocratic, 'pre-capitalist' values among the planters and the violence to which their slaves were subjected.[28] As this example shows, the non-quantifiable factors are often those same cultural and social factors which are excluded from the model as 'irrational'.

There are doubtless many historians who regard the public furore over *Time on the Cross* as a fitting nemesis for the 'cliometric' school as a whole. The book certainly illustrates the dangers of unwarranted inference and of bias in the choice of sources. But *Time on the Cross* is not typical. The 'cliometric' approach has made a real contribution to our understanding of a number of technical problems in economic history (which of course have not hit the headlines). What the record so far suggests is that the range of such problems is limited, and that in attempting to answer the really significant questions in economic history 'cliometrics' has highlighted particular factors of a formal kind rather than furnished comprehensive interpretations.

# VI

## The controversy over quantification

During the 1960s quantitative history was a highly contentious issue. Some of the early proponents of the new approach got 'high' on figures, becoming 'statistical junkies' (to quote Lawrence Stone).[29] There was a certain presumption about their appropriation of labels such as 'the new political history', 'the new urban history' and 'the new economic history'. For a time history's scientific status was affirmed more unequivocally than at any time since the turn of the century; in 1966 a leading American quantitative historian was rash enough to predict that by 1984 the scientific study of the past would have reached the point when historians could set their sights on the discovery of general laws of human behaviour.[30] Comparable hostages to fortune were given by the 'cliometricians'. As a result, some of the traditionalists in the profession were provoked into making equally extreme rebuttals: in 1963 the president of the American Historical Association urged his colleagues not to 'worship at the shrine of that **Bitch-goddess** QUANTIFICATION' (*sic*).[31] Nearly forty years later the claims advanced for quantitative history are more modest, other historians feel less threatened, and a more dispassionate assessment is possible.

One undeniable achievement of the quantitative historians is to have increased the precision of many factual statements about the past, especially statements about people in the mass. In a great many fields impressionistic estimates have given place to rigorously controlled calculation, which has revealed the overall trend, as well as the extent of variations and discrepancies within it. This represents clear gain. Beyond this, the gathering of large bodies of quantitative data on related issues has enabled historians to be much more confident about many of their descriptive generalizations. It is not true, as has sometimes been claimed,[32] that the result has simply been to restate the obvious. A number of generalizations which were formerly taken for granted have been fatally undermined. Thus it seems to be established beyond reasonable doubt that the English household in the seventeenth and eighteenth centuries did not typically take the form of an extended family, and that slavery in the southern states of the United States had not ceased to be profitable to the owners on the eve of the Civil War (this much of Fogel and Engerman's thesis is sound). If these generalizations are cast in a negative rather than a positive form, this is because the effect of assembling comprehensive figures is often to highlight a diversity, or degree of variation from the norm, which confounds absolute pronouncements of any kind. Here too, the disposal of simplistic notions about the past represents a significant advance in knowledge.

## Quantification and human motivation

It is sometimes argued that the preoccupation with aggregates and trends, by emphasizing the common factors in mass behaviour at the expense of the individual and the exceptional, has a 'dehu-

**bitch-goddess**
The phrase is a reference to a quotation from the American writer William James, who complained to H.G. Wells in 1906 of the moral effects of America's obsession with success: 'The moral flabbiness born of the bitch-goddess SUCCESS. That – with the squalid cash interpretation put on the word success – is our national disease'. The analogy with an obsession with collating statistics is apt.

manizing' effect on history. Elton, for example, detected in much of the 'new political history' an assumption that voting behaviour is a conditioned reflex, determined by economic and social conditions,[33] and it is certainly true that questions of motive may appear to be prejudged by demonstrating a correlation between, say, the business interests of MPs and their record in the division lobbies. This argument needs to be considered in conjunction with another related objection – that quantitative history distorts our view of the past by directing attention to those sources which readily respond to statistical analysis at the expense of those which do not; as a result important historical questions may be posed in terms that exclude a total view. The debate that raged in the 1960s over the standard of living of the British working class during the Industrial Revolution brought out this difficulty well: critics of the quantitative approach pointed out that unquantifiable indicators of the quality of life were at least as significant as wage rates and price levels.[34]

## Quantification within the historian's armoury

But neither of these objections can stand unless it is proposed that legitimate historical enquiry be henceforth confined to those areas which can be illuminated by a quantitative approach. Although some zealots, with their talk of 'a revolution in historiographical consciousness', have come very close to adopting this position,[35] the majority of quantitative historians would not wish to claim exclusive rights. They would probably agree with Aydelotte, Bogue and Fogel when they write of quantitative history:

> What is attempted in this approach is to take more effective advantage of selected parts of the evidence: to seize on those parts of the data that can be handled more strictly, by mathematical means, and to subject them to a more refined analysis ... Restriction of focus is the price that must be paid for being more sure of one's ground.[36]

The effect of any new and powerful technique is temporarily to put more familiar approaches at a discount. That phase already lies in the past. Political historians today are hardly less interested in the actions and motives of individual statesmen than they were before the advent of the 'new political history'. Social historians are supplementing broad quantitative surveys with 'in-depth' studies of particular communities or episodes for which rich documentation survives: the trend is exemplified by the shift in Emmanuel Le Roy Ladurie's work from the quantitative *Peasants of Languedoc* (1966) to his village study, *Montaillou* (1978), which depends on the evocative power of verbatim personal testimonies.

Underlying the more modest aspirations of quantitative history is a growing recognition that its contribution to historical explanation – as distinct from the verification of historical facts – is marginal. The generalizations yielded by analyses of numerical data tend to be descriptive rather than explanatory. To plot a trend, or to demonstrate a statistical correlation between this trend and another, does not *explain* it. Cause and significance remain matters for the interpretative skill of the historian in command of *all* the sources – not merely those which lend themselves to quantification. In the case of major historical problems, the effect of deploying quantitative techniques has been to clarify a number of relevant issues without 'closing' the question. Thus, after all the quantitative work which has been carried out on the economic position of the English aristocracy and the composition of the royal bureaucracy under Charles I, historians are no nearer a consensus on the origins of the English Revolution of the seventeenth century. The prospect that lies before historians, then, is not the solution of major questions by quantitative means but new possibilities of synthesis, in which statistical inference is combined with the perceptions of traditional 'qualitative' history. On these more restricted terms the place of quantitative methods in historical enquiry seems assured.

## The statistics of slavery

The campaign for the abolition of the slave trade made much of the fact that slavers talked of 'cargo' and calculated the conditions on board the slaving ships in terms of profitability; one of the most widely produced pieces of evidence was a plan of the slave ship *Brooks* produced for a parliamentary enquiry into the trade, which showed individual slaves packed into the ship like sacks. Ironically it is these coldly calculated slavers' statistics which helped Curtin to make a realistic estimate of the actual number of people transported in the infamous 'Middle Passage' across the Atlantic. Historians have long argued over the importance of slavery in causing the American Civil War (1861–5). At the time of the Civil Rights marches of the 1960s, which coincided with the centenary celebrations of the war, there was a tendency to stress slavery; later historians reacted against this and argued that the war had been mainly about the rights and status of the southern states. They held, wrongly, that slavery was in fact proving increasingly unprofitable in the years leading up to the war. The cliometric school of history has exploded that particular myth and helped to restore the importance of the slavery issue at the centre of the dispute between North and South.

## Further reading

Pat Hudson, *History By Numbers: an Introduction to Quantitative Approaches*, Arnold, 2000

Michael Drake, *The Quantitative Analysis of Historical Data*, Open UP, 1974

Roderick Floud, *An Introduction to Quantitative Methods for Historians*, 2nd edn, Methuen, 1979

C.H. Feinstein & Mark Thomas, *Making History Count: a Primer in Quantitative Methods for Historians*, Cambridge UP, 2003

Edward Higgs, *Making Sense of the Census Revisited*, Institute of Historical Research, 2005

## Notes

1 Roderick Floud, *Height, Health and History: Nutritional Status in the United Kingdom, 1750–1980*, Cambridge University Press, 1990, p. 29.

2 Curtin's figures are the subject of continuing debate among quantitative historians. See Paul E. Lovejoy, 'The volume of the Atlantic slave trade: a synthesis', *Journal of African History*, XXIII, 1982, pp. 473–501, and J. Inikori (ed.), *Forced Migration*, Hutchinson, 1982.

3 G.M. Trevelyan, *English Social History*, Longman, 1944, p. viii.

4 See, for example, Emmanuel Le Roy Ladurie, *The Peasants of Languedoc*, University of Illinois Press, 1974.

5 E.A. Wrigley and R.S. Schofield, *The Population History of England, 1541–1871*, Arnold, 1981.

6 E.A. Wrigley (ed.), *An Introduction to English Historical Demography*, Weidenfeld & Nicolson, 1966, p. 97.

7 See, for example, David Levine, *Family Formation in an Age of Nascent Capitalism*, Academic Press, 1977, which contains a detailed methodological discussion (pp. 153–74).

8 Peter Laslett (ed.), *Household and Family in Past Time*, Cambridge University Press, 1972.

9 The methodological issues are fully discussed in E.A. Wrigley (ed.), *Nineteenth Century Society*, Cambridge University Press, 1972.

10 See, for example, Leo F. Schnore (ed.), *The New Urban History*, Princeton University Press, 1975.

11 See J.R. Vincent, *Pollbooks: How Victorians Voted*, Cambridge University Press, 1967.

12 Allan G. Bogue, 'The new political history', in Michael Kammen (ed.), *The Past Before Us*, Cornell University Press, 1980. For the application of quantitative methods to British political history, see W.O. Aydelotte, *Quantification in History*, Addison Wesley, 1971.

13 The clearest statement in English is Emmanuel Le Roy Ladurie, *The Territory of the Historian*, Harvester, 1979, ch. 2.

14 G.N. Clark, *Guide to English Commercial Statistics, 1696–1782*, Royal Historical Society, 1938.

15 B.R. Mitchell and Phyllis Deane, *Abstract of British Historical Statistics*, Cambridge University Press, 1962, p. 466. For an account of the problems raised by cost-of-living indexes, see Roderick Floud, *An Introduction to Quantitative Methods for Historians*, 2nd edn, Methuen, 1979, pp. 125–9.

16 W.O. Aydelotte, 'On the business interests of the gentry in the parliament of 1841–47', in G. Kitson Clark, *The Making of Victorian England*, Methuen, 1962, and his *Quantification in History*, ch. 5.

17 For a preliminary account, see Michael Anderson and others, 'The national sample from the 1851 Census of Great Britain', *Urban History Newsletter*, 1977, pp. 55–9.

18 Lawrence Stone, *The Crisis of the Aristocracy, 1558–1641*, Oxford University Press, 1965, p. 130.

19 Floud, *An Introduction to Quantitative Methods for Historians*, pp. 88–122.

20 My example is adapted from one in Edward Shorter, *The Historian and the Computer*, Prentice Hall, 1971, pp. 5–8.

21 Peter Burke, *Sociology and History*, Allen & Unwin, 1980, p. 40.

22 For a discussion on this and related issues, see Michael Anderson, *Approaches to the History of the Western Family, 1500–1914*, Macmillan, 1980, pp. 33–8.

23 W.O. Aydelotte, A.G. Bogue and R.W. Fogel (eds), *The Dimensions of Quantitative Research in History*, Princeton University Press, 1972, pp. 10–11.

24 R.W. Fogel, 'The new economic history: its findings and methods', *Economic History Review*, 2nd series, **XIX**, 1966, pp. 642–56. For the application of this approach to British economic history, see G.R. Hawke, *Railways and Economic Growth in England and Wales, 1840–1870*, Oxford University Press, 1970.

25 Peter Mathias, 'Economic history: direct and oblique', in Martin Ballard (ed.), *New Movements in the Study and Teaching of History*, Temple Smith, 1970, pp. 83–4, and E.H. Hunt, 'The new economic history', *History*, **LIII**, 1968, pp. 15–16.

26 John Habakkuk, 'Economic history and economic theory', *Daedalus*, **C**, 1971, pp. 305–22.

27 Roderick Floud (ed.), *Essays in Quantitative Economic History*, Oxford University Press, 1974, p. 2.

28 See Herbert G. Gutman, *Slavery and the Numbers Game*, University of Illinois Press, 1975, and Paul David *et al.*, *Reckoning with Slavery*, Oxford University Press, 1976.

29 Lawrence Stone, *The Past and the Present Revisited*, Routledge & Kegan Paul, 1987, p. 94.

30 Lee Benson, *Toward the Scientific Study of History*, Lippincott, 1972, pp. 98–104.

31 Carl Bridenbaugh, 'The great mutation', *American Historical Review*, **LXVIII**, 1963, p. 326. For a more extended attack, see Jacques Barzun, *Clio and the Doctors*, Chicago University Press, 1974.

32 G.R. Elton, *The Practice of History*, Fontana, 1969, pp. 49–51.

33 G.R. Elton, *Political History*, Allen Lane, 1970, pp. 48–9.

34 For a review of the controversy, see Arthur J. Taylor (ed.), *The Standard of Living in Britain in the Industrial Revolution*, Methuen, 1975.

35 François Furet, 'Quantitative history', *Daedalus*, **C**, 1971, p. 160. See also his *In The Workshop of History*, Chicago University Press, 1985.

36 Aydelotte, Bogue and Fogel, *The Dimensions of Quantitative Research in History*, p. 9.

# CHAPTER TEN

# Theories of meaning

The sources of history can be read for their content, but they can also be used as a way into the mind – the mentality – of the people and society that produced them. What started as an intellectual study of the history of ideas has now progressed into a much more comprehensive study of the history of human culture and the multi-layered meanings that underpin it. Historians can call on the specialist knowledge of anthropologists, cultural and literary scholars, and psychologists. But to what extent can a historian really evoke the mentality and emotions of people in the past?

## The search for meanings

The interpretation of meaning is at the heart of the historian's work. Without it the primary sources are mute and the past will remain forever beyond our reach. Classical historicism was built on the conviction that technique and intuition could together uncover the meaning of past texts and hence allow us to reach across the gulf of time. Apprentices to the profession spent many years perfecting their skills in this area before they were encouraged to give much thought to larger issues of historical explanation, and textual knowledge remained the mark of the true scholar. Today the quest for meaning enjoys, if anything, an even higher profile. But the emphasis is rather different. For Ranke and his followers, the interpretation of meaning was a means to an end – the recreation of human action and the destiny of nations; the sources were central because they yielded authenticated detail out of which that story could be told. Present-day scholars increasingly study meaning as an end in itself, in the belief that how people interpreted their world and represented their experience is a matter of intrinsic interest. This means that they depart from Ranke's practice in another respect. Whereas he regarded textual meaning as the property of the individual (whose background and attitudes were accordingly central to the enquiry), it is the shared or collective meanings which historians value today. The key term is *culture*, here understood not as **'high' culture** but as the web of meaning which characterizes a society and holds its members together. It is a vast and absorbing field, embracing everything from formal belief through ritual and play to the unacknowledged logic of gesture and appearance.

**high culture**
i.e. established art forms such as painting and sculpture, classical music, ballet, opera, theatre and literature.

There is nothing especially innovative about the aspiration to cultural history (less, in fact, than there is in the appeal of quantitative history). Curiosity about – and respect for – the cultural difference of the past is completely in keeping with the spirit of historicism, and the attention to meaning as an end in itself corresponds to the dominant tradition in the humanities generally (as for example in the study of literature). But there is intense debate among historians about the theoretical approaches which are relevant to the task, and here historians find themselves in a challenging and uncertain terrain, in which there are few familiar toeholds. In this chapter I outline the principal strands of cultural history, broadly conceived. I weigh up the contribution of three distinct bodies of theory to this enterprise – psychology, textual theory and cultural anthropology. I conclude by showing how the recent vogue for cultural history opens up a conflict with the broad explanatory thrust described in Chapter 8. Academic history is currently going through one of its periodic struggles over how the agenda of the discipline should be defined, and the outcome is still unclear.

# I

## The history of ideas

The approach with the longest pedigree is the *history of ideas*, or intellectual history. It includes political thought, economic and social thought, theology, scientific thought, and the values and assumptions expressed in the writing of history itself (i.e. historiography). At its most ambitious, especially as practised in the

United States, the history of ideas amounts to an attempt to capture the intellectual climate of an entire epoch. However, the bulk of the work in this field probably continues to be about the history of political thought and as such is rooted in a tradition which was firmly established during the nineteenth century. Most of the great political historians from Ranke onwards were agreed that what gave history its coherence and continuity was the power of ideas to shape human destiny – ideas about nationhood, the state, constitutional liberties and religion. From this it was a short step to regard the history of ideas as a valid specialism, and to trace the origin of concepts such as natural rights, representative democracy and the national community. To explain their evolution was to explain the process of history itself.

## The challenges from Freud and Marx

In the twentieth century confidence in this approach has been undermined from two directions at once. On the one hand, the stress on the unconscious by Freud and the popularizers of psychoanalysis has given rise to some scepticism as to whether formal professions of belief or principle bear much relation to what people actually think or do: Namier's fascination with Freudian theory certainly accounted for much of his hostility to the history of ideas and his preoccupation with less elevated explanations of political action.[1] On the other hand, Marx's materialist interpretation of history represents a full-scale attack on the autonomy of intellectual history. Although the different schools of Marxist thought vary in their stance on this issue, the implication usually drawn from Marxism is that ideologies are essentially an expression of the tensions inherent in class-ridden societies (see Chapter 8). It is certainly true that today's historians are interested not only in the social impact of ideas in history but also – and perhaps more – in what those ideas tell us about the societies which give rise to them. The result of these changes in the intellectual climate is that the pretensions of today's historians of ideas are more modest than those of their predecessors, and they do not claim the same autonomy for their field. Their work continues to be significant because, although social and material conditions may place limits on the range of ideas which can gain acceptance in any age, they certainly do not determine the precise form those ideas take. Much can only be accounted for by the inventiveness of the human mind and by the power of tradition.

## The ideas of ordinary people

Until quite recently the history of ideas has been dominated by the great thinkers from **Plato** to Marx, whose works can be seen as building blocks in a single Western tradition. Today, however, a much keener awareness is also shown of the fact that the intellectual landscape of a period is not primarily composed of the handful of great works which have inspired posterity; almost by definition, these were inaccessible to all but a few. The common wisdom of the day against which the great names were judged (and in many instances condemned) was what contemporaries had retained, often selectively and incoherently, from earlier traditions of thought. For the political historian especially, what counts is the set of ideas within which people with no claims to intellectual originality operated, and from this perspective the diffusion of new ideas through second-rate and ephemeral literature is as important as their genesis in the mind of a great thinker. The intellectual context of periods of revolutionary change, when ideas are often particularly potent, can be properly understood in no other way. In *The Ideological Origins of the **American Revolution*** (1967), for example, Bernard Bailyn reconstructed the political culture of ordinary Americans from four hundred or so pamphlets bearing on the Anglo-American conflict which were published in the thirteen colonies between 1750 and 1776. His research revealed the influence of not only the **New England Puritan tradition** and the thought of the Enlightenment, which had long been taken for granted, but also the anti-authoritarian political thought of the Civil War period in England, kept alive by English radical pamphleteers of the early eighteenth century and transmitted across the Atlantic. At this point the history of ideas enters the marketplace, as it were, and becomes part of the common culture of the day.

**Plato (*c.* 427–*c.* 347 BC)**
Athenian philosopher, regarded as the founder of Western philosophy. His *Republic* outlined an ideal society, with different classes of citizens, their roles rigidly laid down and enforced.

**American Revolution**
For many years the conflict between Britain and the nascent United States was known in Britain as the War of American Independence and in America as the American Revolution. The British term is probably the more accurate of the two for the war itself; however, the political changes which followed the end of the war, and especially the drawing up of a written constitution based upon Enlightenment principles and English constitutional law, can be said to justify the more ambitious American term.

**New England Puritan tradition**
The colonies of New England were originally founded by Protestant dissidents – Puritans – fleeing religious intolerance in England. The colonies they established were conceived as religious communities, which often proved more intolerant than the English political regime they had fled.

## II

## Getting into the mind of the past

Dissemination is an important issue, but by itself it is not an adequate framework for the study of popular culture, which is about more than trickle-down from the political and intellectual élite. The history of ideas offers rich insights into the intellectual world of the highly educated, but it is not an adequate way of studying the history of popular culture. Nor does conventional social history necessarily make a useful contribution in this area. As we saw in Chapter 5, much social history has been concerned with structures and institutions, often entailing a high degree of abstraction from human experience. It is one thing to categorize people according to their place in a given structure by indicating their occupation, status and wealth. It is quite another to enter into their assumptions and attitudes, to see them as 'sentient reflecting beings'.[2] The history of the treatment of mental disorders is a well-established theme in social history; only recently have historians tried to enter the mentality of the insane and of those who labelled them so – in recognition that the history of madness is, in Roy Porter's words, 'centrally about confrontations between alien thought worlds'.[3] Of course historians have for a long time taken pains to portray the prominent personalities of the past with some degree of empathy; the study of an individual's private papers is important because it allows the historian to see the world through his or her eyes. But it is only quite recently that historians have faced up to the need to make a comparable effort in the case of people in the mass. How, in any given society in the past, did people apprehend their daily experience? What were their attitudes to time and space, the natural world, pain and death, family relationships and religious observance? How should we characterize their ambitions and anxieties? What were their common values?

## The *Annales* school: a historical psychology?

The first historians who tried to answer these questions in a coherent fashion were those of the *Annales* school (see pp. 126–7). One strand of this school is an interest in structures – demographic, economic and social – as in Braudel's books and the early work of Emmanuel Le Roy Ladurie. But the founders of *Annales*, especially Lucien Febvre, had a different emphasis. They called for a *history of mentalities*. In Febvre's view the worst kind of historical anachronism is psychological anachronism – the unthinking assumption that the mental framework with which people interpreted their experience in earlier periods was the same as our own. What, he asked, were the psychological implications of the differences between night and day and between winter and summer, which were experienced much more harshly by medieval men and women than they are today? Febvre called for a 'historical psychology', developed by historians and psychologists working together.[4] There is obviously a connection with the history of ideas, but instead of looking at formally articulated principles and ideologies, the history of mentalities is concerned with the emotional, the instinctive and the implicit – areas of thought which have often found no direct expression at all. Robert Mandrou has probably come closest to fulfilling Febvre's programme. In *Introduction to Modern France 1500–1640* (1961) he characterized the outlook of ordinary French people as 'the mentality of the hunted':[5] helplessness in the face of a hostile environment and chronic under-nutrition produced a morbid hypersensitivity, in which people reacted to the least emotional shock by excessive displays of grief, pity or cruelty.

## Freud and 'psychohistory'

Historical psychology raises large theoretical issues, given that human psychology is such a heavily theorized area of study. Febvre himself was not specially drawn to theory, but since his day one of the key questions for historians in this area is how far they should make use of the findings of psychoanalysis. Freud claimed that, as a result of his clinical work with neurotic patients, he had arrived at a theory which placed our understanding of the human mind on an entirely new and more scientific footing. His theory turned on the concept of the unconscious – that part of the mind imprinted by the experience of traumas in infancy (weaning, toilet-training, Oedipal conflict, etc.) which determines the emotional response of the individual to the world in later life. For Freud and the many followers who modified or extended his theory, the primary use of psychoanalysis lay in the treatment of psychiatric disorders. But Freud himself believed that his theory also offered a key to the understanding of historical personalities, and in a famous essay on **Leonardo da Vinci** (written in 1910) he in effect carried out the first exercise in 'psychohistory'. From the 1950s onwards this approach to biography enjoyed a considerable following, especially in the United States, where psychoanalysis was more widely accepted than in any other country. At its best psychohistory introduces a valuable element of psychological realism into historical biography, as in Bruce Mazlish's controversial study of **James and John Stuart Mill** – two lives in which the intellectual is otherwise particularly likely to obliterate the emotional.[6] With the benefit of hindsight it is all too easy to bend the lives of people in the past to a satisfying shape which emphasizes rationality and steadiness of purpose. Psychohistory, by contrast, dwells on the complexity and inconsistency of human behaviour; in Peter Gay's words, it depicts people as

> buffeted by conflicts, ambivalent in their emotions, intent on reducing tensions by defensive stratagems, and for the most part dimly, or perhaps not at all, aware why they feel and act as they do.[7]

In this way the inner drives can be restored to historical figures, instead of confining their motives to the public sphere in which their careers were played out.

## The psychology of the collective

The insights of psychoanalysis are not confined to individual lives. Indeed from the perspective of the cultural historian, the main contribution of psychoanalysis has been to direct attention to *cultural* patterns of parenting, nurture and identification, and to the play of the unconscious in collective mentality. In *The Protestant Temperament* (1977), one of the most wide-ranging applications of a psychoanalytic perspective, Philip Greven has identified three patterns of child-rearing in colonial America: the 'evangelical' or authoritarian, the 'moderate' or authoritative, and the 'genteel' or affectionate. While these labels signal the directing influence of theology and social position, the impact of each pattern is traced through the characteristic psychic development of children raised in these ways. Greven describes the

**Leonardo da Vinci (1452–1519)**
Italian artist and engineer. His work was based upon close observation of the natural world; his notebooks are full of anatomical sketches as well as designs for works of engineering, although some of the most apparently far-seeing of these, such as his design for a helicopter, have been shown to be later forgeries.  ·

**James Mill (1773–1836)**
British philosopher and follower of the utilitarian ideas of Jeremy Bentham, which stressed the need for modernizing social and administrative reform in order to ensure the greatest happiness of the greatest number. His 1817 *History of British India* criticized the 'backwardness' of native Indian culture. He was the father of John Stuart Mill.

**John Stuart Mill (1806–73)**
British philosopher. His 1859 work *On Liberty* argued the case for individual freedom within the growing hold of the state. Mill was a committed believer in female emancipation and in widening the parliamentary franchise into the working class.

ensuing personalities or 'temperaments' by reference to attitudes towards the self: hostility in the case of the evangelicals, control in the case of the moderates, and indulgence in the case of the genteel. Within a common Freudian framework Greven's approach makes allowance for the cultural diversity of seventeenth- and eighteenth-century America without insisting that every American enacted one of the three models. The appeal of psychoanalytic categories is particularly strong in the case of those facets of the past which we consider irrational or pathological but which made compelling sense to those involved. Racism lends itself to this approach. Models of repression and projection have been used to excellent effect to explain white attitudes to other races during the heyday of colonial expansion – as for example in **Jacksonian America**.[8]

## Objections to psychohistory

Of all the technical and methodological innovations made in the past thirty years, psychohistory has attracted the most curiosity outside the profession, but it is also open to quite serious objections, for two principal reasons. First, there is the problem of evidence. Whereas the therapist seeks to recover the infantile experience of the patient through the analysis of dreams, verbal slips and other material produced by the subject, the historian has only the documents, which are likely to contain very little, if any, material of this kind and very few direct observations about the subject's early infancy. Much personal material which we might consider highly relevant is completely unobtainable, yet this is the bricks and mortar without which a psychohistorical theory of personality cannot be devised. Secondly, even if the claims of psychoanalysis are accepted – and they remain hotly contested among psychologists to this day – there is no reason to assume that they are valid for previous ages. Indeed, the assumption should rather be the reverse: Freud's picture of emotional development is very culture-bound, rooted in the child-bearing practice and mental attitudes (especially towards sex) of late nineteenth-century middle-class urban society. The application of Freud's insights (or those of any other contemporary school of psychoanalysis) to individuals living in any other period or society is anachronistic. For the structure of human personality over time

**Jacksonian America**
The period 1828–37, covering the presidency of Andrew Jackson (1767–1845). Jackson, a successful general from North Carolina, adopted a robust approach to politics. He was a firm believer in keeping the powers of the federal authorities to a minimum; paradoxically, he enforced his view by using his presidential right of veto far more than his predecessors had done. He engaged in a long and generally popular battle against the Bank of the United States, believing it to be an example of centralized tyranny.

is precisely what needs to be investigated, instead of being reduced to a formula. Even the notion of the self, which we (like Freud) may regard as a fundamental human attribute, was probably quite foreign to Western culture before the seventeenth or eighteenth century. As one particularly trenchant critic has put it, psychohistory can easily become a determinist form of 'cultural **parochialism**'.[9] Psychoanalysis is a powerful tool with great potential for illuminating the human mind, but historians who employ it have to be particularly careful to temper their interpretations with a respect for historical context.

**parochialism**
Narrow-minded concern with one's own immediate locality and concerns without regard to their wider context. 'Parochial' means literally 'referring to a parish'.

# III

## Literary theory and the cultural reconstruction of the past

The second body of theory which bears on cultural history is drawn from literary studies. This is the critical stance towards texts variously known as deconstruction or discourse theory. We saw in Chapter 7 how literary theorists, drawing on Saussure's theory of the materiality and arbitrariness of language, have rejected the notion of the authentic authorial voice and instead view the text as open to a multiplicity of 'readings' in which different audiences find different meanings. In Chapter 7 I dwelt on the exceedingly troubling implications which the indeterminacy of texts holds for the epistemological status of history. But it is important to recognize that, at a practical level, the new theories of the text open up the prospect of significant advances in the cultural reconstruction of the past. Traditionally historians regarded their primary sources as a point of access to events or states of mind – to what had an 'objective' or demonstrable existence beyond the text. Literary theory teaches historians to focus on the text itself, since its value lies less in any reflection of reality than in revealing the categories through which reality was perceived. From this perspective, primary sources are essentially *cultural* evidence – of rhetorical strategies, codes of representation, social metaphors and so on. Literary theory gives historians the confidence to move beyond the letter of the text (the traditional focus of their scholarship) and listen to a wider range of voices which goes well beyond the scope of Marc

Bloch's injunction to treat the sources as 'witnesses in spite of themselves' (see p. 62). Close reading – or reading 'against the grain' – is even more time-consuming than the time-honoured procedures of historical method, and for this reason it tends to be applied to smaller bodies of source material of considerable textual richness.

## Linguistic discourse and the language of politics

These conditions are exactly what the historian of ideas is familiar with, and the effect of discourse theory on the study of political thought is already marked. For if language facilitates certain modes of thought while excluding others, and if there is a sense in which language determines consciousness (rather than the other way round as common sense declares), then the political order must depend on linguistic as much as administrative structures: politics is constituted within a field of discourse, as well as within a particular territory or society. That discourse must itself be viewed as a field of contention, and the key texts as (in Dror Wahrman's phrase) 'a **palimpsest** of different and not necessarily compatible "political languages"'.[10] In modern polities there are usually a number of alternative and interlocking discourses jostling for ascendancy – expressing, for example, reverence for the state, class solidarity or democratic rights. A well-documented example is the English Revolution. Kevin Sharpe has argued that prior to 1642 the language of politics had not been recast, both Crown and Parliament still sharing a set of common values expressed in law and custom. What was truly revolutionary about the Civil War was that men were led to act in ways which their language could not as yet represent; the political prize proved to be a new discourse of rights and contract which by the end of the seventeenth century was firmly in the ascendant in England.[11] The French Revolution, legitimized under the banner of *liberté, egalité, fraternité*, was among other things 'the invention of a new form of discourse constituting new modes of political and social action'.[12] Language, then, is power. In taking on board this central perception of discourse theory, historians are redefining their understanding of political thought. They are demonstrating how the members of a **polity** experience, reflect and act politically within the conceptual boundaries of particular discourses, and

**palimpsest**
A parchment which has been written on more than once, i.e. the original wording has been scratched out and other writing has been superimposed upon it. Here used metaphorically.

**liberté, egalité, fraternité**
'Liberty, equality, fraternity', the slogan often inscribed on buildings, documents and other forms of officialdom during the French Revolution. It attempted to sum up the essential spirit of the *Declaration of the Rights of Man*.

**polity**
A state or other entity run by some form of civil government.

how these discourses are themselves subject to contestation, adaptation and sometimes total rupture.

Discourse analysis also has much to contribute to the historical understanding of nationality – a category traditionally used by historians almost without reflection. It was pointed out in Chapter 1 how national identity is never 'given' but arises from specific historical circumstances, which change over time. If nations are forever being constructed anew or 'invented', it is discourse in the broadest sense which accomplishes this – through the elaboration of cultural symbols and the celebration of a highly selective reading of the national past. The dissemination of this material to a mass audience is fundamental to nationalism in the modern world. For this reason in *Imagined Communities* (1983) – one of the most influential recent analyses of nationalism – Benedict Anderson places great weight on 'print capitalism' as a prerequisite for the growth of nationalism since the sixteenth century. More detailed work on the languages of patriotism shows how the content of particular nationalisms has changed over time. In England since the **Reformation** it has had a shifting relation to the monarchy, popular liberties and foreigners – to name just three indicators of political hue. Because 'the nation' is more imaginary than real, the metaphors in which it is expressed have great potency, and their popular meaning – be it democratic or authoritarian – becomes a battleground between rival conceptions of the political order.[13]

The language-led approach to texts is also evident in the attention which some historians are now giving to the literary form – or genre – in which their sources are written. Here the argument is that our interpretation of the ostensible content of a text may need to be considerably modified in the light of the genre to which it belonged – and which conditioned the understanding of its readers. When Natalie Zemon Davis studied the **letters of remission** submitted to the French courts in the sixteenth century by supplicants seeking a royal pardon, she soon realized that they could not be regarded simply as direct personal statements. They were drawn up by **notaries** in an avowedly literary way which reflected several contemporary genres, including fictional ones, each with its own conventions. 'I am after evidence of how sixteenth-century people told stories', she writes,

**Reformation**
In England, the process of religious change in the early sixteenth century in which the English Church first renounced the authority of the papacy in favour of that of the monarch and then established a form of Protestantism known as Anglicanism.

**letters of remission**
Official letters requesting a royal pardon or a reduction in the sentence imposed by a court.

**notaries**
Legal clerks with the authority to draw up legal documents.

... what they thought a good story was, how they accounted for
motive, and how through narrative they made sense of the
unexpected and built coherence into immediate experience.[14]

Davis calls her book *Fiction in the Archives*, not because she
regards the letters of remission as fabrications but to draw attention to the essentially literary issues which they pose. The
question of whether the supplicants were guilty is here subordinated to questions of meaning and representation.

# IV

## The anthropology of historical culture

But for recent historians the most fertile source of ideas in the area
of collective mentality has been not textual theory but *cultural
anthropology*. Although the relevance to history of the study of
exotic small-scale societies of the present day may not be readily
apparent, there are several reasons why historians should be alert
to the findings of anthropology. These reasons are most obvious in
the case of those historians who are themselves specializing in
some area of Third World history, but they also apply to their colleagues in more conventional fields. The findings of anthropology
suggest something of the range of mentalities to be found among
people who are acutely vulnerable to the vagaries of climate and
disease, who lack 'scientific' control of their environment, and
who are tied to their own localities – conditions which obtained in
the West during most of the medieval and early modern periods.
Certain long-lost features of our own society, such as the **blood
feud** or witchcraft accusations, still persist in some parts of the
world today; direct observation of the modern variant prompts a
sounder grasp of the relevant questions to be asked about comparable features in our own past for which the direct evidence may be
very sparse or uneven. The classic demonstration of this is Keith
Thomas's *Religion and the Decline of Magic* (1971), which drew
on the studies of Evans-Pritchard and other ethnographers to
define a new agenda for the study of witchcraft in early modern
England. For historians encountering a past society through the
medium of documentary sources there is – or ought to be – the
same sense of 'culture shock' that the modern field-worker experiences in a remote and 'exotic' community.

**blood feud**
A bitter conflict, often
involving the families and
friends of the protagonists
and stretching over more
than one generation.

## The anthropology of mentality

But since Thomas's path-breaking work the relevance of anthropology to the cultural historian has broadened to become one of method and theory, not just a source of suggestive analogies. The key issue is how anthropologists get to grips with the world view of their subjects. Because they conduct their research by combining the roles of participant and observer, anthropologists can hardly fail to register the vastly different mental assumptions which operate in pre-literate, technologically simple societies. Indeed 'mentality' is at the heart of their specialist expertise, and the concept of 'culture' as used in this chapter is essentially an anthropological one. In fieldwork anthropologists pay special attention to symbolic behaviour – such as a naming ceremony or a rain-making ritual – partly because the sense of strangeness is then most challenging and partly because symbol and ritual are seldom one-dimensional but express a complex range of cultural values; the seemingly bizarre and irrational tend to reflect a coherence of thought and behaviour which in the last resort is what holds society together. The influential American anthropologist Clifford Geertz refers to his own cultural readings of very densely textured, concrete facts as 'thick description': one episode – in the best-known case a Balinese cock-fight – may provide a window on an entire culture, provided we do not impose on it a coherence which makes sense in our terms.[15] There is an interesting convergence with literary theory here: just as a text is open to many readings, so a ritual or symbol may yield a range of meanings. Geertz himself regards culture as being like an assemblage of texts, and he explains the goal of cultural anthropology in terms of 'the text analogy'.[16]

Since descriptions of ritual provide some of our best evidence for pre-literate societies of the past, it is not surprising that historians have welcomed the insights of cultural anthropology. Natalie Zemon Davis is one of many historians who acknowledge the influence of Geertz. She invokes the 'text analogy' in describing her work on sixteenth-century French society:

**lying-in**
Childbirth.

> A journeyman's initiation rite, a village festive organization, an informal gathering of women for a **lying-in** or of men and women for story-telling, or a street disturbance could be 'read' as fruitfully as a diary, a political tract, a sermon, or a body of laws.[17]

The mass in late medieval England, the carnival in early modern France and the rituals of monarchy are just some of the symbolic material which has attracted enquiry along these lines. In a bravura demonstration of the technique of 'thick description', Robert Darnton has analyzed the trivial episode of a cat killing by apprentice printers in Paris during the 1730s. By placing the reminiscences of one of the printers in the context of a varied range of contemporary cultural evidence, Darnton shows how the massacre of cats combined veiled elements of a witch-hunt, a workers' revolt and a rape – which is why the apprentices found it such a hugely amusing way of letting off steam. 'To get the joke in the case of something as unfunny as a ritual slaughter of cats is a first step towards "getting" the culture.'[18] In this kind of history, carefully observed detail really counts, often several times over.

## The limitations of anthropology

Darnton's cat massacre demonstrates the excitement of this approach – but also its dangers. Whereas the anthropologist, as a participant observer, is in a position to observe the ritual and generate additional contextual evidence, the historian has to accept the limits of the sources. The cat killing is described in only one account, and a retrospective one at that. When the documentation is so one-dimensional, it is open to an even greater variety of readings, which means that the authority of any particular reading is more difficult to sustain. Darnton treats the cat killing as a workers' revolt which prefigured the French Revolution. But, as Raphael Samuel points out, the story could just as well have served an analysis of adolescent culture or a study of social attitudes towards animals; a single source lends itself all too readily to 'symbolic overloading'.[19] Cultural historians are for the most part thrown back on oblique and ambiguous evidence of what went on in the minds of ordinary people, and it is appropriate to recognize these limitations before wholeheartedly embracing the interpretative procedures of cultural anthropology or textual theory.

In fact the value of the anthropological approach lies as much in its general orientation as in its handling of detail. It serves as a strong reminder that history is not just about trends and structures which can be observed from the outside; it also demands an informed respect for the culture of people in the past and a readiness to see the world through their eyes. Anthropology also represents a change of emphasis in the way historians try to achieve these goals, by shifting the emphasis away from individual statements to collective behaviour in contexts of cultural significance.

# V

## Gender and the cultural history of meaning

The impact of the cultural approach to history could be measured in a number of different fields: popular culture, religion, consumption and attitudes towards the natural world spring to mind. The fact that a great deal of original work is going on in these and other fields testifies to the importance of cultural history. I can best indicate what this means in practice by exploring one field in more detail: the history of *gender*.

In Chapter 8 gender was presented as a form of radical social theory originally developed by feminist scholars but with a widening appeal in a post-Marxist world. It was clear from that discussion that the material inequalities between the sexes are crucial to the understanding of historical societies and their dynamic over time. But gender is not only a structural question. It touches on subjectivity and identity in profound ways. These issues have come to the fore as the emphasis in contemporary Western culture has veered away from seeing sexual difference as a biological given. Once the traditional binary distinction between male and female is modified to take account of the gender diversity which actually exists, the articulation of masculinities and femininities becomes more and more a matter of psychology and culture. Gender is now something that has to be explained, instead of being invoked as a ready-made explanation for everything else.

## The cultural creation of gender

In practical terms, this shift means two things. First, if gender difference is not principally a matter of nature or instinct, it must be instilled. Parents may experience this as an individual task, but it is essentially cultural in character, since those who are charged with childcare operate within certain cultural understandings of sexual difference and personality development. Gender, in short, is knowledge. Until the very recent past, sexual difference was naturalized (and simplified) into predetermined scripts which most people did not question. Those forms of knowledge took a variety of forms: explicit knowledge about the body, as in sex manuals such as *Aristotle's Masterpiece* (repeatedly reprinted in England throughout the eighteenth century and beyond); or heavily moralized teaching about sexual character, as in nineteenth-century writings about **manliness** and about the proper lady; or again the assumptions about sexual difference which pervade literature in both its élite and popular forms. Recent historians have given close attention to all this material, tracking the contradictions and subtle shifts of emphasis against the bedrock assumptions which remained firm for generations.[20]

The second dimension of the cultural approach to gender takes up the issue of difference. All social identities work partly by a process of exclusion. We are defined as much by what we are not as by what we are. Often the negative stereotyping of those beyond the pale is just as powerful as the corresponding belief in what members have in common: this was true of British national identity during the Second World War, for example, and it has been a recurrent theme in class politics over the past two centuries. In the case of sexual difference, defining the self in relation to 'the other' is particularly pronounced because the social consciousness of most young children is predicated on a fundamental distinction between male and female. All attributes can be mapped onto this binary opposition. Hence all gender definitions are relational, in the sense that they arise from interaction with the other sex and express assumptions about that sex: the enduring discourse of 'effeminacy' as a boundary for men's behaviour bears ample witness to that. Discourse is vital to this process of 'othering', partly because binary structures are deeply embedded in language (good v. bad, black v. white, etc.), and partly because language registers this opposition between male and female in an endless variety of culturally specific forms. In psychoanalysis the tradition associated with Jacques Lacan also places prime emphasis on language as the means by which children acquire their sexed identities. There is now a great deal of

**manliness**
A now obsolete term for the qualities and attributes expected of men. In the late nineteenth century manliness was strongly influenced by militarism: it emphasized physical strength and rigid self-control, both of which were thought to be promoted by sport.

theoretical support for the proposition that language 'constructs' gender difference.[21]

## The dissection of gender identity

The turn towards cultural theory in gender history reflects a significant political shift. Early work in the field focused on oppression and inequality. It was strongly influenced by Marxism, and many of its exponents acknowledged the label of 'socialist feminist'. Whether fully integrated with class oppression or not, the historical subordination of women was essentially seen as a predicament common to the sex as a whole. The proper concern of historians was the nature of that subordination and the growth of organized resistance. The political direction of recent work is not so sharply defined. Political engagement in Western societies has traditionally been seen to express strong collective identities, like 'the British' or 'workers' or 'women'. But once discourse analysis is given full play, 'identity' cannot be frozen at this macro-level; dissecting the complex web of meanings in which individuals situate themselves has the effect of fracturing these large categories by opening up **fissures** along lines of class, nation, ethnicity, region, age, sexuality and so on. Not only is the notion of women as a collectivity hard to sustain; even 'woman' as a consistent self-evident identity can be called into doubt.[22] A comparable process of deconstruction is at work in the history of ethnicity, where the whole concept of 'race' invites radical reappraisal along these lines.

**fissures**
Cracks, gaps.

## Gender and the new polarities of power

However, the emphasis on language and representation does not so much drain gender history of political content as reflect a different kind of politics. Gender today is increasingly articulated in terms of differences that go beyond the basic polarity of male/female; the politics of identity is also expressed through distinctions of sexuality, ethnicity and age. In that sense the Postmodern fracturing of identity reflects actual changes in social consciousness. Moreover, the deconstructionist approach has an obvious bearing on the commonplace feminist observation that most recorded discourse is 'man-made' language. Joan Scott argues strongly that a linguistic approach serves to expose the gender dimension of all power relations. Her argument hinges on two closely related propositions. First, gender is a structural (or 'constitutive') element of all social relationships, from the most intimate to the most impersonal, because there is always an assumption either of the exclusion of one sex or of a carefully regulated (and usually unequal) relationship between the sexes. Secondly, gender is an important way in which relationships of power are signified in cultural terms.[23] To take a recurrent case, the uncompromisingly 'masculine' terms in which war is referred to have for a very long time served to legitimate the sacrifice of life which young men are called upon to endure. In the Victorian era the idea of state-funded welfare was damned as 'sentimentality' – a feminine attribute – by its enemies.[24] Many other comparable examples could be cited. Furthermore, these gendered meanings should not be seen as static and given, and an obvious task for politically informed analysis is to trace their reinterpretation and contestation in different contexts. Gender history of the

The notorious 'Jack the Ripper' murders of 1888 provide a case study not only of crime and prostitution in late Victorian London but also of the collective cultural mentality which found the murders so fascinating. (Topfoto/Topham/Picturepoint)

**draconian**
Excessively harsh.

**Jack the Ripper**
The nickname current at the time and since for the perpetrator of a series of extremely brutal murders of prostitutes in Whitechapel, in the East End of London, in 1888. Speculation about the identity of the murderer, which has led to accusations against, among others, a famous painter and a member of the royal family, has spawned a virtual industry of 'ripperologists'. The fascination the case continues to exert is as interesting to historians as the original murders themselves.

cultural variety may be resistant to the solid collectivities of old, but it has much to contribute to an understanding of how power is articulated in personal and social relations.

This point can be illustrated with reference to the scholarly career of Judith Walkowitz. Her first book, published in 1980, analyzed prostitution in Victorian society through the prism of class and gender: it documented the double sexual standard of the day, the material exploitation of the prostitutes, and the political strategies of those who wished to repeal the **draconian** legislation which regulated the trade. Its political sympathies were plain – indeed the help of the women's liberation movement is explicitly acknowledged.[25] Twelve years later Walkowitz followed this up with *City of Dreadful Delight* (1992), a study of sexual scandals and sexual discourses in London during the 1880s. Within the perspective of the earlier book, child prostitution and **Jack the Ripper** – the main subjects here – would have invited a materialist analysis of the vice trade and the power relations between procurers, prostitutes and clients. These matters are not ignored, but Walkowitz is now less interested in what happened than in what was *represented* as happening. The book's subtitle, 'Narratives of Sexual Danger in Late-Victorian London', accurately reflects her concern with which stories prevailed and why. But, as she emphasizes, this is a deeply political question, since popular notions of sexual character and sexual morality were contained within a regulatory discourse, of which the newspaper press was merely one element. *City of Dreadful Delight* may lack the political bite of the earlier book, but it is a fine study of the cultural processes which make some discourses hegemonic while marginalizing others.

# VI

## The redundancy of class, race and nation?

The shift in the orientation of gender history represented by Walkowitz's two books corresponds to a much broader change in the theoretical underpinnings of historical writing. Twenty years ago most social history, and much political history also, was confidently written in terms of coherent collectivities such as class and nation. It made sense to write about 'the working class' or 'the French nation' because these groups were grounded in a shared material existence from which they derived a common, defining consciousness, extending beyond the life-span of the individuals who happened to constitute the group at any one time. This was most explicit in the case of the Marxists' handling of class and class consciousness, but liberal scholarship was little different in its treatment of political parties, religious denominations and nations as historical actors spanning the generations. In both liberal and Marxist writing these social identities acquired an almost material reality, which served to drive forward 'grand narratives' of progress or revolutionary destiny. By the 1970s this social, material and progressive paradigm may not have taken over the mainstream, but it undoubtedly represented the cutting edge and was the focus of the most important historiographical debates.

That social paradigm has come under attack from two directions. First in the field were the *Annales* historians with their emphasis on collective mentalities. They had, from the beginning, asserted that no picture of the past could be complete without a reconstruction of its mental landscape. Braudel incorporated mentalities into his structural scheme by including them alongside geographical factors in his *longue durée*. By the 1980s the leading *Annalistes* were claiming more than this, declaring that mentality was the fundamental level of historical experience and culture its principal expression. As Georges Duby has put it,

> Men's [sic] behaviour is shaped not so much by their real condition as by their usually untruthful image of that condition, by behavioural models which are cultural productions bearing only a partial resemblance to material realities.[26]

By the 1990s the main impetus for the attack on the social paradigm came from textual theory, with its assault on referential notions of representation. It proved to be a short step from rejecting authentic meaning in texts to fracturing accepted social identities, since what does identity depend on if not a shared language and shared symbols? Class, race and nation all lost their 'hard' objective character and became no more than unstable discourses. Culture itself was now seen as a construction, rather than a reflection of reality. The Postmodernist attack on 'grand narratives' completed the job of demolition by discrediting the persistence of active social identities over time. What is left is the study of representation – of how meanings are constructed, not what people in the past did. Cultural history is the principal beneficiary of this shift in historical thinking because the priority it gives to language makes questions of meaning and representation more important than anything else.

## The benefits and limitations of the cultural agenda

If taken to extremes, it is clear that cultural history – and the 'linguistic turn' in particular – would undermine much of the traditional agenda of historians. The idea that representation should be the *only* legitimate field of historical study is entirely new. A recent article by Patrick Joyce advocating just this is provocatively titled 'The end of social history?'[27] By this he means that the history of class and class relations in the mould of E.P. Thompson no longer has validity, and in his own writing Joyce has, for example, analyzed the subject of industrial work in cultural rather than economic terms, thus detaching it from labour history.[28] For all its rhetorical skill, Joyce's position has found little favour with historians. It amounts to an acceptance of the Postmodernist charge-sheet against history as usually practised. Most of the profession is little inclined to see the scope of their work pared down to the indeterminate dimensions of discourse, and this goes for the majority of cultural historians too. Taking representation seriously does not necessarily mean disparaging everything else. Nor does a cultural agenda signal a minimalist position on the issue of historical truth. Most historians working in the field acknowledge the positive ways in which textual theory has enriched the subject, without taking on board its destructive epistemology.

Yet the difference of emphasis remains. The historian who analyzes industrial relations as a ritual bound by the conventions of a game is doing something very different from the historian of class conflict; emphasizing the malleability of gender identities produces different results from a commitment to the reality of patriarchal oppression; and so on. This difference is crucially one of theory. For the first group of historians, the subject of their research usually holds interest because of its place in a social narrative, which in turn is interpreted by reference to a dynamic theory of social change, usually Marxist. The second group, on the other hand, is essentially interested in contextualizing – in making cultural connections within a single plane, as it were, often with scant attention to changes over time. Theories of the mind, of the text and of culture itself provide the conceptual underpinning for this work, and they too serve to enrich contextual understandings rather than illuminate historical process. Once again, as in Chapter 1, we see the tension in historical writing between the explanatory mode and the re-creative mode. Social theory continues the agenda set in the Enlightenment of interpreting the direction of human history; events and processes are deemed significant in terms of the place they hold in a larger narrative. Cultural theory takes up the historicists' emphasis on the inherent strangeness of the past and the need for intellectual effort to interpret its meaning. This chapter and Chapter 8 have described two quite different kinds of history, and the conflict between them is very much of our time. But the tension they reflect is as old as the discipline itself.

## Freud and psychoanalysis

The Austrian neurologist Sigmund Freud (1856–1939) developed the process of *psychoanalysis*, whereby patients were first relaxed and then encouraged to speak freely about their feelings and memories, often going far back to childhood. His 1900 work *The Interpretation of Dreams* argued that dreams bring out mental pain and trauma which is otherwise repressed in the mind. There was fierce controversy over his tracing of the development of sexual feelings and desires to early childhood, including the *Oedipus complex*, named after the figure in Greek mythology who unknowingly kills his father and marries his own mother, by which a young boy experiences a powerful desire to possess his mother and a fear that his father might retaliate by castrating him.

Freud held that the mind is divided into three parts: the *id*, which represents inherited, innate instinct; the *ego*, which represents the individual's sense of his or her own self within the world; and the *superego*, which reflects those wider social values and ideals which have been learned from parents or through schooling or experience. The Swiss psychiatrist Carl Gustav Jung identified different types of personality, notably the introvert and

▶

the extrovert, and formulated the theory of the 'collective subconscious', those hidden attitudes and fears which are shared by the members of a particular cultural grouping. Freud's theories proved a major inspiration to artists and writers and were particularly popular in the United States, where by the late twentieth century psychoanalysis had become a virtual industry. Although the basis for Freud's theories has come under increasing attack in recent years, public interest in psychology and the working of the mind remains as strong as ever.

## Nationalism

The idea of the nation-state was a product of the French Revolution, where it was seen as the embodiment of the will of the people. One of the leading theoreticians of European nationalism was the Italian revolutionary Giuseppe Mazzini (1805–72), who believed that national self-determination would produce international peace and respect for individual liberty. In practice, European nationalists proved unable to defeat the forces of the established European dynasties, and their cause was taken over by much less liberal-minded leaders in Italy, Germany and France. By the end of the nineteenth century Europe was dominated by major national units, though a number of national groups, such as the Poles, Hungarians and Slavs, had only limited autonomy or none at all. The 1919 peace settlement was drawn up along the principles of national self-determination laid down by US President Woodrow Wilson (1856–1924), which he believed would avoid the national rivalry that had produced the war. Unfortunately, it proved impossible to draw up equitable frontiers along national lines, which helped to provoke the Second World War in 1939. After 1945 there was a move away from nationalism in favour of the internationalism of the United Nations and the Cold War alliances, NATO and the Warsaw Pact. The end of the Cold War, however, saw a major resurgence of nationalist sentiment, especially in Central and Eastern Europe and the constituent republics of the former Soviet Union.

# Further reading

**T.G. Ashplant** & **Gerry Smyth** (eds), *Explorations in Cultural History*, Pluto Press, 2001

**Peter Burke**, *Varieties of Cultural History*, Polity Press, 1997

**Lynn Hunt** (ed.), *The New Cultural History*, California UP, 1989

**Paul Rabinow** (ed.), *The Foucault Reader*, Pantheon, 1984

**Peter Gay**, *Freud for Historians*, Oxford UP, 1985

**T.G. Ashplant**, 'Psychoanalysis in historical writing', *History Workshop Journal*, **XXVI**, 1988

**Dominic La Capra**, *History and Criticism*, Cornell UP, 1985

**Robert Darnton**, *The Great Cat Massacre and Other Episodes in French Cultural History*, Allen Lane, 1984

**Stefan Collini**, *English Pasts*, Oxford UP, 1999

# Notes

1 See, for example, Namier's essay, 'Human nature in politics', 1955, reprinted in Fritz Stern (ed.), *The Varieties of History*, Macmillan, 2nd edn, 1970.

2 I have taken this phrase from Margaret Spufford, *Contrasting Communities: English Villagers in the Sixteenth and Seventeenth Centuries*, Cambridge University Press, 1974, p. xxiii.

3 Roy Porter, *Mind Forg'd Manacles: A History of Madness in England from the Restoration to the Regency*, Athlone, 1987, p. x.

4 Lucien Febvre, 'History and psychology', 1938, reprinted in Peter Burke (ed.), *A New Kind of History*, Routledge & Kegan Paul, 1973.

5 Robert Mandrou, *Introduction to Modern France, 1500–1640: An Essay in Historical Psychology*, Arnold, 1975, p. 26.

6 Bruce Mazlish, *James and John Stuart Mill: Father and Son in the Nineteenth Century*, Hutchinson, 1975.

7 Peter Gay, *Freud for Historians*, Oxford University Press, 1985, p. 75.

8 Michael P. Rogin, *Fathers and Children: Andrew Jackson and the Subjection of the American Indian*, Knopf, 1975.

9 David E. Stannard, *Shrinking History: On Freud and the Failure of Psychohistory*, Oxford University Press, 1980, p. 30.

10 Dror Wahrman, *Imagining the Middle Class: the Political Representation of Class in Britain, c. 1780–1840*, Cambridge University Press, 1995, p. 11.

11  Kevin Sharpe, *Politics and Ideas in Early Stuart England*, Frances Pinter, 1989, ch. 1.

12  Keith Baker, 'On the problem of the ideological origins of the French Revolution', in Dominick La Capra and Steven L. Kaplan (eds), *Modern European Intellectual History: Reappraisals and New Perspectives*, Cornell University Press, 1982, p. 204.

13  Raphael Samuel (ed.), *Patriotism: the Making and Unmaking of the British National Identity*, 3 vols, Routledge, 1989.

14  Natalie Zemon Davis, *Fiction in the Archives*, Polity Press, 1987, p. 4.

15  Clifford Geertz, *The Interpretation of Cultures*, Hutchinson, 1975, ch. 1.

16  Clifford Geertz, *Local Knowledge: Further Essays in Interpretive Anthropology*, Fontana, 1983.

17  Natalie Zemon Davis, *Society and Culture in Early Modern France*, Duckworth, 1975, pp. xvi–xvii.

18  Robert Darnton, *The Great Cat Massacre and Other Episodes in French Cultural History*, Allen Lane, 1984, p. 262.

19  Raphael Samuel, 'Reading the signs: II', *History Workshop Journal*, 33, 1992, pp. 235–8, 243.

20  Roy Porter and Lesley Hall, *The Facts of Life: the Creation of Sexual Knowledge in Britain, 1650–1950*, Yale University Press, 1995, ch. 2; Leonore Davidoff and Catherine Hall, *Family Fortunes: Men and Women of the English Middle Class, 1780–1850*, Hutchinson, 1987, ch. 2–3; John Tosh, *A Man's Place: Masculinity and the Middle-Class Home in Victorian England*, Yale University Press, 1999.

21  For a discussion of the implications of Lacan for gender historians, see Sally Alexander, *Becoming a Woman and Other Essays in 19th and 20th Century Feminist History*, Virago, 1994, pp. 105–10, 225–30.

22  Denise Riley, *Am I That Name? Feminism and the Category of 'Women' in History*, Macmillan, 1988.

23  Joan W. Scott, 'Gender: a useful category of historical analysis', *American Historical Review*, **91** (1986), pp. 1053–75.

24  Stefan Collini, 'The idea of "character" in Victorian political thought', *Transactions of the Royal Historical Society*, 5th series, **XXXV** (1985), pp. 29–50.

25  Judith R. Walkowitz, *Prostitution and Victorian Society*, Cambridge University Press, 1980, p. ix.

26  Georges Duby, 'Ideologies in social history', in Jacques Le Goff and Pierre Nora (eds), *Constructing the Past: Essays in Historical Methodology*, Cambridge University Press, 1985, p. 151.

27 Patrick Joyce, 'The end of social history?', *Social History*, **XX** (1995), pp. 73–91.

28 Patrick Joyce (ed.), *The Historical Meaning of Work*, Cambridge University Press, 1987.

# CHAPTER ELEVEN

# History by word of mouth

In recent years historians have made increasing use of oral testimony, either interviewing people about their memories or tapping into the oral tradition and folk memories of pre-literate societies. Oral sources have had a major impact on social history, and on the pre-colonial history of Africa. Such material can give an exhilarating sense of touching the 'real' past, but it is as full of pitfalls and difficulties as any other sort of historical material. What questions should historians ask of oral material, and what role do they themselves play in its creation?

## Oral testimony and oral tradition

The growing interest of historians in cultural meaning has produced one novel departure which merits more extended treatment. This is the development of a methodology for interpreting oral evidence. Long neglected by professional historians, oral material is now drawn on in two quite different ways, each presenting a distinctive challenge to the conventionally trained researcher. The first and more familiar category is oral reminiscence – the first-hand recollections of people interviewed by a historian, usually referred to as *oral history*. Since the late 1960s oral history has been increasingly exploited in Britain and other Western countries, particularly for the light it can shed on recent social history. Then secondly there is *oral tradition*, that is, the narratives and descriptions of people and events in the past which have been handed down by word of mouth over several generations. Although practically extinct in highly industrialized countries, oral tradition is still a living force in those countries where literacy has not yet displaced a predominantly oral culture; since the 1950s it has been studied with growing assurance by historians of Africa. Both oral history and oral tradition were initially valued as a means of direct access to the past. Today they are increasingly regarded as evidence of how non-élite communities construct and modify cultural meaning over time.

# I

## The pedigree of oral history

It is only very recently that professional historians have acquired any experience of collecting oral sources. Even today the mainstream of the historical profession remains sceptical and is often not prepared to enter into discussion about the actual merits and drawbacks of oral research. Arthur Marwick's otherwise comprehensive list of primary sources in his *The Nature of History* (1970) made no mention of oral sources.[1] As recently as 1995 John Vincent remarked that 'history is not about pre-literate societies'.[2] Yet oral sources of both kinds provided the bulk of the evidence used by those who are now looked back to as the first historians – **Herodotus** and **Thucydides**. The chroniclers and historians of the Middle Ages were hardly less dependent on oral testimony; and although written sources grew rapidly in importance from the Renaissance onwards, the older techniques still survived as a valued adjunct to documentary research. It was only with the emergence of modern academic history in the nineteenth century that the use of oral sources was entirely abandoned. The energies of the new professionals cast in the Rankean mould were taken up by the study of written documents, on which their claim to technical expertise was based, and their working lives were largely confined to the library and the archive.

Ironically, many of the written sources cited by today's historians were themselves oral in origin. Medieval chroniclers such as **William of Malmesbury** in the twelfth century incorporated oral traditions as well as first-hand testimonies into their writings. Social surveys and official commissions of enquiry, which loom so large in the primary sources for nineteenth-century social history, are full of summarized testimonies which historians draw on, often with little regard for the selection of witnesses or the

**Herodotus (c. 485–425 BC)**
Greek historian, sometimes known as the Father of History. His history of Greece's wars with Persia is regarded as the first work of genuine history, based upon critical analysis of the sources, many of which were first-hand accounts gathered from interviews. Herodotus also incorporated into his account many local and geographical details gathered from his extensive travels.

**Thucydides (c. 460–400 BC)**
Greek historian and military commander. He fought in the Peloponnesian war between Athens and Sparta and used his experience and interviews with other veterans as a basis for his history of the war. Unusually, Thucydides considered the war's long-term causes rather than simply providing a series of heroic set-pieces.

**William of Malmesbury (c. 1095–1143)**
English monk and historian, the first major figure in English historiography after the Anglo-Saxon historian, Bede (673–735). William wrote a history of England, taking over from where Bede's account breaks off, in two parallel volumes, one covering the deeds of England's kings and the other those of England's bishops.

circumstances in which they were interviewed. Yet the idea that historians might add to the volume of available oral evidence by conducting interviews themselves continues to arouse misgivings. The reason is partly that historians are reluctant to see any compromise with the principle that contemporaneity is the prime requirement of historical sources – and oral sources have an inescapable element of hindsight about them. But perhaps there is a more deep-seated aversion to any radical change in the habits of work required for historical research, and a reluctance to grapple with the implications of scholars sharing in the creation (and not just the interpretation) of new evidence.

## The anthropology model

In the meantime the interview method has become an important research tool in the social sciences. In anthropology, which came to maturity during the 1920s and 1930s, researchers typically adopt the role of participant observer. They aim as far as possible to lead the life of a member of the community under study, and in order to make sense of their experience engage in constant dialogue with their hosts, including the collection of life histories. In studying contemporary Western society, sociologists have tended to become less personally involved with their subject matter, but the in-depth interviewing of respondents has nevertheless been an important source of data alongside the more commonly practised social survey by questionnaire. The interview techniques of social anthropology and sociology have proved helpful to historians, though – as we shall see – they have needed to develop their own distinctive approach to the material recorded.

## The need for oral history

The fact that oral techniques have made any headway at all among professional historians is due almost entirely to the reticence of conventional written sources on a number of areas that are now engaging scholarly attention. Recent political history is one such topic. Whereas in the Victorian and Edwardian periods public figures commonly conducted a voluminous official and private correspondence, their modern counterparts rely much more on the telephone, and when they do write letters they seldom have the leisure to write at length. There have been major public figures in recent times who have left no private papers to speak of – **Herbert Morrison**, a leading member of the Labour Party in the 1930s and 1940s, being a notable example.[3] In order to fill out the evidence to the proportions appropriate to a biography, historians have had to collect the impressions and recollections of such figures from their surviving colleagues and associates. The same applies to many lesser figures in political and other walks of life. The British Oral Archive of Political and Administrative History was set up at the London School of Economics in 1980 to collect this kind of material in a systematic way.[4] The second area concerns what might be termed the recent social history of everyday life, and particularly those aspects of working-class life in the family and the workplace which were seldom the subject of contemporary observation or enquiry. In Britain the oral history movement is dominated by social historians, whose interest in these topics is in many cases sustained by an active socialist commitment, evident in their house journal, *Oral History*. The third area which cries out for an enlargement of the conventional historian's technical skills is the history of pre-literate societies, which have generated little or no written evidence of their own and are known in the documents only through the statements of literate – and usually prejudiced – outsiders. In the African case, not only is the everyday experience of Africans themselves recoverable by no other means; much of the more formal content of history, such as the rise of entrepreneurial trade or the evolution of political institutions, requires substantial oral work too. Of these three broad areas, it is in the last two that the most substantial contribution has been made and the most significant implications for historical method have arisen.

**Herbert Morrison (1885–1965)**
Labour politician. He was a major figure in the development of London between the wars, especially the capital's public transport network. He served in Ramsay MacDonald's 1929 Labour government, and as Home Secretary in Churchill's wartime coalition. He was Deputy Prime Minister in Clement Attlee's postwar Labour government and was in charge of steering the programme of nationalization through the House of Commons. He was the grandfather of the Blairite New Labour former minister, and EU Trade Commissioner, Peter Mandelson.

# II

## The voice of the people?

> When I came to this village with my father, I was in lodgings as well, so there were no real home comforts to come back to after the pit. I remember being in one set of lodgings: there were six or seven other miners lodging there. It was only a house with three bedrooms, so you can imagine that we were sleeping on a rota basis.

If five or six of us were on the same shift, as soon as I got out of the pit I'd gallop home to be the first to have a bath. There were no bathrooms: all you had was an old zinc tub, and the landlady would have a couple of buckets of water on the fire. If there were five or six of you together, first of all five of you would bath the top half of the body. Everybody bathed the top half of the body in a rota, and then you stepped back into the bath and washed the bottom part of your body. What used to amuse me in those days – well, not amuse – what used to embarrass me was that you'd get the women from next door or from each side of the terraced house. They'd come in there, and they'd sit down in the kitchen, and they wouldn't bloody move – when even you were washing the bottom part of your body. As a youngster and not being used to that, I was not only shy but embarrassed, because you learnt the differences even in those days between the sexes.[5]

This narrative, collected from a retired collier in South Wales as part of a research project on the history of mining communities, conveys something of the qualities which recommend 'oral history' to historians. It is a fragment of autobiography by someone who would never otherwise have dreamed of dignifying his reminiscences in that way. As an individual experience that is commonplace and yet at the same time particular, it offers a vivid insight into a way of life that now survives in Britain only in the memories of the very old. Contemporary written sources for the Edwardian period – the reports of social investigators and charitable bodies, for example – provide copious information about the homes of the poor, but it is information derived at second hand and glossed by 'expert' opinion, a description from outside rather than a product of experience. Oral history allows the voice of ordinary people to be heard alongside the careful marshalling of social facts in the written record.

Domestic routine is only one of the many aspects of the past for which oral history can provide a corrective to the bias of the written sources. Social history aspires to treat the history of society as a whole, not just the rich and the articulate. But, as we saw in Chapter 5, the records to which the social historian instinctively turns carry the stamp of the organizational preoccupations that brought them into being. As a result, labour history features the full-time union official rather than the rank and file; the history of housing emphasizes speculative building and sanitary reform rather than the tenants' quality of life; and agricultural history is taken up with estate management and the rural economy, not the working conditions of the farm labourers. Written documents are also primarily the work of adult men: women who did not belong to the leisured letter-writing class wrote little that has survived, and the experience of childhood finds almost no overt expression in the documentary record. And some social groups which were prominent only seventy or eighty years ago are almost entirely absent from the conventional sources – itinerant traders, unorganized wage-earners of all kinds, and poor immigrant communities.

The testimony which can be gleaned from surviving members of these groups, like the memories of most old people about their youth, is often confused as regards specific events and the sequence in which they occurred. Where it is most reliable is in characterizing recurrent experience, like the practice of a working skill or a child's involvement in a network of neighbours and kin. The routines of daily life and the fabric of ordinary social relationships were commonplace and therefore taken for granted at the time, but now they seem of compelling human interest, and oral enquiry offers the readiest means of access – as in *A Woman's Place* (1984), Elizabeth Roberts's fine study of working-class Lancashire women during the half century before the Second World War. What oral history also uniquely conveys is the essential *connectedness* of aspects of daily life which the historian otherwise tends to know of as discrete social facts. Through the life histories of the very poor, for instance, the way in which casual labour, periodic destitution, undernourishment, drunkenness, truancy and familial violence formed a total social environment for thousands of people before the First World War (and later) can be vividly portrayed. Oral history, in short, tries to give social history a human face.

## Oral history and local history

How do oral historians come by their informants? The sampling techniques of sociology have had some influence here. In one of the most ambitious attempts yet made to incorporate the findings of oral history into a general social history, Paul Thompson took a carefully constructed sample of 500 surviving Edwardians from all classes and regions of Britain, and some of the resulting material is presented in his book *The Edwardians* (1975).[6] But few historians have followed his example. Most recent oral history has been emphatically local in focus, and for this there are sound practical reasons. In a strictly local study all the elderly who are willing and able can be canvassed; less trust has to be placed in the reliability of the individual informant, since the testimonies can be tested against each other; and the purely local references which always feature prominently in life histories can be elucidated with the help of other source materials. But it is also significant that oral history has from the outset been practised by amateur local historians. The English tradition of amateur local history (which extends back to the sixteenth century) has stressed **topography** and the world of the **squire**, parson and – more rarely – businessman. Oral history promises a sense of place and community accessible to ordinary people, while at the same time illuminating broader features of social history. Very fine work of this kind has been done under the auspices of the History Workshop movement. Raphael Samuel reconstructed the economic and social milieu of Headington Quarry near Oxford before it was enveloped by the expansion of the motor industry in the 1920s; without the rich oral testimony he collected, Samuel would have found it difficult to penetrate far beyond the stereotype of 'Quarry roughs' in newspapers of the time to understand the range of trades and social networks which sustained the independent spirit of the villagers.[7] In the field of urban local history, perhaps the best oral work has been the two London studies by Jerry White, an accomplished amateur: one on a notorious Holloway street between the wars, the other about a single tenement block in the East End around the turn of the century.[8]

## The authentic past?

Underlying the current practice of oral history are two powerfully attractive assumptions. First – and most obviously – personal reminiscence is viewed as an effective instrument for *re-creating* the past – the authentic testimony of human life as it was actually experienced. Paul Thompson revealingly entitles his book on the methods and achievements of oral history *The Voice of the Past* (1978), and – notwithstanding all the reservations made in the text – the notion of a direct encounter between historians and

**topography**
The study of the physical features of a location.

**squire**
The general term used for a member of the gentry, the major landowner in a particular village. The term is usually reserved for those whose influence was limited to one particular locality, as opposed to nobles and aristocrats, whose landholdings might be very extensive.

The collection of oral testimony about Campbell Road in Holloway belied its reputation as 'the worst street in London'. (Topfoto/Topham/ Picturepoint)

their subject matter is central to Thompson's outlook and is even more explicit in his principal foray into oral history, *The Edwardians*. At one level, therefore, oral history simply represents a novel means of fulfilling the programme laid down by professional historians since the early nineteenth century – 'to show how things actually were' and to enter into the experience of people in the past as fully as possible.

But many oral historians are not content with being grist to the mills of professional history. They see oral history rather as a democratic alternative, challenging the monopoly of an academic élite. Ordinary people are offered not only a place in history but a role in the *production* of historical knowledge with important political implications. In East London the People's Autobiography of Hackney is an open group of local residents who record each other's life histories and publish the transcriptions in pamphlets marketed through a local bookshop. Although educated people participate, no academic historians are involved; if they were, the confidence of people in their own perceptions of the past might be undermined. The idea is that through oral work the community should discover its own history and develop its social identity, free from the patronizing assumptions of conventional historical wisdom. Ken Worpole, coordinator of the group, recalls the circumstances in which it began in the early 1970s: 'producing shareable and common history from the spoken reminiscences of working-class people seemed a positive and important activity to integrate with various other new forms of "community" politics'; he sees this and other similar projects as essential to the task of 'reviving the historical component of an affirmative class consciousness'.[9] The same might be said of ethnic consciousness, and it is quite likely that black history in Britain will develop along these lines, as blacks draw on their recent experience of migration, settlement and discrimination.[10]

# III

## The dangers of oral history

However, both these formulations – oral history as 'recreation' and as 'democratic' knowledge – present major difficulties. The problems which arise from the oral method are perhaps most evident in the research project conducted by a professional historian. It is naïve to suppose that the testimony represents a pure distillation of past experience, for in an interview each party is affected by the other. It is the historian who selects the informant and indicates the area of interest; and even if he or she asks no questions and merely listens, the presence of an outsider affects the atmosphere in which the informant recalls the past and talks about it. The end-product is conditioned both by the historian's social position *vis-à-vis* the informant, and by the terms in which he or she has learned to analyze the past and which may well be communicated to the informant. In other words, historians must accept responsibility for their share in creating new evidence.

But the difficulties are far from over when the historian is removed from the scene. For not even the informant is in direct touch with the past. His or her memories, however precise and vivid, are filtered through subsequent experience. They may be contaminated by what has been absorbed from other sources (especially the media); they may be overlaid by nostalgia ('times were good then'), or distorted by a sense of grievance about depri-

Historians have learned the techniques required to get hold of the oral testimony of witnesses to the past. But how much care is needed in dealing with first-hand accounts inevitably influenced by hindsight?
(Topfoto/James Marshall/Image Works)

vation in childhood which took root only in later life. To anyone listening the feelings and attitudes – say of affection towards a parent or distrust of union officials – are often what lend conviction to the testimony, yet they may be the emotional residue of later experience rather than the period in question. As one critic of Paul Thompson's work put it:

> His 'Edwardians' after all, have lived on to become 'Georgians' and, now, 'Elizabethans'. Over the years, certain memories have faded, or, at very least, may have been influenced by subsequent experience. How many of their childhood recollections were, in fact, recalled to them by their own elders? What autobiographies or novels might they have since read that would reinforce certain impressions at the expense of others? What films or television programmes have had an impact on their consciousness? . . . to what extent might the rise of the Labour Party in the post-war decade have inspired retrospective perception of class status and conflict?[11]

Whatever the evidence it rests on, the notion of a direct encounter with the past is an illusion, but perhaps nowhere more than in the case of testimony from hindsight. The 'voice of the past' is inescapably the voice of the present too.

## The limitations of oral history

Yet even supposing that oral evidence were somehow authentic and unalloyed, it would still be inadequate as a representation of the past. For historical reality comprises more than the sum of individual experiences. It is no disparagement of the individual to say that our lives are largely spent in situations that, from our subjective perspective, we cannot fully understand. How we perceive the world around us may or may not amount to a viable basis for living, but it never corresponds to reality in its entirety. One of the historian's functions is to advance towards a fuller understanding of the reality of the past; access to a much wider range of evidence than was available to anyone at the time, together with the discipline of historical thinking, enables the historian to grasp the deeper structures and processes which were at work in the lives of individuals. The vividness of personal recall which is the strength of oral evidence also therefore points to its principal limitation, and historians need to be wary about becoming trapped within the mental categories of their informants. It is not that those categories are necessarily wrong, merely that they are more confined than they need be. In the words of Philip Abrams:

> The close encounter may make the voices louder; it does not ... make their meaning clearer. To that end we must turn back from 'their' meanings to our own and to the things we know about them which they did not know, or say, about themselves.[12]

This limitation applies with particular force to the democratic or populist tendency in oral history. The idea behind projects of the 'people's autobiography' type is that an articulate and authentic historical consciousness will enable ordinary working people to take more control over their lives. But to do so they need an understanding of the forces which have actually moulded their world – most of them not of their making or directly manifest in their experience. The problem with collective oral history is that it is likely to reinforce the superficial way in which most people think of the changes they have lived through, instead of equipping them with deeper insights as a basis for more effective political action. Jerry White makes this point cogently:

> Because it [the group project] is locked in an autobiographical mode – with absolute and inviolable primacy given to what people say about

themselves – it does little, if anything, to capture those levels and layers of reality outside individual experience.[13]

## Interpreting oral history

What place, then, does oral history have in the practice of historians? The problems raised here are not grounds for having nothing to do with oral history. What they suggest is rather that oral evidence, like all verbal materials, requires critical evaluation, and that it must be deployed in conjunction with all the other available sources; in other words, the canons of historical method described in Chapter 4 apply here too. Transcriptions of testimonies, such as Thea Thompson's *Edwardian Childhoods* (1981) or the *Working Lives* published by the People's Autobiography of Hackney (1972, 1976), are not 'history' but raw material for the writing of history. Like some other primary sources, they often display evocative and expressive qualities which make them well worth reading for themselves, but they are no substitute for the work of historical interpretation.

Oral sources are in fact extremely demanding of the historian's skills. In his book *The Edwardians* Paul Thompson, by introducing the oral evidence alongside his findings from more conventional sources, may appear to have done all that is required; but for the most part quotations from interviews are presented in an impressionistic manner as illustrative support for the various themes discussed in the book.[14] If the full significance of an oral testimony is to come across, it must be evaluated in conjunction with all the sources pertaining to the locality and people spoken of or else much of the detail will count for nothing. Sometimes oral research itself unearths new documentary material in private hands – family accounts or old photographs – which add to the amount of supporting evidence. It is mastery of the local context which makes the oral work of Raphael Samuel and Jerry White so striking. White describes his book on tenement life in London's East End, *Rothschild Buildings* (1980), in these terms:

> This may be primarily a work of oral history but documents have
> played a large part in its conception. Written sources and oral sources
> interact throughout: finding a new document has led me to ask
> different questions of the people I interviewed, and the oral testimony
> has thrown fresh light on the documents. The rules printed on the

first tenants' rentbooks led me to ask if they were obeyed and how; finding the original plans of the Buildings made me wonder what was kept in the fitted cupboard behind the living-room door; people's memories of shopping led me to take street directories with a large pinch of salt; autobiographical details cast doubts on census classifications, sociologists' assumptions and standard historical reference works, and so on.[15]

Command of the full range of relevant sources is no less important for 'democratic' oral history. The more traditional inventory of local historians' sources – business archives, news-papers, census returns, the reports of charitable bodies, etc. – provides an entry into the economic and social context of the informants' lives and may reveal something of the historical pro-cesses which have shaped the observable changes in the locality. The limitations inherent in the amateur group project mean that, to be politically effective, it requires the participation, if not of professional historians, at least of people familiar with the methods and findings of mainstream social history.[16]

## The construction and distortion of social memory

*histoire vérité*
(French) 'truth history', derived from the phrase *Cinéma vérité*, a style of film pioneered by French directors which attempted to show gritty and unpolished 'reality' rather than the carefully composed images of conventional cinema.

But there is an important sense in which the anxiety about the accuracy of oral testimony is beside the point. More recent work suggests that oral research may be less important as *histoire vérité* or as an expression of community politics than as precious evi-dence of how social memory is constructed. From this perspective it is the very departures from faithful recall that give the content of oral history its full significance. We saw in Chapter 1 how social memory is moulded by political requirements and thus often diverges from the version of events verified by historians. Oral history can reveal that process of divergence and in so doing shed light on the political culture and historical consciousness of ordinary people. The very subjectivity of the speaker may be the most important thing about his or her testimony. The sense of the past that individuals carry around with them comprises a selec-tion of their immediate experience, together with some conception of the nature of the social order in which they live. Historical biographies sometimes show how these two elements bear on each other in the thinking of leaders and intellectuals, but we know much less about their place in the historical awareness of ordinary people. Yet the way in which social groups assimilate and interpret their own experience is a historical factor in its own right, at the heart of political culture.

From this perspective, the mental transition from 'Edwardians' to 'Georgians' and on to 'Elizabethans' is an object of study for its own sake, instead of being merely an obstruction in the way of a direct encounter with the past. Recent work on popular memory demonstrates the kind of insights that flow from this approach. In Australia the participation of Anzac troops in the Gallipoli campaign of 1915 is an important component of the modern sense of Australian nationhood and has been officially promoted as such since the 1920s. Alistair Thomson's oral study shows how the men who had experienced the trauma and sense of inadequacy in combat subordinated their personal memories so as to match the accepted picture of loyalty, bravery and camaraderie on the front line, which most Australians accept to this day.[17] In Alessandro Portelli's study, 'The Death of Luigi Trastulli', the political adjustments of social memory are even clearer. Trastulli was a steel-worker killed by police during a demonstration in the Italian town of Terni in 1949. This event administered such a shock to the workers that very soon appropriate causes and circumstances were being improvised to render it explicable. Whereas Trastulli had been killed during a protest against Italian entry into NATO, many of the memories current during the 1970s relocated the event as part of a later demonstration against the mass lay-off of workers, a much more critical issue for most of the participants. Trastulli was also portrayed as having been pinned against the factory wall by police fire, in an image that emphasized his status as a martyr. As Portelli explains,

> the discrepancy between fact and memory ultimately enhances the value of the oral sources as historical documents. It is not caused by faulty recollections ... but actively and creatively generated by memory and imagination in an effort to make sense of crucial events and of history in general.[18]

Oral history provides a unique insight into that 'making sense'. It reflects an active relationship between present and past, between individual memories and public tradition, and between 'history' and 'myth'. Oral history, in short, is the raw material of social memory.

**Edwardian**
Relating to the reign of King Edward VII (1901–10).

**Georgian**
Here, relating to the reign of King George V (1910–36). The term is more usually used of the reigns of the first four Georges (1714–1830); it was only rarely used to refer to George V, and then usually in conjunction with 'Georgian' painters and writers.

**Elizabethan**
Although usually used to refer to the first Queen Elizabeth, it here refers to Queen Elizabeth II. There was a vogue at the start of her reign in 1952 to speak of a 'New Elizabethan Age', though the term was not current for long.

**Anzacs**
Properly, ANZAC: Australian and New Zealand Army Corps. Anzac troops were involved in the disastrous allied landings at Gallipoli in Turkey during the First World War, where their heavy casualties sowed much bitterness towards the British planners of the operation.

**Gallipoli**
The amphibious landing of allied troops in 1915 at the town of Gallipoli, on the narrow Dardanelles strait in western Turkey,

was one of the most disastrous allied operations of the First World War. The plan, proposed by Winston Churchill as First Lord of the Admiralty, was bold in conception but poorly planned and executed, and resulted in very heavy casualties. The troops had to be evacuated, never having been able to advance inland from the landing beaches.

**NATO**
North Atlantic Treaty Organization. An American-led military alliance of the Western powers created in 1949 and aimed at containing and counterbalancing the threat from the Soviet Union and its allies, which responded the following year by forming their own alliance structure, the Warsaw Pact. Adherence to NATO was controversial with those who sympathized with the Soviet Union in the Cold War, or who distrusted the increasing reliance on military alliances and atomic weaponry.

**district commissioner**
A government official under British colonial rule. District commissioners, who were often young men not long out of university or the army, were entrusted with full administrative and judicial responsibility for vast

# IV

## Oral history and oral tradition

While oral history has been enlarging the scope of recent social history in industrialized societies (and not only in Britain), a comparable exercise in recovery has been going on in sub-Saharan Africa (and other regions of the Third World). Yet although the oral nature of the material means that the two share several common problems of technique and interpretation, there has been little scholarly contact across the North–South divide, mainly because the circumstances in which the two enterprises began and their characteristic subject matter are quite different.[19] In fact Africa is as good a territory as any other for the practice of 'oral history' in the sense understood in the West. The memories of the colonized are an essential corrective to the written sources, which so often reflect the view from the **district commissioner's** verandah or the **mission compound**. In many parts of Africa the colonial period was so brief that until a few years ago first-hand testimony about the imposition of white rule was still widely available. Several studies of colonialism in Africa have deployed oral material to very good effect.[20] But the greatest challenge to historians has been to equip Africa with a more extended past – to demonstrate that modern Africa, like all other societies, is the outcome of historical processes whose roots lie deep in the past. Given the almost complete ignorance that prevailed only fifty years ago, this has been a formidable undertaking, in which the development of a scholarly approach to oral tradition has featured prominently.

## Oral sources in African history

The first manifestos for African history during the 1960s called for an ambitious multi-disciplinary approach to pre-colonial history: **linguistics, ethno-botany, palaeoclimatology** and **epidemiology** were all invoked, as well as the more familiar archaeology, so that African history looked set to become 'the decathlon of social science'.[21] But the more **esoteric** disciplines have on the whole remained the province of their respective specialists, and most of them relate to environmental changes measured in millennia rather than centuries or generations – the relevant time-span for most historians. In Africa as elsewhere, verbal materials have retained their central position in historical research. This is partly because the documentary base proved much broader than had at first been supposed. The European trading companies and missionary societies, which had been in contact with Africa since the fifteenth century and by the nineteenth century had penetrated deep into the interior, were found to have extensive records. In the Islamic regions of the Sahel, the western Sudan and the East African coast, where the frontiers of literacy extended far into black Africa, there are local chronicles dating back in some cases to the sixteenth century, and even – in a few states such as the Sokoto **caliphate** of northern Nigeria – a nucleus of administrative records. But the veneer of literacy was very thin in Islamic Africa, and interest in conservation – in an environment where documents do not easily survive – was slight. At the same time, the European sources, although much more plentiful, present essentially an outsider's view of African culture: they may document the external relations of a kingdom and major milestones such as a rebellion or the death of a ruler, but by themselves they are quite inadequate for understanding the structure and evolution of African societies. And many parts of Africa had no contact with literate outsiders at all until the arrival of the first colonial administrators at the very end of the nineteenth century. Inevitably, therefore, historians found themselves drawn to the other main type of verbal source – oral tradition.

## The nature of oral tradition

Oral tradition may be defined as a body of knowledge that has been transmitted orally over several generations and is the collective property of the members of a given society. In those parts of the world which have known near-universal literacy for two or three generations, oral tradition has practically died out. One of the few forms in which it survives in Britain is the rhymes and riddles of schoolchildren – precisely because they are too young to be fully assimilated into the prevailing literate culture.[22] But in many African societies ethnic identity, social status, claims to political office and rights in land are still validated by appeals to oral tradition; what in Western society would be formalized by written documents, in oral societies derives its authority from the mem-

areas, where they might well be the only Europeans for hundreds of miles. They were required to keep meticulous records, which offer a rich vein of historical material to the historian. They did indeed often live in comfortable houses with shady verandahs.

**mission compound**
Missionaries played a crucial role in developing and shaping Britain's colonial empire. Mission stations, often built around a compound, usually consisted of a chapel with a school or hospital attached. Missionary records are another important historical source for the history of colonized areas, though they offer a very particular, and Western, perspective.

**linguistics**
The study of the nature of language.

**ethno-botany**
The study of human society through its use of, and impact on, plant life.

**palaeoclimatology**
The study of climate in prehistoric times.

**epidemiology**
The statistical study of the causes of epidemic disease.

**esoteric**
Open only to the initiated; hence, in common usage, heavily specialized.

**caliphate**
The status and seat of a
caliph, successor to the
Prophet Muhammad.

**ethnographers**
Those who study the
distinctive society and
culture of other
communities.

ories of the living. Historians are by no means the first observers
to record oral tradition in Africa. Since the beginning of the colonial period it has attracted the interest of **ethnographers** – and
indeed of literate Africans too. More recently social anthropologists have studied oral tradition for the light it sheds on the social
values of African societies today. But only in the 1950s did historians begin to evaluate oral tradition carefully for its historical
content and to lay down procedures for its collection and
interpretation. From the start their work carried a note of
urgency: as literacy spread and young men increasingly left the
countryside for the town or the labour compound, the chain of
oral transmission was evidently nearing its end, and the traditions
would die with the elders unless recorded in the field. (Literacy
and labour migration made less impact on women, but the transmission of traditions in African society is nearly always a male
preserve.)

This was an immensely exciting enterprise. Historians collected detailed bodies of tradition which by genealogical
reckoning extended back four or five centuries, complete with
named individuals and their exploits – the very stuff of conventional historiography. Their faith in the reliability of the
traditions was greatly strengthened by the discovery that in the
more centralized and elaborate chiefdoms the recital of traditions
was the business of trained specialists; fixed texts with vivid
poetic imagery helped to imprint tradition in the memory, while
in some instances material relics such as royal tombs or regalia
were used as **mnemonic** devices to ensure that the reigns of earlier
rulers were recalled in correct sequence. The high point of this
new-found confidence was the publication in 1961 of Jan
Vansina's methodological treatise, *Oral Tradition*.[23] On the
strength of his fieldwork in Rwanda and among the Kuba people
of Zaire, Vansina maintained that the methods required to evaluate a formal oral tradition were in principle no different from
those required by written documents. He likened the African historian's position to that of the medievalist confronted by several
corrupt variants of an original text (see p. 95): through close
analysis of the form of the document, the variant texts and the
chain of transmission, the historian could in each case arrive at
the original 'primary' version. At the same time, comparison of
the traditions of neighbouring chiefdoms sometimes revealed a

**mnemonic**
An aid to memory.

striking degree of agreement, and the independent evidence of archaeology provided further confirmation of the truth of tradition. In the case of the Bantu-speaking kingdoms of pre-colonial Uganda (**Buganda** and its neighbours) the outcome was a continuous political history of some four centuries' depth.[24] Although oral tradition could hardly be viewed as a *direct* encounter with the past in the manner of 'oral history', it was hailed as a truly indigenous source – the voice of the African past uncontaminated by colonialism.

**Buganda**
East African kingdom taken over by Britain in 1894 and subsequently subsumed into the British colony of Uganda. The Baganda people of Buganda were given special status within Uganda.

# V

## The unreliability of oral tradition

Unfortunately longer experience of oral tradition and reflection on the nature of oral society have shown that the position is not nearly so straightforward as this. Some of the reservations expressed earlier about the re-creative claims of oral history apply here too – notably the new and potentially distorting presence of the professional historian as the recorder of the testimony. But there are more serious problems peculiar to tradition. These arise from the repeated tellings through which any tradition has been transmitted to the present and from its social function, which is a much more central issue here than in the case of personal reminiscence.

However much the recital of a tradition may be governed by a wish to repeat accurately what has been handed down, it always entails an element of *performance*. Like storytellers everywhere, the performer is alert to the atmosphere among his audience and his sense of what is acceptable to them. Each retelling of the story is likely to be textually distinct from the one before, as the content becomes subtly adjusted to social expectations. Traditions are not kept alive by storytellers who, by some mysterious faculty beyond the grasp of literate people, are able to remember great epics and lists without effort; they are handed down because they hold meaning for the culture concerned. In the last resort, the traditions are valued not for themselves but because other more important things depend on them.

# The purpose of oral tradition

Broadly speaking oral traditions fulfil two social functions. They may be a means of teaching the values and beliefs which are integral to the culture – the proper relationship between humans and animals, for example, or the obligations of kinship and **affinity**. Secondly, they may serve to validate the particular social and political arrangements which currently prevail – the distribution of land, the claims of one powerful **lineage** to the chiefship, or the pattern of relations with a neighbouring people. Traditions about origins and great migrations usually fall into the first category, while those which recount the doings of particular groups and individuals belong to the second, but there is no hard-and-fast division: many traditions are both cosmological statements and political charters. By the time a tradition has been handed down over four or five generations, its social function is likely to have modified the content considerably by suppressing detail which no longer seems relevant and by elaborating the rhetorical or symbolic elements in the story. And this process can continue indefinitely, as changes in social or political circumstances leave their imprint on the corpus of oral tradition. It may be politic to **excise** certain rulers from the record, or to alter the **genealogies** which 'explain' the present relations between lineages.[25] Sometimes these adjustments are made quite deliberately. Among the Kuba a dynastic tradition could only be recounted after its content had been carefully vetted in private by a council of notables; as one of them put it, 'After a while, the truth of the old tales changed. What was true before, became false afterwards'.[26] More commonly, the process of assimilating tradition to current realities is more gradual and less calculated. David Henige sums up the position like this:

> In societies that depend on flexibility and ambiguity in their social
> and political activities (and this really means all societies, of course)
> orality can free the present from imprisonment by the past because it
> permits the remembrance of aspects of that past – like the sequence
> and activities of former rulers – to accord with ever-changing self-
> images.[27]

**affinity**
Relationship by marriage.

**lineage**
Descendants from a
common ancestor.

**excise**
To cut out or erase.

**genealogies**
Family trees and lists of
ancestors.

# The impact of colonialism

The experience of colonialism introduced further distortion. European over-rule in many instances changed the balance of power between neighbouring societies and led to a remodelling of their political structures to fit administrative needs – with predictable consequences for oral tradition. In British territories astute African rulers soon realized how respectful of 'tradition' their new masters were, and they manufactured king lists and supporting traditions to demonstrate the antiquity of their authority and so advance their claims for special treatment. Furthermore, the new schools run by Christian missionaries introduced a novel element into the conditions of oral transmission. In societies where literacy is a recent accomplishment and is associated with the ruling group, the written word carries immense and indiscriminate prestige. In Africa the earliest published versions of oral tradition, regardless of quality, acquired authority at the expense of other versions, and they often became the standard form in which the tradition was repeated orally. The outcome was a permanent distortion – particularly serious if, as in Buganda, the African chiefly élite propagated an 'official' version designed to buttress its own political position.[28] Far from being a pristine 'authentic' source, oral tradition – like most features of African culture – has been deeply affected by the experience of colonialism and the social changes that came with it.

The sensitivity of oral tradition to the demands of its audience and the prestige of the written word was strikingly borne out when the black American writer Alex Haley went to the Gambia in 1966 in search of his slave-boy ancestor, Kunta Kinte. Although the oral traditions current in the region do not contain information about real people before the nineteenth century, Haley duly found an elder who recited a tradition about the boy's capture into slavery by 'the king's soldiers' in the mid-eighteenth century. Haley had made no secret of his story and what he was looking for, and there seems little doubt that the 'tradition' was concocted for him. Several years later, as a result of the publicity surrounding Haley's bestseller *Roots* (1976), many more specialists in tradition were able to recite the story of Kunta Kinte with further lively embellishments.[29]

## The interpretation of oral tradition

Using oral traditions for historical reconstruction therefore raises major problems. Not only are they mostly narratives intended for the **edification** of posterity – and thus rather low down in the historian's hierarchy of sources; they have also been constantly reworked to articulate their meaning more clearly, and sometimes to change it. Unlike primary documentary sources, oral tradition does not convey the original words and images from which the historian may be able to re-create the mental world of the past. In fact it makes more sense to regard oral tradition as a *secondary* source, but with the added twist that it has erased all the earlier versions. It is as if the publication of the latest historical monograph was marked by the destruction of all copies of the previous work on the subject.

The remodelling over time which all oral traditions undergo is such that the basic facts are in doubt. Among the Lango people of northern Uganda, most recitations of tradition begin with the statement 'We Langi came from Otuke' – the impressive hill in the extreme north-east of their country. This may mean that 500,000 people are descended from migrants who came from Otuke *en masse*; it may be a compressed statement referring to a gradual movement of people from a general north-easterly direction; or – as was probably the case – it could mean that the dominant groups within Lango society came from the north-east and later were able to impose the Otuke tradition as a badge of Lango identity on everyone else; it could conceivably have no historical content at all and reflect a world view in which, say, the north-east represented cattle-keeping – the most prestigious form of subsistence in Lango – as against the south (fishing) and the west (crop husbandry).[30] To interpret the significance of such a tradition requires considerable immersion in the culture of the people concerned. Placing it in time may be even more difficult, in view of the arbitrary lengthening and telescoping of genealogies and lists which is so characteristic of oral tradition.[31] Perhaps most frustrating of all is the tendency for oral tradition to validate the social institutions of the day and only rarely to admit that these institutions have ever been different, for it is in just this area that other types of evidence such as archaeology and external documentary sources have least to offer.

**edification**
Education and moral improvement

The result is that historians are now very cautious indeed about advancing interpretations of oral traditions which purport to refer to events several centuries ago. They know the danger of accepting at face value what may be no more than the community's present-day self-image put into time perspective. Indeed there are signs of convergence here with the preoccupations of some of the more advanced exponents of oral history. For if the subtle modifications by which ordinary people reinterpret their individual life experience provide insight into the formation of historical consciousness, how much richer must the evolving oral tradition of an entire community be as evidence of how the past can be manipulated for social ends. Here the concern is less with oral tradition as historical evidence than with seeking to understand the cultural and political context in which images of the past are constructed.[32] This has very promising implications for the study of collective mentality in Africa.

## The uses of oral tradition

Valuable though this perspective on historical consciousness is, it does not, however, exhaust the scholarly uses of oral tradition. As a historical source in the conventional sense, oral tradition will continue to be exploited for at least three reasons. In the first place, it is wrong to assume that there is necessarily a complete 'fit' between present and past. In fact the representation of society in tradition is more likely to lag behind the reality, particularly in times of rapid social change such as Africa has lived through in the past hundred years. We all interpret the present in the light of models derived from past experience, and oral societies are no exception. Thomas Spear points out that the values and assumptions which are manifest in the traditions of the Mijikenda peoples of Kenya relate to circumstances around 1850, before their social system had been disturbed by the new wealth earned by young men from the caravan trade with the coast; the time-lag offers valuable insight into their earlier political culture.[33]

Secondly, traditions which have been glossed time and time again are unlikely to have been changed in every particular. Stories about the distant past may have been moulded to conform to changing social perceptions, but they also carry information which is incidental to the meaning of the text and affords a glimpse of conditions in the past, such as archaic styles of dress and weaponry, or the arrival of the first exotic goods by long-distance trade from the coast. Even stories whose significance seems to be primarily as mythical symbols may yield valid historical inferences. A case in point is the tradition told by the Shambaa of north-east Tanzania about the foundation of their mountain state. This is attributed to a heroic leader called Mbegha who killed wild pigs, distributed free meat and settled major disputes. Steven Feierman concedes that at one level this story is a myth rich in symbolic statements about Shambaa culture (expressing, for example, the opposition of wilderness to homestead, and of meat to starch); but reference to the traditions of neighbouring peoples confirms that the tale of Mbegha also deals with the resolution of a crisis in Shambaa society in the eighteenth century, caused by the arrival of large groups of immigrants from the plains.[34] Oral traditions, like written documents, can be 'witnesses in spite of themselves'.

## Oral tradition and the recent past

Thirdly, and perhaps most important of all, many of the features which make the interpretation of oral tradition so problematic are much less evident the nearer they approach the present. Myths of origins have a fascination all of their own for both fieldworkers and armchair scholars, but the area in which oral tradition has made the greatest impact on historical knowledge is nineteenth-century African history. All oral tradition, however stylized and abstract it eventually becomes, begins as description of actions and events as they were experienced in life. From the historian's point of view, the great merit of traditions pertaining, say, to the lifetime of the grandparents of today's elders is that the process of abstraction has not yet gone very far: details which meant a great deal to the original participants may have been dropped, and the stories may have been affected by the perspective of hindsight, but the exploits of named individuals and their social world remain clearly visible. In a valuable discussion of how oral tradition evolves, Joseph Miller refers to this material as 'extended personal recollections', implying an intermediate category between first-hand testimony and oral tradition proper.[35] The experience of many historians shows that shallow traditions about the nineteenth century respond well to the critical skills in which the profession is trained.

The historian of the nineteenth century holds another advantage, namely the *plurality* of traditions surviving from that period. For more remote epochs the only traditions likely to survive are those associated with the ruling lineage or – in the case of chiefless societies – tribal epics of migration and warfare. But the period immediately preceding the Scramble for Africa lies within the remembered past of smaller social groups – the clan, lineage or petty chiefdom. This material not only allows the historian to apply the principles of comparative source criticism by setting one tradition against the others; it also does much to offset the otherwise pronounced tendency for oral tradition to portray African society from the top as seen through the eyes of the ruling élite. Something of the tension which divided opposing interests and rival centres of authority can be reconstructed from the varied oral materials surviving from the nineteenth century, as David Cohen has demonstrated so well in his micro-study of Bunafu.[36] In short, historians can now attempt a broader social analysis than the mainstream court traditions permit by themselves.

In Africa the nineteenth century was a period of major social change, owing to the spread of long-distance trade, the renewed expansion of Islam and – in the south and east – the convulsions set in train by the meteoric rise of the Zulu kingdom. As the work of recovering the oral traditions for this period proceeds, historians are greatly enlarging their understanding of these themes and of the circumstances in which Africans confronted the colonial intrusion at the close of the century.[37]

# VI

## Conclusion

The use of oral evidence by historians began as a means of restoring the particularities of human experience to their central place in historical discourse. A technique which owes its modern development to sociology and anthropology has been enlisted in support of an enterprise foreign to the generalizing, theory-oriented nature of those disciplines. In fact the practice of both oral history and oral tradition has had more to do with the re-creational than the explanatory side of historical enquiry. Like other academic innovators oral historians have tended in the past to advance exaggerated claims for their expertise, maintaining that they are uniquely – perhaps exclusively – qualified to recover 'lost' areas of human experience. Both oral history and oral tradition have been presented as the voice of those who have been denied a proper hearing by the conventional materials of historical research – in one case the bottom tier of industrialized society, in the other the non-European peoples who were at the receiving end of colonialism. In both these areas the vital contribution of oral sources can hardly be denied. What cannot be sustained, however, is the notion that the historian, by listening to 'the voice of the past', can re-create these neglected territories of history with an authentic immediacy. The term 'oral history' – sometimes used to cover work on oral tradition as well as personal reminiscence – is particularly unfortunate, suggesting as it does a new specialism analogous to diplomatic or economic history. Oral history is not a new branch of history but a new *technique* – a means of bringing into play new sources to be evaluated alongside written sources and material remains.

But at the same time oral sources merit more attention than they currently receive from the profession at large, or the wider public. They are, after all, *verbal* materials, and they share many of the strengths and weaknesses of written sources – the wealth of detail and nuance of meaning, as well as the distortions of cultural bias and political calculation. Oral sources are therefore particularly appropriate materials for the exercise of the historian's traditional critical skills. And they have the further attraction of affording a unique insight into the formation of popular historical consciousness – something that should be of abiding interest to all historians.

## Gathering oral history

As oral history has grown in popularity so historians have become more sophisticated in how they set about collecting reminiscences. Museums and archives specializing in the history of the twentieth century (for example the Imperial War Museum) often invest in the gathering of oral memory interviews while potential interviewees are still alive. Television history has long made use of oral history interviews, often with figures who played a leading role in important events of twentieth-century history. Such important first-hand testimony can be invaluable, but it needs to be treated with caution: interviewees can be wanting to get 'their' version of events on record.

Oral history societies publish handbooks to give advice to novices in the field. The oral history researcher needs to bear in mind that interviewees may be very elderly and frail, and unable to take being interviewed for any lengthy session. Few interviewees can launch immediately into detailed reminiscence about events they might not have thought about for years. Historians have learned the value of approaching the main theme of the research carefully, sometimes providing artefacts or music from the period to help to trigger the memory. Memory itself has to be treated with great caution. It can be remarkably clear, even after a very long time; on the other hand, memory can play tricks, and what seem to be firm and detailed memories can be disproved by other evidence.

## Writing pre-colonial history

The Europeans who arrived in Africa in the nineteenth century to colonize it tended to adopt a dismissive attitude towards indigenous culture and history. This was partly born out of feelings of racial and cultural superiority and partly from the inherent difficulty for Europeans to comprehend a non-literate society. Almost of necessity, this imbalance was perpetuated when historians began to write about colonial history: the 'story' was usually deemed to begin with the arrival of the first Europeans, and even the most anti-colonialist accounts effectively wrote off the pre-colonial history of the continent, leaving it to anthropologists and archaeologists. More recently, there has been a marked shift in attitudes towards bringing the pre-colonial history of colonized areas into the historical record. This has come about partly because of the way in which other disciplines have provided keys and ways into the indigenous culture, and also partly because a new generation of indigenous scholars are able to marry their awareness of their cultural identity with a thorough understanding of the discipline of academic history.

## Further reading

Paul Thompson, *The Voice of the Past: Oral History,* 3rd edn, Oxford UP, 2000

Robert Perks & Alistair Thomson (eds), *The Oral History Reader,* Routledge, 1998

Stephen Caunce, *Oral History and the Local Historian,* Longman, 1994

Sherna B. Gluck & Daphne Patai (eds), *Women's Words: the Feminist Practice of Oral History,* Routledge, 1991

Raphael Samuel & Paul Thompson (eds), *The Myths We Live By,* Routledge, 1990

Alessandro Portelli, *The Death of Luigi Trastulli and Other Stories: Form and Meaning in Oral History,* SUNY Press, 1991

David Henige, *Oral Historiography,* Longman, 1982

Jan Vansina, *Oral Tradition as History,* James Currey, 1985

Joseph C. Miller (ed.), *The African Past Speaks,* Dawson, 1980

## Notes

1 This omission is partly rectified in one paragraph on oral sources in the third edition of *The Nature of History*, Macmillan, 1989, pp. 215–16.

2 John Vincent, *An Intelligent Person's Guide to History*, Duckworth, 1995, p. 3.

3 Bernard Donoughue and G.W. Jones, *Herbert Morrison*, Weidenfeld & Nicolson, 1973.

4 Anthony Seldon and Joanna Pappworth, *By Word of Mouth*, Methuen, 1983.

5 Christopher Storm-Clark, 'The miners, 1870–1970: a test-case for oral history', *Victorian Studies*, XV, 1971, pp. 65–6.

6 Thompson describes his sampling procedure more fully in his methodological work, *The Voice of the Past: Oral History*, 2nd edn, Oxford University Press, 1988, pp. 124–31.

7 Raphael Samuel (ed.), *Village Life and Labour*, Routledge & Kegan Paul, 1975.

8 Jerry White, *The Worst Street in North London: Campbell Bunk, Islington, Between the Wars*, Routledge & Kegan Paul, 1986; and *Rothschild Buildings: Life in an East End Tenement Block, 1887–1920*, Routledge & Kegan Paul, 1980.

9 Ken Worpole, 'A ghostly pavement: the political implications of local working-class history', in Raphael Samuel (ed.), *People's History and Socialist Theory*, Routledge & Kegan Paul, 1981, p. 28.

10 *Oral History*, **VIII**, 1980, no. 1, reports the proceedings of a conference on black history and oral history in 1979 which was attended by both professional historians and black activists.

11 Stephen Koss, review of Paul Thompson's *The Edwardians* in *Times Literary Supplement*, 5 December 1975, p. 1436.

12 Philip Abrams, *Historical Sociology*, Open Books, 1982, p. 331.

13 Jerry White, 'Beyond autobiography', in Samuel, *People's History and Socialist Theory*, p. 35.

14 See the review of Thompson's book by Robert Gray in *Social History*, **V**, 1977, pp. 695–7.

15 White, *Rothschild Buildings*, p. xiii.

16 For a small-scale but promising example of this approach, see Tottenham History Workshop, *How Things Were: Growing Up in Tottenham 1890–1920*, 1982.

17 Alistair Thomson, *Anzac Memories: Living with the Legend*, Oxford University Press, 1994.

18 Alessandro Portelli, *The Death of Luigi Trastulli and Other Stories: Form and Meaning in Oral History*, State University of New York Press, 1991, p. 26.

19 Oral history and oral tradition are considered together in a fruitful way, however, in B. Bernardi, C. Poni and A. Triulzi (eds), *Fonti Orali: Antropologia e Storia*, Franco Angeli, 1978: some of the major contributions are in English.

20 John Iliffe (ed.), *Modern Tanzanians*, East African Publishing House, 1973, includes a number of recorded life histories. Oral evidence is skilfully woven into Charles Perrings, *Black Mineworkers in Central Africa*, Heinemann, 1979.

21 Wyatt MacGaffey, 'African history, anthropology, and the rationality of natives', *History in Africa*, **V**, 1978, p. 103.

22 See Iona and Peter Opie, *The Lore and Language of Schoolchildren*, Oxford University Press, 1959.

23 Published in French in 1961, the English version appeared as *Oral Tradition*, Routledge & Kegan Paul, 1965. Vansina has completely revised the book as *Oral Tradition as History*, James Currey, 1985.

24 M.S.M. Kiwanuka, *A History of Buganda*, Longman, 1971, and S. Karugire, *A History of the Kingdom of Nkore in Western Uganda to 1896*, Oxford University Press, 1971.

25 In this and the previous paragraph, I have drawn heavily on Joseph Miller, 'Listening for the African past', which forms the introduction to J.C. Miller (ed.), *The African Past Speaks*, Dawson, 1980.

26 Jan Vansina, *The Children of Woot*, Wisconsin University Press, 1978, p. 19.

27 David Henige, 'The disease of writing': Ganda and Nyoro kinglists in a newly literate world', in Miller, *The African Past Speaks*, pp. 255–6.

28 Michael Twaddle, 'On Ganda historiography', *History in Africa*, I, 1974.

29 Donald R. Wright, 'Uprooting Kunta Kinte: on the perils of relying on encyclopaedic informants', *History in Africa*, VIII, 1981.

30 John Tosh, *Clan Leaders and Colonial Chiefs in Lango*, Oxford University Press, 1978, pp. 13, 24–34.

31 David Henige, *The Chronology of Oral Tradition*, Oxford University Press, 1974. See also his *Oral Historiography*, Longman, 1982, pp. 97–102.

32 See, for example, Paul Irwin, *Liptako Speaks*, Princeton University Press, 1981.

33 Thomas Spear, 'Oral traditions: whose history?' *History in Africa*, VIII, 1981. See also his *Kenya's Past: an Introduction to Historical Methodology in Africa*, Longman, 1981.

34 Steven Feierman, *The Shambaa Kingdom: a History*, Wisconsin University Press, 1974, ch. 2–3.

35 Miller, 'Listening for the African past', p. 10.

36 David W. Cohen, *Womunafu's Bunafu: A Study of Authority in a Nineteenth-Century African Community*, Princeton University Press, 1977.

37 Notable examples are Andrew Roberts, *A History of the Bemba*, Longman, 1973, and Jan Vansina, *The Tio Kingdom*, Oxford University Press, 1973.

# Conclusion

## Other fields of history

The last four chapters have assessed the contribution to historical scholarship of sociological and economic theory, the quantitative analysis of historical data, the impact of cultural theory and the use of oral evidence. But this list is very far from being exhaustive. Other new departures such as the use of landscape and film as historical sources, the adoption of a post-colonial perspective and the history of the environment, have been only lightly touched on in this book, because until now their impact has not been so pronounced; but in a comprehensive survey each would merit extended discussion. Together all these innovations amount to the most significant methodological advance since Ranke laid the foundations of modern historical scholarship more than a century and a half ago. As a result the content of historical study has been vastly extended too. It now embraces social structures in their entirety, the history of collective mentalities, and the evolving relationship between society and the natural environment. Although much further work remains to be done, women are now more present in the historical record than they have ever been. And for the first time historical research now extends to every corner of the globe; no culture is deemed too remote or too 'primitive' for the attention of historians.

## Has history surrendered?

This record of innovation over the past forty years is open to different readings. It can be seen as a surrender by historians to the promise of topicality offered by other, more 'relevant' disciplines – a line of attack that Elton made very much his own.[1] According to this view, every enlargement of history's scope represents a departure from the central concern of the discipline (for Elton this remained the constitutional and administrative history of England). To the extent that the current turn to cultural themes is associated with a Postmodernist epistemology, it invites dire warnings of the **end of history**.[2] A more optimistic and generous verdict would cite the occasions in the past when historians have successfully assimilated the insights of other disciplines, for example philology and the law in the nineteenth century. Everything depends on whether openness to contributions from elsewhere is compatible with upholding the essentials of historical awareness. There is certainly a danger that overarching social theories may obscure the particularity of the past, or that textual theory may wrench primary sources from their historical context, or that oral history may unwittingly read present-day attitudes into the remembered past. But these dangers are well understood, and one of the things which this book has sought to demonstrate is how historians, forearmed with that awareness, have tended to resist the less digestible implications of innovations from outside the discipline. One thinks of E.P. Thompson's long campaign against the determinist tendencies of Marxism, or the carefully qualified welcome given to modern textual theory by Appleby, Hunt and Jacob.[3] A great deal of the excitement of historical study derives from its pivotal position where the concerns of many other fields converge. Historians make those concerns their own by submitting them to the disciplines of historical context and historical process. They relinquish those intellectual positions which stand above or outside history; the rest they assimilate and in so doing enrich the subject beyond measure.

**end of history**
The phrase 'the end of history' was also used by the American commentator Francis Fukuyama to describe the apparent triumph of American liberal democracy in the light of the collapse of the Soviet Union in 1991. What Fukuyama meant was the end of the dialectical conflict between East and West, which had been resolved in the West's favour. However, further conflicts have followed on from the end of the Cold War, including a new dialectic between the values and policies of the Western democracies and those of fundamentalist Islamic groups. Fukuyama's confident assertion excited much comment at the time but is now regarded as something of a period piece.

## A fragmented discipline?

But the enlargement in the scope of historical enquiry presents one undeniable problem: history has become a discipline with very little apparent coherence. During the nineteenth century it was possible in practice to fence off history from other disciplines and to confine its brief to the narrative presentation of political events. The rise of economic history in the early twentieth century would have imposed greater strain on this convention had it not been for the fact that political and economic history tended to remain in separate compartments. But today the situation is very different. Not only has the range of approaches to the past expanded with the maturing of social history and the arrival of cultural history. More and more research is conducted on the frontiers between thematic specialisms, and the traditional claim of political history to be the core of the subject is almost impossible to sustain any longer; history has become a house of many mansions, with numerous doors and passageways inside.[4]

History has always been inimical to the definitions of the logician. But now more than ever it can only be adequately characterized in terms of paired opposites. It concerns both events and structures, both the individual and the mass, both mentalities and material forces. Historians themselves need to combine narrative with analytical skills, and to display both empathy and detachment. Their discipline is both re-creation and explanation, both art and science; in short – to return to one of the starting-points of this book – history is a hybrid which defies classification. These distinctions should be seen not as warring opposites but as complementary emphases, which together hold out the possibility of grasping the past in something like its real complexity. Nothing is to be gained from defining history in terms of lucid absolutes – except perhaps rhetorical support for some new approach whose credentials have yet to be established. A great deal will be lost if, in the interests of a spurious coherence, historians close their eyes to a whole dimension of their subject.

## The purposes of history

Last but not least, the diversity of current practice reflects a central ambivalence in the function of history. For as long as men and women retain any interest in human nature and human creativity, they will recognize that every manifestation of the human spirit in the past has some claim on their attention, and that history is worth studying as an end in itself. Some of the new approaches during the past forty years are recognizably part of this humanistic tradition. The study of collective mentalities is concerned in the first instance to re-create the emotions and intellect of people living in conditions very different from our own, so that their humanity can be more fully realized. Oral historians in Britain and other industrialized societies are committed to the recovery of everyday experience in the recent past as something of value in itself.

But the innovative strain in recent historiography has also been strongly influenced by the conviction that the record of the past holds lessons for contemporary society. The almost total retreat from topical concerns which characterized the historical profession in the first half of the twentieth century has ended. Quietly but persistently, historians are now reasserting their subject's claim to offer guidance and perspective. The conviction is there, and it influences research priorities, even if the results are seldom communicated to a lay readership as forcefully as they should be. **Macro-economic** history, and the quantitative methods which it has brought to greater sophistication than any other branch of history, is principally concerned to explore the dynamics of growth and stagnation in national economies. The sense of crisis about the management of the world's natural resources has prompted the growth of environmental history, just as the entry of black Africa into the international arena has directed attention to African history. The theories of social structure and social change which historians have drawn from the social sciences were originally propounded by thinkers such as Marx and Weber as a contribution to contemporary problems; it is no accident that they have been applied with such interesting results to areas such as urban history and the history of the family which directly address contemporary problems today.

**Macro-economic**
Concerned with the large study of economies, on a national or international level.

## History for all?

Of course if historians are to fulfil their potential as providers of social wisdom, they must reach out to a popular audience. On this count the profession is much given to pessimism. Historians in Britain periodically lament their loss of **lay appeal** and look back fondly to a time when their predecessors were widely read – even if their books were short on scholarship. David Cannadine,

**lay appeal**
Appeal to the general reader, outside the academic profession.

for example, has testified to his colleagues' 'intellectual timidity and antiquarian pedantry', qualities which in his view have driven away readers and students alike.[5] It is certainly true that the relentless pursuit of professionalism makes little allowance for a non-professional audience, but in fact this self-defeating attitude is far from universal among historians. On closer inspection the problem turns out to be one for certain kinds of history, rather than the whole subject. Technical political history may be little read outside the academic world, and the attempt to remove from British history familiar landmarks such as the English Revolution of the 1640s or the Industrial Revolution is little to the taste of the wider public; but those scholars who endow their history with meaning and coherence continue to receive a ready hearing. One has only to call to mind Olwen Hufton's panorama of women's experience in Early Modern Europe, or Eric Hobsbawm's sobering and wide-ranging reflections on the 'short' twentieth century.[6] Historians with a message have not been confined to the ivory tower in the past, and there is no reason why they should be in future.

What gives most cause for optimism about the future of historical studies is that more and more historians are now investigating themes of topical relevance. They do so not as a propaganda exercise but in the conviction that there are valuable insights to be learned from the findings of historical scholarship. No doubt those insights are less clear-cut than the champions of 'scientific history' would care to admit. If society looks to historians for 'answers' in the sense of firm predictions and unequivocal generalizations, it will be disappointed. What will emerge from the pursuit of 'relevance' is something less tangible but in the long run more valuable – a surer sense of the possibilities latent in our present condition. For as long as historians hold that end in view, their subject will retain its vitality and its claim on the support of the society in which they work.

## Notes

1 See especially G.R. Elton, *Return to Essentials*, Cambridge University Press, 1991.
2 *Ibid.*; Arthur Marwick, 'Two approaches to historical study', *Journal of Contemporary History*, XXX, 1995, pp. 5–35.

3    E.P. Thompson, *The Poverty of Theory*, Merlin Press, 1978; Joyce Appleby, Lynn Hunt and Margaret Jacob, *Telling the Truth About History*, Norton, 1994.

4    For some stimulating reflections on this theme, see Theodore K. Rabb, 'Coherence, synthesis and quality in history', in T.K. Rabb and Robert I. Rotberg (eds), *The New History: the 1980s and Beyond*, Princeton University Press, 1982.

5    D. Cannadine, 'British history: past, present – and future?' *Past & Present*, **CXVI**, 1987, p. 178.

6    Olwen Hufton, *The Prospect Before Her: a History of Western Women, 1500–1800*, HarperCollins, 1995; Eric Hobsbawm, *Age of Extremes: the Short Twentieth Century, 1914–1991*, Michael Joseph, 1994.

# Index